The Brothel Boy
and
Other Parables
of the Law

The Brothel Boy
and
Other Parables
of the Law

Norval Morris

New York   Oxford
OXFORD UNIVERSITY PRESS
1992

Oxford University Press

Oxford   New York   Toronto
Delhi   Bombay   Calcutta   Madras   Karachi
Petaling Jaya   Singapore   Hong Kong   Tokyo
Nairobi   Dar es Salaam   Cape Town
Melbourne   Auckland

and associated companies in
Berlin   Ibadan

Library of Congress Cataloging-in-Publication Data
Morris, Norval.
The brothel boy and other parables of the law/Norval Morris.
p.   cm.
1. Criminal law—Philosophy.   2. Punishment—Philosophy.   3. Burmese fiction.   I. Title.
K5018.M67   1992   345—dc20   [342.5]   91-32351
ISBN   0-19-507443-2

9 8 7 6 5 4 3 2 1

Printed in the United States of America
on acid-free paper

To H.A.B.

Integrity at its highest level

Preface

Why Burma for these parables? Why Eric Blair as the central character? A book should speak for itself and not require an apology, but a brief answer to these questions might not be amiss.

For five years Eric Blair, later to become famous as George Orwell, was indeed a district officer in Moulmein, Burma, being both policeman and judge for a diverse populace of Burmese and Europeans. He is a superb embodiment of the moral and ethical values to which I aspire; so I borrowed his *persona*, and his setting in the Moulmein of his early twenties, and in imagining these stories I tried to live up to his values.

It is my experience that when a serious moral or ethical question arises in conversation, or even in the university classroom, an answer is immediately and dogmatically given, based on knee-jerk political, religious, or social attitudes. Answers are offered before questions are completed. When, however, the identical question is moved to a different time and place, it is possible to escape those cultural blinders and at least to get the relevant issues presented. In these stories I have tried to introduce all the major aspects of a set of currently contentious ethical-moral-legal issues in a way that, I hope, holds the reader's attention until the whole package can be considered. I believe that this amalgam, casting back I suppose to the morality plays of the Middle Ages, lends itself well to the parable form.

I should qualify my calling these stories parables, since they make no claim to reflect revealed or higher truth. They are secular, agnostic parables, posing problems, but uncertain in their solution. District Officer Blair had Veraswami to guide him on medicine and philosophy and U Tin Hlang on law and politics, and thus in each parable got the question comprehensively phrased. As to the answer, he was on his own.

A decade of writing about and discussing the moral dilemmas presented in this book generated the helpful advice of more people than I can possibly acknowledge properly. I have been privileged to have two efficient and generous support systems, one at home and the other at this excellent university. But if exceptional assistance may be acknowledged, let me in particular thank Michael Tonry, Marc Miller, Gordon Hawkins, Franklin Zimring, and Sarah Carrig.

University of Chicago   Norval Morris
Chicago, February 1992

Contents

The Brothel Boy
and
Other Parables
of the Law

Prologue

I tend to resent authority, its confident manner and plump bum, yet in Moulmein in my early twenties I exercised the combined authority of a district officer and a police magistrate over nearly one hundred thousand Burmese, Indians, and Chinese, and a few hundred Europeans. The seeds of my hostility to authority had been planted at St. Cyprian's and Eton; but in Moulmein, as policeman, prosecutor, and judge rolled into one, I came to feel its temptations within myself. Dr. Veraswami thinks I succumbed; perhaps I did.

There could hardly be a lovelier setting in which to shape one's fledgling responses to power. Moulmein is in lower Burma on the banks of the river Salween. Encircled by hills some thirty-eight miles inland from the Gulf of Martaban, it is, by Burmese standards, a large town, with a population while I was there of about 60,000, of whom about 45,000 were Burmese, mostly Karens and Mons; but it was difficult to count Burmese villagers, since Moulmein dwindles off into outlying villages, particularly along the Salween, which meanders in sweeping bends around the outskirts of the town.

I was to report to the district officer at Moulmein within a fortnight of graduating from a one-year course at the Burma Provincial Police Training School in Mandalay. I was given to understand that it was an easy but important posting, suitable to one of my inexperience but possible promise. The officer I was to relieve, Captain Humphreys, had started the district office in Moulmein and was therefore in the best possible position to tell me all I would need to know about Moulmein and the surrounding villages that were to be my suzerainty; there was no need for any briefing at Mandalay headquarters. My suspicion was that ignorance dictated this reticence.

I was assured that this first posting was a great opportunity for me. Though the Burmese in and around Moulmein caused fewer problems for the administration than the Chins and Karens of the North, and hence presented little challenge to the district officer, Moulmein was a centre of teak production and, to a lesser extent, of rice and rubber cultivation, so there were important commercial interests to be protected and assisted. If those in commerce were pleased with me, the foundations of my career in the civil service would be secure. The thought was, I suppose, that the English growers, millers, and shippers, and even the other European traders, would be flattered to have an Old Etonian as their district officer, even a twenty-year-old Old Etonian. If I could please Jardine, Matheson and Company, I would please the Raj.

My first year in Rangoon and Mandalay had at least taught me how not to travel in Burma. Kipling, on whom I had first relied as a travel guide, had proved disastrous. On my first journey I had found that there were no flying fishes "On the road to Mandalay," none at all, playing or otherwise, as he had suggested. And this was not surprising, since that road ran well inland, parallel to the Irrawaddy River. Nor did the river provide any better passage. It, too, entirely lacked flying fishes—probably they had succumbed to the wide mud flats through which the river made its excruciatingly leisurely way. Early on, I had risked the river journey from Rangoon to Mandalay on what was fancifully known as an "Express Steamer" of the Irrawaddy Flotilla Company: six interminable days of crowded and unrelenting discomfort to carry me and a diverse mass of smelly humanity, and their vegetables, stoves and livestock, a distance achieved overnight by train.

I decided this time to avoid both road and river and to hurry by train to my first posting. It would be good at last to take on responsibilities for others than myself: it seemed a passage to adulthood. I had been a child and youth too long; duties would put an end to adolescence.

I could have spent a few days on leave in Rangoon—my travel voucher allowed it—but instead I took the express train to Pegu, just north of Rangoon, and changed there for a sweaty and sooty night on a train that stopped at every village on the 170 miles to Martaban. There, the next morning, surprisingly untired by the journey, I boarded a ferry for the half-hour trip up the Salween to Moulmein.

In contrast to the mud flats and relentless rice paddies of my last ferry journey, the Salween ferry glided between high banks of varied and luxuriant foliage into the Gulf of Martaban. Close to each bank of the river were low hills plentifully dotted with pagodas. Unlike the sluggish, humid Irrawaddy, the Salween was a river of fresh delight and gentle breezes, providing a cool, green passage to my tour of duty for the Raj.

On my graduation from the training school, the one "pip" on each epaulette had grown by automatic progression into the two stars of a lieutenant. There was, I suspect, little to distinguish me from the stream of other young Englishmen given premature authority in the service of the Raj, except perhaps that in appearance and manner I was more gangling and unsure than most.

Only one event had set my career in the civil service at all apart, and that event didn't make my task in Moulmein any easier. In my first weeks in Burma I had acquired a nickname, a nickname with contemptuous overtones, which had preceded my arrival both in Mandalay and in Moulmein—"The Rickshaw Wallah."

I had seen rickshaws in Colombo but had not ridden in one until we docked in Rangoon. In both cities, the rickshaw men persistently clamoured for my custom, pulling at my clothing, grasping for my hand, trying to lure me to their chariots. It was impossible to ignore their importunings; toothless, gum-rotten smiles from pocked and scarred faces, arms gesturing toward the seats of their rickshaws, demanded at least some response and induced a vague sense of guilt in me in declining their services. But in Colombo, since I did not disembark from the Herefordshire, I didn't need their help; in Rangoon I was carrying so much luggage that I did.

Rickshaws were comfortable vehicles to ride in, quite well sprung. The rickshaw wallahs seemed to trot along happily enough between the shafts, easing to a walk up inclines or in close traffic. I found I enjoyed the novelty and did not think much about the life of the rickshaw wallahs. They had certainly solicited my custom vehemently. They didn't seem forced to pull me, though of course they were.

As the novelty wore off I found myself increasingly uncomfortable with someone literally dragging me around the streets. There was an element of physical subjugation which troubled me, so that I used rickshaws less and less as the months passed. That was not particularly helpful to the rickshaw wallahs, who needed customers to survive. I often found sentiment and sense in conflict in Burma and, come to think of it, elsewhere.

One day in Rangoon, in my second week of paying obligatory respects to those who were in authority over me, I was walking back to the officers' barracks around noon when I saw a rickshaw wallah, older than most, stagger slightly, slow to a walk, and then stop. Pressing down on the shafts, he bowed forward slowly to the ground, pitching his portly, pith-helmeted customer forward. The rickshaw wallah then pulled himself to a squatting position in the gutter, the rickshaw resting on its shafts. The customer shouted something I could not hear, paused a moment, and, as I hurriedly approached, got down from the rickshaw, pushed a coin into the coolie's hand, and strode past me saying, "The lazy fool. I told him it was just around the corner."

I stood perplexed. The coolie squatted there, eyes closed, mouth open, breath rasping. I said something like, "Can I help?" but got no reply.

Instead, he folded sideways over one of the shafts of the rickshaw, his worn sandals clinging doubtfully to his flattened and scarred feet. Lying in the gutter in his tattered grey-brown tunic and unkempt lungi (a piece of cloth wrapped and tied around his waist like a skirt—the uniform of a rickshaw wallah), he looked utterly desolate.

None of the few natives in the street took the slightest notice of these events. I saw no European. I had no idea what to do.

Suddenly I recalled that there was a medical emergency room attached to my barracks. I lifted the coolie onto the apron of the rickshaw, took off my uniform jacket, and put it under his head, the badges of rank on my epaulette sticking up above his head like small crowns. I raised the shafts of the rickshaw. It was surprisingly heavy. Pulling him the few hundred yards to the emergency room left me in a lather of sweat.

It was no good. He was dead—so the nurse told me when I managed to get her to look at him and not in amazement at me. But it did make an amusing story, I am told, as it wound its way through the messes of Burma and India. Someone straight from Eton joining the Indian Imperial Police was odd enough; but that on arrival in Burma he should pull a rickshaw for a dead coolie was sheer joy.

The general view was that I had made an awful fool of myself. I still cannot see what else I could have done, though it did blight my time in Burma.

The rickshaw wallah's customer had a plump rear, I recall. And I further confirmed my impression of this correlation between amplitude and authority when the owner of the rickshaw, with a similarly substantial posterior, made formal complaint that I had killed his coolie, driven him to death. I had, he said, deprived him of his property in the rickshaw wallah, who was under contract to him; and, he added, I had interfered in an even worse way. It had taken him several days of searching to find his rickshaw at the barracks. Who would ever expect it to be there? If I decided, for reasons known only to me, to take a dead coolie to the emergency room, that surely gave me no right to take the rickshaw, which I must have known the coolie did not own.

He was fobbed off, but it did help those who wished to embroider the tale.

My early days in Moulmein were not easy. My predecessor, Captain Humphreys, was almost literally that. Considering his affection for alcohol, it was surprising that he had lasted so long in Moulmein and that his reputation at headquarters had not suffered. He had come to Moulmein as a captain, it being customary to start a new district with a more senior officer than a lieutenant; but he had received no further promotion. He had been left in Moulmein too long. Nor had his next posting been gazetted. All that he and I knew was that he was to go on home leave and that he was to be succeeded in Moulmein by Assistant Police Magistrate Blair, who would also serve, for the time being, as district officer.

Humphreys had booked a room for me at the Club. He told me his bungalow would be available if I wanted it when he left. I thus inherited his files—which were in surprisingly good order—and, if I wished, also his bungalow, the staff at the bungalow, and the female Burmese companionship provided on demand for the night from the nearby village. The bungalow seemed clean enough, and the staff did not appear dejected by the likely substitution; the path of sense was to fall in with his plans, including those for his earliest possible departure. I was anxious to get to work.

Each morning he briefed me on local matters. After his alcoholic lunch, he was disinclined for work. My afternoons and early evenings were free to explore the district on my own, on bicycle or foot.

The Europeans I met at night in the Club. The Indian traders and a few of the more prosperous Burmese were described to me by Humphreys, so that I was able to introduce myself to some of them in my afternoon wanderings. I visited the local hospital and the nearby gaol, the former run by an Indian doctor, Veraswami, who had been away on a medical emergency when Humphreys had taken me on a formal visit to inspect the hospital and to meet its staff.

Apparently the only issue of any conflict, when I arrived in Moulmein, concerned this Dr. Veraswami. He had applied for membership of the Club. Why anyone who had a pleasant home for himself and his family, near the hospital where he worked, should want to belong to the Club was beyond me. But, no doubt, membership of the Club was the only mark of social acceptability in Moulmein. Whatever his reasons, he had indeed applied for membership. He didn't play tennis, he didn't play billiards or bridge—but he wanted to join, and two members, apparently grateful for his medical attention, had put him up.

The Club was, of course, for Europeans only, though no sign to that effect was anywhere to be seen and the articles of association did not so provide. But the point was well understood. There were two or three Eurasian members, sons of European fathers and Burmese mothers, who led an uneasy half-life in the Club, but they were particularly vociferous about the need to keep the natives out. And, on occasions when transient princelings or maharajahs came through Moulmein, they had been briefly housed at the Club. But Dr. Veraswami's application raised issues transcending these minor breaches in the dyke.

I met Dr. Veraswami on one of my cycling explorations. I was riding past the hospital when I saw a portly, round-faced, bespectacled, crumpled white-suited figure, about forty years old, matching Humphreys' description of Veraswami, emerge from the main entrance, a stethoscope dangling from his coat pocket.

I rode over to him, dismounted, and offered my hand with the silly enquiry, "Dr. Veraswami, I presume?"

"Mr. Blair, it must be. You make me sound like Dr. Livingstone. You have come a verry long way to find me, Mr. Blair. Not ass far ass Mr. Stanley, of course, but far and hard enough. Captain Humphreys told me you would be relieving him."

He spoke in jerky, sibilant sentences. I was searching for some politeness to offer in return when he hurried on, the words hissing and tumbling over each other: "Do pleass spare me some time. It would be a privilege, a verry great privilege, to come to know you so early in your command of our district."

He certainly exaggerated my role; but then, as now, I was not easily offended by flattery. Still, he did seem on the "pushy" side. How could a middle-aged Indian doctor take other than a contrived or manipulative interest in one of my youth and inexperience? He must want something from me. Yes, "pushy" was probably the right word.

We spent an hour or so together, he telling me of his work at the hospital and at the gaol, where he also served as chief medical officer. His official duties took him, as well, to the surrounding villages as Inspector of Hygiene for the Department of Health. Despite these multiple official appointments, he was permitted some private practice, provided the administration had first call on his services. There was no European doctor in Moulmein, though there were other medically qualified Indian and Burmese practitioners. But Veraswami was, certainly, the only doctor with English training, including an advanced degree in surgery, making him the only Fellow of the Royal College of Surgeons in all of Burma.

He seemed boastful about his professional qualifications, but otherwise easy and interesting to talk to, once my ear captured the lilting, inflected rhythm of his sentences. The reason for his boastfulness and, I now saw, the unease it caused him, became clear to me as we parted: "May I ask a favour of you, Mr. Blair? Even at thiss early stage of our acquaintance? A verry great favour it iss, to be sure."

I must have nodded or otherwise signified my assent.

"I have applied to join your Club. It would be a verry great help to me, in my professional work, you see, to be a member. I know many of your European friends would be troubled to have me in the Club. But I promise to visit rarely indeed, only on public occasions, issn't it?"

I doubted that his membership of the Club would attract more Europeans as private patients than it would repel. Still, if he thought it would increase his practice, I would not stand in the way. The whole thing puzzled me. Why belong if not to use? At twenty I had never belonged to any club, except the officers' clubs at my various barracks, which came with the job.

I mumbled a weak, almost evasive agreement, "By all means, Dr. Veraswami. I shall do what I can."

Veraswami's words gushed gratitude, though his eyes showed less enthusiasm. He watched me as I rode away.

" . . . Fine doctor . . . excellent English degrees . . . important responsibilities . . . educated and witty man . . . congenial member of this club . . . " and so on, hackneyed phrase after hackneyed phrase. I sounded unconvincing even to myself.

"Doesn't our young district officer know the man's black?"

"What did he say? Veryslimey a congenial what?"

"Put the question. Put the question."

No one else spoke. The mover and seconder of Veraswami's application were conveniently absent. "Wisely funked it," was the general view. The chairman didn't let it go to a vote: "Fails for want of support."

My intervention was treated as a lapse of taste as well as a manifestation of poor judgement, the most charitable view being one I overheard when I made the mistake of going to the toilet without making my presence known to two standing outside at the urinals: "I think he's trying to suck up to Veraswami for some reason. He's not a fool. He must know we can't let niggers in."

Afterwards the chairman, seeing me isolated at the bar, spoke to me. He did his brave best, interrogating me about Mandalay to find mutual acquaintances, clutching desperately at the few we found—all "fine fellows," we agreed. Duty done, others lured by his efforts to our proximity, he spoke to me so that they would not hear: "I'm sorry about the meeting, Blair. You should have sounded me out first, you know."

I doubted I would ever fit in; yet, if I was to be an effective district officer, I must.

I soon came to understand how Humphreys had managed to cope with his work while confining his sobriety to the mornings. There really was not much to do. As with all military and paramilitary organisations, the continuities of control and the regularities of discipline that got the work of the Burmese Police done were provided by the noncommissioned officers. They, and the three platoons of policemen serving under them, worked at least as well for me as they had for Humphreys. I interfered as little as possible, but I tried to learn something about each of them and their duties. A policeman's life in Moulmein, as elsewhere, is a daily routine whose largest risk is boredom, interrupted by occasional spurts of violent and sometimes dangerous action. But crises are rare; ennui prevails.

I kept the records straight, made my reports to Mandalay, held the required parades, and learned the orderly judicial processes of settling local personal and financial disputes. My lack of legal training seemed no great disadvantage. The year in Mandalay had prepared me for the routine of my duties; I was less confident of its assistance in emergencies.

I made inspection tours of my district. The country was beautiful, the Burmese reserved but friendly. Even the headmen and the village elders treated me with more respect than my years or knowledge deserved; Humphreys must have been a better district officer than I had suspected.

Quite swiftly I settled into the humid regularities of life in the tropics. I did not often regret my decision to come to Burma, but as yet there was little to give me confidence in its wisdom. I was untested and uncertain, capable of maintaining the facade of a district officer but deeply conscious of my limitations. Further, I was lonely, very lonely. Long letters to and from home were no substitute for friendship, and I lacked friendship until Veraswami slowly and hesitatingly offered himself to that end.

At the hospital, and of course at my office and in public generally, our relationship was formal, excessively so on his part, I thought. But from the first evening when I accepted his shy invitation to his bungalow "for a beer before tiffin, Mr. Blair," and came to a verandah in Moulmein that holds the happiest of my memories of that sweaty town, I hoped that friendship would grow between us.

The evenings on his verandah, the rattan armchairs, the foliage still hanging heavy from the late-afternoon rain showers, the breeze stirring the palms, the smells and sounds of the township and the nearby hospital and gaol, the heat abating, and the bottles of Watney's beer with their wired glass stoppers clinking among the few tired lumps of ice in the oval bucket, all made an oasis of mind talking to mind profoundly different from the relentless ritual phrases of the Club. From Veraswami I learned about many matters my reading had neglected and my experience had not yet encompassed.

I needed and relied on Dr. Veraswami's worldly wisdom, his knowledge of Burma and of the ways of the Raj. He never patronised my youth—the nearest approach being when, occasionally, he called me "my young friend." He critically tested my ideas, he never told me what to do, he guided me to my own decisions. Yet in one way he complicated my life, since to be his friend diminished me in the eyes of most Europeans. After his abortive effort to join the Club, "Doctor Veryslimey" was even less popular; I may not have been his only European friend, but certainly it did not take long to call that roll.

At the time it escaped me, but I now see that there was at least one advantage to my first troubling case in Moulmein: it drew me closer to Dr. Veraswami. It concerned the only entirely nameless person I have known—unnamed, unchristened, unbuddhaed, I suppose. To his face, usually averted, he was simply "Boy"; when speaking of him, he was "the brothel boy."

The Brothel Boy

I wonder—does any other Old Etonian roll his own cigarettes? I'm not sure why I do. They are cheaper, of course, but the taste is not very different, and bits and pieces of tobacco do drift into one's mouth and require picking off the tongue or lips, which seems to disturb some who observe it. In the Club they make no secret of their disapproval—"A frightfully low-bred habit."

"Blair, do take one of mine, it's so much easier."

"No thanks, I prefer these," and I watch their foreheads wrinkle in revulsion.

I had carefully rolled a cigarette and was about to moisten the paper, my tongue protruding, mouth agape, when a native boy burst into my office shouting, "Come, come, Sir. Hurry please. They are killing the brothel boy."

I knew, of course, of the local brothel, but not of any "brothel boy." A homosexual prostitute seemed most unlikely in Burma, quite out of character with local values and prevailing behaviour—but I had mistaken his role. At all events, I hurried to where I was led to find several village men standing over the unconscious youth but desisting now from further violence. They were, it was immediately obvious, the remainder of a mob of assailants.

The boy was unconscious, bleeding from the head and face from wounds inflicted by repeated kicks. His shoulder was twisted, obviously broken. His clothes, when whole scarcely adequate, were now gaping, torn, and bloody. He lay in a foetal curve, clutching his groin. The expression on what was left of his features was of anguished surprise, the lips drawn back, mortal fear apparent. The smell of fear and violence, of sweat and vomit, was pervasive.

Resentfully they stood back to allow me to inspect him. Then, not concealing their reluctance, they helped me to carry him to the police station, where I telephoned Dr. Veraswami at the nearby hospital. By the time Dr. Veraswami had arrived, I knew the outline of the events that led to the brothel boy's beating. Some villagers returning to the fields in the afternoon had heard a girl's screams from a heavily overgrown area near the Salween River customarily used for washing, but not at this time of day. When they reached her the screaming had ceased; she lay, a young girl, naked in the brothel boy's arms. She had been raped. In her struggles she had apparently struck her head violently on a sharp rock. The boy had made no effort to flee.

The girl was taken to her home. More villagers arrived, and the boy was attacked. He might or might not have been killed, or the villagers might have overcome their dislike of the Raj's justice sufficiently to bring him to me. In any event, my arrival may merely have saved him for the hangman. It was, after all, a clear case—a young girl, a virgin, raped and injured by the brothel boy.

And it became an even clearer case when, a few days later, she died from the combined effects of the head wound and septicaemia. A villainous mixture of local herbs that the villagers had applied to her head wound probably hastened her death. Dr. Veraswami had not been called.

The law began its processes. My first few months in Moulmein had taught me what must be done to prepare for a trial. In the preliminary enquiry into more serious cases I usually acted only as judge and prosecutor, avoiding the further incongruous role of defence counsel that I sometimes assumed in the trial of less serious crimes. It was not required, but I had fallen into the practice of asking one or other of the three Burmese in Moulmein claiming some forensic skill to represent indigent natives accused in serious cases. But this time my requests were firmly rejected. There was nothing to be said. He had raped her and she had died. He had been caught immediately. He did not deny what he had done. The only question was whether the villagers would kill him or whether the Raj, with its quaint, imported formality and pretence of impartiality, would do so. They could see no reason to impede the Raj. So I was judge, prosecutor, and defence counsel, equally untrained in all three roles, though with developing experience in minor disputes and less criminal matters. Certainly the boy could not do much for himself.

I interviewed him under close guard in the hospital. I tried to talk quietly to him; I didn't hurry, sitting silent for long periods. He would look down and away, immobile, never volunteering a word or a gesture. The effect was of one cloyingly anxious to please, but not knowing how to. Whenever I asked him what had happened by the river, he would rush to sweaty verbosity, his head and shoulders bobbing forward with exaggerated sincerity, "Please Sir, I paid, I'm sorry Sir . . . Please Sir, I paid, I'm sorry Sir," the words running on with rising inflexion, flooding incoherently into one another, until he would begin to sob. When the crying stopped he would return to his motionless silence. And if I again even remotely probed the events by the river, the same miserable routine would follow.

If I asked him to do something, to stand up or sit down, to open a window or door, to bring me a chair, he would leap to comply, diligence gleaming in his eyes, ingratiatingly obedient, like a well-trained dog. But I could achieve no communication with him beyond his prompt obedience to simple orders. I tried different tacks to relate to him, asking him about many things, always speaking clearly and slowly, but to little effect. Sometimes he would seem to understand and give a monosyllabic reply, accompanied always by a clipped "Sir," and sometimes he would offer a shy and innocent smile, but his words and smiles seemed quite random, having little to do with my questions. And as soon as I approached the matter of the girl, or of washing by the river, or even of money, out would spill the "Please Sir, I paid, I'm sorry Sir" flowing to tears, sometimes preceded by the incongruous smile.

"A 'perseveration,' I believe it iss called," Dr. Veraswami told me. "Over and over and over he says the same things in the same words in hiss mind, believing them completely, I think, but not knowing what they mean. Sometimes he will say it all, sometimes bits and pieces, you will find, but always in the same sequence, going round and round, exactly the same. You will get verry little more from him. It iss all hiss silly mind will let him think about. Perhaps not so silly, issn't it? Safer so. But I doubt he pretends; he doess not malinger, I think. He tells you all he can tell himself."

So it proved. The boy was obviously stupid. And the meaningless repetition and cringing self-pity became increasingly distasteful.

I went to the brothel to try to learn more of the boy. He had, it was recalled, been born there some twenty or so years ago. His mother had worked for the previous owners of the brothel but had died a few years after the boy's birth. His father was, of course, undiscoverable; any one of the fertile male population of this or neighbouring villages could be a candidate for that unsought honour. The present brothel keeper, a smarmy lady of large physique, expressed unqualified praise of her own virtue in having let the boy stay when she bought the brothel some years ago. He was, she said, until now an entirely reliable punkah wallah, willing to keep the fans moving for the more prosperous clients who wanted them and would pay for them, while he faded into the background.

I could understand how unobtrusive he would have been. As interested in him as I was, I found it hard to see him as a person at all. On any subject apart from the crime, he said only what he thought he ought to say. Otherwise, immobile, slight, turned away, he seemed as present as the furniture.

"How did he keep himself?" I asked the proprietress of the brothel. She was lyrical in praise of her generosity: She kept him without charge. Actually let him sleep inside. Clothed and fed him. And sometimes, she said, customers who were anxious to show off would give him a few annas, which, in her bountiful kindness, she let him keep. This was, I supposed, the source of his savings, which he had tried to give to the girl he killed.

"Did he help the girls if they were treated badly by a customer?" I further enquired. Indeed not; that was her job. And, archly, she added that there were always men of the village to whom she could look for assistance if she needed it. But that was very rare. The girls knew they should expect, even encourage, vigour in some customers. They were often the best customers. And the girls knew she would care for them if they were hurt. It would have been most improper for the boy to intervene. He was enough trouble to her without that.

All he was expected to do, she explained, was to keep the punkah moving gently to begin with and perhaps later slightly more swiftly so that, by different methods, he and the girl could cool the customer. She laughed with betel-gummed delight at her own wit and then explained to me that the boy's job was very easy, that often he did it on his back, his arms pillowing his head, his heel in the loop of rattan which, by rhythmic pressure, waved the overhead punkah. She developed this theme of his sloth and her own generosity at some length.

"What of his schooling?" I asked. This question confirmed her view of the idiocy of the white servants of the Raj. Powerful, eye-rolling laughter was her response, so that I had that often recurring sense of how alien and useless I was in this Burmese setting. A brothel boy at school would be more at home than this assistant police magistrate in Lower Burma. And about as useful, I suppose, in her view.

I asked the brothel keeper if she knew how the boy had met the girl he killed. Her already ample bosom rose, swelled, and trembled with indignation. He had met the girl when he helped her with her parents' laundry. Washing was men's work, but the girl's father was often unwell and the girl did it for him. It was, of course, the brothel boy's duty, in return for the brothel keeper's munificence towards him, to do the washing for the brothel, which took him daily to the river. The boy had, she thought, on occasion assisted the girl by helping her carry some of her parents' laundry to and from the river. She had, it appeared, most unwisely chatted and played with him in a friendly way when they met. The proprietress had on one occasion made it her business, indeed gone out of her way, to warn the girl that the boy was a fool, a simpleton, not to be trusted, and that she should behave towards him like everyone else—not talk to the stupid boy except to tell him what to do or not to do or to reprimand him. But the girl would not listen. She was only a child of twelve or thirteen, but even so she certainly should have known better, as the younger girls in the brothel all understood, after the kindly but firm warnings so generously given.

I turned to Dr. Veraswami to try to understand the boy and his crime.

As usual, Dr. Veraswami was pleased to talk to me about this or any other subject. Both of us lacked friends and conversation partners in Moulmein. Dr. Veraswami's children by his first marriage were grown and departed; those by his second were old enough to love but not to talk with. And his present wife would run to hide in the kitchen when she saw me approaching their bungalow. She had, the doctor told me with a gentle smile, "many fine qualities indeed, indeed, but the confidence in conversation of a particularly timid mouse."

Dr. Veraswami was the only person I enjoyed in Moulmein, certainly the only one I felt at all close to since, try as I would, I could never establish a reciprocal warmth of feeling with any of the natives, though I think some of them knew I respected them. My servants would not talk at all of the crime, looking anxiously resentful and falling silent if I mentioned the boy. By contrast, in the Club, it was a subject of unending, energetic, circumlocutiously salacious chatter, the details of which I attempted to spare myself by stressing that, since the matter was *sub judice*, I should not mention it or receive advice about it. This did no good, of course, but it did give me a further excuse to avoid the Club, and confirmed the prevalent view of me there as a posturing outsider, probably a coolie lover.

Dr. Veraswami had, after all, worked in a mental hospital, and he was closer to the Burmese, certainly in their illnesses, than anyone who was not Burmese. So I turned to him.

"The boy iss, I think, quite retarded, but to what level iss hard to tell." Dr. Veraswami seemed perplexed. "Iss not easy to be sure. After all, my friend, he iss quite illiterate. Unlike you, he and the books move in different circles, always have, always will. Measuring such a mind iss beyond me, and others also, issn't it? But he iss certainly far backward, far backward."

The villagers had made much of the girl's virginity; I wondered about the boy's sexual experience. Dr. Veraswami was again hesitant, but did not doubt my speculation that the violence by the river might have been the boy's first experience of intercourse. The boy had witnessed much, of course, but the brothel girls would certainly see themselves as superior to and distant from the boy. Chastity, in the sense of absence of congress with a woman, may well have been forced on the boy.

"Is he mad? Was he mad?" I asked the doctor.

"To be sure, I don't know at all. . . . He iss certainly not normal. But given hiss life, Mr. Blair, how would you know what he thinks . . . if he does think, ass you mean it?"

"Mad or not, is he likely to do something like this again, or has he learned his lesson?" Surely the swift and brutal punishment for his venery, then the arrest and everyone condemning him, had instructed even his dull mind.

Dr. Veraswami was not so sure. "One would think so, indeed one would. But I must tell you that there are cases like hiss where even after verry severe punishment the act iss repeated. You must not, Mr. Blair, underestimate . . . ," and here he grasped wildly in the air for an unembarrassing euphemism, and with triumph found it, " . . . the power of the gonads! Of course, if you hold him in prisson for twenty years there would then be little risk—these fires do with the years burn less intensely, believe me—but I doubt he would survive so long in prisson."

Dr. Veraswami's resignation in the matter began to annoy me. "Well, if you can't help with why he did it, or whether he's dangerous, what should be done about him?"

"He will be hanged, of course."

I protested that we both knew the boy meant no harm, no evil. The more I thought about him and his crime, the less wicked it seemed, though the injury to the girl and her family was obviously extreme; but it was a tragedy, not a sin.

Dr. Veraswami was relentless. "You think him retarded, and he iss. You think him ignorant of what he should and should not do, and he iss. You think he meant no harm, just like an animal, a reaction to the girl. But don't you see, Mr. Blair, all your English colleagues see him ass just the same ass other Burmese, indistinguishable from all other native boys. All look alike. All are stupid, ignorant, cunning, untrustworthy, dirty, smelly, sexually uncontrolled. All are the same. To excuse him because he iss just like the rest would in their minds be madness in you, not in him."

I had no ready answer. "And," he continued, glancing towards the village, "so I fear iss the view of the Burmese. A brothel boy, yess, but in no other way different. They don't let mind speed worry them. You think he iss different and therefore innocent where others who did what he did would be guilty; you may be right, probably so, but the villagers don't agree! You must do what your British friends at the Club and the villagers expect you to do."

My testiness increased. "You seem so content in this, Doctor. The boy is surely less responsible than most killers; he meant no harm insofar as he understood what was happening, and you seem so swiftly to accept his hanging. Surely he is less worthy of being hanged than most murderers."

Dr. Veraswami was waving his head vigourously from side to side as I spoke. This, I had earlier discovered, was a frequent Indian gesture easily mistaken for dissent, but having the larger meaning of a qualified assent—in effect, you are nearly right but not quite. "The gaol, the prisson, perhaps," he said, waving in the direction of the dung-coloured walls of the gaol, still visible in the bright light of sunset. "He could sit there on the other side of the wall with the rest until he died, perhaps. He will learn nothing there, ass you know. Have even less to do than in the brothel. If anything he will become even more idiot than now. And they will prey on him." Then, after a pause to acknowledge my troubled silence, "Or perhaps the place where we lock up the mad. Have you seen it? Worse, I think, than the prisson. Yes, I remember, you have been there."

I had and it was. No psychiatrist could possibly wish to work in such circumstances, and none did. It was indeed the least desirable service for any doctor, Burmese or Indian—and no English doctor had as yet ever drunk enough to find himself posted there. Veraswami did his best for his insane patients, but he had much else to do.

"But iss it not much the same, even in England?" Dr. Veraswami asked. It was not really a question. He knew. I did not know. But what he implied was probably the truth.

"So what, Mr. Police Magistrate, would you have us do with the boy? Shall I take him home with me? Keep him here to serve us beer? Iss it not difficult enough for me to live in this dreadful place without taking him ass a son to my bosom? The villagers would indeed then reject me entirely quite. Or iss he to be a part of the police magistracy? You would be more doubted and even less respected—a most unwise move indeed. . . . "And he trailed off to vague head wavings.

"I wonder, Doctor, if one of us could have talked to the girl before she died—what would she have wanted me to do?"

"She would have been more scared of me than of you—Indian doctors, ass you know, bewitch village maidens and turn them into hyenas or other horrible animals; English policemen merely steal them! I doubt either of uss could have made her understand verry much about the boy. But what if we could? How could she forgive him? How tell him he was forgiven? Take the money from him, perhaps? It iss offensive. No, you will get no help from such thoughts, my friend. It could not in any way have been her problem. It iss yours."

Later, reflecting on the realities Dr. Veraswami had held up to me, I found myself dreaming the reformer's dream, summoning the resources of medicine, psychiatry, prisons without brutality, and a political caring that was ages removed from Burma under the Raj.

Did much change? I was not sure. Certainly the boy would not be executed, since, with the movement towards minimum social decencies, the executioner is one of the first functionaries to be retired. But others tend to take his place. A larger, self-caring bureaucracy often accompanies a larger caring for others. The boy might well be held until cured, but how would one ever know? Only by letting him out. And one can't do that until he is cured. So he must be held. The false language of treatment and cure would replace the Burmese bluntness of condign punishment—and which is to be preferred? If the boy could choose, he would choose to avoid the hangman, but there would be other whips and torments waiting for him even in my dream of the all-loving State.

My daydreams that the boy and I were elsewhere and in another time, rather than here and now in Moulmein, were understandable but gave me no comfort. My decision would have been cruelly lonely had not Dr. Veraswami seemed to enjoy our discussions and to be willing to help me in my thrashings around to avoid hanging the boy. Sometimes, however, he struck home hurtfully. I was pressing him for his opinion of how the boy felt in the act of killing—caring, cruel, lost, bewildered? I suggested confusion and a sense of isolation. Dr. Veraswami looked incredibly embarrassed. "Did you not tell me, dear friend, of some difficulties you and some of your distinguished young friends . . . ass it were . . . experienced at that fine English preparatory school you attended before Eton? St. Cyprian's, issn't it?" I had no idea what he was talking about and remained silent. He blushed. Indians do blush, though less obviously, of course, than Englishmen. "Enuresis, issn't it, I believe? Flogged for what you did not know how to avoid, I think you said." And I knew that I, too, suddenly was blushing, the lobes of my ears scarlet, the guilt of my childhood bed-wetting still upon me.

Dr. Veraswami was sure he had offended me; his agitation increased. He got up, fussing about with bottles of beer, now warming as the bits of ice he had somewhere found melted to fragments.

He was, of course, quite right. In a sense I had been where the brothel boy found himself. I had been beaten for my sins, sins that were clearly both wicked and outside my control, yet nevertheless sins, or so they seemed to me and to Bingo and Sim, who wielded the cane and broke the riding crop on me.

It was possible, therefore, to commit a sin without knowing you committed it and without being able to avoid it. So it had seemed then, and the feeling of guilt undeniably remained, and strong. Sin was thus, sometimes, something that happened—to me as to the brothel boy. You did not, properly speaking, *do* the deed; you merely woke up in the morning to find in anguish that the sheets were wringing wet.

I tried to calm Dr. Veraswami, to assure him that he had not offended me, that I appreciated his directness, that I needed his help. This led me to an excessive confession, one I had made to no one else, and probably no one else knew about it, not even Sim. The last time Sim had flogged me for bed-wetting, I remember with great pain a further loss of control of my bladder and a warm flow inside my short pants, down the inside of my left knee, onto my long socks, and into my left shoe. Sim had me bent over a desk, posterior protruding, but I hoped most desperately, and still now in misery believe, that the desk shielded his eyes from my pants and the pool which may have formed at my feet. The shame, had the puddle been seen and almost surely commented on, would have been beyond bearing. But I still don't know if it was.

Dr. Veraswami's hands were flying about in near frenzy. I tried hurriedly to make the link to the case of the brothel boy, straining thus to calm him. I thought he feared a breach in our friendship, but that is unfair; on reflection I think his only anxiety was that he was troubling me too deeply. Perhaps he was.

Were my feelings then, and the brothel boy's now, at all comparable? Had I become a ponderous, unfeeling mixture of Bingo and Sim, punishing the boy by death because of the harshness of the environment into which he had been flung, compared to which my trials at St. Cyprian's were trivial?

Dr. Veraswami would have none of it. "But, Mr. Blair, bed-wetting and rape which kills . . . how can you compare them at all? Misplaced guilt . . .

childish fears and adversities loom ever large, but no, not at all, not in any way like the brothel boy's guilt."

Perhaps gallows humour would reassure Veraswami that he had not wounded me. "At all events, Dr. Veraswami, after that beating, when I wet my sock and shoe, I did not wet my bed again. I was cured. Sim cured me. The hangman will surely cure any lack of control our brothel boy may have over his burgeoning sexual instincts."

But Dr. Veraswami was hardly listening, "No, no, no, dear Sir. . . . Enuresis while asleep, sexual attack while awake; nothing similar."

So I pressed the analogy, suggesting that precautions might be taken: Drink little late, empty the bladder before retiring; one might even arrange to be awakened during the night if others would help. What were the precautions the brothel boy should have taken against copying what he had seen, and seen as acceptable behaviour, to be purchased when the flesh engorged? The brothel boy could hardly be justly punished for the desire. Obviously he had nothing to do with it; less than I had with the springs of enuresis. And whence was he to find the wisdom and control, in unsought and unexpected heat, not to do what probably seemed to him an obvious and acceptable act? He had observed in the brothel apparent gratitude by both parties, simulation and true appreciation being indistinguishable by him—and often by others more intelligent and perceptive than he. Where were the differences between him and me in our sinning? The distinctions seemed to favour him.

Dr. Veraswami's intensity increased. "No, you are verry wrong; forgive me contradicting you, but you are off a lot. The boy must have known he wass hurting her, dull though he iss. The girls in the brothel fear and complain of violence, they talk to each other about it often, the boy must have known. Once he came close upon her, he knew, he knew; believe me, my friend. The cases are quite different. You do yourself too much injustice. You did not sin; he did, and most grievously. Your comparison with your bed-wetting misses the essential difference, isn't it? He wass conscious of what he was doing; you were not. And being conscious, backward and confused though he iss, mistreated and bewildered though he wass, he must be held responsible. You must convict him, punish him, hang him! He is a citizen of Burma, a subject of your Imperial Majesty; you must treat him ass a responsible adult and punish him. That iss what citizenship iss."

I had never before heard such a lengthy, passionately sibilant speech from Dr. Veraswami. It seemed to have calmed him. Again, it didn't help me.

It seemed to me that the discussion had tilted crazily against the brothel boy. Responsibility . . . citizenship . . . consciousness of what he was doing. . . . Were these sensible standards for a youth of his darkly clouded intelligence and blighted situation? And, if not, what standard should be applied, to what end, with what results?

An all-wise God could by definition draw these fine distinctions, but it was hard to think of the brothel boy and an omniscient God (and even less an omnibenevolent God) as in any way related. And I knew that I was no plenipotentiary of such a divinity; being a minor agent of the Raj was enough for me. My employers had never distinguished themselves in drawing delicately generous moral distinctions; indeed, they seemed to judge entirely by the results and not by the intentions, which surely must inhibit any fine gradations in attributing guilt.

Did this mean that there was no room at all in my jurisdiction for mercy, for clemency? I decided to put the question to Dr. Veraswami.

Unlike my fellow members of the Club, Dr. Veraswami enjoyed my skill in rolling cigarettes. He rarely smoked but occasionally would accept one of my own home-grown cigarettes. He preferred to moisten the paper himself, I holding the enfolded tobacco out to him; but he also cheerfully accepted those that were the product of my own hands and tongue.

When talking with Dr. Veraswami I found I sometimes rolled a cigarette to give me time to phrase a point of delicacy or difficulty, as many who smoke a pipe use the ritual of filling, lighting, and tamping as time for reflection. On this occasion, the cigarette rolling was a preamble to an effort to seek Dr. Veraswami's views on the moral aspects of the problem of the brothel boy. And, if he agreed that the boy was less culpable, to press him why he was so adamant about the hanging.

"Do you know a painting by Peter Paul Rubens of the Last Judgment?" I asked Dr. Veraswami. "It is a huge painting with lovely, though overweight, naked ladies and gentlemen ascending to unclothed inactivity above the right hand of Christ. Just below His left hand there is an interesting Prince of Darkness in control of a lecherous team of demons dragging the damned off to undepicted horrors, with a face at the bottom of the Devil's side of the painting screaming in agony."

Dr. Veraswami said he had seen a poor print of it once, he thought, but in any event he plunged ahead of my circumlocution to the heart of the question. "You ask, I suppose, my friend, where will the boy be if the admirable Mr. Rubens paints truth? Of course, I don't know. I am not a Christian but, if I were, I would guess he will not be among those damned."

"Well then, how can you tell me to hang him?" I asked, pressing Dr. Veraswami for reconciliation of his apparently conflicting positions.

Dr. Veraswami yielded to no difficulty in the reconciliation. Mercy, a full and forgiving understanding of behaviour, was the prerogative of God, if there was one, and if he had so little to do that he interested himself in us after we died—which Dr. Veraswami doubted. Nor did he believe, as did some Hindus and all Buddhists, that we came back in some other form; but if we did the boy was as likely to ascend as to descend in the hierarchy— whatever it was. All in all, if God had made the boy as he was and put him where he was, it was hard to believe that the boy had behaved any better or worse than God must have expected. But all that, he argued most vigourously, had nothing to do with Assistant Police Magistrate Blair, who admirable though Dr. Veraswami knew he was, educated and wise beyond his years, could not now help the boy. "Justice, Mr. Blair, iss your job. Justice, not mercy." And his gesturing hand fell and was still, simulating the fall of the gallows.

"Surely, Doctor, mercy can be a part of justice. They are hardly in opposition. Cannot mercy infuse justice, shape it, direct it?"

"Sometimes, sometimes, but often it iss beyond our competence." And he launched again into a lengthy speech, his plump, white-clad behind balanced against the verandah rail, his black thumb and forefinger nipping at the air as if to capture ideas as they floated by. The tenor of his argument was, so far as I followed it, Freudian. If we knew all we could about any murderer, including the brothel boy, all about his inherited capacities and all his life experiences, we would find more than sufficient explanation for all his actions, including the rape which killed. Conduct was apparently "overdetermined," once you included the unconscious and the subconscious. And for most of these pressures, which collectively and inexorably determine everyone's behaviour, it would seem unfair to hold anyone responsible. "But, Mr. Blair, fair or not, it is essential to do so! Within justice there may be room for clemency, for mercy, for human understanding, providing only that the essential purposes of punishment under law are not frustrated. Here they would be. He hass killed while deliberately doing what iss a verry serious crime. There iss no room for mercy, no room at all." And then, as if he thought it would clinch the matter: "Why, even the good Viennese doctor himself, Sigmund Freud, said you are responsible for your unconscious. There it iss!"

"But surely, Doctor, if we can distinguish degrees of fault, or think we can, sufficiently to reduce or increase the punishment of the guilty, to be merciful or to be severe, why can't we—why can't I—by the same means reduce guilt itself? After all, sometimes we do that. When people kill accidentally, we call it manslaughter if they have been very careless indeed; and if they have not been careless and yet have killed it is usually no crime, and never murder. We may not be very good at judging moral fault, but in a rough-and-ready way we can. And surely the boy is nearer innocence than guilt."

"No, no, my magistrate friend, you make the same mistake, forgive me, pleass. We are talking only of intentional acts, not of acts of carelessness—they are quite different. That iss what distinguishes the boy's acts from your enuresis, issn't it? And for such acts . . . ," and here Dr. Veraswami grabbed two handfuls of ideas from the air around him, " . . . the boy iss either to be treated ass a responsible man or he issn't. There iss no half-man for guilt in the eyes of the law. If there were a choice of punishments for what he hass done, perhaps you could be merciful, because he hass been much abused and iss of weak mind. But there issn't, there issn't. It iss circular, you see."

I didn't see at all, but he pressed on, now almost skipping about with the released energy of uninhibited talk, which I suddenly realised was an even more cherished luxury for him than for me. "Man iss defined by hiss capacity for moral choice. That iss what man iss, nothing else, otherwise an animal." And then, chuckling at the cruel pointedness of the joke: "Dr. Freud and the law agree, you see. For hiss unconscious mind and for hiss conscious mind, such ass they are, the brothel boy is twice responsible. Otherwise, you would have to excuse everyone, certainly everyone you took the trouble to understand."

Though a painful conclusion, the point was strong. Justice cannot excuse everyone, obviously. And if our judgement of moral guilt reflects mainly our degree of ignorance of the relevant moral facts, then all we would do in a mercy-controlled system of punishment would, in effect, be to excuse or be merciful towards those we know a lot about or decided to find out about—and not towards the others. To my dismay it seemed to me, therefore, that if Justice stands in opposition to Mercy, we are damned (or, certainly, this Assistant Police Magistrate is); and if Mercy is to infuse Justice, to be a part of it, we probably claim beyond our competence.

Dr. Veraswami understood my difficulty in this whole matter, my search for some principle to guide me. "I think a lot about it, Mr. Blair, since it iss such a worry to you. And, if I may, pleass, I hope you agree, here iss my conclusion." And after a pause, a thumb-and-forefinger, tweezer-like nip in the air to catch his words, "There iss no steady principle to guide you, none at all. You must be a man of principles, not of principle."

Dr. Veraswami seemed to be becoming more elliptic than before, and in annoyance I told him so. "No, you misunderstand me," he replied; "I mean there iss no moral principle to guide you, moral, *moral*. There are, of course, other guides, other principles. The main one iss that you English should use the executioner ass little ass you can—rarely, if you use him at all. And how to know how little iss 'ass little ass you can'?" Here he paused again, hands still, achieving impressive rhetorical effect. "I have it! If the British do not wish him killed, there iss no problem unless the natives want him killed verry much, and the British think they should let them have their way. If it iss a native to be executed they will not care too much. But if the British and the natives *both* want him killed, ass with the brothel boy, unless he iss so verry mad as to be obviously mad to all, natives and British alike, you can do nothing unless you also wish to leave the service of the Raj and be seen by all ass a treasonable fool."

Hesitantly, regretting the force of "treasonable fool," he added: "I would like to help you, but I can't. Perhaps you should leave here. . . . I would miss you. You would be happier in England, I think, but iss this the way? Iss this the way to go? And even if you do save the boy, what can we do with him? Ass I said, the gaol? The madhouse?"

It appalled me to realise that I was in Pilate's role, at least as Pilate may have seen it, though otherwise the comparison made no sense. Nor, increasingly it seemed to me, did I. Perhaps it was for me the madhouse that Dr. Veraswami saw as useless for the boy. No, I understood the issue all too well; it was now clear and I was not confused. Dr. Veraswami was right. As a moral issue, the boy was nearer to innocence than most of us; at the

Last Judgment I would back his chances over most. But as a legal and political matter, what a weak reed he had in me to sustain his life!

I recalled another recent occasion in Moulmein when I had failed to stand for the right against public pressures. Was it to become a habit? A recidivist Pilate indeed! A few months ago, very much against my better judgement and every inclination, I had shot a working elephant that had recovered from a period of "must" in which he had damaged some property and killed a native. As soon as I saw the elephant, I knew with perfect certainty that I ought not to shoot him; but the natives expected it of me and I had to do it. I could feel their dark, sweaty wills pressing me forward, irresistibly. If I did nothing, it was quite probable that some of them would laugh. So I shot the elephant.

I had to contend then only with native opinion; the Europeans would have divided on the question, some holding it to be a damn shame to shoot an elephant for killing a coolie, because an elephant was worth more than any damn Coringhee coolie. Now, with the brothel boy, the forces pressing on me were different, and greater. No one would laugh if I did not hang the boy, but European and native opinion were agreed and vehement—that is what I ought to do, what I must do.

Memories of St. Cyprian's again swept in. I remembered how Latin was beaten into me, and I still doubted that a classical education could be successfully carried on without corporal punishment. Bingo, Sim, and the boys all believed in its efficacy; as in Moulmein, public opinion was unanimous about the value of physical punishment. I recalled Beacham, a boy with a dull mind—not as dull as the brothel boy's, but certainly not bright— whom Sim flogged towards their joint goal of a scholarship for Beacham, as the heartless might flog a foundered horse. And when Beacham was severely beaten yet again for his failure in the scholarship exam, his words of poignant regret came back to me: " I wish I'd had that caning before I went up for the exam."

As I walked with Dr. Veraswami into the gaol yard I caught sight of him. Six guards were getting him ready for the gallows. He stood, surrounded by the guards, slim and muscular, with shaven head and vague, liquid eyes. He seemed genuinely bewildered, uncomprehending though deeply fearful. The guards crowded close to him, with their hands always on him in a careful, caressing grip, as though all the while feeling him to make sure he was there. He seemed hardly to notice what was happening. His eyes caught mine and paused while it dawned on him that he knew me and that I had been gentle with him. The vague eyes shaped a semblance of communication.

No marks remained of the beating. His body had repaired itself, but the intervening weeks had not helped my mind to repair its anguish. I walked behind him to the gallows. Though his arms were bound, he walked quite steadily. And once, in spite of the men who gripped him by each shoulder, he stepped lightly aside to avoid a puddle on the path. The puddle—and I understood why—brought me back to the unreasoning St. Cyprian's guilt. That I should be destroying a healthy, conscious man, dull and dangerous though he may be—the unspeakable wrongness of cutting short a life in full tide! The struggle for rational judgment came as a minor anodyne. How can I refashion the world of the just and the unjust, of the forgiving and the prejudiced, myself an uncertain observer rather than a shaper of justice, a player without influence on the rules? Only by my own death would I escape the pain of these cruel games if I stayed long in the magistracy.

So that when he was dead, and the superintendent of the gaol asked Dr. Veraswami and me and the rest of the little procession to join him in a drink—"I've got a bottle of whisky inside. We could do with it."—I found myself drinking and laughing with the rest of them, quite amicably, but perhaps too loudly.

Commentary to
"THE BROTHEL BOY"

Few now favour the execution of all murderers; but if not all, then how to choose? Abolitionists have a simple answer, but for those who wish to retain the death penalty the question has powerful force.

There are now more than 23,000 murders per year in the United States of America, of which at least 10,000 are "capital murders," that is to say, killings where the murderer faces the death penalty as the law stands. Yet, in no year in this country have there ever been two hundred executions, and the present rate runs below twenty a year. How is that 0.2% to be chosen? And even if the percentage be substantially increased, as some retentionists advocate, the problem remains fundamentally the same, since most reject a lottery and few wish for the bloodbath of the execution of all such killers.

Traditionally, two broad philosophic concepts have interacted to help different people at different times decide which convicted murderers should be executed. The interaction is between the concepts of guilt and blame.

These words, "blame" and "guilt," have no agreed technical meaning. I use them because they make sense to me and help me to understand the thought and feeling processes that move people when they seek to determine an appropriate punishment for a crime, to distinguish the grave offence from the venial. They talk of the gravity of the injury to the victim and of the evil intent or recklessness of the criminal, of blame and guilt. They talk of what the criminal "deserved," of the talionic law of an eye for an eye, a tooth for a tooth.

Both concepts, blame and guilt, look backwards. They are based on what has happened and what is deserved by way of punishment. The discussion proceeds to forward-looking concepts, to utilitarian ideas, to the belief that what is done to the criminal as punishment may deter others who are like-minded, may deter the criminal himself from future criminality or teach him conforming ways, and may be used to separate him temporarily or permanently from the community in whose name the punishment is to be imposed.

The story of the brothel boy explores these issues in sharp form. His *blame* is great; without justification or valid excuse he has taken the life of an innocent young girl in a brutal way. His *guilt* is very doubtful; given what he is and what the world has made him, he may well not, when he comes to divine judgement, stand among the damned. Then there are the utilitarian considerations facing District Officer Blair as he comes to exercise his several discretions which may save the life of the boy or send him to his execution.

If we can sort out which considerations properly weigh, and how heavily, in determining what should be the punishment of the brothel boy, we will have gone far in understanding the legitimate purposes of criminal punishments.

One must not be too hopeful. Consensus is unlikely to emerge, and indeed "The Brothel Boy" is deliberately fashioned to tease out issues on which thoughtful people have differed for centuries.

Here, then, are some of the ideas, and some of the decisions and studies, that have weighed with philosophers, lawyers, psychiatrists, and social scientists as they have tried to fit the punishment to the crime, to the criminal, and to the legitimate needs of social safety. Far from all that is relevant to District Officer Blair's decision is explored, only a few of the major issues to launch reflection and discussion.

There are two broad and sharply different patterns of discourse about capital punishment, as about other punishments—deontological and utilitarian. The former does not treat questions of social advantage or disadvantage; it focuses on the moral deservedness of the punishment, on issues of blame and guilt. The latter treats questions of the social cost-benefit of capital punishment—questions of deterrence, of prison administration, of alternative punishments—and it takes into consideration the views of the public. A few comments on each will link this ongoing debate to "The Brothel Boy."

The Deserved Punishment: Blame and Guilt

Blame and guilt interact, I have suggested, to produce the deserved punishment. This does not mean that the deserved punishment should in all cases be imposed—it is a great mercy for all of us that we don't always receive our just deserts. What it does mean is that the punishment imposed should never exceed that which is deserved. Blame and guilt together define the upper limit of a just punishment; reasons of penal policy should set the punishment within that limit.

Blame is related to the harm done or risked—the injury; guilt is related to the mind of the criminal, or what the lawyers call *mens rea*. Blame is objective, guilt subjective. It is the product of the interaction between blame and guilt that primarily distinguishes those murderers who will be selected for execution from the mass of available candidates.

There is no serious crime without *both* blame and guilt, each to some degree. No matter the extent of the injury that your actions caused, unless you intended it, or were reckless as to some risk of injury related to what you did, you are not a criminal. Likewise, no matter the depravity of your wicked intentions, unless you expressed them in actions or words, you are not a criminal.

The blame in "The Brothel Boy" is great, the guilt slight. But, as Veraswami insists, guilt is there to some degree; the brothel boy's behaviour is not the same as Blair's childhood enuresis—or so Veraswami argues.

Many of the nicest issues in the substantive criminal law revolve around this relationship between blame and guilt. "The Brothel Boy" raises it in sharp form, but it has troubled men and women for centuries. For example, a Greek infant of royal blood is given to a poor peasant to rear. Entirely ignorant of his true parentage, the infant grows to lusty manhood, kills his father in a chance roadside encounter and then weds and beds his mother. As a result of these events—in the opinion of the general populace and also of the wisest seer—plague descends on the land. Oedipus would seem entirely to lack guilt, though if the populace and the seer are correct he is properly to be blamed. The story of the brothel boy is another example of the popular tendency to seek a scapegoat for a grievous injury and to press for his punishment. But whatever the pressures of popular opinion, the law and the lawyers have insisted on the need for some showing of guilt, of mindful wrongdoing, before punishment may be imposed. Does the brothel boy qualify?

The Law and the Lawyers

The original definition of a felony in the Common Law was an offence punishable capitally. For centuries all felons risked execution. Gradually the range of capital offences was reduced. Gentler manners, a doubt of the efficacy of this punishment for lesser offences, the refusal of juries to convict when they thought the punishment excessive, the development of alternative, less severe punishments, and many other factors led to the present situation where, in practice, only the most blameworthy and most wicked of murderers are thought to be properly subject to the death penalty. Legislation in all states of the Union has tried to achieve this result, but there is substantial diversity in the legislative definitions of the principles to be applied by judges and juries to reach this end. And the judges and the juries differ widely in their interpretations of the legislative mandates.

In the United States the matter is further complicated by the Bill of Rights, with its insistence on equal protection under the law (by which, for example, it is prohibited to impose the death penalty on a racial basis—though every study reveals that it is so imposed), on due process of law in the trial of those to be selected for this punishment, and on the prohibition of cruel and unusual punishments. A substantial jurisprudence of death has been developed to narrow the constitutional range of the death penalty, a jurisprudence you do not wish to examine unless you are a lawyer or a convicted murderer. But this at least may be said—and here I irresponsibly lapse into the dogmatic: it is presumptuous for eight men and one woman to think that they have moral calipers of such precision that they can in advance define that delicate balance between guilt and harm which alone can justify such a selection. I am sure St. Peter finds it quite difficult; for the rest of us it is impossible.

By that statement I mean, of course, no personal criticism of the Justices of the Supreme Court. They do their best with this impossible task; but it would be refreshing if there were a clearer recognition on their part that they, like us, lack the sensitivity, the knowledge, and the purity of heart to make such fine distinctions.

Deterrence

Is capital punishment a uniquely effective deterrent punishment? Does it save innocent lives? Affirmative answers to these questions are the most frequently advanced justifications for the death penalty. What, then, are the answers?

The retentionist argument is not the superficially false proposition that other criminals like the brothel boy, far from a rationally planning offender, will be deterred from killing by the brothel boy's execution. Rather it is that the existence of the death penalty, and its application to what are seen as the gravest crimes, will give a signal to all who may contemplate killing another that this may be their fate too, and will thereby cause at least some of those who are rationally motivated to desist. Thus the lives of some potential victims will be saved.

Cardinal Newman expressed the skeptic's view of the above argument: "As well try to bind the rage, pride, and passion of man by threat of punishment as try to guide the ship in a storm by strands of silk."

So much for speculating about the efficacy of a rational motivation basis for the deterrent effects of capital punishment. What do we know, as distinct from what we speculate about? Surely, this question of general deterrence, of the brothel boy being executed to reduce the incidence of murder, is responsive to empirical analysis. Is it?

Dogmatism should be avoided on both sides of this argument. The best available evidence is not decisive.

Since the 1950s, with Thorsten Sellin's finding that the death penalty appeared to exercise "no influence on the extent or fluctuating rates of capital crimes," platoons of scholars have studied this question, applying a diversity of research techniques, some of them quite sophisticated. Sellin came to what he called "the inevitable conclusion that executions have no discernible effect on homicide death rates." Later scholars have been unable to refute his conclusion, although they have modified it toward caution.

The latest scholarly assessment of the available evidence on the deterrent effect of capital punishment is that by Roger Hood in his study for the United Nations, cited below. His conclusion was: "Research has failed to provide scientific proof that executions have a greater deterrent effect than life imprisonment. The evidence as a whole still gives no positive support to the deterrent hypothesis" (Hood, *infra*, at 167).

It is not as though scholars have been remiss in searching for such evidence. Careers are to be made if it is found. And the United States of America, where most of this intensive research has been pursued, is a natural laboratory for finding such deterrent effects if they exist, since the laws and practices vary profoundly between the states, from abolitionist to retentionist, and from retentionist states that never or rarely execute murderers to those with bulging death rows and regular executions.

Perhaps more troublesome for the retentionist who seeks evidence of the uniquely powerful deterrent effect of the death penalty is the conclusion of a panel of the National Research Council of the National Academy of Sciences that "the available studies provide no useful evidence on the deterrent effect of capital punishment" (Blumstein et al., *infra*, at 9). The panel further advised that "any policy use of scientific evidence on capital punishment will require extremely severe standards of proof. The non-experimental research to which the study of the deterrent effects of capital punishment is necessarily limited will almost certainly be unable to meet those standards of proof" (*Id.*, at 62-63). So, in terms of scientific knowledge, as distinct from reasonable speculation, we are unlikely ever to *know* that capital punishment saves innocent lives.

How, then, stated as objectively as an abolitionist can, does the deterrence argument stand? Capital punishment may or may not have a deterrent effect on the murder rate greater than that possessed by the alternative punishments. Capital punishment may or may not save innocent lives. But it certainly does not save a sufficient number of lives to be detected or measured by our present research methods. At best, it can be uniquely effective as a deterrent only at the margins of the homicide rate, certainly less significant in its life-saving effect than a variety of other social processes that could reduce that rate.

This does not, of course, dispose of the retentionist position. As we have seen, there are deontological reasons to be advanced in favour of capital punishment, and the retentionist can validly argue that in a situation of extreme blame and guilt, with the life-saving capacity of capital punishment in doubt, it is better to err on the safe side and to retain the death penalty for its possibly marginally greater deterrent effect.

Incapacitation, Cost, and Prison Administration

One thing is clear about the death penalty; the murderer will not kill again. The brothel boy will rape no other young girl. And there are cases, though they are rare indeed, of a convicted murderer serving a prison term, being released, and then killing again.

Of course, if life-saving is the overriding concern of punishment, then it is not the murderers who should not be released; their post-punishment homicide rate is miniscule compared with that of released robbers and of other felons who have used a gun in the commission of their last crime.

Nevertheless, it is true that holding convicted murderers in prison for protracted periods is expensive, and it is further true that exceptional mistakes are made and a rare released murderer kills again. Should, therefore, all be executed?

The facts on the question of the costs of protracted imprisonment and of capital punishment are reasonably clear, though they are counterintuitive and not well known. Our present capital punishment regime, with its crowded death rows, frequent appeals, and excessive media attention is clearly more expensive than the alternative punishments favoured by abolitionists. Comparisons between countries and between abolitionist and retentionist states in this country confirm that fact.

As to the prison regime for convicted murderers: they turn out, as a group, to be an entirely manageable segment of the prison population. There are exceptions, of course—turbulent and intractable convicted murderers—but not nearly as many as there are turbulent and intractable robbers and burglars. Long acquaintance with prison regimes in abolitionist countries and in states of this country, and many years of wandering the yards and cell-houses of our prisons holding those convicted of the major felonies, have convinced me that the correctional authorities have no more difficulty with this category of convicted offenders than with any other; indeed, the contrary is the case.

Public Opinion

Among western industrialised nations, only the United States of America still retains capital punishment. Worldwide the situation is different, with a majority of countries remaining retentionist. Studies supported by the United Nations over the past two decades have established, however, that the steady trend is towards abolition.

An interesting aspect of this movement, one which confronted District Officer Blair in pointed and personal form, is the force of public opinion. Blair did not want to shoot the elephant; he knew its "must" was past, knew it not now to be a threat to person or property, yet he shot it under the pressure of public opinion. In every country that has abolished capital punishment in the past fifty years, public opinion has favoured the retention of that punishment; yet the movement toward abolition continues, with legislatures—not generally regarded as palaces of independent judgement—recognizing and acting upon the force of the abolitionist case even at the risk of thereby losing votes. The issue thus compels consideration of the role of the elected representative in a democratic legislature. The United Nations study by Roger Hood concludes on that question: "popular sentiment alone should not determine penal policy, that task being the responsibility of elected representatives exercising their own judgment."

There is, as you see, almost as heated an argument about the determinative role of "the popular will" on the capital punishment debate as there is about deterrence. It was clearly the popular will and the vacillation of District Officer Blair that disposed of the brothel boy.

Selected References

The following references will assist those who wish further to pursue the issues raised in "The Brothel Boy":

Bedau, Hugo Adam. *A Capital Punishment Reader*. New York: Anchor Books, 1967.

Blumstein, A., et al. *Deterrence and Incapacitation*. National Academy of Sciences, National Research Council, 1978.

Hart, H. L. A. *Punishment and Responsibility*. Oxford: Clarendon Press, 1968.

Hood, Roger. *The Death Penalty: A World-Wide Perspective*. Oxford: Clarendon Press, 1989.

Zimring, Franklin E., and Hawkins, Gordon. *Capital Punishment and the American Agenda*. Cambridge: Cambridge University Press, 1986.

This is, of course, a very brief bibliographic guide. The justification for its brevity, despite the libraries of books and articles on this topic, is that four of the books cited above encompass the most recent worldwide and American studies on capital punishment and contain comprehensive bibliographic guidance to the scholarly literature on that topic. The fifth, the H.L.A. Hart book, is the definitive statement of the punishment philosophy that influences this commentary to "The Brothel Boy."

The Best Interests
of the Child

It had happened swiftly, safely, and to the noisy delight of the Chinakans. The distance between the beach and their fishing village was about a hundred yards; we were inundated midway on our journey, providing a perfect view for all.

When we pushed off there seemed ample clearance between the calm waters and the gunwales, though the barque was heavily laden with the tins of bully beef, of dried biscuits, of jam and condensed milk, and a wide variety of other groceries to which the Burmese villagers were reputed to be partial. I doubt that Mr. Plimsoll would have been suspicious, unless perhaps he was wise in the ways of Burmese fishing villagers.

I had built so many dreams around those tins and bottles. Of course I would not bargain; no vulgar barter for me. I would simply give gifts—not all at once, but in a steady flow of beneficence. The natural tendency of the Burmese to extend hospitality to a European who had unbent to the point of wishing to visit their humble fishing village for a day or two would be powerfully reinforced by my munificence. Images of feasts, of wise old Burmese gentlemen beaming with approval at the young white man come to live temporarily among them, of the less proper passages in *The Golden Bough*, had haunted me for weeks; and I confess it had not escaped my daydreams, and even an occasional more real imagining of the night, that one or more of the slender, lovely Burmese girls might take it into her heart and passionate nature to express her gratitude in those ways they were reputed to favour for this purpose. And now, now nothing would remain. Not a single biscuit, not a pot of Marmite, none of Jardine's diverse and, I ruefully remembered, expensive produce remained above the waves.

A sinking feeling, I thought as the barque sank, and was amused by the trite pun. Looking, I am sure, a total fool, pith helmet still squarely in place, left arm raised to preserve my father's watch, his parting gift to me, I trod water while boats pushed off from the village. I was soon pulled aboard and carried dripping to the landing stage, where I had expected to arrive in dignity and wealth, not soggy poverty.

They treated me kindly. There were a few muffled laughs but most of my audience had disappeared into their huts to minimise my embarrassment. The headman welcomed me with a word and led me to the hut set aside for me facing out into the Gulf of Martaban. Tall for a villager and carrying himself with almost military rigidity, he was dressed in a long white *longhi*, the cylindrical shirt to the ankles, folded over in front and tucked in, and a single-breasted *eingyi*, a short-sleeved jacket, also of white and almost transparent cloth, the more formal dress of male villagers of the South of Burma. His dignity contrasted starkly with my soggy squalor. In pidgin English he directed me to divest myself of my clothes and to substitute the two pieces of village attire like those he wore which were waiting for me, neatly folded on the sleeping mat in my hut. He gestured for a young man to gather up my clothes and suggested that I might like to rest for a while.

I remember what an idiot I felt. It had been ludicrous to think I could manage on my own. Here I was stranded—well, hardly "stranded," rather "at sea," though in a hut—without even an interpreter. What a miserable emissary of the powerful Raj! What a fool the natives must think me! I would have to ask San Thay to join me, rather than leave him on the beach with the police sergeant. Or wouldn't it be better, I recall thinking, to call the whole visit off and crawl back to Moulmein, birthday or no birthday? How presumptuous I had been to think that my schoolboy affectation of a benevolent visit to a Burmese village would be acceptable to the villagers. Undecided, I walked around the edge of the huts, along one narrow companionway and another, to the landing stage where I intended to gesture or shout to the beach or somehow get a message to San Thay.

They had wasted no time! The youth of the village were at work and play between the village and the beach. Three or four fishing barques and a cluster of dark diving heads were assembled over the scene of my inundation. Bully beef and biscuits, jams and condensed milk, the imperishable cornucopia of Jardine and Sons was being rescued by the young men and women of Chinaka. My immediate anger turned to amusement and then to laughter, and a new flood, this time of goodwill, engulfed me. Suddenly the village was populated, not deserted as it had been when I walked from my hut to my view of the salvage operations. My amusement had generated acceptance. And it was clear to me that it did not matter if San Thay joined me in the village or not; either way I would be treated kindly.

My laughter turned to quiet amusement and then to interest in the salvage operation. I wanted to swim out to assist, but the loin cloth and jacket seemed inappropriate to the purpose, and my swimming costume, which I had brought in my bag, was of course intermingled with the groceries on the sands at the bottom of the shallow bay. So I watched, and pointed, and laughed at the joy of the young divers, and applauded as tin after tin emerged to be tossed into one or another of the boats.

My bag rose to the surface in the arms of two young men. Into a boat it went and was brought to where I stood. I reached for it. Firmly, but gently, I was denied its possession. Reawakening anger quickly calmed as I was made to understand that washing and drying might be necessary and that the clean contents would soon be in my hut.

I saw a lighter skin among the children playing around the divers, slim and swift in the water like the rest, but with a honey-coloured body and brown hair. I pointed to him and asked the headman about him. "He JiHan. His mother speak English. She work for Sahib Cunningham in Moulmein. She help you talk." And so it was. JiHan's mother, Shin Yalat, served throughout my visit to Chinaka as an erratic but conscientious translator on the few occasions when translation was necessary.

But it was her son, JiHan, who had attracted and held my immediate attention. He seemed to me about seven years old, but I am never sure of such matters. It was clear that he was Eurasian, of light brown skin, browner than the sun can achieve for the European, but lighter and tanner than the Burmese. He was beautiful, as only a very few European children are ever beautiful, and Burmese children never—though the average pulchritude of the Burmese, child and adult, clearly exceeds that of Europeans. He glowed with the soft radiance of the young and privileged—bright blue eyes, light brown hair, and fine Nordic features set in an envelope of honey-coloured skin. Slender yet sturdy, swift of movement, he was compellingly visible among the children of the village.

I would never forget the date of this, my first failure as an entrepreneur. It was the twenty-fifth of June, 1926, during the rainy season in the month the Burmese call Nayan—I don't know the year in their calendar. But it was also my first birthday in Burma and I had been planning its celebration for months, building too much on it, no doubt.

It had seemed to me important to mark the passage of the year by some ceremony and yet to avoid, if possible without offence, the usual alcoholic celebrations at the Club. Obviously, I would have to be away from Moulmein on the twenty-fifth of June.

Since my duties obliged me to visit all villages within my jurisdiction at

least once a year, a trip to Chinaka, in the curve of a bay on the coast facing the Gulf of Martaban, had seemed to me an excellent excuse for a private birthday celebration of a type I would be likely to enjoy and to
remember. I would take San Thay, my houseboy, and stay at Chinaka for
two or three days. San Thay and the policeman could stay on the beach
while I went out to Chinaka itself.

I had visited Chinaka on occasions before, but they were always formal
and brief visits, an hour or so with the headman, asking through an interpreter if there were any police problems I should address. He had had no
idea at all, and I not much more, of the frame of reference of such an
enquiry.

My earlier visits had been confined to the two buildings on the shore.
One was a large structure in which the villagers kept the tools for tilling
their gardens and in which they shaped the barques that were the capital
equipment of this fishing village; the other, a simply constructed but
ornately decorated pagoda, fell outside my lay jurisdiction.

The sense of cleanliness, peace, and relative prosperity about Chinaka,
as well as its graceful setting, had attracted me to it for more than a formal
visit. The village consisted of between 150 and 200 inhabitants, and forty
or more bamboo and thatch huts, connected by wooden walkways and
built on stilts over the shallow waters of the bay. Their economy was simple but sufficient: mostly fishing for food and for barter, with some small
vegetable gardens near the beach, and a few pigs penned ashore.

Those who lived in Chinaka and the other stilted fishing villages in the
delta were regarded as primitive and simple by other Burmese, not only by
the town dwellers but also by those in the agricultural villages. The
Chinakans and the others who made their homes over the water seemed to
have come from waves of migration earlier than the movements west from
Siam and south from India.

When I had last visited Chinaka my perception of its beauty must have
been apparent. The headman had invited me to return and, gesturing
toward a hut on the outer perimeter of the village, urged me to use it and
had seemed to mean it. Many Burmese villages have rest houses for travelers (it is an act of Buddhist religious merit to provide one), but for a fishing
village built offshore it is unusual—travelers don't pass that way. He had
seemed sincere in the invitation, so I accepted and planned the birthday
visit.

It was the beauty and simplicity of the place that attracted me, I told
myself, but greed was not entirely absent. Some of the villagers produced
hand-carved model boats, replicas of their fishing barques, delicate and of
precise detail, and much prized by Europeans and Burmese alike. I had
intended to acquire several of these. But in the event, these plans, too,
proved trivial.

When the drama, anger, and amusement of my arrival were over, I settled with quiet contentment into the life of the village. I was cared for in
the sense that I was fed and allowed to be a part of the village without

much fuss being made. There were no feasts, no gifts, none of the uninhibited entertainments I had stupidly expected; just a shy acceptance. I accompanied the crew of a fishing boat one morning, wandered about a bit on the beach and in the gardens, and chatted a little with San Thay and the sergeant, who also seemed to be enjoying our stay in Chinaka. And I slept a great deal, the reed mattings on the springy floor of the hut proving unexpectedly comfortable.

In the later evening of the day of my arrival at Chinaka I had changed back into my now washed and dried shorts and an open-necked shirt, finding embarrassment in any simulation of native dress. Shin Yalat had come to me, confirming what the headman had told me: that she worked as a maid in Moulmein for the Cunninghams and that she would help me talk to the villagers. She did her best. It was not very good. I concluded that it was not so much that she could not remember the simple English words to which I tried to limit my conversation but rather that she was of no great swiftness of mind—of a soft and generous disposition, eager to please, but not very adept linguistically or, I suspected, in any other way. JiHan's English was vastly better than his mother's, really quite excellent for his age, but he did not seem to wish to play the role of interpreter for me. He was less than at ease with the adults in the village, though the children obviously accepted him as one of their own. In the end, neither Shin Yalat nor JiHan spent much time with me during my visit to Chinaka.

It was a wonderful time when words were not particularly needed, an experience very different from my expectations but, as birthdays go, I could think of none better. There was no bitter aftertaste; I was pleased with what I had done. I did not regret the loss of the supplies. Indeed, they had not been lost; they had been traded in an exquisitely gentle way, a lesson to the economist and to the administrators of the Raj that few, no doubt, would accept. I congratulated myself on the delicacy of my sensibilities when, of course, none of the virtue of the transaction lay with me. I recall that several of the meals I had been served had indeed been enriched by foodstuffs salvaged from the gentle shallows between the beach and Chinaka. My fair share or more, I was sure.

The memory that clings closest to my mind is of one evening sitting on the walkway, my back resting against my hut. Soft, spicy smells of fish cooking for dinner sharpened my appetite, while I looked out across the deep curve of the bay and its encircling palms, and watched several twin-oared barques, each propelled by a man sitting in the stern, his oars crossing and uncrossing in front of him as he pushed his boat lazily home to the peace of a Chinakan evening.

In such a calm setting the Cunningham case came to me on soft tread. Yet Dr. Veraswami was right: "It iss a difficult decision for you, Mr. Blair, ass difficult ass you will ever have to make."

I had met the Cunninghams on occasion at the Club. The relatively few children of Europeans in Moulmein were welcome at the Club during the daytime, when they used the tennis court and the swimming pool; but it was not common for them to be there in the evenings, when I tended, occasionally, to visit. I had never seen the Cunningham boy there, though I understood in a vague way that he swam there often in the afternoon, the only people remarking on this being the two adult Eurasian members, who were quick to spot and comment on one of their own being so unqualifiedly accepted, as they clearly were not. So far as I knew, the Cunningham boy was treated like any European child of his age; certainly the other young children saw nothing of note about him, except perhaps his energy and agility in play. But I did not know him at all and had forgotten our meeting in Chinaka until I visited the Cunningham bungalow, and that visit was not social, rather in the line of duty.

Coleen Cunningham had telephoned one morning to police headquarters to report that their bungalow had been broken into and that some money and a few relatively valueless pieces of personal jewelry had been stolen. Bruce was up the river at the teak plantation—would someone come to investigate the matter and do whatever had to be done?

There was not much to be done. There rarely is with burglaries, if they are burglaries and not thefts by servants. One has to determine the outer limits of time when the offence occurred, who was in the bungalow over that period, and whether anyone saw or heard anyone or anything suspicious. It means a series of rather pointless interviews in which little is discovered beyond what is blurted out by the first reporter of the loss.

My morning was free. The Cunninghams were, after all, the most prosperous of the nongovernmental Europeans in Moulmein. I had found them quite pleasant when we had met at the Club, and there was no reason—other than sloth—for delegating the investigation, such as it would be, to anyone else. So I went myself, taking a recently recruited Indian policeman with me to add an air of authority to my likely inefficiency.

My assistant and I were shown into a sitting room leading out onto a verandah immediately beside the main entrance to the bungalow. A maid had obviously been expecting us and led us into the empty room, saying that the memsahib would be with us in a moment. But the boy, whom I immediately recalled seeing at the Chinaka village, was the first to arrive. He stood immobile in the doorway, surveying us, hesitant yet curious, in the manner of bright children, the striking blue eyes moving rapidly in his oval face. He could not have been more than seven years old, yet he seemed taller than the usual seven-year-old, his slight frame held erect, the head tilted back. He was not a child to be ignored—and he knew it. He moved with confidence into the room, it being clear to even a first-time visitor like me that, despite his light-brown skin, he was at home.

I acknowledged his courteous "Good Morning, Sir" and asked if he recalled our earlier meeting. "Of course, at the village." But the current events preempted his interest: "Will you catch the thief?" It seemed unlikely, but as Coleen Cunningham hurried into the room, her hand reaching for the boy's shoulder, I assured him that we would try.

"I see you have already met John," she said, and squeezing his shoulder added, " He seems to be enjoying this burglary." Nor did Coleen Cunningham seem greatly disturbed. She had seen no one, had not lost much of value, and had not felt threatened personally. Of course, her room had been broken into during the night and this caused her understandable unease, but she was a sensible, confident person who recognised that the intruder had gone to some effort not to disturb her and hence likely meant her no harm—though she would have to make arrangements for better security in the future.

And she was clearly right about the boy's enjoyment of this minor criminal drama. His shiny eyes watched everything that was being done; he was more than willing to run errands or to fetch anyone of the household I or my assistant might wish to interview. He had his own theory of the burglary; he had found an unexpected footprint outside the window of the Cunninghams' bedroom and what he said was a mark on the shutter that had not been there the day before. Whether these findings were the precocity of an incipient sleuth or the products of childish fancy I never found out, since this proved to be one of my many failures as a detective. The responsible criminal was never brought to book, certainly not for this crime, though I supposed it likely he would eventually be caught for some other similar crime. I rarely did catch burglars, unless someone had seen them or informed upon them, on which occasions my capacities as a detective invariably took great leaps forward.

Mrs. Cunningham served coffee to me soon after my arrival that morning, my Indian constable being given similar courtesies in the kitchen, the boy acting as his escort. There was not much to tell. She had left her purse on the dressing table in the bedroom with a few notes and some small change in it—she did not know how much—and in the morning she found the purse empty, on the floor. The only other things missing seemed to be some imitation jewelry taken from a drawer in the same dressing table.

Bruce had left for the interior earlier the day before. She had dined at the Club. She had gone to bed on returning from the Club, after checking that John was asleep in the room next to hers. He had come into bed with her in the morning as he often did, whether Bruce was home or not. She had half wakened and taken him in her arms. They had both slept for some time. The offence was discovered when they woke.

As I say, I never found the thief. I think the boy's explanation captured all the truth of it we would ever discover: "Someone watched and waited outside, broke the shutter catch very quietly, and sneaked in; but he didn't get much."

Later I made the usual formal report to help the Cunninghams with their insurance claim, the main constabulary duty in such matters. The boy had impressed me with his charm and intelligence so that in the next few weeks, whenever I met Coleen or Bruce Cunningham, I asked after him. They responded warmly to these enquiries and always had one or another story of the boy's wit or success to relate. But I didn't see him again until the crisis of decision was upon me.

I saw Bruce Cunningham soon after he returned from the interior and talked about the burglary with him. He seemed as unconcerned as his wife. I expressed my pleasure in meeting the boy and risked asking him about the boy's name—I had met him as "JiHan" and then he had been introduced by Mrs. Cunningham as "John." Was this merely an anglicisation of his name, or was there more to it? And what did the boy call himself? And his friends?

Apparently, though without intending to, Bruce Cunningham had solved this minor problem for the boy and for others. A few weeks before the child's birth, Shin Yalat's husband, a Karen from the fishing village of Chinaka, had been killed in an accident upriver at the teak estates owned by Cunningham's firm. Shin Yalat's grief was obvious, and the Cunningham household cared for her with solicitude; but it later became clear that she had been spared some awkward explanations since the boy, when born, was obviously not the son of her husband. The Karens are darker skinned than most Burmese—the boy's father was undoubtedly European. Nevertheless, when he was born Shin Yalat gave him the name she and her husband had agreed upon for a boy, "JiHan," a name reasonably common among the Karens of the South of Burma, though not so common in Chinaka as to be confusing. And "JiHan" he was called by his mother, Shin Yalat, when they were alone or on the occasions he had been taken to his late father's family in Chinaka. However, from his early infancy he was known as "John," as a formal matter, in the Cunningham household. The Cunninghams had seen him within hours of his birth and from their first sight of the light tan skin, the blue eyes, and the straight features, the awkward Burmese "JiHan" had translated itself into the easy English "John." But in his second year these appellations too had been changed, and largely by the boy himself. Amused by the two names, Bruce Cunningham had found a commonality between them and had called the boy "J.J.," in the manner of the moguls of American business. The boy latched on to this and shaped it to his personal style so that he called himself and became generally known as "JayJay"—in the Cunningham household (except to Coleen), at the Club, and throughout the European, Burmese, Indian, and Chinese communities of Moulmein. But Shin Yalat stuck to "JiHan" and Coleen to "John."

The crisis came quietly to the Cunninghams, though they should have expected its arrival someday. It came in the form of a promotion. Bruce was to be in charge of the company's interests in Kenya, itself a secure stepping stone to a directorate in London. There was no question about it; he must grasp this opportunity, which would mean moving to Kenya via some leave in London three months hence.

If Coleen Cunningham had been calm about the burglary, she certainly was not calm now. Pushing aside the hesitant restraining hand of the duty officer, she burst into my office. "Bruce is up the river again, and I can't find John. I think his amah, Shin Yalat, has taken him. Some of his clothes and toys are gone. You must find him and bring him back immediately."

I did not bridle at her peremptory tone; she was on the edge of tears and her blustering manner did not cloak her anguish. I tried to calm her, but she would have none of it. There was nothing more to tell me, she said. John had probably been taken to Chinaka. I should fetch him.

Everything had been normal the night before, she told me. John went to bed at his usual time. She read to him until he went to sleep. She then wrote a letter home—by which she meant, of course, to her family in England, since Burma and Kenya would never be thought of by her as providing other than transient residences. And then she went to bed herself. She heard nothing in the night. In the morning John was gone and so was Shin Yalat.

"Did Shin Yalat speak about this to the other servants?" I asked.

"They say not."

"Did Shin Yalat know that you and Bruce are leaving Burma?"

And here she hesitated, not, I thought, to polish an untruth but to be precise about an uncertainty. "We have not spoken of it yet to the servants, but I think they may know. I don't know how. But I have the impression they do."

"Shin Yalat is his mother, is she not? I knew the answer, of course; but the enquiry might help Mrs. Cunningham see the difficulty of the situation and lessen the pressure on me for an immediate police solution.

"He was born to her, yes, but since then I have been his mother. We kept her on because she looked after him well. But he is obviously half European. It is absurd to think of him as a Burmese village boy. You have talked with him. Surely you know. She has kidnapped him. You must bring him back. I'll come with you to Chinaka."

The thought of what I should say and do in Chinaka was bad enough without the added threat of the now relentless Coleen Cunningham to complicate my task. With some effort I persuaded her not to come to Chinaka with me, which is, I suppose, a tribute to the swift success of her effort to compel me to go there. She agreed to stay at their bungalow, certainly until Bruce returned. I suggested sending a message to Bruce to return as soon as he could—she had already done so.

It seemed to me that at least I should see that JayJay was safe and find out what Shin Yalat's intentions were if he were with her. And if he were not, then indeed I had an urgent police matter on my hands—so I had bet-

ter go immediately to Chinaka. If he were there, whether I should bring
him or them back to the Cunningham bungalow perplexed me. Did I have
authority to do that? Probably not. And yet there seemed a genuine issue
about the boy's future. Who should decide? Surely not me.

Coleen Cunningham rejected my offer to have a policeman accompany
her back to her bungalow. When she left the police station she was less dis-
tressed than when she had arrived, but it seemed to me also less in doubt
about what had happened and must now happen. Shin Yalat had kidnapped John; he must be brought back and she discharged, at the very
least. My earlier enquiry as to whether John had been formally adopted by
Bruce and herself had been brushed aside as absurd. "We will do that when
we are back in England on leave before going to Kenya. You can't rely on
courts or records here. Everyone knows he is our child and has been since
he was born—we have made no secret of that to anyone. Shin Yalat knows
it too; she has been his amah, his nurse, his nanny. You must have seen
that for yourself."

How should I travel to Chinaka? The road from Moulmein to Mudon
and on to Chinaka was hardly a road, more a track really, and a track often
swallowed by the jungle and rutted by tropical rains—not gentle English
ruts to trip the wandering inebriate, but chasms to stagger an elephant. To
carry larger loads, even trucks were at risk; bullocks pulling bamboo sleds
on heavy teak runners were better suited to avoid the bogging and tipping
that beset all other conveyances.

There were, of course, motor cars in Moulmein. One could not drive
the direct route from Rangoon to Moulmein, but the roads from Rangoon
to Mandalay, and from Mandalay to Moulmein could be negotiated. It was
hardly sensible, however, to do so. Leave those adventures to one's driver;
let him wrestle with the punctures, the boggings, the overheatings. When
the car arrived in town it would be useful, but between towns it was a misery. In any event, the only motor vehicles that were available to me in
Moulmein were a few army lorries, and then only in emergencies and with
the permission of the military authorities at the garrison.

These matters troubled me as I wondered how to go about bringing
Shin Yalat and the boy back to Moulmein. I could get permission to take a
military lorry, but it would be a chancy journey. On horseback I could be in
Chinaka about noon, if I started early, and perhaps back by late afternoon
on the evening train from Mudon. Yes, that would be the best plan. If I
took a policeman with me as an interpreter, he could bring the horses back
to Moulmein while Shin Yalat, the boy, and I could return by train.

But I felt the need of advice and counsel before leaving. It would not
do to rush off with no idea what to do when I got to Chinaka. If Shin Yalat
and JayJay were not there it would be obvious what to do—but what if, as I
hoped and believed, they were there? Dr. Veraswami was too busy to talk

to me until the evening. There was no one else to turn to in Moulmein. Much as they and I disliked it, I would have to try to seek advice from my superiors in Mandalay by telephone—caution and good administrative practice seemed to converge on this result.

The long-distance telephone had come to Burma with the military, the signal corps festooning lines along the roads and railways, talking to one another while lying on their bellies by shouting into gunmetal orifices actuated by desperately rotated cranking devices. The railway authorities had carried matters further, substituting less fearsome wooden boxes affixed to walls in the stationmasters' offices, requiring less cranking, having earpieces to be lifted to the side of the head rather than requiring the assumption of a recumbent posture, and with little, protruding rounded metal mouths into which one shouted. And then these machines moved into homes and offices. I hated them all, and they seemed to hate me. Those in the capital cities who arranged the switching requests obviously resented my interrupting the usual military, railway, or commercial business to which their lines were largely devoted; they patronised me and seemed to go out of their way to misunderstand me. My usually too verbose efforts on the telephone always reminded me of Laocoön's desperate struggles with the serpent; but if I was to be advised on what to do at Chinaka it would have to be by telephoned advice or not at all.

So, soon after Coleen left, I wound the handle, shouted into the little metal mouthpiece, and put through a trunk call to Mandalay Regional Headquarters. Mandalay listened, could offer no help since the legal adviser was on leave, but authorised me to call Rangoon Headquarters even up to the second in command of the Burmese Police, a presence I had actually met some months earlier when he paid an inspectional visit to Moulmein.

To my astonishment my call to Rangoon was expected. There had been a call from Mandalay, but also, and more surprising to me—though had I then more judgment of human behaviour it should not have been— Rangoon headquarters had already heard about the alleged kidnapping from elements of the commercial community in Rangoon associated with the company for which Bruce Cunningham worked. There was no doubt about what I was to do—it was not a matter at all of my judgment—I should understand it to be a direct order: if Shin Yalat and the boy were in Chinaka when I got there, I was certainly to bring the boy back to the Cunningham bungalow and hand him over to Mrs. Cunningham and to Mr. Cunningham, who would probably be there by then. Shin Yalat should be persuaded to return to Moulmein too, but I was not to see that as an order—I should not use force to compel her return, but the boy must come back.

It was hardly a conversation at all, more a series of unambiguous directions. My search for advice, for some understanding of the relevant law, of the attitude I should take to the boy and to Shin Yalat, was swept aside. In due course I would receive, I was assured, a Memorandum of Law to guide me to the relevant law and to support what had been done. But, for the time being, I was to fetch the boy home and to take with me whatever police force I thought necessary to that end. No, there was no need to alert the army authorities in the matter; surely I could handle it with the police force available. After all, it was only a Burmese woman with a child.

I began to regret that I had sought advice; it might well have been better to leave it to the inspiration of the moment in Chinaka. Now I had no choice. But I did have some choice as to how to carry out the orders. Remembering the friendliness of my earlier visit to Chinaka, I decided to confine myself to one Burmese policeman as an interpreter to accompany me.

We arrived at the beach looking across to Chinaka, hot and tired, in the late forenoon.

My policeman-interpreter was a Shan, but he spoke fluent Karen. It was a painful session for me and, I gathered, also for him. The headman and the priest met us in the shade of the storage hut on the beach. There were no chairs, no mats or other signs of hospitality, just the area beside the large hut where grassy vegetation became sand to squat or sit on.

When we arrived, activities on the shore ceased. By the time our horses were unsaddled and tethered, the few women working in the vegetable gardens had rowed back to the village. Soon the headman could be seen rowing himself to the shore. The priest emerged from the pagoda and we were assembled.

I could see children playing around the walkways of the village, but no adults were taking any obvious interest in our meeting. I could not see JayJay among the children, but at that distance I could hardly be sure.

The headman, erect, cold-eyed, had apparently misplaced what little English he had found on my earlier visit. He spoke in Karen in what seemed to be brusque and complex sentences; certainly the few words of Karen I knew were of no use to me. And the priest did not participate at all in the discussion; for all he said he might as well have been a Trappist. He was a youngish man in a less-than-spotless saffron robe who spent most of the time he was with us digging abstractedly in the rough sand with a preternaturally large and dirty big toe equipped with a broken nail. His contribution to the parley was to distract me, in which he was very successful.

It was not only his small stock of English that had deserted the headman; his earlier cordiality to me had also quite disappeared. I did my best to explain our business in neutral terms. "Are Shin Yalat and JiHan at Chinaka?"

"Yes."

"The Cunninghams are worried about them. They do not know Shin Yalat and the boy are visiting the village. JiHan must come back to Moulmein so that he can go back to school."

There then followed a lengthy exchange between the headman and my interpreter from which I felt excluded as they chattered back and forth. I interrupted, rebuking the policeman for carrying on the discussion himself: "Tell me everything he says; don't talk on like that."

This both upset my only ally and confirmed the headman's growing hostility, his eyes and posture revealing his complete understanding of my miserable mission, and of my unease in it. He pressed me firmly to the truth. "Shin Yalat and JiHan must return with you—is it so? Are you taking her child from her and her family?"

In reply, I made the task of the interpreter impossible, talking on and on until in desperation he stopped me and I had to retreat from my earlier direction to him just to interpret. "Tell the headman, please, in your own words, that the boy must now come back to Moulmein with us, that Shin Yalat may if she wishes to, and that I promise that the boy will not ever be taken away from her without a careful, legal decision as to whom he should live with." The promise was self-serving and weak; I had no such authority. A direct order from Rangoon could hardly be resisted. I wondered where I gained the courage to make these uncertain promises.

As the talk lengthened between the headman and my interpreter, I felt more and more helpless and excluded. They both warmed to what was clearly to them an interesting if troublesome matter, centering, I suspected, on the obtuseness and probably the cruelty of the English.

It was all very painful. We were rowed out to the village. I was taken to the hut of Shin Yalat's ex-husband's family, which was now her family, though she was a Shan from the North and had not seen her own parents and siblings for years. The hut was crowded; all the family lived there, I gathered. Shin Yalat and JayJay were there. I tried to be pleasant to them but the boy was stiff-backed and hostile, the mother withdrawn and hostile.

The boy's response was direct and clear: "School opens on Monday. It is Friday today. Shin Yalat and I will come back in time for school. I am allowed to come here with Shin Yalat when there is no school. Why are you taking me back?"

I felt years his junior. There was a clear-eyed directness about him that outfaced me, and he did have the better case to argue. My mumblings that "everyone is worried about you" sounded weak and childish to me. But there was no better line to pursue.

As he gradually appreciated that I would not relent, that he had no choice in the matter, that Shin Yalat and the villagers were equally unwilling to help him have his way, and that he might even be taken from Chinaka without Shin Yalat, the tears came to his eyes. He did not wipe them away. He turned from me and asked Shin Yalat to take him back to Moulmein. His request was wordlessly accepted. She stood. He took her hand and glared, damp-eyed, at me. They were ready.

I turned and walked out of the hut. My interpreter, who had remained silent during my talk with the boy and his mother, walked out after me. No one else followed. I waited on the walkway.

The headman spoke at length and quite loudly to Shin Yalat and her family. He knew he would be overheard by the interpreter and made no effort to lower his voice for confidentiality. My interpreter later told me the headman had tried to reassure the family that I would not let the Cunninghams steal the boy, but my interpreter thought that he did not sound as if he had much confidence in this. He told them of my promise but did not seem to understand exactly what it meant—nor, it seemed, did my interpreter.

It was a disagreeable return journey. Shin Yalat and JayJay rode on the two horses to Mudon, the policeman and I leading them. I had thought that the horseback ride might cheer up JayJay, but he made it clear that he had learned to ride and did not need to be led, and that if I thought he would run away, by all means let me lead the horse as a punishment for my stupidity.

The journey passed largely in silence. JayJay did not talk much to Shin Yalat, and neither spoke to me. At Mudon, the policeman left us, riding one horse and leading the other, to return to Moulmein. On the train, the boy slept most of the time, cuddled up beside his mother. Her eyes were closed; whether she slept or not I was not sure.

I had time to think. The Cunninghams should not take Shin Yalat with them to England and Kenya, even if she would be welcome in Kenya, which was doubtful. She would be utterly lost in England with nothing whatsoever to do, isolated and superfluous. And seeing her in Chinaka had made it clear to me that Chinaka must be her home. Setting any questions of sentiment aside, she would be taken into her ex-husband's family in Chinaka, another mouth to feed, but accepted because the husband's widow is, by custom, part of the husband's family. She would work with the other women in the few shoreside fields and in household duties, but she would be a substantial drain on the family. If JiHan were with her it would be very different. Soon he would begin to work as a fisherman. He was obviously strong and intelligent. He would make a fine fisherman, a productive and promising member of the village, the stuff of which village elders and headmen are made. With JiHan, Shin Yalat was an asset; without him, a customary obligation to be borne.

And letting sentiment seep in, the mother and child seemed deeply attached to one another, and the boy seemed accepted and successful in Chinaka. Why not let nature rule? It would be cruelty to wrench the boy from his mother, and surely it would confirm the emerging and occasionally expressed Burmese opinion of the tyranny and insensitivity of the Raj. Had we not undertaken to protect and respect their customary laws and their religious practices? Here was a deep-set custom, essential to family and village relationships, expressed in the life of the Buddha himself: the mutual obligations of the husband's family and his wife and children; and I was thinking of tampering with it!

My calming reverie was shattered by our arrival in Moulmein. The Cunninghams, Coleen and Bruce, met us in a company lorry. The boy ran excitedly to them. There were tears from Coleen. To my surprise, the Cunninghams seemed pleased, too, to see Shin Yalat. But the same affection did not envelop me. My morning's hesitancies with Coleen Cunningham and the telephone call to Rangoon, which I am sure had been reported to Bruce Cunningham, had made them doubtful of me.

It was arranged that Bruce would soon call upon me to discuss the whole matter, and the four of them clattered off in the lorry, Bruce driving, Coleen and the boy beside him, Shin Yalat in the rear.

The memorandum came when I was tired. All I wanted to do was to sit on the verandah, have a whisky, perhaps another, talk to no one, not even to Veraswami, and go to bed, to sleep I hoped, and not to spend the night awake thinking how tired I was. But the memorandum came and demanded attention by its very bulk.

Rangoon, in the person of one Douglas Sharp, had promised a Memorandum of Law to help me with the Cunningham case; what had come seemed more like a legal training manual, a blow-by-blow description of the cases and the statutes, and, like all such, it was painfully careful to avoid any remotely helpful conclusions. But it did have the merit of honesty, if not of brevity. There was a covering note which reported what appeared also to be the memorandum's final conclusion: "In sum, the current case law and statutes do not give any clear guidance in the problem you must decide. They tell you the principles to apply but not how these principles apply to your case."

In the covering note, Sharp added, though it was omitted from the memorandum, that I could rest assured that whatever I decided would certainly be severely criticised by the authorities in Rangoon, himself included, since it was a problem whose solution could not but alienate important interests in Burma, and that he was entirely delighted that he did not have to make the decision himself. Solomon, he suggested, had it easy by comparison to Blair. As an afterthought, he wished me luck; though where he thought I might find it did not appear. He requested that I regard this covering note as strictly personal comment, not to be treated as any part of his official legal advice to me. He annoyed me, but I rather warmed to him.

I allowed myself the whisky and, as the sun began the rapid final descent typical in the tropics, I sat on the verandah, my back to the light the better to read, my chair tipped back, waiting to see if the fading light would give me some understanding of what the lawyers had to suggest. "The best interests of the child" was the phrase that resonated through Sharp's document. This must be given predominant weight, but other matters must be considered also. Parental rights were not to be ignored. Everything, so it seemed, was to be judiciously weighed, the child's interests being given prominence but balanced in some mysterious fashion against everything else. What a help these lawyers are!

Sharp was adamant that this lengthy memorandum was only a first installment; there was much more law I would need to know before deciding the case. All he had so far canvassed was English law, English statutes, and English cases. He would now promptly search out whatever he could about Indian and Burmese law and practice in a case of the type I had to decide. But he did add one confident conclusion that confirmed my sense of being captured by the Cunningham case: it was already clear to him that both in England and in Burma a question of custody of the type I faced could in the first instance be brought before a Magistrate's Court. There was no way I could shuffle the problem off to the certainly more qualified judges in Mandalay or Rangoon. They, of course, could hear appeals from my decision, but the general practice in such cases in England as in Burma was to give great weight to the discretion of the magistrate of first instance. After all, he, more than any more-senior judges, would be close to the contending parties and would therefore, so it was argued, be better able to achieve this fine balance between many competing interests.

I could have swallowed all this with less misery if Sharp had not managed to convey his amused satisfaction that the problem was mine, mine alone. It was too late to try to master the details of his memorandum. The darkness had drawn the paper to my sweaty nose. I would read it in the morning and then decide what should next be done.

A most restless night. Never really awake but hardly asleep; the line between dreams and half-awake self-hatred wavering through the night. My dreams were of fragments of my own childhood interlaced by a waking sense of helplessness in being so futilely situated in Burma, neither writing nor learning, far separated from all that interested me in the world. And then, in the last soft sleep before dawn, when peace comes to the troubled, I dreamt of the secure warmth of my mother's love, only slightly perturbed by my father's protracted military absences. I woke with the sense that` Shin Yalat and JiHan were as one and that the lawyers' cases were as nothing to that sweet tie.

The morning and early afternoon went by in administrative trivia, the Cunninghams, Shin Yalat, and JayJay pushed from my mind by the warm certainties of my dream; and it was not until late afternoon that I gave Sharp's memorandum a careful reading.

Sharp's words recreated many of my repressed uncertainties. He told me a lot about the way the law, in particular English law, approached problems of adoption and custody of young children, but he also managed to convey an air of indisputable direction without openly saying so—the boy should go to the Cunninghams for reasons any sensible Englishman would know without having to labour them. He wrote with the educated young Englishman's typical patronising attitude toward the Burmese. It seemed clear to him that, if the Cunninghams really wanted the boy, there were ample grounds for me to find in their favour, some quite legitimate and some less so—such as his heavy suggestions that, by virtue of the birth of the boy, sired other than by her husband, Shin Yalat might be thought unfit to be his mother; unfit, at least, if the Cunninghams were to be weighed morally in the balance with her as parents. He softened this blow, he thought, by speculating that no doubt she merely reflected the moral values of all Burmese women, and that therefore this might be an unworthy individual moral assessment—which seemed to me rather to stress than to minimise the insult. His further innuendo that she might well know more than she had admitted about the earlier alleged burglary and theft seemed to me wild and improper guesswork.

But I could not dismiss all of his memorandum so lightly. He did tell me a lot about the values that were brought to bear on these custody conflicts in England. Much of what he wrote seemed sensible and helpful in my quandary. One comment in particular leapt from his neatly handwritten pages, so carefully and repeatedly marked "Confidential—Without Prejudice—Not for Distribution." It was this: "There was one proposal by the 1921 Committee which did not find its way into the report of the Second Committee that I believe has a lot of sense in it. It was recommended that the judge or magistrate in an adoption proceeding avail himself of the advice of any reputable person who had experience in the instant case. The Committee assumed that this person would be some sort of public health officer, probably a woman, who would be at an advantage in a confidential interview. Why don't you enquire whether there is anyone in Moulmein who can serve in this capacity?"

What an idiot I had been! Surely Dr. Veraswami would be able to guide me to people who had maturity of judgment and who also already knew something of the life of the boy in his Chinakan and Cunningham settings. It was certainly worth the enquiry. In the end, it gave me my best insights into the extraordinarily difficult decision I faced, for the more I learned, the harder, not the easier, it became. And it was Veraswami himself who led me into these further decisional complexities.

I hurried around to Veraswami's bungalow in the later afternoon, unusually early for such a visit. Fortunately, Veraswami had returned home from the hospital before I arrived so that I was spared the awkward embarrassment of a meeting with his servants while his wife and children hid in anxiety. He greeted me as effusively as usual, enquired if the sun was sufficiently across the yardarm for a beer, and we sat to drink and sweat and talk on the verandah, looking across to the hospital and the gaol through the dripping undergrowth, while the late afternoon shower steamed in the remaining heat of the swiftly setting sun.

Yes, of course he knew the Cunninghams and JayJay. Had I not realised that the Cunninghams were one of the few European families that consulted him on a regular basis? Where did I think he got the money to keep me supplied in beer? And then, troubled by his own directness, "Of course, Mr. Blair, I am teasing, ass you know. It iss a privilege and one of my few pleasures that you feel at ease to visit me and consult me ass you do about yourself and your important work." His hand-waving took on great circular sweeps of benevolence, and he rummaged about for more beer, so as to demonstrate what I already knew—that he was pleased by my company, a sentiment I reciprocated with an intensity he could hardly know. Moulmein would have been impossible without him.

"Mr. Blair, I will do all I can to help you about the boy, his mother, and the Cunninghams. I know the problem you face. I have seen it looming, approaching, inexorably, so it hass seemed to me, for some time, ever since the boy wass born—or even possibly before, to be precise, if you do not think I am ass usual my overly boastful self."

"Before JayJay was born? How could that be, Doctor? Not more of your Indian predestination, I hope."

"Indeed not, no, not at all, by no means. Rather the common sense to which you English lay such frequent claim. You see, I attended Mrs. Cunningham's accouchement when she first came to Moulmein."

It took me a moment or two to understand what he was talking about. I had heard nothing of Mrs. Cunningham ever having been pregnant. Certainly she had never been so while I was in Moulmein, or rather, I never knew about it if she had. What Dr. Veraswami was telling me was that she had arrived in Moulmein pregnant, close to the date of expected parturition. She and her husband both worried that she should not have traveled out from England so late in her pregnancy and so on arrival in Moulmein they had enquired who was the best doctor in the town. They had taken the trouble to look behind the recommendations in the Club guided by skin colouration, to the realities of training, experience, and reputation in crisis that confirmed Dr. Veraswami's preeminence. And what was more remarkable, when the Cunningham baby died within hours of its birth, and the complications of the birth were such as to preclude Mrs. Cunningham from ever again bearing a child, they did not turn on Dr. Veraswami with accusations of incompetence, but, rather, recognised his skill and effort in their service and his regret in the baby boy's death. So he had remained the doctor to them and their household, including Shin Yalat and her son when he was born, a few weeks after the death of the Cunningham baby. "I could not say, Mr. Blair, that the Cunninghams see me ass a friend, but I do know that they trust me with their personal problems, medical and psychological, and that I am verry glad to serve them. And they are generous patients. So please have another beer and forget my offensive joke." A lugubrious staccato noise, meant to be a laugh, escaped him.

"Psychological problems, you say, Dr. Veraswami. Of what sort?"

"I am not sure you should ask, my friend, and I am quite sure I should not answer—Hippocratic oath, confidences of patients, and all that."

Embarrassed by my gaffe, I hurriedly changed the subject and told Dr.

Veraswami of the Memorandum of Law I had received from Sharp in Rangoon and of the fact that it was recommended by an English committee, advising on matters such as I had to decide, that it was proper for me in my role of judge to consult someone who might be better able to find the facts I would have to weigh than I could by ordinary court processes; that I had come to him to seek advice about who in Moulmein might be helpful in this way; and that here he was, the obvious person, trusted by the Cunninghams and I supposed by Shin Yalat and certainly by me. Surely he should help me.

Veraswami was both silent and still—a most unexpected combination in such a bouncy, energetic person. I waited. The silence became difficult. I fidgeted, I suppose, which pushed him to a response. At last he did speak, but with none of the open directness I had come to expect: "I do not know. I am too tired to make up my mind now. If you will excuse me now, I will think about the matter; perhaps talk to the Cunninghams and Shin Yalat if I have your permission to do so, perhaps not. I shall let you know in a day or so if I think I can be of any help. Iss that satisfactory, Mr. Blair?"

I began to feel a pushy outsider, loading onto him what should be my burden. But surely the matter was too important for such delicacies. It would be best to take him at his word. I finished the remaining warmish dregs of my beer, stood up, said that of course what he proposed was most acceptable to me, and thanked him, perhaps too formally, for his hospitality.

"Oh, Blair, don't be so stiff and English with me. I am in doubt. I need time to think and perhaps to talk to others. I know how much you care about this decision and I am ass ever moved by your warmth of heart and sincerity of purpose. Don't, ass the Irish say, 'treat me like company.'"

I had never before wanted to hug him—indeed, any male—but I wanted to then. But, of course, years of restraint won out. I offered what must have been a somewhat sickly smile, and said good evening.

"It hass not been easy, not easy at all, quite difficult, but I have decided what I should do, and I have the agreement of Mr. and Mrs. Cunningham and of Shin Yalat—JayJay I did not ask. I will tell you everything I know, and everything I think, about whether the boy should stay with Shin Yalat or stay with the Cunninghams; but I will not try to decide thiss question. That iss for you. Only for you. It iss your burden, a heavy burden, and it iss right that no one should share it, I think. But I will conceal nothing I know from you. And I think I can tell you in a sentence what the problem iss—the problem, not the answer. The problem iss one aspect of the question of cultural neutrality."

The words were pouring out of him, his hands waving frantically forwards and outwards. I was not finding it easy to follow him, though I was delighted that I would have his help and guidance. But he pressed on, stopping for no elucidation.

"That iss it, Blair: are all cultures equally to be respected? Are they to be equal in your judicial eye? Or are there neutral principles by which you can properly decide the superiority of one culture over another? Or are the determinants of advantage or disadvantage themselves culture-bound, culturally determined, so that what iss considered advantage or disadvantage iss itself dictated by the competing cultures? If thiss be so, it iss hard to see how you, an Englishman, with your peculiarly privileged view of the world, can at all fairly decide on the boy's custody between the Cunninghams and Shin Yalat if hiss best interests are to guide you, for from the point of view of which of the two competing cultures are those interests to be determined? How can you, how can anyone, know how to choose, if all of uss wear these cultural blinkers? What an appalling problem for you, Police Magistrate Blair! No one really knows the answer, yet you must decide it in the case of the child of Shin Yalat. I will help you all I can, but I am quite delighted that the problem iss yours, not mine."

It was not immediately obvious to me how Dr. Veraswami was characterising my task of deciding who should have custody of the boy, but I was much relieved by what he said. At the least it meant that I would have the guidance of a wise counsellor about matters other than the law, and though Sharp annoyed me with his arrogant assumptions about the Burmese and also, it seemed to me, about the likelihood that I was merely looking for the easiest way out of a politically delicate case, nevertheless, he was obviously informed about the law and interested in its principles and origins. If, in remote Moulmein, I had to take on this sort of decision, I was relieved to have both Veraswami and Sharp assisting me.

I pressed Dr. Veraswami to be sure I understood the terms on which he would help me and the way he thought the problem of deciding the boy's custody should be defined.

Veraswami insisted that he was unsure what he would do in my situation, but he trusted me in the sense that he believed I would do better the more I knew—he was prepared to complicate the problem for me, not to try to simplify it, which I took for a compliment. He claimed to be ignorant of the English and Burmese and even the Indian laws of adoption and custody, but he hoped that what he knew of the Cunningham household and of Shin Yalat and the boy would help me.

"I don't know much about the law either, Dr. Veraswami, but Douglas Sharp in Rangoon has been trying to teach me—at considerable length; lawyers do not seem to lack for words—and I think I understand some of it. Let me tell you."

"No. Not now, if you do not mind, Blair. Let us meet soon when we are not tired, ass we both are now, and talk quietly without rush or hurry. . . ." His hands opened outwards in a gesture of leisurely reflection.

He was clearly right. I was burdened and anxious to be rid of the problem, ready to grasp at straws in order to pull myself comfortably one way or the other. I needed time, ample advice, calm discussion, and balanced reflection so that I could with more inner peace withstand the harsh criti-

cisms that would follow whatever I decided. So we arranged what had surely not been done ever before in Moulmein under the suzerainty of the Raj:
we would meet late the next afternoon, an Indian doctor and an English
acting superintendent of police, himself a magistrate to boot, on the verandah outside the police station, overlooking the parade ground—in full
view of anyone who cared to observe from the residential quarters of the
police on the other side of the parade ground, or anyone who had need to
visit the police station—and talk as equals and friends into the night. It
seemed a most revolutionary plan, and I was delighted I had made it.

We did attract stares of interest from some of the European and
Burmese police, and of disapproval from two or three Europeans who
chanced to visit the police station, but it proved a relaxed and helpful
venue. Nor was there delay in our approaching the case of JiHan-John—I
never could settle upon either title in my mind.

"It is good of you, Dr. Veraswami, to play Solomon for me in this matter."

"It iss not surprising, Mr. Blair, that you mention that name, Solomon,
though I think the story you had in mind about him was a much earlier
Indian folktale that the Jews liked. Something very like it iss often told in
India and not about Solomon."

My eyebrows must have expressed my skepticism; Veraswami often
told of what was earlier and better in the history of India than of anywhere else. He looked puzzled. "No, really, I have read the story in the
Book of Kings, and it iss like many western Indian folktales, only, if I may
say so without offending you, not ass subtle ass most of them. Perhaps I
am quite wrong in one way about that—Solomon himself was the fifth
counted son of David's verry many children, and David's relationship with
Bathsheba, except in hiss dotage when she prevailed unfairly on him to
appoint Solomon hiss successor, does lend the story a reflected complexity
missing in most folktales and, if I may add, in most English discussions of
Solomon's alleged wisdom. He certainly had a scheming mother and
seemed to inherit that skill from her. But all that does not matter now,
not at all; what matters now iss whether the story about him you had in
mind, about the two women contesting bitterly for the baby, iss like Shin
Yalat and Coleen."

I agreed that Solomon's solution to the problem I faced had crossed my
mind, though I was doubtful how to apply it to present circumstances without being charged by my superiors with uttering threats to murder, which I
strongly suspected they would see as grounds for a severe reprimand, if not
worse. Assistant superintendents of police, even when clothed in magisterial robes and duties, must not threaten to bisect a young boy with a sword,
ceremonial or otherwise. Solomon's solution seemed for me a path away
from earning a reputation for wisdom, as he had, and toward prompt dismissal from the civil service. I said as much to Veraswami.

"You take it too literally, Blair. If the story guides you at all, it iss only" —and his pudgy hands searched for a phrase—"ass a metaphor, a test to help you, an idea, not a procedure. Why, not even the exalted magistrate of Moulmein has such unlimited authority of life and death ass did Solomon." And he smiled happily at me.

"Please, Dr. Veraswami, I am not proposing to cut JayJay in half. To the contrary, I wish he were twins—preferably twins who disliked one another. But how does Solomon help? After all, the story has lasted over two thousand years, more if you are correct about its Indian origin—there must be some useful and truthful ideas in it."

I cannot recall the words of the lengthy analysis of the story in the Book of Kings that Veraswami developed with obvious pleasure, but I do recall its broad thrust and a few of his phrases.

Most people, he suggested, read the story as literally as I had, whereas it had endured because it was a parable speaking to deeper truths than one prostitute's lies about another—for that is what both mothers were. No matter to which of the two women Solomon gave the baby, the child could expect no fine future as the bastard of an inmate of a brothel in Jerusalem. Perhaps Solomon, if he had been as generous as he was supposed to be wise, should have intervened to arrange a more promising future for the baby. And it had been such a simple problem for Solomon, much easier than mine: neither claimant mother had known much of the baby; it was newly born to one of them, so that neither had demonstrated a caring capacity. The only difference between the two mothers was that one had given birth to the child and one had not—though each had on the same day given birth to a baby. That must be so, Veraswami stressed, for even in Solomon's kingdom, three thousand years ago, a doctor and a midwife could tell whether or not a woman had recently given birth, so that Solomon would have no need of the threat of a sword to find any necessary facts unless they both experienced parturition at about the same time. "So, my friend, Solomon had it much easier than you. Neither Shin Yalat nor Mrs. Cunningham is telling you any lies, as far as I know. Solomon only had to find out one fact and let his decision follow it, and he knew a way to find the fact, or thought he did; while you, Mr. Police Magistrate, have a much harder problem because you know all the facts and they don't clearly tell you what to do. Solomon's was a problem of evidence; yours iss one of substance, an ethical decision—so verry much more difficult."

"So, I have nothing to learn from that story to help me now, Dr. Veraswami?"

Veraswami's head waved from side to side in his distinctive gesture signifying perhaps yes, perhaps no. "Ass a literal story I have always been suspicious of it, Blair. Solomon may have shown statistical wisdom—sound gambler's instincts—since most mothers would prefer life for their child with another to the child's death, but he did not have to possess any profound psychological understanding to know that."

"What, then, does it show, Dr. Veraswami? Why has the story lasted if there is no more to it than you say?"

"Because, my friend, it speaks, I think, to a deeper truth, harder to accept, but one which we all grasp within ourselves. The true mother does not mean the natural mother, the mother who gave birth to the child. Motherhood is more than parturition. The baby Solomon did not bisect was one "mother's" possible means of escape from the brothel, a most valuable future asset. To be a true mother, so goes the parable of the wise Solomon, iss to be prepared to deny oneself for the welfare of the child, and that denial can be shown by anyone who cares sufficiently for the child. Solomon may have got it wrong (it iss possible, iss it not?) about who really was the baby's natural mother, but not, it seems to me, about which of the two cared most for the child." Chuckling to himself, Veraswami added, "And, by the way, ass the story iss told, I have always thought that he did get it wrong. Have you met many Jewish mothers, Blair? I am not at all sure which was which." He held his right index finger vertically beside his forehead and said, "But the point iss, whether or not, it doesn't matter, you see."

Veraswami's syntax had trailed off badly, but his theme had grown more interesting. However, it didn't solve my problem, but merely shifted its ground. Why did it matter whether Shin Yalat or Coleen Cunningham cared more than the other for the boy? And what about Bruce Cunningham's caring, which also seemed strong and clear—did that not count in the balance? These degrees of caring and sacrifice, should that be called for, spoke only, I suppose, to what would serve the best interest of the boy in times of crisis in his life and in the steady tenor of his growth.

I recalled that Sharp's memorandum had suggested that the different "degrees of solicitude " of those contending for the child might be determinative. What an extraordinary idea! How could one measure such sentiments? Who loved the child most? Those who protested most powerfully? Those who wailed the loudest? But trying to think about different degrees of caring for JayJay pushed me to the further troublesome thought: Why should anyone want to adopt a child? I knew that many children were adopted and that sometimes adults fought bitterly over the custody of children. But why? For the child's sake? For themselves? For their own advantage? But what possible advantage could there be in having to care for, and pay for, and shape one's life around, a child? On the face of it, it seemed a remarkably selfless act—altruism in powerful form.

It was surely one of God's more cunning jokes to link sexual pleasure to procreation. He must have concluded that, absent such a powerful incentive, animals would not choose the altruistic path of child-bearing and child-rearing. And He must have concluded further that, of all animals, men and women would need to be tempted to procreate every day and night of the year, not just during brief periods of heat. So God must have foreseen that no one would want to be a parent unless coerced to that role—and yet here were people, not so coerced, fighting for the right to be parents.

Shin Yalat had surely not wanted to conceive when she copulated with whoever was JayJay's father; but from the child's birth onward she had devoted herself to him, built her life around him. Now the situation had changed, and she needed him more than he needed her. If she were to live in Chinaka, life would be a great deal better for her with than without JiHan. So was it altruism that moved her? She could hardly know. The deep imprint of genes over the millennia had shaped her behaviour toward her child—who was sacrificing and who was being sacrificed seemed hardly relevant. And yet it was unavoidable, if JiHan were to stay with her, that his life would be narrowed for her sake. The sacrifice, objectively, would be his.

But even that possible insight didn't help much since it also seemed that the Cunninghams were in no objective sense altruistic in wanting to keep John with them. It was not that they wished to be generous to a child with ability and grace who otherwise would be an illiterate fisherman in a Burmese village—they wanted John. They wanted John because he was a fortuitous substitute for the child they had lost. The same kind of genetic imprint that was in Shin Yalat determined the behaviour of Coleen Cunningham and, I assumed to a lesser degree, of Bruce Cunningham.

I am told that among certain animals the mother will drive off the other children of her species so that she can suckle and care for her own. If necessary, she will kill the others, the better to be able to rear her own. But if she makes a mistake and takes under protection a baby not her own—and apparently this does occasionally happen—then the infant she thus adopts will be cared for and fought for as her own. Genes do not recognise and protect genes; rather, they use their host vehicles, which are acculturated to protect whomever they take to be their children. The Cunninghams had made no mistake in taking JayJay as their own, but the cases seemed parallel. Between Shin Yalat and Coleen Cunningham, as loving mothers, there was nothing to choose. And there was no reason to think that Bruce Cunningham was any less a father to JayJay than if the boy were genetically half his.

I began to wonder if the whole problem posed in terms of self-sacrifice for the sake of the child made any sense. At a certain level all motives are self-serving. If that be so, then in my obligation to judge between Shin Yalat and the Cunninghams, I should not consider the strength of their motives except insofar as they might work to the advantage of JayJay.

What sense is there, then, in this idea of "degrees of solicitude" for the child? Very little, I came to think. Such an idea might be relevant if one were contemplating whether JayJay would be neglected or cruelly treated by any of those seeking his custody; but plainly all three wishing to be JayJay's parent had deep affection for him, and his being neglected or treated cruelly seemed most unlikely whatever I decided.

JayJay's happiness seemed to be the touchstone, but how to measure happiness? It was even worse than trying to measure the likely degrees of solicitude for him of Shin Yalat and the Cunninghams.

I remember our conversation that evening overlooking the parade ground. The Solomon story helped to focus my mind more on the boy than on the adults contending for his custody. They had strong interests, of course, but, in the context of Veraswami's version of the Solomon story, theirs seemed secondary to JayJay's. On the other hand, Veraswami's confirmation of the views I had formed about the Cunninghams and Shin Yalat, the interests of these adults, the ties of love and service they had formed with the boy, became of predominant importance.

Veraswami's close acquaintance with the Cunningham household served only to confirm the opinions I had formed from my briefer contacts with them in Moulmein and with Shin Yalat in Chinaka. The Cunninghams did not appear to recognise that John was a Eurasian; they acted in every respect as if he were their natural child. I found it hard to imagine what different treatment the baby boy who had died soon after birth to Coleen would have received. They were loving, considerate parents. Indeed, if they were to be criticised as parents, it was for lavishing possibly excessive love on an only child—if love can ever be excessive, though certainly it can be smothering and inhibiting. But here I had to admit that they were not overly protective of the boy to the extent of denying him youthful adventures. After all, they did let him go with Shin Yalat to Chinaka on occasion, which I had no doubt they could have prevented; they did let him ride horseback at an age when too solicitous parents might have denied him that experience; they let him play freely with his European and Burmese peers, which few if any other children in Moulmein, European or Burmese, were allowed. And clearly they loved and cherished him. He was the very focus of their home, his needs timing their days when this was possible, his presence in the morning in their bed most welcome. Their care for his education and the growth of his person and character seemed unqualified.

Nor could one, in fairness, fault Shin Yalat in her care of JiHan. Would she have treated him any better, loved him more, if he had been her husband's child? How could I know that? How could Shin Yalat herself know that? He obviously was not her husband's child. What the circumstances of his procreation had been I neither knew nor could enquire; but by no outward and visible conduct and by no word did she do other than serve and care for JiHan in Moulmein as an amah, in Chinaka as a mother—or so it seemed to me. Did she, in Moulmein, behave as more than an amah to JiHan? How could I know? Amahs often seemed to love the children they cared for with a love that was deep and enduring. The same could be said for, and was reported of, many English nannies. Should I ask Shin Yalat if she loved JiHan as a son or only as a child she devoted her life to? What a silly question! How little I could build on the answer, whatever it was.

I asked Dr. Veraswami whether the boy had suffered any grave illnesses, my thought being that in such crises the depth of sentiment of Shin Yalat and the Cunninghams might be more manifest. "The usual childhood ailments: a few high temperatures, a few minor accidents." And then, seeing the point of my question, Veraswami added: "It hass been my experience that both Shin Yalat and Coleen were in anxious and loving attendance whenever I arrived and that the boy had gone to whichever of hiss three parents wass nearest whenever he wass hurt. I think you will find it verry hard to distinguish between them in degrees of solicitude for JayJay, once you recognise that you English and the Burmese have verry verry different ways of expressing love. The only difference in expressions of love that I can see between them iss that Shin Yalat undoubtedly conceived, carried, and bore JiHan, and that the Cunninghams did none of these things. Many would think that that wass the decisive difference between them. Now tell me, we have put it off too long, what does your much vaunted English law say about these things? Does it make that difference between Shin Yalat and Coleen the central guide to your decision? If so, you will not need anything like Solomon's wisdom to solve your problem and to earn the hostility of the Cunninghams and, no doubt, of your superiors who rely on you to do what important commercial interests in Burma want you to do. Ass I well know, the Cunninghams are important and influential people."

"I have Douglas Sharp's letters and memorandum from Rangoon in the office, if you would care to glance through them," I answered, and rose from my seat to get them. Veraswami raised a courteous palm: "No. Let me look at them after you have decided the case. I could be no help to you with the law. But it might help me if you could give me some rough understanding of how much guidance the law gives you. Are there past cases and opinions of wise judges to guide you to what you should do?"

"Would that there were, Dr. Veraswami. There aren't, but a few do help a little, I think."

I did my best to summarise what Sharp had written to me. What it came to was that English law had, surprisingly, not approached these problems until the mid-1920s—there was no law at all about adoption until then—and then only by way of two Committees of Enquiry leading to the first Act of Parliament on adoption in 1926. This Act of Parliament had received the Royal Assent a few months before Veraswami and I sat talking beside the parade ground. Previously, these matters had been, in law, questions only of inheritance of property, or they had been confined to litigation among the very wealthy concerning Wards in Chancery.

As far as Sharp knew, no case precisely like the one I faced had been reported; but there had emerged the general view that the governing value was the best interest of the child, balanced against what seemed like the quite strong rights of natural parents to the control and custody of their children. The cases told me, in other words, what I already knew: the natural parents had a strong claim; they could lose it by neglect or cruelty, in which case the State might assume their responsibilities or might give the child to others. Natural parents could, of course, also lose these rights by agreeing to give them away, by contracting to give them to others, apparently even to sell them, and then the matter would be a simple one of enforcing whatever the agreement or contract said—but there were no litigated examples known to Sharp of this giving or selling of children, just assumptions from general principles.

If a parent or parents let others, say relatives, care for their child over a substantial period, pay for the child's keep, and educate and care for the child, then the natural parent or parents might lose their custodial rights, the child becoming the child of those who raised, educated, or cared for him. But there seemed to be no English case in which this assumption of responsibility for the child by anyone other than the natural parent or parents had led to a change in custody when, as with Shin Yalat and the Cunninghams, the natural mother was also caring for and living with the child. Still, the principle might be more important than this difference of detail.

"Why," Veraswami asked, "did England have no statutory law on adoption until thiss year? Did not India have some laws on thiss matter much earlier, and Burma, I suppose? And what about other countries? Why does the so-called Mother of Parliaments move so late to this question of mothering? You would think she would be quick to worry about her children."

"Sharp claims ignorance of what law there might be in Europe other than in England. He tells me that America acted earlier in this matter, with some case law and statutes. He thinks it was one aftermath of their Civil War, and that the end of the 1914 to 1918 war explains why England moves in the matter now. I am not clear about the connection, but Sharp suggests that the mass of orphaned children after these wars, the desire to get them out of institutions, the sheer cost of those institutions, and the wish of families to try to replace their slaughtered youth, all together pressed the law to an interest in adoption. It makes sense, though it is speculative.

"As to India and Burma, Sharp claims ignorance, but I have asked him to give me advice about the traditional law and practice in these countries and I think he will. He has suggested that Indian law is well developed concerning the adoption of male children, but its main purpose is to provide male children to pray for the souls of their adoptive fathers after their deaths. It sounds like one of his many prejudices, but I am unsure. Anyhow, he will let me know, he says, and also about Burmese law. You see, Dr. Veraswami, I am not even sure whether English or Indian or Burmese law governs in these matters. Sharp is also to advise me about that.

"In the end, Doctor, I fear the legal directions will come to this: the best interests of the child weigh most heavily, but the rights of the natural parent or parents are to be given very great weight. Indeed, they are to be protected unless the parents have been cruel to the child, have neglected the child, have displayed some moral fault or faults making them unfit to be parents, or have entrusted the child to others who have formed familial relations with the child that also must be greatly respected. Shin Yalat would seem in law, at any event in English law as Sharp advises me of it, to be entitled to remain JiHan's parent and keep custody of him unless it can be said that by her actions she has entrusted the child to the Cunninghams to be treated as their child. If she has, then I have to begin that awful process of trying to decide what is in JayJay's best interests. How, in Heaven's name, can I know?"

"So, Mr. Magistrate, where the lawyers lead you iss to a procedure of thought, issn't it? They tell you what you may think about and what you may not—but to decide thiss custody question there iss not much they tell you to leave out. Over all iss the best interests of the boy; but then you must not overlook the powerful claims of the natural mother, just because she iss the natural mother, nor of the Cunninghams, because they have for several years treated the boy ass their own, looked after him, paid for his care. All these matters you can weigh ass well ass any middle-aged Indian doctor with a taste for London, but perhaps I can help you with the question of the boy's interests—not the answer, I don't know that—but the question."

"Does it not come to," I asked, "where the boy will be happier?"

Dr. Veraswami was clear that this was the wrong way to approach the matter, though I found his argument hard to follow. The defect in this approach, he argued, was that it was too positive, too confident. It was like looking for a world of lasting love. It claimed too much for the life of anyone. "You are too young to know yet, my young friend, and I can only sense the truth of it without feeling it, but I suspect that those who tell uss that either love or happiness are the lasting satisfactions do not know much of what they say. I have watched older married people: it iss clear that the fever of love iss not upon them, but there iss a quiet mutual support, a friendly affection, a comfortable tolerance which seems to me to be a much warmer and more lasting sentiment than love. Love, if one iss verry fortunate, grows into affection and becomes enduring in the change. No, it iss not happiness you must seek for JayJay; it iss a quiet acceptance of the limits we all feel and the pains and disappointments we will all endure no matter how well we do. Love becomes affection; ambition becomes satisfaction in one's work. And that iss, I think, the real anodyne for the human condition—work—the only anodyne, the only sure comfort."

Veraswami seemed to be drifting from one sentiment to another, but I did think his point about the central importance of work to happiness made good sense.

Work in Chinaka for JayJay would be completely predictable and utterly reliable: the work of a fisherman and probably the responsibilities of an emerging leader of the village. But how dull, how repetitious! Work in

Kenya for JayJay would be a small school with the often painful task of growing up to colonial and British ways, certainly less supportive and easy than the paths, or rather paths and channels, of a Chinakan childhood and youth. His work later in England also seemed predictable in its early years.

He was intelligent and energetic; the Cunninghams would press him, if he should need pressing, which I doubted, to University and a profession. Conformity and achievement, intellectual and physical, would be expected of him, while he carried the burden, not mitigated by the excessive politeness of his peers, of a skin of different colour—so that he would never quite belong. If work was the anodyne, he might need a lot of it if I set him on the English path.

Distracted by these speculations, I missed the beginning of what Veraswami was saying. "I'm sorry, Doctor; my mind had drifted."

"Perhaps it iss ass well that it had; perhaps it should stay away. I am not at all sure whether I am being verry helpful, but I wonder should you consider something else we have not talked about—I think of it ass a doctor, but I suppose it iss true for any profession and for many avocations. Perhaps the boy is creatively gifted, one cannot be sure, but he iss very promising, do you not think so? And if he iss, then his happiness does not, I suppose, matter ass much ass his having the opportunity to develop those gifts. If so, I suppose, you must send him off with the Cunninghams and leave Shin Yalat in failure, to be merely tolerated in the village."

"But is it not important to have creative people in the Burmese village, Dr. Veraswami? Could he not help his people there, too?"

"Not verry much, I think. A few more fish, perhaps better boats or houses, perhaps a more peaceful existence, but it iss hard to see how he or anyone else could make much change. Some educated Burmese will no doubt lead their country away from England toward political independence and, one hopes, economic prosperity; but they will come from the cities and from the city schools and from English universities—not from fishing villages."

It was true that JayJay was intelligent and energetic, but there were, certainly as yet no signs of any creative genius. I started to say as much to Veraswami but he pressed on in another direction: "It iss interesting, most interesting, that the boy may go to Kenya, near where it all began."

"Where what began?" I asked.

"You know, Mr. Blair, the human experience, you, me, us, *Homo* supposedly *sapiens*, isn't it so? I am told that some three million years ago the first *Australopithecus Africanus* began to wander the grassy savannahs where you may send the boy."

I supposed that courtesy precluded asking Veraswami directly what he was going on about—but why not? "Tell me, Doctor, what has our long-named ancestor to do with JayJay?"

"I think it is quite relevant, quite, perhaps even a fundamental point; tell me if you do not agree." He got up from the table and walked over to the balcony so that he could prop his rump on it and address me even more directly. When Dr. Veraswami decided to engage one in close conversation, he took it literally. "The point iss that we are not here for happiness, or of a certainty not only for happiness, or even for our own best interests, even if we were sure what they are. We are a species, the same species, you and me, though the English may find that most hard to agree to; and that species iss distinguished from all others in that it hass developed a most unusual brain. The early African hominid of which I spoke wass distinctive in that it moved about carrying tools—other animals used tools, but this animal took tools about with it where it went. And by means we only poorly understand, in three million years it developed an astonishing reasoning and communicating capacity from which all that iss distinctively good and bad in man emerges. The boy, JayJay, iss a part of that species, as much a part as all others over those millions of years, and he hass to grow so that the species will grow. I find it interesting indeed that he might go back to where it all began, if you decide he shall live hiss childhood with the Cunninghams."

It remained farfetched to me, but I could see how an argument could be made that my decision about the boy was part of a larger cosmic pattern involving everyone, though it did not comfort me much. Dr. Veraswami saw that I found his anthropological meditations unhelpful. "I will not continue to trouble you with these possible sillinesses of mine, Blair, but at least one thought from the biologists may help you. Thomas Huxley, who you will remember supported Darwin when hiss views of man's origins were most unpopular, said that we must learn what iss true in order to do what iss right. I think that the truth of man's origins and the development of the species remain important to many more decisions than you might think, including whether JiHan stays or John goes.

"Yes, yes, whether you like it or not, there iss one more species point that my conscience tells me I must press upon you about your decision. It iss probable that the growth of the brain in the hominids, of which I spoke, came from their behaviour, from what they did, and not from any chance mutation of their genes. It iss clear to me that people learn and grow by doing, by trying—not by mere acceptance of what others do and try. The human condition iss a struggle, and I do not mean a struggle to survive, I mean a struggle to grow. And I am not at all sure—quite unsure, in fact, that it iss possible to grow in that way ass a fisherman in the Gulf of Martaban.

"It iss behaviour that determines growth, Mr. Blair, not the other way around, if you follow me, please. You will have noticed, I am quite sure, that when people pray, whatever their beliefs, Hindus, Muslims, Buddhists, Christians, even Jews, they behave in verry similar ways. Oh yes, I agree, to be sure, that they do not behave in identical ways; some prostrate themselves, some do not; some bend their knees, while some regard genuflection as a sign of idolatry; some clasp their hands together above or in front of their heads, and some do not; most bow their heads. But my point iss that those are the sorts of things that all people do when they pray.

"You would know a person was praying if you knew nothing whatsoever of his religion, had never seen one of his tribe or cult or persuasion before. One type of behaviour for all people is praying. It iss like laughing or crying—common to all, all humans. Though some animals also laugh and cry, they do not pray, or so it seems to me. And what I am trying to say iss that the praying shapes their beliefs, gives form and importance to them. The behaviour, the praying, in all its forms makes people more perceptive of matters larger than themselves, makes them think less selfishly, makes them contemplate the force they choose to call divine, and their place in the human story. I am sorry to sound like a preacher, but you will surely see that it iss the praying that fashions the intensity of the belief, not the other way around; it iss not the belief which compels the praying."

"What has this to do with the boy, Dr. Veraswami, even if you are right? I agree it is an interesting idea."

"Thiss, I think. You will give the boy more opportunities to develop, through many different forms of behaviour, as a European than as a Burmese fisherman. He can grow more because he will be expected, encouraged, pushed, and prodded to behave in more ways. He will grow more. That iss the point."

"One minute you have him a cell in the evolution of a species, the next a plant to be grown in a hothouse so that he will spread, swift and large. He is just a little boy, Dr. Veraswami, and perhaps will grow best unprodded beside his mother. Many little boys do. And now you are asking me, as I understand you, to treat the boy as if I were considering the placement of an animal in a laboratory designed to make the largest contribution to all the other animals there, though none would make any more than a miserably small contribution."

"It iss worse than that, Blair: a miserably small contribution to all the other animals there now and all those that will be there in the future."

"If you are right, Doctor, should I be here in Moulmein? Should you? Should any European or Indian?"

Veraswami bounced up from the balcony, arms thrown upward in delight. "You mock me well, Blair. Certainly I don't think you should be here, except to talk to me. And I am sure that I should not be here, except perhaps to be of some slight help to you. Though this evening I think I have failed even in that. You pleass, pleass, must not think that I have been arguing that you should give the boy to the Cunninghams or to Shin Yalat. I find it a verry troublesome problem. But I put these ideas to you, such ass they are, in the hope that they will help you to ass full an understanding ass you can have and will need."

We were both tired, tired absolutely and of the subject; it seemed too hard, beyond the decent boundaries of any decision that anyone should have to make for others.

Veraswami made one last effort cryptically to sum it up. "Ass property, the boy belongs to Shin Yalat; even though the Cunninghams have contributed to hiss life, they did not give him life. If life is a search for happiness, my guess iss that he will be happier in Chinaka than in London—

though I certainly would not be. If the purpose of life iss to contribute to the welfare and happiness of others and to take resigned comfort in those contributions, then he must go with the Cunninghams."

As we said good night, I found that what most stuck in my mind was the vehemence of Veraswami's preference for London over Chinaka, were he the child at issue. And yet here he was, slaving away at the miserable hospital in Moulmein, when he could, I assumed, have been at a palatial London hospital, had he wished.

Veraswami walked off across the parade ground, or rather around it. I knew the feeling. I always preferred the circuit to the walk across. I have never felt at all at ease on a parade ground, and to Dr. Veraswami crossing a parade ground must have felt even more incongruous.

I sat for a while on the verandah after Veraswami had left. What I found myself concluding from his involved talk about the human species, and the ways in which we live and grow, was that I might be facing a choice between JiHan's happiness and his obligation to pay that small token of tribute to the development of the species that some can make.

Perhaps the solution to my problem might be found in what I had so far seen as its greatest difficulty. The very distance between the two cultures of upper middle-class England and of a Burmese fishing village had until now intensified the challenge to me; but that very distance might also provide the clue to the better decision.

First, that distance must have been as clear to Shin Yalat as it was to Coleen Cunningham. The Cunningham household demonstrated it and lived it every moment of the day and night. Shin Yalat could hardly have failed to recognise that her son was being brought up in a home of a very alien culture, a culture from which she was excluded other than as an observer and as a foreign servant. She might not have phrased the fact of her increasing separateness from her son in that way, but she could not have been blind to what was happening to him and to her relationship to him.

But more important, the two cultures represented what some would see as polar opposites in the relationship between the individual and the group. Success in the Burmese village lay in conformity, in being deeply a part of the group; the group would grow through the collectivity. It was of course true that, in many respects, the English culture, which JiHan would join if he accompanied the Cunninghams, also had its rigid expectations of how one should behave, how dress, how speak, with whom associate; but it also, more perhaps than any culture other than the brash and as yet uncultivated Americans and the even more uncouth Australians and Canadians, encouraged and gave its highest respect to the creative and uniquely contributing individual. Individual thinkers and leaders, provided they reasonably conformed in outward behaviour—in dress, speech, and manners— were the bedrock of English science, of English letters, and of English industrial strength. By contrast, the Burmese fishing village was the epitome of group life, where group development was the only acceptable agent of change.

This did not mean that the Chinakan fisherman might not know a great deal. Some thought that he might know as much about the complex life of the shoreline of the Bay of Chinaka as any modern marine biologist—he might know as many facts. But his was knowledge of a different order, a knowledge shared with all the fishermen in the village. It was not the knowledge of the individual discoverer.

All this should not weigh much in my decision, I supposed, unless I believed that JiHan might be one of the chosen few blessed with capacities for individual creativity, in which case the warmly supporting group of the Burmese village would dampen and drown those unique qualities. He might well be happier in Chinaka, but the chance of his there being, even a small part, individually creative seemed quite unlikely.

But how very unhappy JiHan would likely be in England. I remembered the miseries of my prep school and of Eton, and I, too, had been seen as clever and independent, and hence the appropriate butt both of schoolboy cruelty and of the affected irony of the less secure teachers. JiHan would be seen by some as a "Boong," a native, a lesser breed without the law, a monkey dancing to the tune of an English organ grinder, but never quite making it. Was that the misery to which I was to commit this warmly happy boy when the charm and ease of Chinaka, and the role of leadership in the village, awaited him?

To my astonishment, it was the Officer in Charge of the Imperial Police in Burma on the telephone. He assumed I knew what he wanted to talk to me about and seemed hesitant, almost shy, in his approach to it: "I hope you don't mind my calling you on this matter, Blair?"

"Not at all, Sir. Certainly. What matter, Sir?"

"That child and the Cunninghams, of course. But if you think it improper for me to discuss it with you because it is *sub judice*, I want you to know, Blair, that I don't wish to influence your judgment at all, believe me, but you had better know the range of problems you have in hand. His Majesty's Government is watching the matter closely."

The fan was rotating more noisily than usual in the public area outside my office where the telephone was located; I had expected more advice from Sharp, not these embarrassed animadversions of the most senior officer of my service in Burma. As I say, the telephone always terrifies me—the two words, telephone and terrify, run euphoniously together and resonate in my mind as I clutch the instrument to my face—but the authoritative rumblings from Rangoon made me realise that I was in the eye of the political hurricane and had better concentrate with some determination on what was being said.

He put it circuitously but vigourously. The last thing in the world he would ever consider doing was to interfere in the exercise of judicial discretion by one of his subordinates. I must understand that the great reputation of English law, at home and abroad, was built on that secure impartiality of the English judge and his sturdy independence from political interference. Nevertheless—and the word seemed to crop up quite often in his conversation—nevertheless, I must realise that the case I had to decide might have important consequences quite beyond the parties before me. He phrased it well; I could hardly forget its force: There were some with commercial interests of importance to His Majesty's Government who would wish for local support of a major industry and of those who run it; but also of considerable importance was the growing nationalistic sentiment in Burma, feeding on the same turmoil as in India, a sentiment which would delight in making a *cause célèbre* of my little matter by suggesting that even Burmese children were not safe from the larcenous ways of the Raj. So what was important was that justice should be seen to be done and that no suggestion of political influence should be thought to have been brought to bear—it was obvious that I should ensure that whatever words I uttered in court should not be capable of misconstruction to that effect, and yet at the same time it was impressed upon me that "the right thing should be done."

Douglas Sharp would, of course, be ready to guide me on the law, but it had been concluded in Rangoon that I should not be assisted in the actual hearings by any legal representatives beyond those the Cunninghams might decide to employ, lest it be thought by the Burmese radicals that I was being unduly influenced. On the other hand—and the Officer in Charge seemed to have as many other hands as neverthelesses—he had given directions that I was to be allowed priority use of the trunk line telephone and it was expected that I would, over the next day or two, before I heard the case, consult regularly with Sharp and other legal officers in Rangoon, who had been working diligently on the relevant law and would advise me on it.

"Do you understand? Do you have any questions?"

I did, and I did not.

"Oh yes, one other thing, Blair. Captain Taylor will be coming to Moulmein tomorrow on a general inspection of your section. He will be no trouble. He will come straight back after the Cunningham case is decided. We need someone there to report back promptly on the political and commercial implications. No interference, you understand."

He regretted that he would be away from Rangoon for the next few weeks, but he had no doubt that he could leave the matter safely in my able hands. The peremptory quality of his farewell made me think that he shared my doubts in his concluding statement.

"I hear you got your marching orders, Old Boy, from the head shebang Burma Police, no less. He told me to call you."

Sharp infuriated me sometimes, and I told him so. I told him that it had been impressed on me that I was not confined to his advice but that I could search more widely in the legal affairs section in Rangoon or even Mandalay if I wished. And I thought I did.

"Oh, don't be so stuffy, Blair. I'll play the charade with you if you want."

"It's not a charade. I need technical advice on the law, not schoolboy teasing, Sharp. I don't really understand all the implications of the difference between adoption of a child and custody or guardianship of a child. I want help like that, not your brilliant repartee. So, if you will help me, do so."

Sharp seemed chastened but not troubled at all by my words. Or rather, it seemed to me he was suddenly quite troubled, sensing that I was wrestling with the case, not just trying to find a discreet way through it.

By Burmese standards, Moulmein was a large town and, hence, on the itinerary of every wandering dance and folktale-acting troupe in Burma. While I was in Burma there must have been a *pwe*, a performance by such a group, two or three nights almost every month, though less frequently at the height of the rainy season. Occasionally I would attend their performances and stay for a short time. I did not know the stories they mimed well enough to follow them in detail, and my Burmese was certainly not adequate to the task. The dancing, though graceful, had a repetitive pattern that I soon tired of. The dancing girls were young, extremely supple, and graceful, but I had no need of stimulus for my sexual inclinations; they were enough trouble without my going out of my way to encourage them.

Moulmein had a high reputation among the wandering dancers and actors because of a natural theatre near the town. The river Salween made a firm U curve close to the main road to Mandalay. The actors and dancers would pitch their wooden boards and their bamboo and canvas stage at the curve of the U, close to the road, so that with generators and simple arc lamps their Bamboo U would serve as well as Shakespeare's Wooden O, which, after all, had been the primitive site of some great plays. The audience would gather on the road and the side of the road, squatting and lying on mats, or sitting in a few scattered chairs, the close view across the narrow river lending to the stage and the performers on it an air of a separate and magical world. From a police point of view the *pwes* caused no trouble whatsoever, though some of the Europeans expressed anxiety. The *pwes* blocked the roadway and stopped traffic, of course, but in the evenings that hardly mattered; there was so very little traffic to stop, and they never generated any disturbances.

I was surprised when the mayor, Ba San Chi, asked me if I would join him one evening a few days hence at a *pwe*. There seemed no reason to decline. We were on cordial if distant terms, and this gesture of personal hospitality should not be rejected. He told me he would meet me at the *pwe*, if I did not mind, since he had to be there earlier to welcome the actors and dancers and see that everything was in order—apparently this was a group of some distinction.

I should have known. I did know as soon as I arrived. There was a large gathering at the road across from the Bamboo U and, as I edged through to the seats obviously reserved for the mayor's group, it was clear that it was more than a hospitable gesture that had motivated Ba San Chi. There was another guest, well known throughout Burma, and Ba San Chi should have told me of his likely presence when he invited me.

I had seen the man's face often in the Rangoon papers. It was an unusual face, the shiny light brown skin of the privileged Burman, neat symmetrical features, and then—a most singular feature—a curved indentation, as if from a hatchet wound, slicing from above the right eye over the bridge of the nose and down under the right eye high on the cheek bone. It gave his face at once a sinister and a sincere air. It seemed to be both a straightforward injury and a mark of cunning and perfidy. I recalled his name before the mayor introduced him to me—U Tin Hlang—and remembered that he was one of the leaders of the G.C.B.A. For the past year one could hardly pick up a Burmese newspaper without seeing his face.

He expressed the formalities of salutation in tones appropriate to my public school rather than to a Burmese politician. But he softened the formality beyond the "How d'y do" to an assertion of pleasure in meeting me, as if he had heard of me before. I asked what brought him to Moulmein.

"You do, Mr. Blair, you and the Cunningham case." I tried to raise an enquiring eyebrow. "Mrs. Shin Yalat's solicitor has briefed me; I plan to call on you tomorrow to give notice of appearance." I turned to the Mayor. His party, it seemed, consisted of three, and he seemed anxious to separate himself from his guests—somewhat shamefaced, as if he were conscious of having taken advantage of me unfairly, which he had.

There seemed nothing for me to do but to sit down, be as silent as courtesy would allow, and escape when I decently could. Clearly I should not be seen plotting with Shin Yalat's counsel, particularly such a notorious counsel. So I tried to turn my attention fully to the performance, which was already under way with much banging of the drums, the euphonic wailing of a high-pitched wind instrument, and, of course, total disregard for European tonal scales. A dancer was twisting prettily in a tight-fitting, severely cut, red silken skirt and loose, white, open-buttoned tunic. Her extraordinarily long fingernails, when turned back on flexed hands, almost touched the arms above her wrists.

My mind wandered from the performance. The presence of U Tin Hlang in Moulmein should not be taken lightly. Why had Rangoon not warned me that he might involve himself in the case? Perhaps they didn't know.

I knew, of course, that the G.C.B.A. was an activist group plotting Burmese independence, but I regularly forgot what the acronym stood for. With effort I could work it out: General Council of Buddhist Associations. It was regarded in the Club as a seditious organisation, and I was glowered at as inept whenever the G.C.B.A. was mentioned—surely the police should have the guts to protect us from such rabble rousers!

There had been little nationalist activity in Moulmein during my period there, though some rioting had occurred in Rangoon by Burmese against Indians that, as I understood it, had an underlying political significance—the aspiration of members of the G.C.B.A for independence both from England and from India. They apparently feared—and with good cause, I later came to understand—that if India gained independence, Burma might remain as it had been administered under English rule, as a part of India. The grant of dyarchy to Burma in 1923, the same form of dual government that had earlier been given to India, by which there were local elections to the legislature as well as English nominations to it, with power being apparently shared but in fact remaining firmly within the control of the English authorities, did nothing to reassure activist Burmese of the imminence of self-government.

I had never actually talked with a senior member of the G.C.B.A. What little I knew came from the Rangoon and Mandalay newspapers, which made their leisurely way to Moulmein bearing a heavily slanted Raj perspective on the news, from the wireless broadcasts that also originated with the administration in Rangoon, and from the more neutral comments of Dr. Veraswami, who was interested in both the Indian and the Burmese nationalist movements, though not as a participant.

In the Club there was talk of the Burmese "barristocracy." I gathered that a coterie of Burmese had eaten their dinners at and passed their examinations for one or other of the Inns of Court in London, had hobnobbed with members of the English aristocracy and upper-middle class, and had returned to Burma with a strong sense of their equality, at least with anyone in authority in Burma. The view was strongly asserted that the pusillanimity of the Rangoon and Mandalay authorities succoured this barristocracy and spelt the end of all that was sensible in the relations between the races ordained by God.

The dance stopped. The stage was cleared. There are no intervals in the European sense in such *pwes*, but rather breaks of action of a length to suit the stage of the performance, the weather, and the inclinations of the actors. Politeness moved me to try to make a courteous chatter with Mr. U—the weather, the performance, and such matters. He smiled and responded briefly, but made no pretence of wishing to talk about anything other than the case that had brought him to Moulmein and me into his company—again a circumstance he made no attempt to conceal, saying he had asked the mayor to invite me so that he could talk to me about the case.

"Surely, Mr. U Tin, it is wrong for us to discuss the case out of court. You tell me you will be appearing on behalf of Shin Yalat; I will listen carefully to you at that time, but not now, not about the case."

"You have such difficulty with 'Mr. U Tin.' Perhaps you would care to call me 'Mr. Lang,' which was what was preferred in England, or 'Tin' as a sort of Christian name, which also found some favour there. But on the question of our talking about the case, have your own way, of course, but after all, you have talked of it a great deal with Rangoon, even with the eminent officer in command of Imperial Police Burma, I am told. Why not with me? If Douglas Sharp can go on and on to you with his smart repartee, why not me?"

His knowledge of my telephone conversations astonished me, as did his allusion to "repartee," a word I recalled having used to Douglas Sharp as a reprimand. Surely my telephone conversations themselves had not been intercepted!

I did my best to hide my anxiety and growing annoyance. "There is surely a difference. My department and its staff were trying to help me with a difficult case; they were not trying to influence my decision—you would be trying to influence my decision."

Utter delight spread over Hlang's—or U's—or Tin's—bisected face and I realised what a ridiculous thing I had said. He was obviously not uninformed about my relationship to police authorities and the Legal Section; it was ingenuous for me to pretend.

When the next interval came we made our way through the sweaty, squatting throng of Burmese and slowly walked the mile or so back to my bungalow. I listened carefully to him. It seemed to me important that I see the case in its full political significance now that it had been raised to that level. What U Tin Hlang had to tell me was not really at all complex—if the Burmese boy was given to the Cunninghams, it would look to the villagers like simple larceny.

"I had thought of arranging for the dancers tonight to present a folktale which is very popular in the country, for reasons which you will understand. It would have made the point dramatically for you, Mr. Blair, that I wish to make about the boy JiHan. But the mayor thought you would be revolted by its indecency. He has most odd ideas about the tastes of English gentlemen, but I did not argue with him. I think you would have enjoyed it. It is called 'The Young Man Who Changed Sex.'"

U Tin Hlang fell silent. He knew how to lure one on. Curiosity compelled me to ask him what the story was about.

Apparently, a young man was powerfully attracted to the daughter of a rich man, who kept her in golden but secure custody, in the manner of the folktales of the world. The rich man denied the young man's suit and turned him away. The young man went to a sorcerer, who prescribed a potion that allowed the young man to change into a young woman and back again. So equipped, he changed to a young woman and gained access as a servant to the rich man's house. Diligence, intelligence, and a clear sense of purpose were rewarded when the servant was appointed the personal maid of the daughter. The potion was then further imbibed, and the servant returned to his original state of virile young manliness, so that instant love arose and was promptly consummated between the daughter and the young man. (I could see why the performance might be somewhat unusual to European eyes; the Burmese like realism in the presentation of their stories.) The daughter became pregnant. Losing his nerve, the young man ran away. The daughter told all to her father, but he still refused permission for her to marry the young man. Instead, he married her off to another rich man, a friend of his in a neighbouring village, telling him the whole story. When the child was born, the young man, the natural father, petitioned the Princess Learned-in-Law for custody of the child. The Princess Learned-in-Law was, of course, the ultimate authority on all questions of law in Burma. The Princess Learned-in-Law denied the young man's petition; any child born in wedlock was conclusively presumed to be the son of the husband no matter what the evidence to the contrary. "Every Burman knows that story, Mr. Blair; every Burman approves of its message."

"So, in your eyes, I am dealing with the case of a Burmese child simply being stolen by a childless European couple. Is that it, Mr. Lang?"

"What I think doesn't matter, Mr. Blair. I am trying to tell you what the Burmese in general will think, and it is jolly decent of me to be taking the trouble to inform you in this way. And, as you know, English law has a similar presumption, though it is not so compelling. The boy may look half European to you, but for my purpose he is entirely Burmese; the English court will be stealing a Burmese child."

U Tin Hlang went on to argue that even the more informed Burmese, less moved by the Princess Learned-in-Law, would hold a similar view: They had often heard English authorities say that local customs and local laws would be respected unless they were in some sense repugnant to ethical and legal values held to be inviolable by English law. That could hardly be the case here. Adoption was better known in Burma than in England, which only this year had its first adoption law. How could it possibly be allowed that the boy could be wrenched from his mother?

"So you think, Mr. Lang, that the Cunninghams should not take the boy and educate him as you have been so well educated in England?"

Again a look of unqualified delight spread over his beaming round face. "Oh dear no, not at all, not at all. I hope you give him to the Cunninghams. Probably it will help the boy, and it will be a great help to the movement. We need that sort of stimulus now. I will be most appreciative, though I will denounce you from every box I can find to climb onto."

He saw my annoyance. I did not reply. I was outraged that everyone seemed to be using the child, his mother, and the Cunninghams for their own ends.

And then he continued: "You see, Mr. Blair, this is a wonderful case for me. I shall speak movingly to you in the court, words that will be interpreted by those who report me as powerful attacks on your employers. And then, whatever you decide, I shall win the case. If Shin Yalat keeps the boy, it will be due to my compelling advocacy—another victory for the G.C.B.A. and for my position in it; if the boy goes to the Cunninghams, the G.C.B.A. will be strengthened greatly by my heroism in so gallantly struggling against such determined wickedness as you have demonstrated. It is a great case, a great case for me."

Veraswami's instructions had been quite clear: Do not talk to the boy about whether he would prefer to grow up as a Burmese fisherman or as an English gentleman, but talk to him so that *you* will be able to decide whether he would prefer to grow up as a Burmese fisherman or as an English gentleman. Quite clear; wonderfully unhelpful, but quite clear. Why should I talk to the boy at all? How could he know the answer to that question? I could see no point in embarrassing the boy and even less in embarrassing me. I was never any good at light chatter with children, and this seemed hardly the occasion for light chatter even if I could manage it. And how could I ask whom of the adults contending for him he loved more? In any event that seemed less important than the equally hopeless task of trying to assess the intensities of their love for him. Why had I let Veraswami talk me into this dreadful interview with JayJay?

It had been a single sentence of Veraswami's that had persuaded me. "Perhaps it iss improper to involve the boy, perhaps unfair, but I suppose you must try if only to be sure for yourself that he cannot help in your decision."

"But it will upset him, Veraswami; deeply, I should think."

"Of course, but whatever you do he will soon be deeply disturbed by one or another separation. He iss a strong and resilient boy, I am sure. Your interviewing him will make little enough difference to him in the long run. You should do it for yourself, Blair, even if you hate it, ass perhaps you will—or perhaps not; he iss a rather sweet young man, easy to talk to, even for me."

The Cunninghams and Dr. Veraswami agreed that I should talk to the boy in some informal setting, perhaps while swimming at the Club or playing French cricket with him before an evening meal at the Cunninghams. I had decided that the boy was old enough to talk to me, if talk to him I must, in my office, where he would know I was involved in serious concerns about his future, even if he did not understand their full import.

I dredged my memory for how I felt and thought at his age, but the only impression that welled up was of adults not taking me seriously, trying to make baby jokes of things I thought important. In my few earlier contacts with JayJay in Moulmein and Chinaka, and on that hostile journey bringing him and his mother back to Moulmein, I had gained the sense of a maturity beyond his years, so that the formal setting of my office at the police station seemed appropriate to me.

The Cunninghams agreed, with marked lack of enthusiasm, to my request that John should be brought to see me; they mistrusted my judgment in what they saw as a simple decision, obviously in John's best interests, and they feared—as I also feared—that I would, quite unnecessarily and for my own purposes, upset the boy. But they were sensitive and, I thought, wise in having Shin Yalat accompany him to my office and in making no attempt in any way to prepare him for the interview. I knew this to be so from the moment I saw the boy and his mother walk past my window to the entrance of the police station. He was clearly pursuing with joy an engaging adventure—a surprise which could only be to his advantage, since such had been the case with all surprises given him by adults during his life. He was a much loved boy and showed it in the confidence and directness of his every movement.

Shin Yalat sat quietly and still outside my office. I am sure she knew the purpose of the interview but she preserved the calm immobility of countenance of a Burmese woman on formal occasions.

How should I start the conversation with the boy? The weather? School? Yes, that seemed a possibility. "I want to talk to you, JayJay, for a while, to get to know you better. I hope you don't mind."

A smiling shake of his head did nothing to put me at ease. By contrast, he seemed quite at ease, the hostile attitude he had demonstrated on the forced return journey from Chinaka being either forgotten or controlled. His eyes wandered around my office and lighted on the line of rifles locked in an extended rack along one wall.

"Why are those guns there, Sir?"

"If we have to arm the police, say to chase some dangerous criminal, or to shoot a tiger that has been raiding a village, I unlock the rack and give the rifles to the policemen. I have one of the keys to the rack; so does each Duty Sergeant."

"Could I hold one of them, Mr. Blair? My father would let me . . . I think." The statement was saved from prevarication by the note of extreme doubt in his voice.

Despite my strong inclination to humour him in any way that I could during this interview, letting him play with an unloaded rifle did not seem a good idea, and I told him, truthfully enough for our joint purposes, that it was beyond my proper authority to take the guns from the rack except when there was clear need, and that each time the rack was opened and a rifle taken out a report had to be submitted to Mandalay.

"Really, a report to Mandalay, even when you do a little thing like that?"

"Issuing the guns is not such a little thing, JayJay. They are very dangerous."

He smiled in a friendly way and wandered over to the window of my office and looked out. Nothing was happening. A few police sitting outside their huts on the other side of the parade ground, but nothing to hold his attention. The silence lengthened. "I think I would like Shin Yalat to take me home now, please."

I asked if he minded staying with me a little longer, to which he gave a somewhat neutral assent.

"Do you remember when we first met in Chinaka, JayJay?"

His face brightened. Of course he did; what fun it had been swimming for all the tins I had spilled in the lagoon.

"And do you remember when you . . . when we . . . failed to solve the mystery of the burglary?"

That, too, he remembered and had enjoyed. He had told me how it had happened. He was not sure I had believed him, but he still thought he was right.

I assured him it was as good an explanation as I had; I knew none better. But I wasn't sure. Was he?

"Of course, yes, did not the mark on the shutter and the footprint outside prove it?"

I yielded that it was persuasive evidence. What was becoming even more clear to me than I had previously appreciated was that I was dealing with a child of capacious mind and retentive memory.

He was smiling, friendly but slightly bored, helping me to make conversation, polite but disengaged. We talked of school, of cricket, of horses, of fishing in Chinaka. I would advance each subject, he would respond openly, I would let it trail off. He liked school, though he sometimes found it very dull. Horses were super. Fishing at Chinaka was great fun. He was still polite, but occasionally fidgeted and wandered about the office. We were getting nowhere.

Each time I mentioned the Cunninghams I rather dampened the ease of our communication by the formality of my reference to them—Mr. Cunningham, Mrs. Cunningham—but I found it hard, situated as I was, to talk of his father or mother, which they were not, unless I were now laying the foundation on which the law might later make them so. And how to refer to Shin Yalat other than as Shin Yalat bewildered me. Then, with inner horror at what I heard myself saying, I blundered directly to the issue.

"Have you thought what will happen to you if Mr. and Mrs. Cunningham leave Burma?"

"I will go with them?"

"But what about Shin Yalat? What if she can't come with you?"

"Of course she can. Why shouldn't she?"

"Well, perhaps she wants to stay in Burma, in Chinaka. She would not find it easy to live in England or Kenya, you know."

"Daddy and Mummy would look after her. She would look after me as she always does."

"You won't need looking after much longer. You'll be off to a boarding school soon. You will soon be looking after yourself. Then what is Shin Yalat to do?" And then he must have realised from my face or my demeanour that this was no idle conversation but a matter of deep concern—that the pattern of his life might be shattered and that our conversation had something to do with it. His eyes filled with tears though no noise of pain escaped him. "They wouldn't be so cruel, I am sure." But the last phrase had an uncertainty similar to that he had expressed about his father's view of his freedom of access to a rifle. Cruel or not, he suddenly knew what was upon him.

And now there was no possibility of making an easy exit. He walked, baby footed, to the door of my office, opened it, and ran crying to the arms of Shin Yalat.

I think, but am not sure, that I saw them both to the door of the police station. All that I had learned was that, whatever I decided, the boy would be scarred by it. But it was also clear from our conversation, as well as from everything I knew and had heard about JayJay, that the odds were that he would grow up to be a fine Chinakan fisherman or a fine English gentleman. And no compromise was possible.

The evening before the hearing I dined alone at the Club. Captain Taylor was there, but without discussing the question we both thought it better not to dine together.

After dinner I walked around to Dr. Veraswami's bungalow to tell him of my talk with JayJay, of the unexpected interventions of my superiors in Rangoon, and of U Tin Hlang.

I did not stay long. I knew it was necessary for me to try to order my thoughts on the law so that I could be ready to listen with understanding to whatever would be said to me tomorrow. But I found myself complaining somewhat childishly to Dr. Veraswami about the extent of the pressure from outside that was being brought to bear on me.

"It is quite maddening, Dr. Veraswami. Whatever I do will be thought corrupt: bowing either to political pressure or to pressure from commercial interests."

"So it iss, Blair. You cannot avoid those suspicions. It iss even hard for you to avoid the reality of being improperly influenced, let alone the appearance. You will just have to try to set them aside." He waved my superiors and the G.C.B.A. away with a slow sweep of the hand. "But, of course, it will not be easy."

There was a reflective silence between us, broken in time by Veraswami recalling some words of an English poet and playwright, T. S. Eliot he thought, to the effect that the greatest sin is to do the right deed for the wrong reason. "You may well be thought to have sinned after this case because you did the right deed for the right reason. The wrong reason will be . . . presumed, issn't it?"

I was not at all sure I knew what he meant. Was he suggesting his view of the right decision? At all events I knew he had more confidence in the sincerity of my effort at impartial judgment than did Sharp and the others in Rangoon, and that comforted me. On second thought, perhaps the problem was that in Rangoon they did have a sense of the risk of my independence of judgment, and that was what troubled them. It had become too complicated by half. I had better fix my mind on the boy, his mother, and the Cunninghams, and do what was right in my conscience—to the devil with their politics!—even if that meant doing what I concluded was the right thing for the right reason and yet being thought a spineless flunkey in the doing.

As I walked home to my bungalow, and for the next hour or two, I tried to draw into some focus my understanding of the law I would have to wrestle with tomorrow. The facts concerning JayJay and Shin Yalat and the Cunninghams now seemed clear to me, and so did the commercial and political interests warring around them; but in the last resort the relevant law surely had a lot to do with what I must decide. I was not a saint sitting in the wilderness deciding with wisdom on abstract principles of justice; I was a junior magistrate, untrained, prone to error, uncertain of my judgment. I had to seek what guidance I could from established law.

From what I could ascertain before the hearing, Burma had a substantial law of adoption that had developed for the singular reason that a Burmese Buddhist was unable to make a will; his only way of influencing the passage of his property after death was by adopting those he wished to benefit. Adoption in Burma required no court hearing and no formal registration; but it did require consent to the adoption by the natural parent, parents, or guardians of the child, and the consent of the child if of a sufficient age. It also had to be made obvious that the adopting parents intended the child to inherit; this had to be clear to others in the community—after all, that was the purpose of Burmese adoptions, inheritance.

Under Burmese law, JayJay could hardly be adopted by the Cunninghams. Shin Yalat obviously did not consent, and under Burmese law her consent could not be dispensed with.

The Guardians and Wards Act of 1890 was an Indian statute which, of course, applied also to Burma as a province of India. Any time the custody of a child was at issue, including when an adoption was contemplated, this Act applied. It made the best interests of the child the controlling consideration.

The Indian law on adoption, in particular the predominant Hindu law, differed greatly from the Burmese law. Indian law provided for adoption of males by males solely for the purpose of arranging lineal succession and for the new son's necessary activities in the funeral rites for the father. None of this seemed applicable to Burma, since it was clear that Burmese customary law, and not Indian law, governed adoption questions in Burma.

English law had recently—very recently—been changed. A few months earlier England had passed her first Adoption Act. Previously all adoptions had been informal or contractual, and all that was ever litigated were questions of inheritance and of custody or guardianship. Under the new English statute, Shin Yalat's consent to the adoption would have to be proved, unless the Cunninghams could show that a *de facto* adoption had taken place. This would seem unlikely in that the Cunninghams and Shin Yalat had each contributed to the rearing of JayJay. Therefore, under English law, Shin Yalat as the natural mother would have her rights as a mother protected unless it could be shown that she had neglected JiHan or been cruel to him—which she had not.

The English law of custody or guardianship was less formalised. It had grown in Chancery for rich Wards of Chancery and was a freewheeling, unencumbered, discretionary body of law in which the "best interests of the child" were the paramount consideration, despite the extraordinary difficulty of defining what that meant.

Custody or guardianship, of course, is only temporary. It can be challenged at any time, certainly by a natural mother like Shin Yalat if custody of JayJay were awarded to the Cunninghams. By contrast, adoption is as permanent as the legal relations springing from natural birth.

That is where I stood, with, however, one complicating factor. The law of adoption I should apply was clearly Burmese law, since JayJay's birth was in Burma. Thus, I was precluded by both English and Burmese law from treating him as other than a legitimate child, the son of his dead Karen father, since he had been born in wedlock, despite the obvious fact of his partly European parentage. Under the law of adoption, then, the Cunninghams had little chance of becoming the boy's new parents. However, they hadn't asked me for an adoption order, but rather for custody of the boy so that he might lawfully accompany them to England and Kenya. Indeed, had not Shin Yalat taken the boy to Chinaka without their permission, I do not think that the matter would have come before me at all. The Cunninghams would simply have taken him away with them, leaving Shin Yalat to whatever remedies she could find—and there would have been none. No, perhaps that was unkind; I had no reason to doubt that the Cunninghams would deal fairly with Shin Yalat, including taking her with them if she insisted on that—which, of course, she would not.

In briefest form: I could treat the matter as a Burmese adoption, in which case JiHan would stay with Shin Yalat, or I could treat it as simply a question of custody, in which case the best interests of JayJay would govern, if I could assess them. My Magistrate's Court was not bothered by the forms of action; that is one reason why the English statutes of adoption and custody gave these matters to courts of such lowly jurisdiction—so that the family realities, rather than the legal forms, could govern. If the

Cunninghams were given custody of John, then, in due course, some years later, an adoption could be formalised in England.

So the difference between adoption and custody might be at the heart of the matter. Suppose it had come to me as a custody question, in another way? Suppose the Cunninghams had decided to make their home permanently in Burma and wished to send JayJay to an English public school, and Shin Yalat did not wish to go. Or suppose Shin Yalat decided to remarry and settle with her new husband and JiHan away from Moulmein. Or suppose the Cunninghams for good cause had decided to discharge Shin Yalat, or she had decided to leave them, and she proposed taking JiHan with her back to Chinaka. In all these situations the problem would have come before me just as a custody question; I would have had considerable discretion under the Guardians and Wards Act to decide in JayJay's best interests as well as I could determine them. But if the matter had the permanency of adoption, then it seemed that under both English and Burmese law Shin Yalat would be unlikely to be deprived of her parental rights.

Yet was it not self-deceptive, bordering on the fraudulent, to think of this as other than an adoption? Whatever the technical legal forms, once the Cunninghams and JayJay were lawfully in England and then Kenya and then back in England, there was very little likelihood of Shin Yalat's ever seeing her son again, whether or not the Cunninghams later pursued the formalities of adoption. What faced me lay on the border between adoption and custody; what was becoming clear to me beyond doubt was that I did not wish ever to become a lawyer.

There was one possible solution that Sharp insisted I should keep in mind. Under the new English law of adoption, and applying as best one could some of the earlier statements by judges in custody cases, there did seem one realistic way in which the Cunninghams might be granted parental rights over JayJay. There were some cases where natural parents had let their child be looked after for a considerable period of time by others, often relatives, and then sought by *habeas corpus* to have the child returned to them. Courts in such cases had sometimes ruled against the natural parents, finding that the ties of love formed during the protracted entrustment of the child to that substitute family should not be broken. Sharp thought the same argument could be made about the hybrid adoption-custody case I faced with JayJay. There were troubles with the argument, it seemed to me, and Sharp reluctantly agreed. It went beyond any existing English or Burmese decisions, for in none of those cases had the natural mother been in residence with the family to whom her child was "entrusted," and it hardly seemed right that a Moulmein magistrate without legal training should take to himself the right to extend the law in this way—even if it did make sense. Shin Yalat was with the boy as much as were the Cunninghams. Of course, they had paid for his keep and his education, and a mercenary law might regard that as relevant, but I found it hard to think it so. Still, I had to agree with Sharp, this did give me a rationale for permitting the Cunninghams to take JayJay with them when they left Burma, without having to pretend that it was merely a question of his temporary custody.

My office was spacious for one, but cramped, very cramped, for six. Yet, if we trooped into the courtroom, all hope of informal communication would be lost, and I thought it utterly necessary for me, if not for the parties contending before me, to be able to talk with personal meaning Perhaps I deceived myself. Perhaps it was like many other adversarial decisions in which one must win and one must lose—nothing can be said to comfort the loser, and the winner is so delighted to hear the result that he is interested in nothing else.

We gathered in near silence, with words only of formal greeting and courtesy. Captain Taylor and I had been talking perfunctorily before the Cunninghams arrived, what about I do not remember, but certainly not about the case I had to decide.

I must give Taylor his due for circumspection; he most carefully avoided, from the moment he arrived in Moulmein, giving any hint of his own view about the matter, and succeeded, somehow, in leaving me with the firm impression that whatever I decided would be wrong and that its error would be precisely, fairly, and clearly reported to Mandalay. Throughout the hearing in my office he preserved an interested silence, a focused immobility, his only movements being the necessary mopping with his handkerchief at his brow and the open neck of his khaki shirt.

It was indeed fiercely hot. As the Cunninghams, Bruce and Coleen, arrived, and then U Tin Hlang shepherding Shin Yalat, the clouds gathered and released a tropical storm. Sheets of water were hurled onto my office, so that the shutters had to be closed if we were not to be inundated. The weak rotary fan in the ceiling struggled hopelessly to move the hot and humid air. The brutal heat and the strained faces of the people before me gave the scene a cataclysmic air. There was to be a tragedy for some in the room, and I had to be the agent of their despair. The decision was mine, inescapably, and as Dr. Veraswami had rightly said, "It iss a difficult decision for you, Mr. Blair, ass difficult ass you will ever have to make."

When one leaves the tropics one forgets the noise of a tropical storm; the visual memory of the mass of falling water remains with me, but I find it hard to recall the sound other than that it was loud. I do remember that it was not easy to make oneself heard in my little office that afternoon; ideas with which I had struggled to my moral limit had to be offered in a shout. There was no doubt it was an unhelpful venue.

My memories of that afternoon are dominated by U Tin Hlang. Coleen Cunningham did not speak at all. Shin Yalat was silent and self-effacing, as if she herself were on trial for some offence.

Bruce Cunningham had only one point to add to our many earlier conversations. It seemed to him on reflection, he said, "that it would be a rotten thing to do, having treated JayJay as a European child for seven years, educated him as a European, given him the expectation of a prosperous English future, to walk out on him now. It would be as if we had used him as a toy, now to be thrown aside. That really would be the ruthless Raj Mr. U complains about."

That was all that was said for the Cunninghams. They were not represented by counsel, unless the presence of the taciturn Captain Taylor could be regarded as representation. They relied on what they knew I knew of the whole matter.

By contrast, U Tin Hlang, in representing Shin Yalat's interests—or were they his own or those of the political organisation that paid him?—moved with the easy assurance of one at home in the courtroom, confident of the righteousness and persuasiveness of his cause. He knew that it was not customary to appear robed in a Magistrate's Court but, equally, he knew he had a right to appear robed, and robed he was—in the gown of an English King's Counsel—though the heat and humidity led him to eschew the full wig to which he was entitled as a "Silk."

I had gathered from observation of the Courts of Record in Rangoon and Mandalay that this form of dress was acceptable in the tropics—gown but no wig. And it made sense because very little indeed need be worn beneath the gown. But such formality was unnecessary, almost incongruous, in a local Magistrate's Court, before a judge dressed as a police lieutenant.

U Tin Hlang gave an admirable performance. He was attentive to his client, solicitous of her comfort, and respectful in trying to consult her—or at least in appearing to be consulting her. To the Cunninghams and Captain Taylor he was formal and correct, not offering to shake hands but obviously ready to reciprocate precisely any courtesies they might extend. But there were none; we were all anxious to have the hearing done with and were not at ease in such matters, as was our English-Burmese Silk.

U Tin Hlang brushed aside Bruce Cunningham's suggestion that it would be a "rotten thing" for them to abandon the child now: "Mr. Cunningham should have thought of that when he and Mrs. Cunningham so greatly interfered in JiHan's life without bothering to find out from his mother if her child would become their child."

U Tin Hlang's submission on behalf of Shin Yalat must have occupied half an hour. Despite the surroundings and the humidity, it was easy to listen to. He spoke clearly, fluently, gracefully, in low key, without rhetorical flourish but with force. There were, he assured me, only two themes in his submission, and each was sufficient to justify, nay, to compel, the retention of custody and guardianship of JiHan by his natural mother, Shin Yalat. His first submission would be that the best interests of JiHan would be served by leaving him in his own country with his own people; his second submission would be that the law gave me no choice in this regard, that under Burmese law there was no question of shifting custody in such circumstances as faced the parties in this case, and that English law and the frequent statements of English political leaders joined in affirming the respect English law accorded to Burmese customary law insofar as Burmese matters were concerned—and JiHan and his mother were certainly Burmese.

I do not recall the details of the arguments. I know I found them very strong. He carefully avoided any hint of the immediate political significance of the case and gave the impression that it was his deep concern for the Burmese villager that led him to represent Shin Yalat. But his peroration did have political overtones, suitable for publication as it stood in the Rangoon and Mandalay newspapers; it was punctuated with statements from the House of Commons, as well as from leading English administrators in India and Burma, stressing their respect for Burmese law in relation to indigenous Burmese matters. He concluded: "You must do what a village headman would do in this matter. Only if there were clear conflict between English law and Burmese law would there be possible propriety in a contrary order. There is no such conflict. Therefore, may it please the Court, I submit that the custody of JiHan should remain where natural law and Burmese law both say it should remain, with his mother."

At last the Cunningham case was before me. I must decide it. I had, if the truth be known, made up my mind before U Tin Hlang had spoken, but I had hoped that he might say something that would make my decision seem clearly right or clearly wrong. In the latter case, I believe, I would have changed my mind. But nothing new had been said; it had all been said before that dark and steamy afternoon in my office.

Decision could no longer be deferred. The rain drummed on the shutters, the room began to stink, the air had not as yet been cooled at all by the rain, and the fan struggled on utterly unequal to its task. I found breathing difficult, as if I were about to choke or to cough compulsively. To speak, certainly to speak loudly enough to be heard, it proved necessary consciously to draw breath. I seemed lost not only as to what to say but also as to the very mechanics of saying it. Perhaps the best course would be to give my decision in a sentence and offer no reasons for it; Taylor would have less to work with and no one else in the room would hear more than the decision, whatever I said.

But one cannot be that weak. I would not neglect to give the reasons for my decision out of moral cowardice. I began haltingly, outlining what I had gathered about the law from Rangoon as well as from U Tin Hlang, and what I had done to inform myself about the facts of the case. Tension increased; it was as if I were torturing them. Why not get it over and done with? So, I opened my mouth, drew a breath, and, of course, swallowed nervously, wrongly, and precipitated a fit of coughing from which the only words that emerged were a hoarse, "What I have to consider above all else are the best interests of the boy . . . and therefore . . . , " and the choking cough returned in breathless force.

My lungs got no better, the bombing no less—a routine of unproductivity. Though what I broadcast to those on the Indian subcontinent who cared to listen was nearer to the truth about the war than what they would elsewhere hear, it remained propaganda, an encouraging mixture of exaggerations and half-truths. But gradually the momentum of the war was shifting to us. The Battle of Britain was long past. The Russians had lumbered to our side. The buzz bombs had not yet started their crescendos of death. It might take a long time to win this dreadful war, but the ultimate result seemed clear enough. Japan was making no further headway in the Pacific, which must mean that the overall balance there, too, would gradually tip in our favour. But the killing continued, not the least in the saturation bombing of the industrial cities of the Ruhr. All this, in its minor details, sugarcoated for Indian consumption, I read nightly on the BBC.

My routine was firm. There was no need to rehearse what I had to read each evening. A reading through to myself just before the broadcast, mouthing a few phrases, sufficed for such clarity of diction as I could summon. I never had understood why it was thought that Eton, followed by five years in Burma, fitted me to read the news to the Indian subcontinent; but mine not to reason why—or what or how.

The date stuck firmly in my mind; it was the twenty-fourth of December, 1944. The evening bulletin that I had to read to the disinterested Indians, who wished only for independence from the Raj, read in part:

"The marshalling yards at Hamburg were struck again yesterday in a massive daylight raid by American B-29s and English DeHavilland twin-engine light bombers. Six of our planes failed to return. Fires continued to burn in Hamburg through the night. Severe damage was inflicted on Germany's heavy industry and transport systems. It is regretted to report that Group Captain "JayJay" Cunningham, who was in command of the DeHavilland flight, was shot down, presumed killed. "JayJay" Cunningham, D.S.O., A.F.C. and bar, Croix de Guerre, was one of the aces of the Battle of Britain, a Spitfire pilot who converted to service in a bomber squadron and later rose to its command. The Prime Minister expressed his personal grief in this sad loss of "one of the finest and bravest of the few.""

I managed to stumble through the reading and to suppress the fit of coughing that threatened to choke me. I was haunted by the vision of JiHan, now age twenty-five, throwing out his nets in the bay of Chinaka, illiterate, ignorant, and alive. Would anyone think to tell Shin Yalat?

Commentary to
"THE BEST INTERESTS OF THE CHILD"

In deciding disputes between those claiming custody of a child, it is the conventional wisdom that "the best interests of the child" is the deciding value. On close examination it appears that, with very few exceptions indeed, these cases do not turn on the best interests of the child; rather, they turn on the child's least bad interests. Both claimants for custody usually offer a less than ideal setting for the child, often through no fault of their own. So, in teaching Family Law, I came to see these "best interests" cases as "least bad interests" cases, and to discuss them accordingly.

But there was another, perhaps more interesting, side to the problem: what would one do if the choice were between two ideal or excellent familial situations for the child, or even two very good situations? And, in particular, how would the choice be made if it had to be between different cultures and different ways of life? And so I was led to speculate about cultural neutrality.

Can it be said that one culture is to be preferred to another, or must all cultures be seen as equally acceptable paths on the evolution of the human animal?

How to frame this dilemma? Let District Officer Blair have to decide between a privileged upper-middle class English setting and a privileged Burmese fishing village setting for an unusually bright and gifted Eurasian child. Both family settings must have some defects: the English couple are not genetically the parents, but they have raised the child since his infancy; the Burmese family lacks a father, but the extended Burmese family has already demonstrated the child's complete acceptability. In one setting he is likely to grow into a leader of the village; in the other many more paths will be open to him, offering greater opportunities for achievement—but the risks of conflict and failure are also greater.

This is the most ambitious of the parables in this book, since it not only poses the difficult question of cultural neutrality but also compels speculation on what life is for. If the pursuit of happiness, contentment, and safety has primacy, there is much to be said for the fishing village. If maximisation of intellectual potentialities and of contributions to human welfare have primacy, the life of the able English intellectual was to be preferred in the late 1920s and early 1930s.

And how much should the emotions of others weigh in considering the child's best interests? Is Shin Yalat's love for the child, she being the natural mother, a card to trump the quite likely equal affections for the child of the European couple?

Commentaries to the other parables in this collection can perhaps guide the reader on questions that may have been overlooked; but not here. Much of literature and of human experience circles around the issues raised in this story. All that this commentator can do is to throw down the flag of obvious warning that questions like "what is life *for*?" and "are cultures equally acceptable, or can they be ranked on some sort of hedonistic or ethical basis?" are not to be taken lightly. Perhaps they should not be taken at all. Perhaps there are some things one should not talk about, not on grounds of taste but on grounds of recognition of ignorance. But District Officer Blair had no such choice; he had to confront these issues, aided by Veraswami's medical and ethical guidance and U Tin Hlang's legal and political assistance.

Blair made his decision and in the result the child died earlier than he probably otherwise would have. Does this mean Blair was wrong? Surely not. Retrospective prediction is a cheap trick; it is predicting the future that presents difficulty, and that is what Blair had to do.

Blair later married—indeed twice. In Burma he was single. Is the dilemma he faced in this story one on which there is a gender difference? Would most women give the child to the Burmese mother, while most men would favour the English adopters? Scattered empirical research leads me to think that would be so; and, if it is, that raises fascinating issues on which, again, I am unprepared even to try to throw light.

This story poses a dilemma for which its author is in no better position than you to offer informed advice.

Ake Dah

"The Parable of the Old Man and the Young" [1917(?)]

Then Abraham bound the youth with belts and straps,
And builded parapets and trenches there,
And stretched forth the knife to slay his son.
When lo! an angel called him out of heaven,
Saying, Lay not thy hand upon the lad,
Neither do anything to him. Behold,
A ram, caught in the thicket by its horns;
Offer the Ram of Pride instead of him.
But the old man would not so, but slew his son,
And half the seed of Europe, one by one.

Wilfred Owen
War Poems

It would have been disapproved of, frowned on, even perhaps a matter for comment: teaching a Malay sergeant how to roll a cigarette in one of those filthy little tin and rubber machines that leave wisps of tobacco sticking out the end—the type you lick from side to side on the grey, sticky edge of the cigarette paper. But happily none of my superior officers was there to see my childish delinquency, and the Malay sergeant was clearly enjoying the lesson.

That was one very good thing about Moulmein; it was so distant from headquarters and so far down the chain of command that one way or another I was always warned, well in advance, before the arrival of anyone in authority over me.

Still, I did feel somewhat foolish, being so unprofessionally occupied, when a police corporal burst into my office to announce: "A large number of villagers is approaching. You should come, Sir."

I did what we had been instructed always to do first in situations of uncertainty: put on my officer's cap. Then, buttoning my tunic and adjusting my Sam Browne, I stepped into the outer office, which gave a view across the parade ground to the thirty or forty approaching Burmese.

I could not imagine what was happening. I thought I recognised that most of the elders who led the group were from the village of Versali; and that certainly seemed to be the headman of the village, Ake Dah, walking alone in the rear of the crowd, dressed in the saffron robe of a Buddhist priest, but without the priest's shaven head.

The leading group of elders stopped about ten paces from the police station. Ake Dah stopped in their rear. The straggling group of children further to the rear also stopped. I stood on the steps of the verandah of the police station. There was utter silence. Ake Dah seemed entirely at ease; those in front, profoundly ill at ease.

How long we would have preserved this tableau I do not know; eventually I found some words to end it, though they seemed hardly apposite. "What can I do for you?" It must have sounded peremptory, though that was not my intention.

One of the older villagers took a step or two toward me and said, "We have brought Ake Dah to you."

"Yes," I replied, and looked at Ake Dah, standing calm and apparently uninvolved in the rear.

There was no response.

It seemed courteous not to prolong the stagey scene, with me standing on the steps of the verandah looking down on the crowd. I stepped down and walked to the group, who moved aside as I did so, making a rough aisle leading to Ake Dah. As I walked to him, I offered some formality like "Good afternoon, Headman."

He made no reply, but inclined his head toward me.

"Do, please, tell me what all this is about."

The words came with explosive unexpectedness: "Mr. Policeman, I tried to kill my son, Mai Treya, my only son. The village men stopped me and brought me here for you to arrest and punish me. I told them they were wrong, but I came with them. Here I am."

I had no idea what to do. I had not been trained for this type of arrest! I glanced around, nervously I suppose, toward the police station and the two or three policemen peering out from the window and the open door. It seemed weak to call them out, but I did feel exposed and insecure—not about my safety, of course, but about appearances, which so plague young district officers.

The mood of the crowd seemed to be relieved by Ake Dah's words. As I looked at them, several in one way or another confirmed that Ake Dah had told the story they wished to tell. The rest, they made clear, was up to me. So I did and said what I would do and say for any other visitor. Gesturing toward the police station, I invited Ake Dah to come in with me to talk about this. Calmly, he assented, and followed me as he had followed the men who had brought him from Versali.

In my office, I took off my cap and invited him to sit down. By a movement of his head, he declined. He stood there, almost serene; I was fidgety,
not he.

"Would you tell me all that has happened, Headman?"

"I told all, Mr. Policeman. Now no more." He was polite, but utterly
taciturn. Questions not connected with the events that brought him here
were answered courteously but briefly; questions relevant in any way to his
attack on his son, anything to do with his son, elicited no reply.

Suddenly, his neck stiffened, his head turned slightly to the right and
upwards, his glance also moved to the right and upwards, and he did not
seem to hear whatever I was then saying to him. After a few seconds,
though at the time it seemed an inordinate period for immobility, his body
relaxed and his eyes moved back to engage mine.

"Are you feeling ill, Headman?" I asked in some anxiety. He recognised
no point in my question: "No, Mr. Blair."

There seemed nothing else to say or do; I had to arrest him. I did so in
the formal words of arrest—for attempted murder. He made no response. I
called in the duty sergeant and told him that Ake Dah was under arrest. I
asked the sergeant to see that Ake Dah was lodged in the gaol, in a single
cell, not with any other prisoner, and stressed that he should be given
every opportunity to contact me, or anyone else, if he so wished.

Ake Dah listened to all this and offered the one comment to me that
he had allowed himself that afternoon: "You are wrong to do this." He
then made *eyebong* to me, pressing his palms together in front of his chest
and inclining his body and head slightly toward me, and followed the
sergeant out of my office.

It struck me that I should have been worrying more about the son than
the father, since the father gave no indication of evasive intent, and perhaps the son was in need of medical care. I walked out to the group of villagers still waiting outside my office, told them that Ake Dah was being
taken to gaol, and asked them about Mai Treya.

They had done what had to be done without any advice from me. The
boy had been taken to the hospital immediately the attack on him was
interrupted. They had heard no word since, but it was their opinion that
he was not mortally injured—a stab wound in the back near the left shoulder, but clear of the lungs, as they described it to me. I was unsure whether
to go to the hospital or to the village. The latter seemed more sensible: I
could not help at all at the hospital—the boy would be looked after well
without my intervention—but the quicker I found out what had happened
at the village, the better.

I told one of the Burmese policemen to accompany me; we set out on bicycles for the two-mile ride to Versali.

Versali was unique among the villages in my district, and there were few villages like it in Lower Burma. Like most Burmese villages, Versali was surrounded by a low fence of wood and interlaced bamboo leaves, which might inhibit a few wilder animals and was believed to impede hostile *nats*—those thirty-seven animistic spirits that pervade Burmese village life. Also, as in other villages, the houses were predominantly of bamboo and thatch, with stronger woods reinforcing some of the uprights, and an occasional tin roof as a tribute to the English midlands.

A few houses, the more prosperous, were built on wooden stilts, lifting them eighteen or so inches above the ground, cooling them and greatly reducing their insect life.

What distinguished Versali was that, unlike Burmese villages generally, it had been influenced by the economic opportunities of European colonisation. Most villages remained isolated from the economic life of the twentieth century, their rice culture the same as it had been for centuries, each village largely self-sufficient—but not Versali. It had its own timber mill that competed with the European mills. It had its own herd of elephants, trained to work in the forest and at the timber mill.

There were not what you would call roads in Versali—tracks rather, but tracks wide enough to allow an elephant to haul a large wooden sled stacked with logs from the trees felled in the teak forest owned by the village. The mill itself was not modern, but it was efficient enough to bring prosperity to Versali. Versali's houses were better, its sanitation and services more ample, than those of any other village I visited, and much of this prosperity was the result of Ake Dah's energy and intelligence.

He had married the daughter of the previous headman; before his father-in-law's death, he had started the mill and demonstrated his suitability to lead the village. There had been no doubt of the succession.

I had met Ake Dah soon after my arrival in Moulmein. Since then I must have spoken to him on six or seven occasions; I had no particular sense of him. He was reserved, obviously intelligent, and respectful—perhaps too respectful—but no district officer could be other than pleased with Versali and with Ake Dah as its headman. Taxes were collected without apparent resentment, the village was contented and prosperous.; one could hardly ask for more.

There had been only one source of tension I could call to mind as I bicycled to Versali, trying to avoid the deeper ruts in the tracks, and that too concerned Ake Dah and his family. He was openly a leader of the Young Men's Buddhist Association. He travelled regularly to meetings of the Association elsewhere in Burma, and other leaders of the Association sometimes visited him in Versali.

The YMBA had been established in Burma in emulation of the YMCA. If such organisations were suitable for Christian youth, particularly those in the army, then, the Buddhists of Burma thought, a similar organisation for boys and young men of their religion would prove similarly valuable. And given the administration's support of the YMCA movement, they could hardly without open bigotry oppose the YMBA. But from its earliest days, the YMBA had served purposes other than the religious. Devout Buddhists supported it, of course—it had the blessing of what passes for a priesthood in Theravada Buddhism, which predominates in Burma, Ceylon, and Thailand—but its mission soon became political: it was irredentist and in vigourous and open pursuit of independence from colonial rule and influence.

The political purposes of the YMBA were much assisted by an extensive infiltration of younger Burmese barristers who had read law as undergraduates in India, Burma, or, in a few cases, England. Some had also eaten their dinners at an Inn of Court in London and developed the sharper political inclinations of the foreign barrister in England. There was little attempt to conceal the striving toward independence from the Raj nurtured in the YMBAs of Burma.

Ake Dah may have been the perfect headman from the perspective of the district officer, but from Mandalay and Rangoon he was seen quite differently—not as a major threat, by no means a national leader of a hostile political movement, but as locally influential and therefore needing to be watched.

Ake Dah had been the ideal son-in-law to the previous headman, with the exception that at first no grandchildren came to enliven his declining years and to carry on what had seemed an appropriate family succession in Versali.

Soon after his father-in-law's death, when Ake Dah was in his mid-forties and his wife only a few years younger, a son was born to them, a son they called Mai Treya. "Mai Treya" translates as "Son of the Prophet," and suggests one moving close to Enlightenment. To the Buddhist this reflects no particular credit on the natural father nor any sense of divine or immaculate conception—rather that the soul of the child, by virtue of previous life experiences, is of advanced spiritual virtue. It is not a name to be risked for the son of a village headman; the son of a king, perhaps, but only a very confident king, expecting his son to bear the *karma* of the Enlightened One. Other, more conservative, Buddhists disapproved of Ake Dah so naming his son, but the name remained, though shortened in daily use to Treya.

Two daughters were born to Ake Dah and his wife in the years immediately following Mai Treya's birth.

Ake Dah and his family dominated the village of Versali, administratively, financially, and architecturally. Their house was much larger and more comfortable than the others, rather like one of the better European bungalows, though adhering to the outward appearance of a village hut, built on low stilts and with a substantial surrounding verandah.

I knew, too, that Mai Treya had been sent to boarding school in Rangoon, to an English private school, St. Mark's, attended by the more privileged European children in Rangoon and the children of a few wealthy Burmese—it was thought to be the best school in Burma. Though its religious affiliation was Church of England, there was no insistence on religious observance as a condition of enrollment, and children of Buddhist parents who wished their children not to be drawn away from their religion were accepted, with this exception: boys were not admitted or allowed to remain enrolled if they had entered the Buddhist "priesthood" by the ceremony of *shin-pyu* and service in a *kyaung*, a Buddhist monastery, a normal ceremony and practice for Buddhist boys at about the age of nine.

Those who ran St. Mark's professed religious tolerance, and no doubt believed they demonstrated it; but it was inevitable that at St. Mark's the Ten Commandments dominated the Five Precepts, and the ambitious ways of the West displaced the Middle Way.

I had met Mai Treya once or twice. He must be about eleven or twelve now. He had seemed a bright and pleasant young man travelling to and from Rangoon in his westernised school uniform. I had met him only at the ferry jetty, as I recalled; I had no idea what life was like for him at his father's village. At school, I supposed it was like life at a modified English public school—much modified, I hoped.

On the outskirts of Versali I caught the front wheel of my cycle in a deep rut and fell heavily. Elephant-drawn sleds and bullock carts play havoc with jungle trails; I should have concentrated more on keeping myself upright and less on Ake Dah and his family. The policeman helped me up; I arrived in Versali in a dirtier condition than a district officer should.

The village seemed to be sparsely populated, and I suppose it was, with one contingent following me back from Moulmein and another accompanying Ake Dah's wife and daughters to the hospital to see Mai Treya. And I suddenly doubted that I had been sensible to come to Versali at all. Perhaps I should have stayed at police headquarters and interviewed some of the villagers there, or gone to the hospital to talk to the boy himself—if he was fit to be interviewed—or to those who were with him. It was too late for such reflections now; would I ever gain sense to think things through before charging off to useless action?

Ake Dah's house was deserted. I looked in every room. There was no sign of a struggle, no blood, no furniture overturned. No one approached the house.

The timber mill on the edge of the village was working; one elephant was visible, a native riding on its neck, directing the hauling of logs onto the elevated feed that led to the saws. Smoke came from the mill and from a few of the huts. I decided to wait on the verandah for the villagers to return from Moulmein and then to get one or two of them to tell me, *in situ*, what had happened to Mai Treya.

There was a rattan chair on the verandah near the front steps. I sat myself there; my police attendant sat on the steps. We were both shaded by the overhanging, bamboo-thatched roof, but it was steamy hot.

Why not do some detective work while I had the chance? I went back into the house to see whether there was anything like an office. Where did Ake Dah keep his records? And what of his correspondence? My superiors might be interested in what I might find there.

There was an office table on one side of the dining room, with what looked like army ammunition boxes stacked beside it. There was a small bookshelf on the wall behind the table, the books being mainly Buddhist tracts, with a few on milling and on agriculture—certainly no novels. I opened one of the ammunition boxes and started to rummage through the handwritten correspondence, mostly in English. My police assistant came to the door. I found myself pretending to be doing other than what I was. How very ridiculous!

"Let us wait outside," I said. And we resumed our positions on the verandah.

By the early afternoon I had the story of the morning's attack on Mai Treya by his father as clear as I ever would—in its externals, not its motivations. Villagers and family agreed precisely on what had happened; they disagreed wildly about why it had happened.

Ake Dah had awakened his son early, as he often did. They were seen talking on the verandah after first dawn. They then walked to the small pagoda that Ake Dah had had built not far from his house, and assumed positions of meditation on the apron of the pagoda, the boy cross-legged, the father to the son's left in a tight kneeling position. There were a few other villagers worshipping at the pagoda but none close to Ake Dah and Treya. Both father and son appeared to be in deep and prolonged meditation, side by side. Then Ake Dah was seen to take a long knife from his robe and raise it high behind his son. He paused. Villagers saw him and several shouted at him. Simultaneously the knife was thrust forward and the boy turned toward the shouts from the villagers. The knife entered the boy's back, but high and to one side. The villagers rushed at Ake Dah and held him; he made no resistance.

The boy was in severe pain—the muscles and tendons of his left shoulder were deeply cut; but he made no move away from his father. As the villagers held Ake Dah, the boy struggled with them to leave him alone and flung himself toward, not away from, his father's arms, including the arm and hand still holding the bloody knife. The villagers pulled him away and tended his wound.

Before the incident, there had been no harsh words between Ake Dah and Treya; they had seemed particularly close. Treya had returned from Rangoon only a few days before. His father had seemed delighted with him and had, some thought, been neglecting his work for the village to be with his son—but none blamed him for that. Talking to both those in his household and other villagers, I had the sense that Ake Dah was greatly admired, almost venerated, but was also viewed as a distant, almost fearsome, figure—esteemed, but not loved, deeply respected, but not at all a man of the village.

Ake Dah's wife and daughters were distraught and bewildered. They seemed to have no clearer ideas of what had led to this attack on Treya than had anyone else. There did not appear to have been any recent changes in Ake Dah's behaviour; he was as devout and predictable as ever, in fact, more so. And, it appeared, at least as fond of Mai Treya as he had ever been.

It was clear that I would not learn much more that day at Versali. The policeman and I cycled back to Moulmein, and this time I kept my eyes carefully on the road ahead. I sent the policeman back to the police station; I went on to the hospital, intending to interrogate Mai Treya.

Dr. Veraswami said that Mai Treya was well enough for me to talk to him, "But remember, Mr. Blair, I know you will forgive me pleass, the boy hass suffered a terrible experience today. The body repairs quickly, the knife missed its mark, but he loves hiss father, and he iss bewildered. It must be terrible for him. Do pleass be gentle with him."

Veraswami did not come with me to Treya's bedside. I suspected he wished to preserve a different relationship with the boy from that of one who might be punishing his father. I thought he was wise to stay apart from me for the time being.

Treya lay quietly in a single room, reading what looked like boys' twopenny weeklies, to which I had been addicted in my youth but which were known by my parents and at the Club as "rubbishy comics." He hurriedly put them aside as I entered the room. His left shoulder was heavily bandaged. He was reclining on pillows on his back and did not seem to be in pain. A young woman, not dressed as a nurse—more likely a house servant, I thought—rose from a chair in the corner of the room as I entered. I gestured to her to sit down, and spoke to the boy, "Good evening, Treya. May I talk to you for a while?"

The calm almond eyes in the round brown face turned directly to me. "Good evening, Sir. Please come in." The words were of clear, English enunciation, precise and sharp, quite unlike the usual slow and lilting speech of a Burman youth.

I enquired if his shoulder hurt. "A bit stiff, Sir." Had his mother and sisters come with him to the hospital? "Yes, Sir. They left not long ago."

I found myself struggling for questions to achieve a semblance of conversation between us. He was respectful but quiet. I did not wish to plunge immediately into the morning's events.

"Is there anything I can get you? A book perhaps?" No, he had some books and comics—with a shy glance toward what I now clearly saw were the Gem and the Magnet, half-tucked under the sheet on his bed. And, he further assured me, "Ningala," apparently the name of the girl seated in the corner, "will get me anything I want from Versali."

"Will Ningala stay with you here?" I asked, and unwittingly found a clumsy key for opening the attack on him.

"My father told her to stay with me. She will stay."

"Your father sent her though he is not at the village. He is . . . ," and I managed to stop myself blurting out the unpleasant reality of his father's situation.

Treya's calm deserted him, confronted by my tactlessness. He made no answer. His eyes filled with tears. He did not blink. He looked directly at me, wide-eyed, as the tears bathed his eyes and moved to his cheeks.

I was appalled at my insensitivity. "Don't worry, Treya. Everything will be all right." What in Heaven's name that meant, I cannot imagine—mendacious comforting noises, but lies, certainly lies. I didn't for a moment think everything would be all right.

Treya finally cut through my evasions. "There is something wrong with my father. Why don't you help him instead of locking him up? He told Ningala to stay with me to help me. Do please help him."

Ningala had not moved in response to Treya's tears, but she was obviously deeply troubled. Treya spoke to her in Burmese, telling her, as best I could understand, not to worry, that Blair sahib was not hurting or threatening him.

I heard myself trying to reassure Treya that I would indeed be of help to his father—though that hardly seemed my job. "Tell me what you think is wrong with your father. I promise to try to help."

He began to reply, but only a whimpering cry emerged. Apparently he believed me; apparently he felt my sympathy, and that entirely destroyed his control. The contained youth departed, and I found myself awkwardly holding a clutching and sobbing little boy, gulping "I don't know" through his tears.

There was nothing for me to do at the hospital. Ake Dah had arranged, apparently from his cell, all that should be done: someone to sit beside his injured son through the night until his mother and sisters could return the next morning. How extraordinary! In the morning he tries to kill the boy; in the afternoon he makes thoughtful provision for his care and protection.

What stayed with me, resonated in my mind, was Treya's "There is something wrong with my father. Please help him." But that was not my job. To see that he was fairly tried for attempted murder was my job.

I had not been particularly successful with the son; could I do any better with the father? I would have to try.

He was held as I had directed he should be. His cell was clean. The blankets on his trestle-and-canvas cot looked fresh and were neatly folded. There was a table and a straight wooden chair in his cell. The cell was well lit and not in the line of sight of other cells. Ake Dah, still wearing his saffron robe, sat on the chair, quite immobile, eyes cast down, hands resting on his lap.

He raised his head as I approached. He did not seem troubled. He was certainly not outwardly resentful. He did not smile, but his eyes acknowledged my arrival.

I asked the policeman on duty to unlock the door to the cell.

"May I come in?" It seemed a strange request of one in a cell, but it did not feel inappropriate.

"Yes, Mr. Blair."

Ake Dah did not get up as I entered his cell. I took off my cap and looked about for somewhere to sit. He inclined his head toward the cot. I sat there.

"Are they looking after you properly here, Headman?"

"Yes, Mr. Blair. But you should not have sent me here."

I decided with one so utterly in control as Ake Dah that the proper course was one of unqualified directness. "I had no choice, Headman. You and your villagers told me you had committed a serious felony. You had to be arrested. You might have attacked Treya again; he was in danger."

"Treya was never in danger. I know you think he was, Mr. Blair, but he was not—never. It was a wonderful thing that happened—a revelation, not a crime. It is not your fault you did wrong. But you did wrong."

He made no sense to me. Yet he seemed so reasonable, so confident, almost generously forgiving. I must have looked quite lost, for in a burst of words he told me what had happened at the Versali pagoda that morning, as he understood it.

"Mai Treya is to become an Enlightened One, a true Buddha. Perhaps soon, perhaps in many generations. It is told to me. And I have to protect him and test him. He is besmirched at that school, St. Mark's; he is tempted from the Path of Enlightenment. I should never have left him there, but his mother and I were so ambitious for him. The voice of God told me to kill him. God speaks to me often. I have been tested and proved worthy as the protector of the next Buddha, and the divine *karma* of Mai Treya is confirmed. I was told to kill him; I did what God commanded and he spared me and spared my son. The voice of God spoke through the villagers and saved Mai Treya to stay a while with me. It is most wonderful."

There was no response I could make. I sat silent. I do not think I fidgeted. I behaved properly, I think—just listening intently and looking directly at Ake Dah; but this did not, as I had hoped, prompt him to explain further.

"You either understand, Mr. Blair, or you do not. I cannot help you."

"What, then, do you think I should do, Headman? I cannot have one of the headmen attacking his son with a knife. That is a crime. You know it is a crime. You know I must arrest and charge you."

Suddenly it was as if I were not in the cell with him. I do not think he heard my last sentence or two. He was quite still, almost rigid, eyes averted from mine. After a few moments he seemed again to recognise my presence and recalled that I had asked him a question, and with a somewhat condescending smile he replied, "God told me what to do; I cannot help you, Mr. Blair. I did what I had to do. I do not know what you should do."

It had been a dreadfully long day—too much had happened, too much that bewildered me. A talk with Dr. Veraswami might help, and I certainly would welcome a beer.

I walked the short distance from the gaol to Veraswami's bungalow. As I approached, I saw Veraswami's wife and two of his children scurrying away from the verandah—they would never stay to meet me. Veraswami had insisted it was just embarrassment in the presence of a European, though it seemed oddly contrasting to Veraswami's own relative social confidence. But their hiding from me had never made me feel unwelcome, disappointed rather—I would have liked to come to know Veraswami's family, too.

When I reached his bungalow, a servant told me that Dr. Veraswami had not yet returned from the hospital but would be back soon, he thought. Would I not wait? Would I like a beer?

I accepted both invitations and settled in my usual rattan chair to try to think through the turmoil of the day. But whenever I set myself deliberately to think something through, I find fantasy substituting for thought, unreal conversations in my head that can never take place, the past and an unlikely future intermixed. So I did not hear Veraswami until he was quite close to the verandah, startling me by calling out, "What a joy to see you here, Blair! How very kind of you."

I was too troubled for circuity. As soon as Veraswami had found a beer and come out onto the verandah, I accosted him with Ake Dah's attack on his son. "Have you seen the headman from Versali yet, Veraswami?" No, he had seen and treated Mai Treya, as I knew, but had not thought it necessary or proper to go to the gaol to see the boy's father. He had heard stories of what had happened, but had not given them much thought. The boy was not in any medical danger.

"But the father claims he heard the voice of God telling him to do what he did. And further that God then intervened and through the villagers saved his son. Surely that adds up to a medical problem, Doctor."

"If it iss true, it iss a theological matter, not a medical problem. And it iss also a problem for those like you who serve the criminal law, issn't it? Are you going to punish the servant of God?"

I must have looked annoyed. Veraswami seemed to be playing word games with me at a time when I needed his best counsel, not his tasteless jokes. "But he must be mad, Dr. Veraswami. He seems to love his son. He hears a voice telling him to kill the boy. Surely that is madness; I mean technically, medically, madness."

"Many people hear voices in their heads, Mr. Blair. I mean they truly believe they hear voices that others do not hear. I do not doubt them; it iss their truth. And it iss also true that the alienists sometimes lock them up ass mad because of what they say they hear and what they do. I do not know if the boy's father would have been thought mad if he had not tried to kill his son. But then he did try to kill his son, as you and many others tell me, and so you say he must be mad. Perhaps . . . perhaps . . ." and his voice sank to silence.

"Should you go to see him, Dr. Veraswami?"

"But what if he doesn't want to talk to me? I gather he didn't talk much to you. I will try, of course, but for whom do I go?" Obviously agitated, Veraswami paced about the verandah, his eyes turned away from me, looking toward the hospital. "Do I see him for you, ass one serving the criminal law, to consider whether to punish him? Or iss he a patient? Not, I think, unless he wants me to be hiss doctor, and I will be surprised if he does—he hass never called for my help before, and he does know of me."

Veraswami paused, turned to me, and added, "Since he iss in gaol, I will call on him to see if he needs medical help and we will see what happens. He may wish to talk to me."

Veraswami reminded me that he had worked for a time in a mental hospital in London and that he had considered making psychiatry his specialty, "but that iss a verry different story I will tell you one day, not now. Does the headman not need a lawyer as much as a doctor? Hass he a lawyer?"

I had not considered the matter; I should have, but I hadn't. I had better ask him. I found myself rehearsing in my head what I would say to Ake Dah and how he might reply—and I to him—and he to me—and so on. Veraswami cut into my reverie, "You look tired, my young friend. Are you hearing voices yourself?"

"Of course not, Dr. Veraswami. Just thinking what I should say to Ake Dah and he to me."

"Well, you do look tired. It must have been a verry, very long day for you. Much to do. Much to worry about. There iss nothing more to do now.

The boy iss safe. I will go to the gaol. Perhaps you should go to your bungalow or to the Club or wherever you want to go; but no more work today."

He was right. I had better think more and rush about less. No, not the
Club; my bungalow. And I thanked Veraswami and walked home in the
peace of the evening, saddened for Treya, Ake Dah, and, it ought to be
confessed, for myself.

Mid-morning, the next day, my start-the-day routine completed—
inspections, duty rosters, the lists settled for the next sessions of the
Magistrate's Court, including a preliminary hearing into the charges
against Ake Dah—I made my way to the gaol.

Ake Dah responded warmly to news of my visit to Treya, but was barely
interested in what I had to tell him of the hearing I would have to hold on
the evidence against him, the hearing at which I would have to decide
whether the charge should go forward. I managed to hold his attention sufficiently to explain that if the evidence supported a charge of attempted murder, he would be tried in Mandalay or Rangoon before a judge of the Superior
Court, whereas if it were a lesser charge against him—say, unlawful wounding or assault occasioning bodily harm—he could be tried before me, in the
Magistrate's Court, if he wished. I urged him to get a lawyer to represent him
at the preliminary hearing. I told him I was not experienced in these matters,
but that everything I had been taught and everything I had observed led me
to the view that he would be wise to get a lawyer immediately.

"Mr. Blair, I did what had to be done, what God told me to do. I do not
think I need anyone to explain that to you. But I will think about what
you have said."

I recalled the story of the devout Christian, accused at the Old Bailey,
who had declined a dock brief and the assistance of counsel on the ground
that "Jesus was his counsel," and who was nevertheless urged by the judge
to "get local counsel also"; but I did not think it wise to tell that story to
Ake Dah.

Ake Dah seemed uninterested in further discussion of his own situation
and rather brusquely shifted the conversation to conditions at Versali, asking me if a few of the elders of the village could come to the gaol to discuss
what should be done at the mill and in the fields and with the working elephants while he was in gaol. I agreed, of course, and helped him to make
the necessary arrangements for a message from him to be taken to Versali.

I tried again to urge him to get a lawyer and offered to help him do so if
he wished; but he remained disinterested, almost patronising in rejecting
my offer. So be it, I thought; I will not be troubled in court by lawyers'
wranglings. I will hear what a village elder or two report of the attack on
the boy, get a medical report on him, let Ake Dah tell his story if he wishes
to, and then decide what I want to happen and so order. There will be no
chance of my getting into legal difficulties provided I don't give reasons for

what I order—just say I have reflected on the evidence and decided to order so and so. This procedure was probably the best judicial advice I had been given at the Mandalay school; I would follow it.

I went back to the police station, took off my cap as I entered so that I could nod to the duty sergeant without putting him to the burden of a salute, and wandered into my office.

To my astonishment, there was U Tin Hlang, sitting in my least uncomfortable chair, his round brown face with its curved scar beaming at me.

"Mr. Lang! How good to see you here again!" I burst out, for I had found him personally a joy in our time together on the Cunningham case.

He was obviously pleased by the immediate warmth of my greeting. He rose quickly, hand extended, "And it is very good to see you again, Your Honour." He knew that as a junior magistrate I was entitled to no such honourific, other than in the courtroom, but it had become a form of lightly teasing address to me when we were together wrestling with JayJay's future and he had wished to stress the weight of the burdens that fell on my young shoulders.

"What brings you here? Surely you can't still be worrying about the Cunningham case?"

"No. Not that case, though you were a great help to our movement in that case—your perfidious larceny of the Burmese child has been spread far and wide," and he opened his arms to embrace all Burma, "and I am very grateful to you. No; that case is over between us. This time it is your devout Versali headman and his potentially Enlightened Son who bring me into Your Honour's presence. I come at the direction of the General Council of Buddhist Associations—you cannot have forgotten us, the G.C.B.A. It would disappoint me profoundly to be told that we are not a sharp thorn in your district officer's side, a persistent burr under the saddle of your far-flung administration."

I must have failed to conceal my regret at realising that now every decision I might make about Ake Dah and Mai Treya would be under skilled scrutiny. Deciding what was right and ordering it without giving reasons were now forlorn hopes. My genial Burmese barrister might be good, if verbose, company, and he might be instructive about social change and politics in Burma, but he would not make my magisterial task a whit easier. And, at the Club, the combination of Doctor Veryslimey, the U Tin Hlang barristocrat, and my inept self would inspire astonishingly little confidence. And like it or not, what they thought and said at the Club pressed upon me.

The steady certainty of most Europeans I associated with that I was sentimental and weak in my dealings with the Burmese made balanced decisions much more difficult. I was often troubled by the thought that I was either reacting excessively against what was seen as "the right thing to do," which almost always was favourable to the immediate interests of the Europeans, or letting myself be swayed weakly to go along with Club opinion.

I have since learnt that every judge is stirred by similar anxieties, and thus influenced whether he likes it or not, whether he realises it or not; but at twenty-four, with few to support my weak tendrils of independent judgment, I felt these pressures keenly.

Yes, I am sure my face did not conceal the thrust of these reactions from U Tin Hlang. "Do not worry too much, Your Honour; together we will handle these matters peacefully—at any rate without scandal," and he smiled at my negatively shaking head.

"I suppose you want to see Ake Dah immediately," I said. "He told me clearly he did not want legal assistance. Why should I let you see him?"

"You are quite right, Your Honour; you should not authorise my admission to your no doubt excellent gaol. Certainly not until I commit some appropriate offence or until the headman from Versali asks for me as his legal counsel."

I kept silent, sure that U Tin Hlang, with the pompous affectation of a London-Burma barrister, was only circling around what he really wanted to say. He continued, drawing an envelope from his pocket, "But I would be grateful if you would give this letter to your headman prisoner. It is from the Secretary of the G.C.B.A."

I took the letter and promised to get it to Ake Dah within the hour. It did not seem hard to guess what it would contain. I had no doubt that Ake Dah would soon be U Tin Hlang's client and that my judicial task would thus be greatly complicated. I had to admit to myself that when I was thinking of a lawyer for Ake Dah I was not thinking of a lawyer like U Tin Hlang, not a lawyer who would relate village concerns to the larger political realities of Burma—and make these linkages in a case that already seemed more than sufficiently complicated for my taste.

"By the way," U Tin Hlang added, as I put the envelope on my desk, "do you censor incoming mail? I don't think you should, unless you suspect it contains contraband or a file or some complicated plans for escape; but so that you shall not ever doubt me, here is a copy of what is in that envelope," and he handed me a letter.

I put it on the desk, ostentatiously unread.

"Where will you be staying, in case Ake Dah wishes to contact you, as I'm sure he will?" I asked.

"I will go now to the Htun Hla hotel, Mr. Blair, which as you know is not at all like the Savoy; but it will have to serve. Would you perhaps join me there for a drink before dinner—or perhaps also for dinner, if you are not otherwise engaged?" I must have been slow of response, so that he added, "I will not burden you with talk of the case of the headman, I promise you. But I would find it most pleasant to talk with you about other things Burmese and English, if you wish."

I accepted his invitation, saw him from my office, and returned to read the paper he had given me, a duplicate, he said, of what was in the envelope. It was in Burmese script and beyond my comprehension; I don't know

why I had thought it would be in English, considering its Burmese provenance. But U Tin Hlang had added a note of translation for my benefit:
"All this conveys, Mr. Blair, are two propositions: that the Young Men's
Buddhist Association was represented yesterday at an emergency meeting
of the General Council of Buddhist Associations, and at the meeting it was
decided to send me to Moulmein immediately to serve as counsel to the
headman of Versali in any legal proceedings that might arise from the
events at Versali that day involving the headman and his son. I err; there
are more than two propositions when I think about it: the headman is
asked to accept me as his counsel; and, a centrally important final proposition, he is informed that the Association will bear the heavy costs of my
representation."

I suppose that was all that was in the unopened envelope I arranged for
Ake Dah to receive; surely U Tin Hlang would not risk any discrepancies.
At all events, the policeman who delivered the envelope to Ake Dah
returned to me with the request that I approve U Tin Hlang's visiting Ake
Dah in gaol as his counsel.

I knew precisely where the Htun Hla Hotel was situated: on the other
side of town from my bungalow near the statue of the young Buddha from
the Mons period, the statue I most enjoyed in Moulmein. It was not huge
like those in Arakan, not minute as in the Pyu kingdom, but life-sized and
unconventionalised; not posed in formal meditation, but young and alive,
sitting on a bench with his feet swinging free. But it was undeniably a statue of the Buddha and had been treated as such probably since the first century A.D. of our calendar, though history and belief are often intertwined
in Burma as, I suppose, elsewhere.

The Htun Hla had been a hotel, or more probably there had been a
hotel on that site, since a representative of the East India Company had
visited Moulmein and stayed at an inn or resthouse of that name in
1742—and probably long before. It was the best hotel in Moulmein, but
still somewhat seedy and clearly less comfortable than the Government
Resthouse or the Club, both of which were, for different reasons, denied to
U Tin Hlang.

I decided to arrive in style. U Tin Hlang often had that effect on me—
he seemed so lightly to be pursuing larger purposes that I reacted by yield-
ing to the juvenile wish to surprise him. Why not live up to my nickname?
I would arrive in a rickshaw. There were not many rickshaws in Moulmein,
but there were a few.

In the result, the rickshaw, or rather my timing of dressing for the trot
across town, kept me late. I changed out of uniform into a light cotton
safari jacket, light khaki shorts and long white socks, and made sure that
my boy had polished my brown shoes to a gloss. It seemed the right dress,
neither too formal nor too casual—I still cared about such things. But I

timed it badly. It was a steamy evening and I showered and dressed too quickly, so that when the rickshaw arrived and we were no more than a hundred yards on our way, my shirt was ringing wet, odiously wet, impossibly wet. I had to tell the rickshaw wallah to turn back and wait while I dried myself and stood under the slowly rotating fan in my bedroom until I stopped sweating and could put on a shirt that might retain some hint of crispness until I reached the hotel.

It was not U Tin Hlang who was surprised on my arrival; he was nowhere to be seen as I stepped down from the rickshaw in front of the hotel. The surprise was mine, but not mine alone. Veraswami was there, obviously astonished at my behaviour. "What iss it, Mr. Blair? Are you not well? Do you require my professional assistance? Can you no longer walk or ride a bicycle?"

It seemed better to ignore his ponderous efforts at teasing. "Good evening, Doctor. What are you doing here?"

"We are, as one may say, both doing the same thing. Dining with the barrister, U Tin Hlang. Did he not tell you he had invited me?" Veraswami looked troubled, as if it might embarrass me that he was here.

I tried to express my pleasure in his presence, though I did not feel it. The three of us together would make an even odder group than I had anticipated, and, when reported to the Club, our dinner would take on the air of a conspiracy. But there was nothing I could do about it now. I often felt that way when dealing with U Tin Hlang, but I never seemed to learn from these repeated experiences. I found myself thinking that that was why he would prosper politically and I would not.

U Tin Hlang was waiting just inside the entrance to the hotel in its open, scrubbed, but starkly furnished foyer. He had a table for us in the large room that served alike for lounge and dining room, immediately beneath a fan rotating with reasonable speed and only moderate clanking noises. The chairs were upright and wooden backed, but there were cushions on their seats.

There seemed little to link the three of us, little in common to talk about; but there was, of course, one inexhaustible subject, if we cared to stay on it: life in London, particularly life in London for foreign students and youths from the provinces. It sustained us through beers before dinner, through a clear vegetable soup served with a few green leaves floating in it for reasons I still cannot fathom, and then what U Tin Hlang told us was a chicken curry served on rice with what was called *ngapi* or *nganpayay*, a fermented fish paste, which, he claimed, was the regional dish of southern Burma. It smelt powerfully; I took very little. U Tin Hlang noticed my caution and said that he was not surprised: the dish was not often served to foreigners, and when Mr. Kipling had tried it he had offered the opinion that it was "fish pickled when it ought to have been buried long ago." I did my best; in very small quantities it was tolerable.

It was not the beer that made me decide it was ridiculous for us to avoid the topic we all wished to discuss; it was too hot to risk much beer if it were not to pour out of one's pores as from a sieve. I waited for a pause in the conversation. "Let us talk about Ake Dah and Mai Treya. Of course the matter is *sub judice*, but I believe we three have the best interests of the village and of the father and son at heart, and should be able to talk to one another about it."

As I spoke, I had the sinking feeling of one knowing that he is being ingenuous and childish. Veraswami was silent. U Tin Hlang responded with gravity, quite unlike his usual bantering style: "Thank you for your confidence, Mr. Blair. I shall not misuse it. I will remember and learn from what you both say but I shall not use it to embarrass you or to constrict your judicial or medical discretions. Please believe me." And again I could see why high office awaited him.

I turned to Dr. Veraswami: "You saw Ake Dah today. What is your opinion of him? Is he mad?"

"I can tell you the name the psychiatrists are beginning to give to hiss mental disorder, but I do not know what the word 'mad' means, Mr. Blair, and I am not being difficult with you, for sure not. He iss schizophrenic, of the paranoid type. He hass delusions of grandeur. He hass been selected by God to smooth the path of a new Buddha. He hears voices in hiss head telling him thiss in many different ways, but always about hiss son, Mai Treya."

"But," I objected, "he is probably the most successful headman in southern Burma, in all Burma, for all I know. He has made that mill and that elephant herd; few other villages have done anything like it. The village will be lost without him; they're already consulting him while he's in gaol. He's obviously very intelligent and very sensible."

"You are quite right, quite right, but you make the mistake, the very common mistake, of thinking that the mentally ill are unintelligent. He iss verry intelligent. But you must understand, he really believes he iss the servant of God. He doessn't think it; he knowss it. Just like your Abraham said he knew it. It iss, you have long ago understood, the same story. But you must not think that iss surprising. It iss a verry, verry common story. Many people hear voices in their heads, I mean hear them, I do not mean say they hear them, I mean hear them, hear them," and he nodded repetitively until U Tin Hlang interrupted.

"Tell me, Dr. Veraswami, do such voices often tell men to kill their sons?"

Veraswami nodded even more vigourously at the point of U Tin Hlang's enquiry. "To injure or kill themselves, that iss common. To kill their entire families and themselves, iss also reported quite often in the literature. To kill wives they believe are faithless iss also verry common, associated often with their own failing sexuality, issn't it? But you are right; to kill a son to prove obedience to God or, more extraordinarily, to save the son's soul for future godliness iss rarely reported."

We were silent. I was shaping a question as to what he thought had brought Ake Dah to this belief when Veraswami continued, "You must not think Ake Dah iss prevaricating. He speaks truth ass he sees it, and many people will believe he speaks absolute truth, real truth, objective truth, not just subjective truth. After all, the Christians and Jews, and even the Moslems, all believe that Abraham spoke truth in fact about his attempted murder of his son Isaac. Each year Ake Dah has been becoming more devout; each year he spends more time in meditation, more time at the pagoda and less with hiss family, is more anxious about hiss divinely blessed son at that wicked school, and gives less attention to the affairs of Versali—and I don't think he visits his wife's bed at all nowadays. He hass been growing steadily more and more and more troubled, more frequently hears the voice inside him telling him what to do. His schizophrenia and his hallucinations feed on his genuine religious beliefs. It iss verry sad."

"What," U Tin Hlang asked, "do you mean when you say 'the voice inside him'? Is it different from my hearing you talk?"

"Yess, I think it iss. When I hear you talk there iss noise in my head, but I know it comes from outside my head. When Ake Dah hears the voice of God, God speaks directly to him; he hears the noise inside hiss head, but it comes from inside hiss head—ass I say, God speaks directly to him, directly, not from outside."

"Can you cure him?" I asked.

Veraswami smiled at me with warmth. "You ask a kind and gentle question, but I am not sure I can answer it. If by curing him you mean stopping his hearing the voices or stopping his acting on them, I can do that by sedating him heavily and by having him watched carefully and for a long time—until he ceases to hear the voices, which will happen some time hence, perhaps in a few years if he lives so long. But he may not want the sedating or the watching. And why should I try to cure him, Mr. Blair? He iss now even more esteemed in the village, soon perhaps throughout the Buddhist world. Mai Treya iss not in danger. He iss old enough to be separated from hiss father for a while and to be instructed how to care for himself so that he can be with hiss father without danger. Why should we cure him?"

U Tin Hlang began to speculate how those who were paying his fees, the General Council of Buddhist Associations, would like to have a genuine new prophet on their hands, and was suggesting lightly that they had enough trouble with the British without adding any new theological burden, when our dessert arrived—fresh fruit it appeared to be, which seemed excellent to me after the gorge-raising threat of the unburied fish, until U Tin Hlang pointed out that it included the Moulmein specialty *durian*, much prized throughout Burma, though, he added "some Englishmen will tell you that the flavour and odor of this fruit may be realised by eating a garlic custard over a London sewer, while others are no less positive in their perception of it as a delicious blending of sherry, spicy custard, and the nectar of the gods. Do try it, Mr. Blair."

All in all, I was glad I had accepted U Tin Hlang's invitation to dinner. I had struggled through the food—if not a culinary delight, it was certainly a memorable and recountable experience—but I had been pleased by our conversation. Veraswami had given me some glimmering of understanding of this extraordinary crime, if crime it was; I had at least a sense of the psychological pressures on Ake Dah, and U Tin Hlang had meticulously observed the proper limits of extra-court advocacy.

I decided to risk a further step. I told them of my difficulty in understanding the legal aspects of the case, equipped with only the Indian Penal Code, my notes from the Mandalay course, and one or two tired and old textbooks. This led U Tin Hlang, as I hoped it would, to volunteer to lend me, for a few days, some later commentaries that he had brought with him.

I asked U Tin Hlang if he had been involved in any earlier cases where he had advanced the defence of insanity. He said he had, and that what it came to in his view was this: Whatever the words of the test of insanity as a defence to a criminal charge, he had found that if he could bring the jury to identify with his client, to the extent of having some understanding of the psychological tumult inside him, they would find him not guilty by reason of insanity. Generally, the jury wished to avoid convicting the accused if they could say to themselves: "If I were sick enough, I could do that." If they didn't feel like that—and he thought it was a matter of feeling rather than thinking—there would be a conviction.

The last defence-of-insanity case he had been involved in was rather like what Veraswami had been talking about—a man in a psychotic depression who had killed his wife and daughter, and then tried, but failed, to kill himself. He was found not guilty by reason of insanity because, U Tin Hlang thought, the jury had come to understand how those periods of sadness we all have, that sense of uselessness and of the miseries of the world, can become deep and painful and lasting, so that death for those one loves and for oneself seems a kindness. He had found that if the jury could be brought to think about their own depressions, they would have at least a clue to, a distant sense of, a psychotic depression. They had to be brought to see in themselves, in miniature, the depression, the psychotic depression, that would lead a person to kill a member of his family and then to try to kill himself. "If I cannot make them identify with the criminal, have some sense of the awful force of his sickness, see at least a tinge of it somewhere in their own lives, they will convict."

All this seemed safely distant from Ake Dah's attack on his son, but I could see how links could be drawn. U Tin Hlang, I realised, was really being very helpful to me, and without any unethical advocacy; I was grateful to him.

U Tin Hlang got the books for me from his room and saw us to the front steps of the hotel. "No doubt you will want another rickshaw to deliver Your Worship to his bungalow," Veraswami helpfully said. "Tell me, Mr. Lang, if I may so call you, following the uncouth practice of our young judicial friend, is 'Worship' the proper term for him?"

I tried to separate myself from this absurd dialogue. U Tin Hlang offered the helpful view that "Worship" was only appropriate when my great judicial mind was turned, as now, toward theological disputations, toward extrasensory epiphenomena; otherwise, the appellation should be "Your Honour," not "Your Worship."

I had had enough of this. "Goodnight, Mr. Lang. Thank you for dinner. Are you coming with me, Dr. Veraswami?" And I set off to walk home through the now cooler evening, Veraswami falling in quietly beside me.

It struck me that this was the first time since I had come East that I had heard of mental illness in the villages. It was generally said that the pace of village life was such that psychosis was not to be found there. I asked Dr. Veraswami if this were so, and if Ake Dah had lapsed into mental illness because he had parted from the simpler life of a villager and taken on Western competitive ways. He was amused at my question. "My young friend, I know they say that, that there iss no psychosis in the villages, but all that means iss that there have been no psychiatrists in the villages," and his high-pitched giggle expressed his approval of his turn of phrase. "Burmese villagers are quite ass likely to go mad ass the rest of us; they are spared psychiatrists, not psychosis," and the giggle resumed.

As we parted I thanked him for what he had told me about Ake Dah and said I would ask him to advise me again when I had a better understanding of what I would have to decide at the preliminary hearing.

At the time, the year's training course in Mandalay had not seemed particularly well designed, my predominant impression being of the repetition of the obvious, relieved by my unexpected enjoyment in learning how to control a platoon and then a company on the parade ground. But when responsibilities were mine in Moulmein, I found guidance and comfort in many of those repetitions.

Do an "appreciation of the situation," as you would for a military manoeuvre, was one such drumbeat-repeated litany of advice. It's not only in war that you should sum up the enemy and his positions, chart your resources, assess your options, and then make a decision; do it whenever you have an important decision to make.

What were my options with Ake Dah? There was no question of bail; he was properly held on a clearly valid charge until the preliminary hearing. His counsel had made no application for a psychiatric examination; he might, of course, and that would delay the preliminary hearing, but he hadn't yet. Should I be taking any formal steps in light of what Dr. Veraswami had told me of Ake Dah's mental illness? Or should I leave matters as they stood until Ake Dah was arraigned before me in my role as a police magistrate on the charge of attempted murder, and then decide whether he should be held for a Superior Court trial or tried on a lesser charge before me if he wished. Or should something else be done to bring legal finality to his attack on his son? There was clearly a variety of options; an "appreciation" was required.

The simple course, the straight up-and-down-the pitch course, was to do nothing now—often an excellent plan—to wait for the preliminary hearing, and to respond to the evidence that would then be presented. If U Tin Hlang made no mention then of Ake Dah's apparently mad religious beliefs, all I would have to do would be to let trained judges in Mandalay or Rangoon, wherever he was tried, grapple at trial with his defence of insanity if it were made. There would certainly be adequate evidence before me to commit Ake Dah for trial on a charge of attempted murder unless something was said about his mad motive, and I was under no obligation to raise any question about his motives.

That seemed the simple and safe path to follow; it could get me into no legal difficulties and would be approved by my superiors—but it felt wrong. It increased the chance of a substantial sentence of imprisonment for Ake Dah, which did not seem likely to be of much use to his family, to Versali, or to anyone else. And U Tin Hlang might well decide to offer Ake Dah as a martyr to the Raj, advancing a justification of his actions on religious rather than psychiatric grounds, arguing the validity of Ake Dah's religious beliefs and not their psychopathology. That would surely be the way to advance the purposes of the G.C.B.A., who were, after all, employing him. That must be his plan; otherwise he would have been besieging me with interlocutory motions for a psychiatric assessment of Ake Dah prior to the preliminary hearing, trying to get the attack on Mai Treya treated not as a criminal law matter at all, but rather as a problem of mental health that might or might not—he would argue, would not—require Ake Dah's commitment to a mental hospital, and that certainly made a criminal charge inappropriate.

So, if I did nothing but act the remote magistrate, U Tin Hlang had it in his power, given what I knew of Ake Dah's own explanation of his conduct, to use Ake Dah for political purposes, to take advantage of his mental illness and the deep sincerity of his religious beliefs to sacrifice him. It could not be right for me to fall in with such a plan, but it was not immediately clear what I could do to stop it.

The plain fact was that I didn't know enough law to make an effective appreciation of the situation; I had better do some work and try again. And this time I would have to rely on my own efforts with the law. If I sought help from Mandalay I would be told to follow ordinary procedures, which would play into U Tin Hlang's plans if they were as I judged them to be.

Every moment of the next two days that I could tear free from regular duties was devoted to the search; it proved not too difficult and more interesting than I had expected. What Section 84 of the Indian Penal Code, the law applicable in Burma, said about the defence of insanity was clear enough:

> Nothing is an offence which is done by a person who, at the time of doing it, by reason of unsoundness of mind, is incapable of knowing the nature of the act, or that he is doing what is either wrong or contrary to law.

I found that there were two sources for this section. Thomas Babington Macaulay had drafted a proposed section, Section 67, for the Indian Law Commissioners, which had been published in 1837 by order, it proudly read, of "The Governor-General of India in Council":

Nothing is an offence which a person does in consequence of being mad or delirious at the time of doing it.

The other source was obviously the opinion of the judges, given in the House of Lords in 1843 after the M'Naughten case, which provided for a defence of insanity if by reason of unsoundness of mind at the time of the act charged as a crime the accused did not know the nature and quality of his act or did not know that what he was doing was wrong.

Macaulay's Section 67 seemed likely to me to give a defence to Ake Dah—there could certainly be evidence that Ake Dah was "mad" (Macaulay's word) at the time he wounded his son and that he acted as a consequence of that madness. But it seemed much less likely that he would have a defence under the law as it stood, under the Indian Penal Code's Section 84, since he clearly knew that what he was doing was "contrary to law." U Tin Hlang would argue on behalf of Ake Dah, of course, that the law must yield to the command of God, but he would have to admit that Ake Dah knew that the law forbad what he was doing. So, I wasn't at all confident that Ake Dah would have a valid defence of insanity under the law as it stood. Yet it seemed monstrous to think of him as an ordinary violent criminal.

I would have to ask Dr. Veraswami what the principle was behind the defence of insanity. Why were there these differences between one test and another? But there seemed little I could do about it at this stage. And as often happens, at the nadir, a hopeful idea came to me.

There was one order I could make at this stage that would at least delay the trial and might avoid it entirely. At the very least, it would give me time to talk to Ake Dah and his family, to talk to Veraswami, and to better understand the law and what options I had—to make a better "appreciation of the situation."

As a magistrate at a preliminary hearing I could not force a defence of insanity on Ake Dah, but I remembered that the question of Ake Dah's "fitness to plead" to the charge, his mental competency to stand trial, was relevant, even at this early stage, and that I was entitled, as a magistrate, to raise that question even if Ake Dah and U Tin Hlang did not want it to be raised. Yes indeed, Mandalay had been more helpful than I had given them credit for; some things had stuck.

I checked on it; I was right. If there was reason to believe that because of mental illness an accused was "unfit to plead" at a preliminary hearing, the magistrate could order him to be held for a psychiatric report at the nearest mental hospital. Within a week, the hospital was required to report to the court on the accused's mental condition, whether in their view he was fit for trial and, if not, whether he should be committed as insane.

I then checked on what this fitness to plead meant. What it amount-ed to was whether the accused knew that he was on trial and knew the likely consequences of a trial, and whether he could reasonably well defend himself or reasonably well assist his counsel in his defence. It seemed quite clear to me that Ake Dah could do all these things very well indeed, but it did not seem contrived to use this method of holding matters still for a time so that U Tin Hlang and his employers could not use for their own ends what I now found myself thinking of as the tragedy at Versali.

I had a message taken to U Tin Hlang at his hotel that I proposed to call the case of Ake Dah at the next petty sessions, which would be tomorrow, to make an interlocutory order prior to the preliminary enquiry.

I have never enjoyed a court hearing as much. U Tin Hlang appeared robed, as he had in the Cunningham case. It astonished the few litigants before me and amazed their local counsel, but U Tin Hlang was used to making a stir in Burmese courts and was untroubled by his grandeur amidst our simplicities.

A policeman acting as clerk of the court called the case of Ake Dah. U Tin Hlang looked around as if astonished at the absence of his client. I plunged ahead: "On the basis of information that has come to me from the gaol, and on the basis of my own observations of the accused in this case, I am ordering that the headman, Ake Dah, now held in Moulmein Gaol, be transferred to Moulmein Hospital for a psychiatric examination as to his fitness to plead to the charge against him." That was it: as few reasons as possible, just the order.

U Tin Hlang protested grandly and strenuously: an abuse of power, tyrannical treatment of a loyal servant of the State, defamation of religion, gross error of law, intention immediately to appeal, and so on. I knew his rhetoric outreached his authority, and that there was no appeal from such an order except by way of *habeas corpus* application to a Superior Court, which would be most unlikely to succeed and if it did succeed would not help his pursuit of the martyrdom of Ake Dah. I said that his objections were noted, and had the next case called.

My joy in victory was short-lived. For a week, perhaps for a longer time, I had staved off what I took to be U Tin Hlang's plans for Ake Dah, but I still had no clear idea what I wanted to happen to him.

Previously, when I had visited Dr. Veraswami's hospital, I had not thought it necessary to inspect the psychiatric section. I am not sure what I expected, and I am still not sure whether the psychiatric annex for the mad and the retarded at Moulmein Hospital is at all like an asylum for the insane in England, or in India, or in one of the larger towns of Burma— probably not. But Dr. Veraswami told me the problems were much the same—just differences of size which, he said, had a great effect on conditions generally, on sanitation, individual care, the general tone of the institutions, but not on the psychiatric problems they had to deal with. The sad truth was, he said, that quite a lot was known about the general patterns of mental illness and of retardation, but not much was known about the causes of those patterns of behaviour or about their cure.

He said he thought the problems were much the same everywhere because, when careful comparisons were made between different countries, and corrections were made for differences of diagnostic practice, every country seemed to have about the same proportion of schizophrenics and of other mentally ill and retarded people in their populations. Mental illness, in other words, was part of the human condition—like physical illness. We should not be surprised or resentful; God or natural selection or both had done the job they had done and we had to live with it.

At all events, the mental hospital annex at Moulmein Hospital consisted of what seemed to my paramilitary eye a dusty parade ground—Dr. Veraswami called it the "yard"—surrounded on four sides by single-story dormitories, offices, and a few consulting rooms. The distinctive feature was that it was surrounded—huts, yard, and all—by a wire fence about ten feet high, topped by barbed wire, surplus probably from the carnage on the Western Front.

The brutal directness of the sun on the yard was mitigated by a few open shelters made of wooden uprights on which rested corrugated iron roofs to shade the tables and benches where some of the inmates sat dozing or talking. Others walked about in the sun, many talking or muttering to themselves. Some crouched or curled up in the shade of the walls of the surrounding buildings and dozed. It was a scene of inaction. I had expected to be anxious for my safety—to put no fine phrase upon it, scared. I was not; I was outraged. It seemed such a waste of people.

"You must not be surprised, Mr. Blair. There iss not much for them to do. Why not sleep or talk to oneself?"

"But surely there is much that they could do. They could be working; they could be in treatment for their illnesses."

"Perhaps . . . perhaps . . . but I have one doctor to help me with thiss part of the hospital, and he iss a Burmese who hass not been trained in psychiatry—if he had been so trained, he would be in a most lucrative practice in Rangoon, to be sure—and we have eighty patients here, rarely less, and they stay for a long while, some until they die, indeed most until they die."

"It seems such a waste, Dr. Veraswami. Can't we do better than this?"

"You must not be critical, my young friend," Veraswami said, softening any hint of a rebuke by a smile of approval at my indignation. "We do better, so it seems to me, than many places, many countries, your own included, if I may be so bold. Ass you see, there are not many here; many others who are mentally sick are cared for in the villages by their families; in your country perhaps fewer families can care for their sick, or want to."

I had no idea if he was right or not; probably he spoke sense, but it didn't make much difference for what I saw—sick people abandoned and deserted, filling in time, just filling in time.

"Is this what is to become of Ake Dah? I have come to respect him. The thought of his spending years in a place like this, kicking the dust and talking to himself in a sedated way, is awful. Can't we do better than this?"

I was deeply troubled; why, I am not sure, but suddenly Ake Dah was close to my heart. It was terrible to think of his spending perhaps twenty years—and it might be that—in a place like this.

"Where is Ake Dah now, Dr. Veraswami?" I asked.

Veraswami nodded toward a hut on the other side of the parade ground from where we were standing. "He iss in a single room, under observation continuously, which he resents; but if I am to report about him to your court, ass you have ordered, I thought it best to have him watched. And there iss always the risk that the voice he hears might tell him to kill himself—though I think that iss unlikely. Still, better to be safe. . . . "

"I thought you told me, Doctor, that under sedation he would not hear that voice."

"Probably not, but it would be better, would it not, if he iss to be tried, for him to be ass clear in the head ass possible. So I thought we should observe him closely for a time when he has not taken any drugs. And, I must also tell you, I think it verry likely indeed that he will refuse to take any drugs. He will hate them. He doess not think he iss sick; he believes he iss chosen of God. He doess not want to be cured, not at all. Am I to force him to be drugged?"

"Would it be convenient for me to visit him now? If he agrees?" I was not sure why I wished to talk with Ake Dah, but I did. I supposed I should rely only on whatever evidence was brought before me in court; but in my other capacity as chief of the local police, who controlled this prosecution, I had better know as much as I could about him. And also it was my duty to protect a prisoner and to ensure he was treated properly. Perhaps these were all excuses for inquisitiveness.

"Of course you may see him, but I think U Tin Hlang iss with him now. Would you not rather wait until he iss alone?"

I had forgotten that my ordering a psychiatric examination of the prisoner did not at all prevent his counsel seeing him whenever such an interview was medically convenient. U Tin Hlang would be doing a lot of consulting, planning for Ake Dah, I hoped, but also for his political employers.

I asked Dr. Veraswami if he could spare some time to talk to me while I waited to see Ake Dah. "By all means. It iss not a busy day at the hospital. Let us talk here."

It was, I suppose, an appropriate setting in which to learn about a defence of insanity, and about what happens to those who are found not guilty by reason of insanity: a shaded corner of a large yard, dotted with fools and madmen, not uncomfortable since a breeze stirred the palm trees outside the fence, but profoundly depressing—a scene of pain and hopelessness.

We sat on a plank bench. Veraswami leaned his elbows on the rough table and looked up at me, ready to be questioned. I told him I had boned up on the law and its background, that I knew what a defence of insanity involved as a matter of proof, that I knew that most who were found not guilty by reason of insanity were then sent to a mental hospital until they were sane and no longer dangerous; but that I really did not understand how those words of the law worked in practice, here or elsewhere.

Veraswami was slow in replying, obviously making an effort to organise his thoughts. His arms rose from the table, his hands open and pressing inwards as if on a large, invisible ball. "I will try, Mr. Blair. I have seen something of what happens to them in England, and my country, and here; but it iss not easy, it iss all so chancy. I shall try to make it simple."

I bridled at this. "Dr. Veraswami, I know you are more than twice my age, and trained and experienced in these matters, which I am not; but don't oversimplify for my benefit. I shall do my best to understand."

He looked horrified. He probably was. He leapt from his seat and waved his arms like some of the others in that fenced yard. "Oh, pleass, Mr. Blair. You misunderstand. It iss for myself that it must be simple. If I go on, round and round, with long medical words, I will not myself be knowing what I am talking about. For myself, for my own understanding, I will try to make it verry, verry clear. But the trouble iss that in fact these are not simple matters, so that if one makes it direct and simple, one also makes it wrong. But to start with, simple, simple for me, not for you."

I apologised and calmed him down, thinking that he might be a good candidate for one of his own sedatives at this moment; but as usual Veraswami reacted with warmth to my apology, sat himself down opposite me so that the scene of the wandering patients was behind him, and talked to me with unusual directness and understanding.

It came to this: From what he knew already of Ake Dah, if he were found fit for trial, charged with attempted murder, and pleaded the insanity defence, no psychiatrist, no doctor who knew anything about mental illness, would deny that he was a paranoid schizophrenic and that his attack on Mai Treya was related to his illness. So, unless something went wrong, and it often did in sensational trials, he would be found not guilty by reason of insanity and would then be committed to a mental hospital, probably near Rangoon, where he would be held for a long time. The conditions would be much like those I was looking at over Veraswami's shoulder, only worse because the hospital would be more crowded.

If, of course, he did not plead a defence of insanity, and tried to justify his actions as directed by God, the court would do one of two things. It might force an insanity defence upon him, which it could then do, particularly because it would have his, Veraswami's, report, which he would have to present to me since I had ordered Ake Dah's psychiatric examination. (I had not until then realised that I had already unwittingly limited Ake Dah's and U Tin Hlang's freedom of strategy at trial by ordering the enquiry into Ake Dah's fitness for trial.) Or it would simply convict him of attempted murder and presumably impose a sentence of imprisonment.

So, either way, Ake Dah would spend a long time away from Versali, away from his family.

"But all this makes no sense, Doctor. You tell me that Ake Dah is no longer a threat to his son. His son wants him home. His family and the villagers all want him back if he won't attack anyone. What are we doing sending him away for years? Will it help him get better?"

Veraswami said that he did not think Ake Dah would ever change very much, "not until he iss quite old and doessn't care so much about himself."

"What would you do about Ake Dah if we didn't have to worry about these legal processes, Dr. Veraswami?"

Veraswami hesitated, looked about him, and then smiled with pleasure at the idea that came to him. "I would keep him here for a few months, perhaps a year or so, to help me get thiss terrible place into better order—it doess look terrible, doesn't it? Ake Dah iss a fine organiser, an industrious man. He would be excellent here."

"But you just told me every psychiatrist would say he is mad."

"Yes. But that doess not mean he would not be verry useful here."

"Does he think he is mad? You told me he doesn't think he is at all sick. Why should he stay here?"

Veraswami did not immediately respond. He looked about him for a while and then said, "You raise a question which I find verry, verry difficult. At one level I think Ake Dah knows the voice he hears iss a symptom of hiss sickness, but he cannot admit that to himself. He must deny it. It ruins him entirely not to. It diminishes his son if he admits to being ill. It destroys much that he has built around himself. Yet I think he knows, in a sense he knows, but he keeps pushing the truth away. Iss there nothing in your life like that, Blair? Not at all as threatening, of course, but things you know about yourself that you put out of your mind, failures, weaknesses, inadequacies, forbidden temptations which you don't let yourself think about. There are for most of uss. And for Ake Dah these are deeply painful thoughts that must be held down verry strongly; he must act verry calm and wise and divinely inspired to keep them from him. Do I make any sense to you, my young friend? I am not sure of these things, ass I said, though I think we all understand them to a little degree, but without the pain that Ake Dah," and he gestured behind him, "and these others endure."

If what I thought Veraswami was saying was right, then it was very relevant indeed to Ake Dah's state of mind when he tried to kill his son. The idea that Macaulay had suggested in 1837 seemed precisely appropriate in one sense, and his words came back to me—nothing is an offence which a person does in consequence of being mad at the time of doing it. But there seemed a difficulty in the logic. Had Ake Dah not been "mad," he would not have attacked his son; so that on their face Macaulay's words, were they law, would give Ake Dah a defence. But, in a deeper sense, Ake Dah knew that the voice he heard was part of his "madness" and not the voice of God—he knew it, but could not admit it—pride would not let him admit it; he could not reduce himself or his son in that way.

Pride might be too large a word for this type of self-protection, but the principle was clear. Mai Treya had been attacked because Ake Dah was not willing to face the truth about himself. Yet Mai Treya was also attacked because Ake Dah was sick and heard voices. In this situation, which analysis was to be preferred: that which held Ake Dah blameless because the voices were not his and they caused the attack; or that which held that Ake Dah well knew he was not obeying the voice of God but rather his own view of himself and his son as privileged, great beings—so that he preferred to sacrifice his son rather than the Ram of Pride?

And, of course, if enough people believed that he and the voice he heard were expressing objective truth, divinely revealed truth, then he would be seen as a great prophet, as Abraham is seen as a great prophet.

These ideas that Veraswami had launched needed further thought; that, at least, was obvious. I said as much to Veraswami and told him I did not wish to see Ake Dah now. I would get in touch with him soon, well before the hearing next week on the question of his fitness to plead.

Over the next two days, whenever I could escape from routine duties, I tried to write up, for myself, an "appreciation" of the defence of insanity.

Mental illness could be relevant to a criminal charge, quite apart from any special defence of insanity, by helping to disprove the presence of the mental element of the crime—that the killer intended to kill, the taker of property to steal, and so on—but that is quite rare and did not help with the Ake Dah case, since Ake Dah certainly knew he was trying to kill his son.

So it was the special defence of insanity to a criminal charge, the rules made to deal with mental illness as distinct from other pressures toward crime, that I would have to "appreciate."

The Indian Penal Code, the notes I had from the Mandalay course, and the materials loaned to me by U Tin Hlang eventually came together in my mind. There were several competing tests of insanity as a defence to a criminal charge, but they all had the same structure, the same three elements: mental illness at the time of the crime, a causal relation between that mental illness and the crime, and rules about who had to prove the first two elements and at what levels of persuasion. All three elements—the definition of mental illness, the definition of the causal link, and the words to define burdens and weight of proof—were extremely imprecise. Medical definitions would not suffice for the mental illness element; philosophically acceptable definitions would not suffice for the causal element; and the language of the law about the strength of proof required to establish both the illness and that it caused the crime was quite vague.

Macaulay in 1837 had framed the simplest and what seemed to me the most intellectually satisfactory test: "Nothing is an offence which a person does in consequence of being mad," or, to put it more crisply, "Did the accused's mental illness cause the crime?" All other tests were simply variations of this idea: modifying what was meant by mental illness, limiting it to knowledge of wrongness or illegality, and also trying to define the causal relationship between the illness and the crime. This was true of the judges' statements in the House of Lords after Daniel M'Naughten had been found not guilty by reason of insanity; of the Indian Penal Code, which would apply to Ake Dah; and of all other legal tests of insanity as a defence to crime that I could find.

There had also been attempts to give a defence of insanity to those who, though they knew what they were doing, had been unable to control themselves; but, of course, this idea of measuring man's volitional control had proved elusive in the extreme—in fact, impossible.

So, at bottom, what I had to think about was whether Ake Dah's mental illness—which Veraswami assured me was a reality, and which my own observations of his auditory hallucinations had confirmed—had caused him to try to kill Mai Treya. In one sense, the answer was obvious. If he had not heard the voices, he would not have attacked the boy. Is that all there was to it? Surely not, for if that were so, everyone who had any "mental illness" and did an act that was otherwise a crime would have a defence of insanity, for obviously everything he did would have to be to some degree influenced by the mental illness. There must be more to it than that.

I finally concluded that I was on the wrong trail in trying to understand the defence of insanity by refining the issues of definition and causation. The truth was different. What was at issue was attribution of responsibility, not analysis of a definable condition and of a result. The central question was an "ought" question, not an "is" question: Was Ake Dah so sick that he ought not to be held responsible for his act? It was an imprecise question of justice—a question of judgement, not a question of measurable fact.

I felt confident about this, but it did not carry me to any easy conclusion about Ake Dah. It seemed to push me to try to answer a question of enormous difficulty, not only beyond my capacity but perhaps beyond anyone's capacity: Was Ake Dah morally innocent or not? It seemed a question peculiarly within St. Peter's province, if it is he who guards the Pearly Gates. How could I possibly know?

Veraswami had told me of the Dacoits, a criminal tribe of India who had also percolated into northeastern Burma. A young person in that tribe would steal and sometimes murder, since that was what he was expected to do, taught to do as proper behaviour by those to whom he had been born and who had reared him. He should certainly be convicted of those crimes, it seemed to me, but circumstances also seemed to make him morally innocent.

Was Ake Dah any different? He and the Dacoit youth both knew the criminal law prohibited what they were doing, declared it to be the most serious of all crimes. Yet both were morally convinced of the virtue of their behaviour; to St. Peter they would, I suspected, seem very similar. Why, then, did they seem different to me?

I thought, too, of U Tin Hlang's description of some political activists who willingly gave their lives for their political beliefs, carrying explosives on their bodies into the buildings of the Raj to sacrifice themselves there. Were those terrorists as morally innocent as those led to kill by mental illness? Should they, as a moral matter, doubt the validity of their political beliefs more or less than Ake Dah should doubt the divine origin of his voices? Which of the two "prides" was easier to reject? Which merited the larger suspicion and therefore the greater effort at self-control? It seemed an unanswerable question.

I came to the conclusion that I did not need to struggle further with these moral conundrums. The defence of insanity was, properly understood, only a way of extending mercy to some whose sickness led us to wish to forgive them their acts—that was all: a means of extending mercy when we sympathised with what would otherwise be a crime.

And it struck me again that it was a strange sort of mercy. If Ake Dah were found not guilty by reason of insanity on a trial for attempted murder, he would very likely spend many years in a mental hospital, vegetating, not changing other than for the worse, though he was now a threat to no one. It seemed a miserable sort of clemency. If only there were some way of getting him out of the clutches of the criminal law entirely so that his voices and his beliefs could be dealt with as matters of mental health and not as the precipitants of crime.

On Sundays in Moulmein I often went to Morning Service. Perhaps there was an element of doing what was expected of me, although I don't think that was why I went. I doubt that the hope of everlasting life moved me; I find it hard to think about. But I did find comfort and peace in the remembrances of my childhood, of the warmth of ceremonies and hymns closely shared with my mother, and of churchgoing with my family on those occasions when my father was home on leave from India. I have often thought that the Church of England is like the Jewish faith in that folk-ways and customs, a sense of group belonging, weigh far more heavily with its adherents than do beliefs or doctrines. At all events, I went to Morning Service on many Sundays in Moulmein, shook hands with the vicar on the way out, enquired whether I could be of service to anyone in his flock, and sometimes walked on to a light lunch at the Club, thus both prolonging and weakening my nostalgia for England.

This morning, as I turned away from the vicar, having performed my obsequies, a Burmese youth accosted me and handed me an envelope, saying: "Mr. Blair, Sahib, Mr. U Tin Hlang asked me to give you this. I am to wait for a reply." He breathed heavily in satisfaction at a lesson well learned and precisely rendered.

The message from U Tin Hlang read: "I called at your bungalow and was told you were at church. I have laid my hands on a motorcar. If you are free, would you join me for a drive to the hills? I have a well-stocked picnic basket. I will pick you up at your bungalow half an hour hence, unless you tell the bearer of this note you cannot come."

I resented his assumption that I would be so readily available, but in fact I was. Why not? It might be interesting, and he certainly had not embarrassed me by talking too much about our pending case at dinner the other night. So I sent a message of acceptance and hurried back to my bungalow to change into cooler clothes.

U Tin Hlang arrived in what he later told me was a bull-nosed Fiat, a lengthy two-seater touring car with a canvas hood, now rolled down behind the back seat, and long running boards that became mudguards sweeping up over the wheels like surprised eyebrows beside the long green bonnet of the car. The spare tyre was to the right of the driver's seat, outside the cabin of the car, as was the large handbrake on which Hlang's right hand rested as he pulled up in front of the steps of my bungalow, tooting loudly, though he could see me plainly, standing there waiting for him.

A substantial wicker basket rested on the back seat; it appeared he had catered well for the picnic, if there was any relation between the size of the basket and the quantity of its contents. I rather hoped that he had put aside his taste for the Burmese gastronomic exotica of our dinner at his hotel—less moribund fish would not disappoint me.

"Come on, Blair, hop in," and he opened the small U-shaped door on the passenger's side. He hadn't stopped the engine; the dust of his arrival had hardly settled before we were on our way. But to where?

"Where are we going, Mr. Lang?"

I expected a reply, not a song, and for a time did not realise that he was trying to achieve at once both a song and an answer to my question. He threw back his shoulders and mouthed the lyrics roundly to produce a pow-

erful and quite respectable baritone, at least so it sounded over the noise of
the engine, and demonstrated a mastery of cockney intonation as he sang:

> By the old Moulmein Pagoda, lookin' lazy at the sea,
> There's a Burma girl a-settin', and I know she thinks
>   o' me . . .
> An' I seed her first a-smokin' of a whickin' white
>   cheroot,
> An' a-wastin' Christian kisses on an 'eathen idol's
>   foot.

Cheroot and foot rhymed perfectly, to U Tin Hlang's exaggerated satisfaction. He sang it twice, and then switched from the cockney baritone to
his own London-accented speech to add the obvious, "Your own Mr.
Kipling, in 1889, I believe." And then further added, now in his powerful
version of cockney, "Let us see of what he was a-talkin' of."

"The lady or the pagoda, Mr. Lang?" I asked. And we both laughed in
the joy of the adventure.

"The pagoda, you ass, though who can tell? . . . "

I shared the childish pleasure of the moment. How he had managed to
get a touring car for our enjoyment amazed me, but it did not matter. I
had a sense of youthful irresponsibility, like an undergraduate out on an
uncaring prank, which is what I suppose I should have been, not a district
officer worrying about an attempted murder that might disturb the life of
a village.

"Alright, so it's the pagoda. But which pagoda?" I asked. "The country
is littered with them."

"Littered. Do you really mean that?" Of course I didn't and said so; for
they brought charm to every Burmese view, wherever they occurred,
though I thought, without saying so to U Tin Hlang, that their distant
prospect was to be preferred to their sometimes dingy or garishly repainted
appearance in proximity. But even that thought was grossly unfair, I had to
admit to myself, since many of them had stood where they were for far
longer periods than any English statuary other than, perhaps, Stonehenge,
if it can be called statuary.

We settled to the drive, not trying to talk much over the noise of the
engine, with the wind only slightly impeded by the low glass windshield. I
did learn that the car belonged to U Tin Hlang and that he had driven it
down from Rangoon to cheer his leisure while he was in Moulmein. With
the rainy season approaching, he did not much fancy getting about my
town on foot, or even in the rickshaws that I was reputed to prefer for a
variety of purposes: for transportation, as a hearse—he knew not what else.

I ignored these elephantine attempts at humour and asked him which
pagoda was the old Moulmein pagoda Kipling had in mind. He said he was
not sure, but he thought it was the Kyaikthanlan Pagoda on the highest

hilltop overlooking Moulmein. Anyhow, he had declared this to be Kipling's pagoda for today's outing since it gave such a fine view over Moulmein and the Salween.

The road followed the Salween for a distance and then set off straight through paddy fields to the nearest hills, winding dustily into cooler air and lighter vegetation. We drove for about forty minutes before, as we came around a bend, U Tin Hlang pointed over the windshield, "There it is, Blair," and braked to a swift stop.

It was less a pagoda than a series of pagodas, though one sharply arched and pointed pagoda at the summit stood high above the others. The lower and smaller pagodas were a crisp white; the higher and larger, a dark, earth-red colour, topped by a bronze point. In the foreground, on the road, was a Burmese youth, his open umbrella resting on the road, he kneeling on his heels close to it to shield the sun from his neck and back while he gazed across the valley toward the town and the vast view of the winding Salween. The scene has stuck in my mind.

"You like it, Blair?" Indeed I did.

U Tin Hlang started the car, drove quietly round the youth so as not to disturb him or obstruct his view, and stopped the car at some steps at the foot of the low hill on which the pagodas were built. We took the picnic basket between us, climbed the stairs, walked to the left of the main pagoda, and sat under a tree with our backs to the buildings to share the view the boy was admiring from the road.

It was a good lunch, with none of the culinary peculiarities I had feared. Fresh sandwiches, some cheese, cold beer, some fruit—most un-Burmese, except the fruit. Whoever had packed it had been ingenious in keeping the beer cold. Each bottle had been tightly wrapped, when very cold, in layers and layers of newspaper, and then in several thicknesses of cloth to insulate it from the heat. Beer has rarely tasted better to me.

It was most pleasant there with U Tin Hlang. He knew a great deal about Burma and its history, and was happy to instruct me, friend to friend, the difference between our years falling away in the ease of our talk. We wandered around the pagoda, observing but not disturbing the few Burmese squatting in quiet meditation.

The clouds were gathering; the rainy season had arrived, and an early downpour instead of the usual late-afternoon shower seemed likely. U Tin Hlang asked if I wished to be driven back to Moulmein or whether I had the time to see another pagoda. He said there was a famous one not far from where we were.

There was no reason to cut short this expedition. "I'm in no hurry. Why is it famous?" I asked.

"Not so much for what is there, as for what happened there," he replied. "What happened there, or what is alleged to have happened there, is that when young Siddhartha Gautama, the last Buddha, saw the four statues at this pagoda, which you will soon see, he then decided—had not decided before, but then decided—to give his life to the service of others, in particular to trying to find means to reduce their suffering. Anyhow, you will see; it's called the Uzine Pagoda."

We descended to the valley by the same road that brought us up, but took a narrower and rougher road toward Moulmein, almost a dirt track, when we left the hills. Suddenly there was a hissing noise, and U Tin Hlang was braking. Tyres in the 1920s were most delicate; we were lucky to have gone as far as we had without a puncture. U Tin Hlang was efficient in jacking up the car, removing the flattened tyre and the wheel, and replacing them with the spare—and I had done this often enough with army vehicles to be of use. It did not take long. Now we must hope that we would get back to Moulmein without another puncture, compelling us to repair one of the inner tubes and not just change the wheel.

The Uzine Pagoda, the scene of the Buddha's dedication to reducing human suffering and not merely refashioning his soul, was memorable for the life-sized and realistic statues of four men on the paved apron in front of the largest pagoda. One was of a very old man, another of an obviously very sick man, another was dead, and the fourth had the wretched physique of a religious ascetic. All clearly suffered, and suffered greatly. These were the stimuli of the Gautama's self-redirection. They were stark and moving, but did not seem nearly as moving to me as the real sufferings one could all too easily observe elsewhere than in statues. Still, such was the legend, and it gave the statues a better moral than most religious statuary: it pressed upon me the primacy of my own obligation to try to reduce suffering, certainly rather than to strike fine legal or moral postures.

The first heavy drops of rain struck. We rushed back to the car but failed to get the canvas hood up before the deluge hit. At last it was in place and we were in, clipping the celluloid curtains onto the attachments which held them between the hood and the cabin of the car. We were dripping wet, sopping. The road was rapidly becoming a muddy path. U Tin Hlang thought it best to try to get on our way before the road became impassable. We moved slowly back to the main road to Moulmein, which was in better condition, and as the rain settled from the first prolonged downpour to a steady stream, we pulled up at the steps to my bungalow.

I persuaded U Tin Hlang to come in, and to change out of his dripping clothes. I lent him a shirt and pants, which fitted him quite well, while my houseboy dried and aired his. We sat on the verandah watching the rain bend the leaves and weigh down the boughs; tropical storms are noisy on tin roofs and for a time we did not talk. I wondered whether I should talk about Ake Dah; U Tin Hlang had carefully, but not ostentatiously, avoided that topic so far. Clearly, if it was to be raised between us, the initiative would have to be mine. And perhaps, even if I did raise it, he would prefer not to talk about it. But it seemed to me silly not to take advantage of his knowledge, even if I thus risked his bending me to his purposes.

"I know it is unethical for us to discuss the Ake Dah case out of court, but I am troubled for him and for his family—particularly for Treya. Do you mind talking to me about it?"

"You are right, Blair, it's certainly unethical; but I have come to trust you more than you think, and I am prepared to risk it." The risk, of course, was mine, not his, since I had initiated the discussion, but I didn't mind his suggesting the contrary. "Yes, let's talk about it."

I told him why I hoped I would not have to commit Ake Dah for trial for attempted murder. It might suit the G.C.B.A., and even possibly the YMBA, but I could not see what good such a trial could do for Versali, or for other villages, or for Ake Dah and his family. This sort of violent attack on a child, seen by the attacker as divinely inspired, was not one that could be deterred by the threat of punishment. It would do no good to Ake Dah for some to see him as a religious martyr, if he were convicted and imprisoned; or as mad, if he were acquitted as not guilty by reason of insanity. It wouldn't help Treya at all—his life would be blighted more by what happened to his father at trial than by what his father had done to him. So I could see only one way out.

U Tin Hlang was obviously interested. The round, hooded eyes opened in exaggerated enquiry.

"We must keep him at Dr. Veraswami's hospital for about a year—under treatment, I suppose we should say—and then let him go back to the village. I think we can manage that if you will help, Mr. Lang."

"Have you discussed these ideas with Dr. Veraswami or with my client in my absence?" U Tin Hlang asked.

"No, and I suppose I shouldn't be discussing them with you, Lang, but I can't manage it on my own."

U Tin Hlang started to wander about my verandah, carrying his whisky and soda with him. "You know, Blair, I can agree to nothing without my client's consent, and whatever you think about it, I see Ake Dah as my client and not those who are paying me. Just for the moment let us assume Ake Dah would agree. What exactly are you suggesting?"

So I told him. He would not oppose the adjournment of the preliminary hearing into the charge against Ake Dah until Dr. Veraswami would testify that Ake Dah was fit to be tried. I would suggest to Dr. Veraswami, in the light of what he had already told me about Ake Dah's mental condition, that a period of treatment in his hospital would at the very least improve Ake Dah's fitness for trial. U Tin Hlang could return for the preliminary hearing about a year hence, "at a date that suits your calendar," I even more improperly interpolated, and at that preliminary hearing the charge of attempted murder would be withdrawn and a charge of unlawful wounding substituted. If the accused wished it, I could hear that charge; it would not have to be sent on to a Superior Court, as would attempted murder. At such a trial, if Ake Dah pleaded guilty, it seemed to me most unlikely that he would have to serve any prison time; his period in the mental hospital would count as time served in a sentence of, say, one year's imprisonment and two years on probation under suitable conditions. Of course, I could not promise any of these things. Ake Dah might get suddenly worse, more dangerous, but, if things stayed roughly as they now were, that is the sentence I had in mind on his plea of guilty to unlawful wounding.

"Blair, when are you taking up the law? Hurry home to one of the Inns of Court. You will make a most ingenious barrister if you don't find your own way to prison before you are admitted." He was obviously delighted with me, if not with my plan. "You are sure that wily old Veraswami didn't put you up to this?"

Somewhat annoyed, I made no answer. "Do you want another whisky?"

"Please, please," and he held out his glass to me, but made no immediate reply to my proposal.

Put out by his unresponsiveness, I went on, "I am not experienced in these matters, as you well know, but this does seem to me the best result for all concerned. If you disagree, tell me why. Surely we can act sensibly in this matter and don't have to get caught up in trials that will do no good to anyone, and hurt many."

I gave him his refilled glass. We were physically close as I handed it to him. By not grasping the glass he kept me close, eye to eye. "Very well, Blair. I'll trust you completely. We shall talk of this to no one else. I'll tell those who sent me that it was my idea, that Ake Dah and his son needed their support and that this is the best way to give it. And that I lured you into it. You play your role without talking about it to others, including Veraswami, and I'll play mine.

My face must have revealed my pleasure.

"Oh, don't look so self-satisfied, Blair. This will not be easy at all to bring off. You forget I have a strong-willed, if wild-minded, client. I very much doubt that he will fall in with your plan. I will tell him I have persuaded you to it, but I think he will hate everything about it. He sees himself not only as innocent, but as chosen of God to demonstrate the Buddha-like *karma* of Mai Treya and his own noble role in its revelation. But I will try."

U Tin Hlang thought it better to persuade Ake Dah's family to our plan—which was now his plan—before raising it with his client. I decided to go with U Tin Hlang the next morning to Versali.

It required less energy to get to Versali in his grand automobile than on my bicycle, but at one stage I was in doubt which I preferred. Despite the deep ruts in the track, U Tin Hlang drove with undergraduate panache. Swooping around a bend we confronted two working elephants carrying wicker howdahs on their backs, laden with villagers on their way to the teak forest. The car's brakes squeaked; one elephant trumpeted, its trunk curled up above my head; the other glared balefully. We backed off swiftly. I had a glimpse of how Hannibal's enemies must have felt. U Tin Hlang turned off the engine and apologised frequently, to the elephants, not to me, as they lumbered past.

Military trucks were reasonably well known in Versali, but a Burmese driving a large green Fiat sports car and accompanied by the district officer was as surprising to the villagers as he had been to the elephants.

Ake Dah's wife came out of their bungalow as we pulled up. U Tin Hlang spoke to her in Burmese. He knew I understood enough Burmese to follow the gist of the conversation but that I was not fluent enough to carry on a conversation of any complexity. We had agreed that he should be the one to present his plan and that my presence should be taken as a validation of his power to arrange what he had in mind, and that it would be inappropriate for me to advance the scheme myself. With each further step, I became a possible impediment to his ideas, rather than the source of the plan.

The headman's wife did not at first invite us in, preferring the safety of the open ground, surrounded by a small but growing group of children. U Tin Hlang persisted in polite enquiries about her family, reports of Mai Treya's improving health, and statements of his desire to discuss important matters with her, until she had little choice but to invite us both to come onto the verandah of the bungalow. The children drifted off, though their eyes and those of others in the village remained on us for the brief time we talked.

Ake Dah's wife gathered her two younger children, her daughters, to her knees, and listened while U Tin Hlang outlined with precision, and in a strongly caring manner, his belief that it would be better for Ake Dah to stay at the hospital for some months, even up to a year, before returning to Versali. He stressed that she and her children could visit him there as often as she wished, that he would be taken care of, and that Mai Treya could come home from hospital as soon as the doctor thought his shoulder sufficiently healed.

She nodded in understanding, but volunteered nothing.

Would she agree to this?, he asked.

She would do whatever Ake Dah thought best, she replied, though she could not understand why he should stay away so long. He was needed in Versali; it would be hard for her and the children without him.

U Tin Hlang kept pressing, perhaps too strongly, I thought, assuring her that the General Council of Buddhist Associations would see that she and her husband and family were well cared for; but he could get no expression of agreement from her. She intended to walk to the hospital that afternoon and would talk with Ake Dah about what U Tin Hlang had said, if she were allowed to see her husband. She would also be visiting her son in the other part of the hospital. She did not speak a great deal, but I had the sense that she had a clear idea of what was being suggested.

We left the village, the car the center of delight to an attendant crew of running children, U Tin Hlang roaring the engine, though creeping forward slowly, and tooting the horn frequently to increase their delight. We circumnavigated the village in some style, and then attacked the rutted track to Moulmein, accelerating to shake off our tail of laughing youngsters.

"We had better go straight to Ake Dah, before she gets to him," U Tin Hlang suggested, and I agreed.

We did not talk much on the way to the hospital, each planning how to handle Ake Dah. I realised that I must not share my entire plan with U Tin Hlang. For all I knew, he might have been having similar anticonspiratorial ideas about me.

"I think you should see Ake Dah alone, Mr. Attorney," I said. "It would seem better for you to show your client this way out and then together persuade me to it, don't you think?"

U Tin Hlang agreed. So when we reached the hospital, I sat in the office where Veraswami had instructed me when I last visited the psychiatric section, while U Tin Hlang went to his client's cell—or was it a room?—a cross between the two, I supposed.

U Tin Hlang returned in anger. "It's no use, Blair. He really is mad. He insists on going to trial. He's going to be vindicated at trial, seen for the hero he is, the protector of the new Buddha. I had my doubts of your plan from the beginning." Now I knew that U Tin Hlang was destined for high political office. He obviously believed, absolutely and without doubt, that it was now my plan, to which he had tentatively agreed solely to humour me.

I decided to take the plunge. I felt as though I were again entering the courtroom to surprise U Tin Hlang with my initiative about Ake Dah's fitness to plead, but I quickly suppressed any false sense of confidence.

I asked an attendant to take me to Ake Dah and invited U Tin Hlang to come with me. I did not talk to U Tin Hlang en route, staying close to the attendant with U Tin Hlang hurrying behind.

Ake Dah received us courteously, getting up from his trestle bed as we came in. He gestured for U Tin Hlang and me to sit on the bed; he sat on the wooden chair facing us. Saffron robed, without sandals, he still wore an air of calm and dignity.

I knew Ake Dah's English was excellent, but I spoke slowly and clearly in an effort to get my words straight and to accentuate the threat I had in mind. I made no introductory remarks beyond a "Good afternoon, Headman," to which he made the gesture of *eyebong* in reply.

"Your counsel tells me that the suggestion he made to you has been rejected. So be it. We shall hold the preliminary hearing into the charge of attempted murder at the next court sessions. Is there anything else you wish to know? Anything else you would like before then?"

Ake Dah expressed thanks for my concern and said that there was nothing he wanted. U Tin Hlang was looking at me with a surprised expression; why had I dragged him back to the cell if this was all I had in mind? So I pressed on, brutally but quietly, I hoped.

"I must tell you, Headman, that at the same sessions of the court there will be a petition presented by one of my policemen to have Mai Treya declared an abused and neglected child and made a ward of the State. We will have to find a suitable and safe institution for him where he will not be attacked. I am sorry to have to tell you this at such a time, but I thought it better to give you and your counsel as much notice as possible of this petition. It will be served on your wife tomorrow."

I have never seen a face and figure disintegrate so swiftly as did Ake Dah's. U Tin Hlang was on his feet and glaring at me, the curved scar on his face burning red, his arm around the bent shoulders of the now stricken and trembling Ake Dah. I did not wait for any word from either of the men in the cell with me. I walked out of the cell, telling the guard outside that U Tin Hlang would likely be staying with his client for some time.

It worked, of course. When the court convened, U Tin Hlang did not oppose Veraswami's recommendation that Ake Dah should be held for treatment until he was better able to stand trial. After preliminary hostility toward me, U Tin Hlang rejoiced with me in the success of his plan, and we set a tentative date, some months hence, to reconsider when he would plead his client guilty to unlawful wounding or, he suggested, to assault occasioning actual bodily harm, if the attempted murder charge were dropped.

There seemed no need to pursue the neglect petition.

Over the next few months, I asked Veraswami regularly about his head-man patient and about what he had heard of his family. Mai Treya was back at school and the general report was that he was doing well. Versali and Ake Dah's family were not suffering. It seemed Ake Dah made better decisions about the village when he made only a few decisions and those only when consulted at the hospital by the elders; he interfered less and kept his thoughts for the more important decisions, rather than being the pervasive overseer. And Veraswami professed himself deeply grateful. "You should visit the psychiatric section now, Mr. Blair. What you called a prison yard iss now a sweetly blooming oasis. Well, perhaps I exaggerate; but there are trees, and bushes, and running water, and shady corners. It iss verry good of you to give me such excellent staff, and free, even if you do so by blackmail. You may have done wisely; Buddhism will not have its Abraham, but this case hass been a great strain on your character, a verry great strain indeed."

Commentary to "AKE DAH"

What a strange coincidence: the name of the village elder brought to District Officer Blair, "Ake Dah," is startlingly close to the Hebrew name for Talmudic studies of Abraham, "Akedah."

Copying, you say; not at all. In the city where you are, or the city nearest to where you are, there are today several psychotic people who are hearing voices that you could not hear—they are not lying when they tell you of those voices and of what they say. Regrettably, the voices they hear often instruct them to kill or injure themselves or someone they love or have loved. It is by no means a rare event, though it is quite rare for them to act as instructed other than against themselves. But sometimes they do; sometimes they injure or try to injure someone else. And often they tell you in all sincerity that it is the voice of God that they hear.

Offensive heresy, you say—Abraham portrayed as a psychotic old man. Well, this may offend, so let us now firmly put aside the suggestion that this story has anything whatsoever to do with Abraham, the Hebrew patriarch, and his son Isaac, and let us focus instead on secular matters, on the question of what District Officer Blair should have done about Ake Dah.

Since the twelfth century the question has raged, unabated, in the Common Law: should the mentally ill be held responsible for their otherwise criminal behaviour? And in particular, since this is the context in which the question presents itself in its sharpest form, should mentally ill killers be convicted of murder, and, if not, what are the criteria that should distinguish those who should be so convicted from those who should not?

Some suggest that this decision should be left to the doctors, in particular the psychiatrists. If they say the killer was mentally ill, and that the illness was causally related to the killing, that is the end of it—he is sick, not wicked; to be treated, not punished. But that is a simplistic view. It mistakes a moral question, which has a subsidiary content of social expediency, for a question of diagnosis and treatment. The line between the sick and the wicked is not to be drawn for this purpose by doctors, though it must be confessed that the lawyers have not done very well by it.

In fact, philosophers have the most to contribute, but, regrettably, they have given insufficient attention to this problem to be of much use.

So, like it or not, gentle reader, you are in as good a position as anyone to decide this issue for yourself. Let me try to be of assistance to you in this task, if you wish to undertake it, by telling you what the law and the lawyers of the Common Law world—of England, the United States, Canada, Australia, and a variety of other countries that have adopted our legal system—have decided.

In brief compass, I assure you, I can put you in as good a condition for making this decision as most of our judges, psychiatrists, and legal theorists.

What the lawyers call a confession and avoidance is necessary. It is my view that there should be no special defence of insanity to a criminal charge; the sole issue as to the accused's mind should be: did he, with a mind that was or was not "sick," intend or willfully risk this killing? If yes, he is responsible for it; if no, he is not. There are glosses on this theme that turn on the other justifications and defences to crime, but the broad principle has been stated. This is a minority view, though it has been officially espoused by the American Medical Association and by two state legislatures. Others think to the contrary.

Let me, then, as objectively as I can given my declared prejudice, advise you on the development of this defence of insanity, relate what authorities suggest it seeks to achieve, and comment on its definition and administration.

The story of Ake Dah is an ideal vehicle for this purpose, since it raises the most difficult issue of moral responsibility that there is in this area of the criminal law. Blair faced no easy task. He had to decide whether Ake Dah should be tried at all for the attempted murder of his son, whether it was necesssary to indict him and whether he was, in the technical legal sense, mentally "fit for trial." And if he were to be tried, Blair had to decide whether Ake Dah would have a valid defence of insanity to the criminal charge. Further, if Ake Dah were to succeed in that defence, Blair had to think through what Ake Dah's fate would then be.

Fitness for trial, the defence of insanity, the treatment of those found not guilty by reason of insanity—these are not easy questions; but their broad outlines can readily be conveyed.

An accused person may be "unfit for trial" because he is mentally ill or retarded at the time of trial and is, as a result, unable to understand the proceedings against him and to advise his counsel so that he may be fairly defended. In our adversary system of justice, this is an obviously necessary procedural step. It presents itself for decision much more frequently than does the defence of insanity, though it attracts much less public attention and jurisprudential concern. Persons found unfit for trial are held, in conditions of psychiatric treatment when they are available, either until they are fit for trial or, if not, until they are compulsorily committed to a mental hospital or released.

District Officer Blair had no such problem with Ake Dah. Though Ake Dah was, as Veraswami assured Blair, seriously mentally ill, he well understood his situation, knew what a trial was, could advise his counsel on his defence, and had no difficulties with time and place and surroundings. Undoubtedly, Ake Dah was fit for trial, should Blair decide to take him to trial.

The defence of insanity was another matter; here Blair confronted one of the most challenging questions in the criminal law.

Since the twelfth century, and through the assassination attempts on Prime Minister Sir Robert Peel in 1843 (which produced the M'Naughten Rules, the fountainhead of all contemporary Common Law defences of insanity) and on President Reagan in 1981 (which produced our present spread of modified M'Naughten Rules), the several defences of insanity to a criminal charge that have been applied or recommended have the following structure and incorporate the following ideas (though they express them differently):

- they speak to the accused's mental condition at the time of commission of the alleged crime (not to his fitness for trial or his fitness to be executed if he has killed);
- they require that he be seriously mentally ill or severely retarded;
- they ask: Did he or did he not, because of that mental illness or retardation, know what he was doing?
- and, they ask, if he did know what he was doing, did he, or did he not, because of that mental illness or retardation, know that what he was doing was wrong?

If either of the last two questions is answered in the negative by the trier of the facts of the case—judge, or judge and jury—then the accused should be found not guilty by reason of insanity.

To complete this outline, which conceals much dissension as to details: if the accused is found not guilty by reason of insanity, he will be committed to a mental hospital or to a prison to be held until it is safe to release him, which, in the case of one who has killed, tends to be about as long as or longer than he would have been held had he been sentenced to prison after conviction as a criminal.

To focus on the moral, psychiatric, legal, and philosophic issues we face, let us return to the story. Ake Dah was clearly fit for trial; equally clearly, at the time he attacked his son he knew what he was doing—he thought he was commanded to it by God. He also thought that, paradoxically, it was in the best interests of his son, since God often moves by paradox, as all who contemplate suffering in this world must agree. Ake Dah clearly understood the physical act and its likely terrestrial consequences, and he therefore, mentally ill or not, had no defence of insanity based on this part of the defence.

So the focus becomes precise. The determinative question is: Did Ake Dah in his mental condition know that what he was doing was *wrong*?

We will, I believe, penetrate to the heart of the matter if we can decide *why* there is a defence of insanity to a criminal charge. If that be clearly understood, then the moral issues should be laid bare. Unfortunately, there is not much guidance to be obtained from the leading authorities on this question. Here is what they say:

The American Law Institute: "What is involved specifically is the drawing of a line between the use of public agencies and public force to condemn the offender by conviction, with resultant sanctions in which there are inescapably a punitive ingredient (however constructive we may attempt to make the process of correction) and modes of disposition in which that ingredient is absent, even though restraint may be involved. To put the matter differently, the problem is to discriminate between the cases where a punitive-correctional disposition is appropriate and those in which a medical-custodial disposition is the only kind that the law should allow."

This seems to me an excessively wordy description of *what* is done and not at all an explanation of *why* it is done.

The English analogue to the American Law Institute's commentary on the defence of insanity was the statement of the Royal Commission on Capital Punishment: "It has for centuries been recognised that, if a person was, at the time of his unlawful act, mentally so disordered that it would be unreasonable to impute guilt to him, he ought not to be held liable to conviction and punishment under the criminal law. Views have changed and opinions have differed, as they differ now, about the standards to be applied in deciding whether an individual should be exempted from criminal responsibility for this reason; but the principle has been accepted without question."

This seems to me to say no more than that it has long been done and therefore should continue to be done—a very English proposition; it gives no guidance at all as to why it should be done.

Finally, the most attractive explanation of the rationale behind the defence of insanity was offered by Judge Bazelon in the *Durham* case, cited below (at page 876): "Our collective conscience does not allow punishment where it cannot impose blame."

If Judge Bazelon is correct, then it is hard to deny that Ake Dah should not be stigmatised as a criminal, should not be punished, and thus should have a defence of insanity. If he cannot be blamed, it is not easy to say that he has done "wrong," if that word be given an entirely subjective meaning. Should it be so interpreted? Let me offer a problem or two if you are inclined to such a subjective interpretation.

If Ake Dah has not done "wrong," as he sees it, does a political assassin, untroubled by mental illness but convinced of the virtue of his cause, do wrong? We deny him any defence in that situation, but the moral analysis seems very similar. Both Ake Dah and the political assassin are convinced that their views of what should be done are virtuous, serving the greater good. Each may have lingering doubts, but it is not easy to separate the two on that ground, and the strength of their doubts is impossible to quantify. On this analysis, the political assassin no more does "wrong" than does Ake Dah.

If Ake Dah did no wrong, as he saw it, does the slum-dwelling teenage child of a welfare mother—lacking a father, damaged beyond repair before he enters the first grade, denied educative and developmental opportunities, facing the bleakest of futures if he acts within the law—do "wrong" if he sees the commission of crime as the only escape for him and his mother from their grim and otherwise hopeless situation, and acts on that insight? After all, in the world as we know it, severe social adversity is much more frequently a cause of crime than is mental illness. Indeed, the likelihood is that, in the mass, mental illness is not a cause of crime; the mentally ill have no higher crime rate than those who are not mentally ill, unless you count as crimes homelessness, vagrancy, and other products of society's neglect of their basic needs.

So, if you decide that because of his mental illness Ake Dah did no wrong and therefore should be acquitted, you will either have to acquit those whose actions were motivated by political belief and extreme social adversity or you will have to distinguish those cases morally from mental illness cases.

Finally, if you decide that Ake Dah should be found not guilty on the ground of insanity, you will have to consider what should be done with him. Blair and Veraswami discuss this in the story and are perturbed that Ake Dah's situation in the mental hospital will be very little better, if any, than he would face in the prison were he convicted. Though the defence of insanity historically developed in large part as a means of allowing mentally ill killers to avoid the executioner, we now do not execute the mentally ill except in the most egregious of cases. Certainly, Ake Dah was not at risk of execution. So what would giving him that defence achieve? His lesser stigmatisation? But does it achieve even that? Would he not be seen as both bad and mad?

I gave my view of the wisest solution to all these problems in the story. I made Blair act as I would have acted. If you disagree, as well you might, settle the matter for yourself.

SELECTED BIBLIOGRAPHY

There is, of course, a huge literature on the defence of insanity. The selection hereunder is intended only to open up the details of the several debates for those who wish to pursue them.

A. *Case Law*

Durham v. United States, 214 F.2d 862 (D.C. Cir. 1954).
Jones v. United States, 463 U.S. 354 (1983).
M'Naughten's Case, 8 Eng. Rep. 718 (H.L. 1843).

B. *Books*

Goldstein, Abraham S., *The Insanity Defense*. New Haven: Yale University Press, 1967.
Morris, Norval, *Madness and the Criminal Law*. Chicago: University of Chicago Press, 1982.

C. *Articles*

"Incompetency to Stand Trial," 81 *Harv. L. Rev.* 454 (1967).
AMA Committee on Medicolegal Problems, "Insanity Defense in Criminal Trials and Limitation of Psychiatric Testimony," *Journal of the American Medical Association*, Vol. 251, No. 22, June 8, 1984, pp. 2967–81.

The Planter's Dream

"The nightmare suddenly became real," Taylor later told me. "The noise of the gun was no dream, though the dream had seemed very real. I found myself standing there, shotgun in hand, close to the bed, her head and chest blasted, lumps scattered everywhere."

Dr. Veraswami had arrived before me, called by Taylor's boy, Aka Thon, who then came shouting on to my bungalow. Veraswami had bicycled up the hill at top speed through a predawn rainstorm. When I got there, dawn was breaking. Taylor sat slumped forward in a chair on the verandah, Aka Thon squatting anxiously nearby, the details of the scene appearing like a developing daguerreotype as the light increased. They made no move as I hurried inside.

Dr. Veraswami was dressed in his usual crumpled white suit, but without shirt or socks, the suit probably pulled on over whatever he slept in and his feet pushed into his, also usual, black shoes. The effect was macabre, with blood now staining his sleeves and lapels.

I did not have to ask if she was dead. The stench was enough. And a shotgun fired at close quarters into a recumbent and plump female makes a gory mess. It was clear that there was nothing Veraswami could do as a doctor. But he busied himself energetically, cleaning the body and tidying the bed—to no purpose I could see except that somebody had to do it.

Veraswami was relieved to see me. "Terrible, terrible, it iss. You will know what to do, Mr. Blair."

I wished I did. They had not trained us sufficiently for such events. European planters were not expected to blow the top third off their Burmese mistresses. But the first thing to do seemed obvious: "Rest a bit, Dr. Veraswami. Have one of my cigarettes."

As we walked out to the verandah I asked Dr. Veraswami if he thought Taylor needed attention. "No. He iss best left sitting there, I think. He iss unhurt physically but, of course, most upset; though he wass able to speak sensibly enough to me when I arrived, to tell me what happened. He called it an accident. Let us leave him with Aka Thon for the time being."

I rolled cigarettes for Veraswami and myself. We stood awhile, silent, at the other end of the verandah from Taylor and Aka Thon. "When does his wife return, do you know?" I asked Dr. Veraswami.

"Taylor came to see me the day before yesterday—a medical consultation, you see. But it iss not improper for me to tell you that Mrs. Taylor, Mary I believe iss her name, iss returning next week."

"Is that why he did it?" I asked.

It was a stupid question, and Dr. Veraswami waved the hand that was not holding the cigarette about in a circular, rejecting motion. He seemed bewildered and exhausted. I let the silence lie.

The morning sun was now strong on the verandah, steam rising from the surrounding vegetation. Dr. Veraswami peered at his clothes in distaste, fiddled with the buttons on his wet, stained, and wrinkled jacket, and said he would go to his bungalow. He would, he added, send an ambulance for the body and call on Taylor later in the day. "He may need a sedative, you see, or something to calm him, quite likely. He iss, after all, my patient. Where will you hold him?"

The question shook me to action. There was obviously much for me to do—and promptly. I had best begin. I told Veraswami I would later advise him where Taylor was. I tried to thank Veraswami for what he had done, but that didn't make much sense; we each had our duties.

I sent Aka Thon for tea for Taylor and me, and pulled a chair up beside Taylor. I told him that from what I had seen, and what Aka Thon and Dr. Veraswami had told me, I would have to arrest him. He raised an anguished face: "Can it be done before she gets back?" The words were slurred and unclear, and at first I did not follow him. I thought he was talking of the dead girl.

"Can what be done?" I asked.

"Whatever you have to do." I understood: His wife's impending return was the capstone of his misery—he wanted everything settled before her return.

I had not thought what precisely had to be done and how long it would take. I told him I did not know the answer to his question and, as much for myself as for him, rehearsed what I thought should follow. "I will have to hold a preliminary enquiry and write up what are called depositions, signed statements, in effect, of what everyone who knows about her death can tell me about it. You can testify if you want to, but you don't have to. If I find she was killed, and not accidentally, then these depositions will be used at trial at Mandalay or Rangoon Quarter Sessions. You don't have to tell me anything now, but if you do it may be used as evidence. In the meantime, I suppose I have to put you under arrest."

He seemed to understand but responded only by latching on to my mention of an accident. "Blair, it *was* an accident. I didn't mean to kill her. You must know that. Why would I want to kill her? I saw that filthy Black on her and shot at him. She wouldn't have been badly hurt. And then I woke and . . . bloody lumps were scattered everywhere." He slumped forward in his chair, gulping loudly in his reluctance to cry before me.

There seemed no point in pressing Taylor for details. Later would do. So I did my best to calm him, to get him to drink some of the tea Aka Thon had brought, and then to help get him dressed and gather a few clothes and toilet articles together. We walked in silence the mile or so to the police barracks, where I had the sergeant give him a room. I told them both that Taylor must stay in the barracks, and I told the sergeant to have someone keep an eye on Taylor all the time. Taylor gave no hint of suicide, but I could not ignore the possibility. I told Taylor that Dr. Veraswami would come to see him later in the day and that he could send a message to anyone he wanted to call on him. I then went to the railway station to send a telegram reporting to headquarters at Mandalay.

It was midmorning before I got back to my office. Aka Thon was wait-ing: "Mr. Blair, Sir, should I go to her village?" Sickeningly, I realised the depth of my prejudice—the dead girl I had left to Dr. Veraswami. Taylor, I had attended to myself with reasonable consideration. But I had entirely neglected the dead girl's family and her village community.

Aka Thon and I peddled in the heat the few miles to the girl's village. He knew where to go and whom to see. It was less painful than I had feared. Her father was dead; her mother had already been told—by whom, I never discovered; the girl had no siblings. The mother was surrounded by weeping women and would not see me. There was little for me to do. Yes, Aka Thon assured me, it was understood that the mother should see Dr. Veraswami about the body and the funeral. And I pressed him to tell all who cared to listen that Taylor was under arrest and that there would be an enquiry into the death—but this seemed of no interest to anyone.

Intent on piecing together the story of the girl's death, I spent the later part of the afternoon at the barracks with Taylor. Police were about in the barracks, on and off duty; we could not conveniently talk in any of the public rooms. An office seemed too harshly official, so we talked in the white-painted, starkly furnished bedroom that had been allotted to Taylor. A policeman sat outside on the verandah, out of hearing, ensuring Taylor's safe custody as unobtrusively as he could.

Taylor needed prodding to talk. He said he wished to tell me about the killing and gave no hint of trying to conceal anything; but, equally, he volunteered nothing. He answered my questions and that was all. I had to keep at him, and I disliked it. He needed rest, not interrogation; but there was no doubt of my duty, given his repeatedly expressed willingness to tell me all he knew about the girl's death. It was miserable work. The fan, rotating weakly, did little to move the humid air. It seemed unusually hot even for those pre-monsoonal days. By early evening we were both exhausted. As I left, Taylor said he would take a nap. I later learned that he slept until midmorning of the next day—Veraswami's sedative was certainly not needed.

I went back to my bungalow, showered, and dined alone. After dinner I called on Dr. Veraswami. He saw me approaching and, bustling his wife and children off the verandah, greeted me in his high-pitched, fussing way with solicitudes for my comfort, my need for a cold beer, my tiredness, the heat and humidity and their effects on me, and how upset I must be by the morning's tragedy. I made the point that he had got up before me, had had a harder beginning to his day and probably harder work throughout; I didn't see why he should be offering sympathy to me. He chuckled as if my wit were profound and produced the nearly cold beer, settling his ample rump and a clean pair of baggy trousers onto the verandah rail beside the cane chair he had given to me.

"Have you talked with Mr. Taylor yet?" Veraswami asked.

I told him of my visit to Taylor that afternoon and that from what Taylor and Aka Thon had told me I believed I knew what happened—"not why it happened, but what happened."

"We are not likely, my young friend, ever really to know the whys of such sad matters. Glimpses of such truths from the corner of the eye are all we can hope for. But tell me what your diligent police probings detected."

I disliked Veraswami's mocking descriptions of what he knew I had had to do, but I did my best to summarise for him the facts as I saw them.

Only Aka Thon, the girl, and Taylor had been at Taylor's bungalow that night—it was not uncommon for Taylor to let the other servants off at night, particularly when the girl visited him. Taylor had come home from the Club about ten-thirty, and Aka Thon and the girl were already at the bungalow. Taylor had a few drinks but was not drunk. Aka Thon stayed in the servants' quarters. Taylor and the girl went straight to the bedroom. Aka Thon heard no sound of argument, indeed no sounds at all until the gun was fired.

Taylor reported an argument between him and the girl about the return of his wife and about how hard life was for the girl in the village, since so many knew she visited Taylor. Someone wished to marry her, but she must stop coming to Taylor's bungalow if she hoped to marry this man. Taylor had another whisky and began to taunt the girl—and torture himself—by pressing her for details of her relationship with the man in the village. In the end, he told her to do what she liked—stay or leave, come back or not; he didn't care. She cried. He comforted her. They went to bed. Later he went to sleep. Then came the dream. Then the killing.

All this, I told Dr. Veraswami, seemed precise, clear, and likely to be true. Veraswami agreed, saying he knew it was.

"But how can you know, Doctor? He reports a vivid dream. It matches his actions. He sticks to the details. Only he knows. There can be no confirmation or denial of the dream. Not even those Indian mystical perceptions, of which you tell me, let you see what a patient is in fact dreaming— only what he chooses to tell you."

"Not so, my young friend. Not mysticism at all, just facts I know and you don't. You forget, though I mentioned it to you, Taylor consulted me last week. And I think there wass then confirmation, a sort of confirmation in advance, anticipatory confirmation, issn't it, of hiss dream last night. But I am most troubled, most troubled indeed, whether or not I can tell you. After all, you see, medical confidences, Hippocratic oath, the patient's interests, issn't it?" And Veraswami lapsed into gestures and head wavings, and then added, "Would you tell me with your usual care and precision, if you will pleass, what he said about his dream? Perhaps I may be able to help you and him."

I did my best to summarise Taylor's story but made no effort to recapture his alternately halting and gushing words. Taylor had dreamt of the girl being fondled by a dark-skinned man of northern Indian colouration and build, certainly not a Burmese. He thought the man was a Pathan, of a tribe now in revolt in the Northwest of India. He laboured this matter of the man's origin; he could see the man plainly—well built, craggy features, turbaned, loose-robed. Taylor's anger and sense of helplessness grew; he could not move. Then the man and the girl were naked. He could see it all; the man was rampant. And they were on his bed in the bungalow, on Mary's bed. The squalor and shame grew, rage grew; rage and self-loathing overcame him. He struck at the figures on the bed, but his blows touched nothing and had no effect. The pair on the bed did not cease their wild copulation. The girl on the bed responded more than she ever had to Taylor. Taylor floated to the wardrobe, took his loaded shotgun from the top of the wardrobe, floated to the bedside, and shot the filthy Black in the back of his head. The shot woke Taylor. Aka Thon came rushing in. We knew the rest.

"So you see, Doctor, it all makes sense if you believe him. And if you don't, it seems such a crazy story to make up, such an unlikely and unhelpful way of getting rid of a native mistress." I could have swallowed the word "native" as I said it, but I had forgotten that Veraswami seemed even more colour conscious, almost colour obsessed, than my fellow Europeans at the Club.

Embarrassed, I pressed on: "At the Club, of course, they see it as a simple story: Taylor got drunk and told the girl to leave because his wife was returning and he was suffering alcoholic remorse. She tried to blackmail him but asked for too much money. He shot her—damn fool act on his part. Others vary the story slightly by adding that the so-called girl wasn't all that young and was getting on the portly and blowsy side, even for a native mistress (that damn word would not go away), and that Taylor was tired of her; though they admit he chose an excessive way of dismissing her. All emphatically agree that you have to be careful when you take up too long with these village tarts. A few say that Taylor must be mad, bonkers, insane; but the only reason they give is that anyone who kills as he did must be mad. So far as I can tell, he seems clearly to understand what he did and, within his dream, why he did it."

Dr. Veraswami was uncharacteristically silent, almost ill-mannered. Even his head and hands were still. I waited, drinking my beer.

"Can you tell me, Blair, from your legal studies at Mandalay, whether as a doctor I may tell you, a district officer, what my patient, Taylor, told me last week?"

"I don't know, Doctor. Certainly if it would help to stop a serious crime in the future you may and should tell me—I believe the law is clear on that. But about matters of past guilt or innocence, which I suppose we have here, I don't know. I have a telegram from Mandalay that a lawyer from the Police Service will be coming here tomorrow, and I suppose he will know. He may even ask you about it in court—I don't know."

Dr. Veraswami fell silent again for a time. Then he looked up at me with affection gleaming in his eyes behind the glasses that were always askew—a glance I had come to cherish: "Well, it iss to help Taylor. I will tell you. Ass you know, I trust you. If I have to forget it, you will be able to forget it too—we will help one another to forget." And grinning at his own wit he launched into what was a considerable confirmation either of Taylor's story or of the depth of cunning of his plan to kill the girl.

Taylor had consulted Veraswami the week before. He had been sleeping badly, finding himself unable to concentrate on anything for very long during the day, dozing off unexpectedly, drinking too much, generally feeling shaky and disturbed. And the night before he consulted Veraswami he had awakened (yes, the girl was with him—he had managed to tell Veraswami of her) to find himself brushing at the girl's face. Actually, she had wakened them both, startled by his pawing. He had dreamt that spiders had invaded his bungalow, many of them, large and loathsome, and that they were on the girl's face. He had fought them off.

Taylor had some memories of somnambulism in his youth—of being awakened by his parents as he apparently sleepwalked towards their bedroom. But nothing like this had occurred for over thirty years. Could Dr. Veraswami help him? Did Dr. Veraswami think that a nervous breakdown or mental illness threatened?

Dr. Veraswami did his best to reassure Taylor that he was not suffering from any serious mental illness, that he was not losing his mind—he had

rational reasons to be troubled and rational steps could be taken to minimise or eliminate his anxieties. Veraswami urged Taylor to try to regularise
his life in a variety of ways and to take a few days' holiday with his wife
when she returned from England; the doctor also prescribed and dispensed
a sedative and advised him to reduce his drinking. Veraswami now blamed
himself vaguely for not having done more, but I couldn't imagine what
more he should have done.

"You think, then, Doctor, that Taylor told me the truth; he didn't tell a
fake story to cover up a planned murder."

Veraswami nodded his head slowly, his eyes half-closed, in a manner
indicating that he unqualifiedly believed Taylor's story. He began to
explain about "fugue states," in which people act out their fantasies.
Veraswami had studied these conditions, particularly one called "running
amok," during his earlier medical training in India, and had even observed
a case of such a condition after his hospital residency when he served for a
short time on a freighter. A stoker, overcome by the heat in the boiler
room while the ship was steaming through the Red Sea, had "run amok"—
a well-known, though rare, form of behaviour in some Malayan villages.
"To run amok" had become a popular phrase, its origin rarely understood.
The stoker had come rushing up from the laddered purgatory of the boiler
room onto an upper deck, wielding his shovel. With it he struck the head
of an officer who chanced to be in his path, doing him no lasting injury,
and then jumped overboard and drowned, still clutching the shovel. Dr.
Veraswami thought that the stoker was not conscious of what he was
doing. Those who run amok in this way rarely remember anything of what
they have done when they come to their senses. Certainly, he said, some
actions of those under hypnosis may be completely repressed. The same is
true for acts done by those in epileptic fits. By contrast, somnambulists
who act out their dreams, about whom Dr. Veraswami had read when he
was interested in the phenomenon of running amok, do remember their
dreams when they wake from the somnambulist condition.

So Taylor's story blended well with what is known about these conditions—he was most unlikely to have made it up.

"If we believe Mr. Taylor," Dr. Veraswami asked, "what of hiss guilt? Did
he murder the girl? Did he murder the dreamlike Pathan? Can you murder
someone who issn't there? Or murder someone lying under someone who
issn't there?"

"For the life of me, I don't know," I replied. "Do you think they worry
about questions like that at the Mandalay Police Training School? Things
there were simpler, not as complicated as fugue states, somnambulists, and
running amok. So let me ask you the questions they would have advised
me to ask. Do you think Taylor would have killed her if he had not had a
few drinks at the Club—I still don't know how many—and then a last
whisky at his bungalow?"

Dr. Veraswami allowed that probably the girl would still be alive if
Taylor had been, "ass you say it, 'on the water wagon.' But surely to be con-

victed of murder and, I suppose, executed, iss a considerable punishment, a verry considerable punishment indeed, for not being entirely sober. Or even for having what you were pleased to call a 'native mistress' and not being always entirely sober. Few of your European colleagues would escape the hangman! That cannot be right. Iss Taylor any different from the rest?"

Nettled by Veraswami's deferred reference to my use of "native mistress," I responded brusquely. "Of course he's different, Veraswami. He killed her."

"So he did; but it iss hard to see how he can be responsible for hiss dreams. Are you? To be sure, you don't act them out—I assume not; I hope not—but what iss he to do? He had no idea at all he would injure her that night. I am glad it iss your decision, not mine."

The telegram from Mandalay had advised that Arthur Grantham would arrive in Moulmein on the Wednesday evening ferry. Grantham was attached to the Legal Section of the Burma Police. Mandalay apparently did not trust me to run the preliminary hearing into a murder charge without legal advice. I did not resent this; I needed the help.

Presumably Grantham would interrogate the witnesses at the preliminary hearing, leaving me to preside and to see that the depositions were transcribed in a reasonably accurate manner. It certainly would make my task easier.

I set out to meet Grantham early, well before the ferry was due, so that I could go to the railway station en route to send a telegram to Mrs. Taylor, who was aboard ship somewhere between Colombo and Rangoon. Taylor had given, it seemed to me, more thought to softening the blow to his wife than to his own situation. He had talked to me more about this than about the killing, on which he seemed to think he had said all that he could say or indeed that anybody could say. The cable he asked me to send to her read:

SERVANT KILLED IN GUN ACCIDENT STOP IMPORTANT YOU STAY RANGOON STOP WILL JOIN YOU THERE STOP DO NOT RETURN MOULMEIN STOP SEE YOU SOON LOVE PHILLIP.

When he asked me to send this cable I had commented that Mrs. Taylor could not believe the first word for long. He knew that, he said, but he could not stand the thought of how she would be received in Moulmein—the false sympathy, the cloying, effusive comforting, such a misery for her. He wanted to tell her about it himself, though he did not know how he would. He appreciated that in Rangoon, too, such is the capacity of scandal to spread that his wife would soon be told of more ample facts than were revealed in his cable, but he thought it worth the risk to try to lessen the hurt to her in this way. So I sent the cable.

The ferry was on time. Grantham was younger and of more junior rank than I had anticipated. Like me, he was a "two-pipper" assistant police magistrate. He was fresh from Gray's Inn, after a classics degree at Cambridge, with scant courtroom experience but some knowledge of legal theory. I was glad to see him and told him so, going beyond the figure of speech to welcome him. He seemed pleased, but embarrassed.

He later told me he had thought he was coming to Moulmein as a young interloper, wet behind the ears, to advise an experienced and sage police magistrate, in his phrase, "how to suck eggs." My obvious uncertainty and appreciation of his assistance had cheered him greatly. But he had found it difficult—he always found it difficult—to express himself with any warmth on such matters. He knew he was on the taciturn side, and indeed he was, but there was not much he could do about it. He always rehearsed inside himself what he wished to say, so that by the time he was sufficiently confident of whatever it was, the moment had passed and there was no point in saying it. He agreed that this did not make for an easy conversational style and, daringly for him, allowed that I might suffer from a mild form of the same malady—which was true.

There was a further odd embarrassment between us which inhibited our first meeting: We looked rather alike. Of course we were wearing the same uniform and were of similar age, but there was more to it. He was an ungainly figure, unusually tall and of lean build, with feet and hands marginally but perceptibly oversized, of slightly stooped posture, with straight dark hair cut quite short—all physical qualities I shared without enthusiasm for any of them.

His features were more regular than mine but of the same general balance or, rather, imbalance. He sported a thin moustache, while I was clean shaven—perhaps I should try a moustache! Our similarity of appearance did not pass unnoticed at the Club and provided the butt, I suspected, of many laboured jokes. Putting us together did not add to the presence of each separately; we both knew this immediately and well.

After a day or two, with these realities recognised between us and circuitously discussed, our early embarrassments turned to the beginnings of a bond of friendship which, sad to say, did not survive the Taylor case. It has been a disappointment to me. As I think about it, I realise I came closer to forming a lasting bond with Grantham than with anyone, other than Veraswami, since the transient ties of childhood and adolescent friendships. Had we met other than through the Taylor case, perhaps it would have been different. The fault must be mine; certainly Grantham has friends, as do most of my contemporaries, whereas I do not. And this is not because I wish it so.

Grantham did fail, it still seems to me, in the Taylor case, but not in anything he did or said to others. It was how he felt about it and talked to me about it that irked me. But others would say he acted at least as effectively and honourably as I did. All that was in the future, however.

On the evening of Grantham's arrival in Moulmein I had a horse-drawn personnel cart waiting at the ferry landing for him, and with few words passing between us I saw him to the Club, where I had reserved a room for him, and arranged to join him later for dinner.

Grantham listened determinedly, almost immobile, giving little help to my effort to tell him all I knew of Taylor, his wife, Aka Thon, and the dead girl. He interrupted me only to push me to confirm that neither Veraswami nor I thought Taylor was in any way mentally disordered, that Taylor impressed everyone as a sensible, if somewhat stolid, chap—no one saw any fires of mental illness below his dull exterior. Grantham seemed regretful of this: "It would," he said, "be such an easy out."

Grantham was not forthcoming with information on how the law bore on the facts I had recounted. His ruminative style—he didn't actually move his jaws laterally as does a cow chewing the cud, but I kept expecting it—did not make for an easy extraction of information, and there was a good deal I wanted to know. What it amounted to, in sum, was this: Was Taylor guilty if his story was true?

Grantham said that there was some law on the matter, a few cases, but that they were not dispositive. He stressed that we didn't have to decide whether or not Taylor was guilty, which I knew. After some uncertain but determined prodding by me, he agreed that though we would not have to decide the matter, how he and I approached the preliminary hearing might help either to condemn or to spare Taylor, and that it did no harm for me, with his help, to try to form an opinion about Taylor's guilt even though my duties did not require me to do so.

There was no doubt that Grantham was exceedingly difficult to talk with at our early meetings—a hippopotamus would have been of lighter conversational foot. But I was able to wrench a few lines of cases and threads of legal analysis from him.

Apparently the law does not hold one responsible for an act of which one is unconscious. This is not a defence of insanity—there is simply no criminal guilt. As examples, Grantham offered an epileptic giving a blow while in a *grand mal*, or a person fainting and falling on someone—neither would be a criminal assault, no matter what the injury.

Grantham could call to mind no case directly concerned with somnambulist acts and would not risk concluding that they were precisely like the acts of an epileptic or of a person who fainted. There were differences, he thought; and after all, even if one completely believed his story, Taylor had a motive for what he had done, unlike the epileptic and the person who fainted, who did not choose their victims.

I pointed out that Taylor said he hadn't chosen his victim—his "victim" was the virile Pathan. Grantham's jaws moved but no words came.

Another difference Grantham suggested was that the epileptic and the person who fainted did not later remember what had happened, whereas in a way, a clouded sort of way, Taylor did. Grantham did not know, in his phrase, "which way that cut."

The case nearest to Taylor's that Grantham knew of concerned a Londoner who was working with his young son in a second-story room overlooking a river. The son was painting the windowsill, the father doing some carpentry work. Without warning, the father struck the boy on the side of the head with a mallet. The boy fell in the river. Dazed but not seriously injured, the boy scrambled from the river and went to the police station for help, saying, "Come quickly. Something has gone wrong with Dad." He was right. The father had a tumor developing on his brain. The father was acquitted of assault with intent to kill and of assault with intent to inflict grievous bodily harm—since he lacked those intents. He was, however, convicted of simple assault. Grantham allowed himself the criticism, lengthy for him, that it was "an unimaginative, silly decision." Why this was so eluded me.

Grantham seemed to think it might be important to try to determine whether Taylor could have predicted any danger to the girl if he drank before having her share his bed. The general line of argument, as I understood it, was that Taylor, if his story were believed, might be guilty not of murder but of involuntary manslaughter—not intending to kill but doing something knowingly that risked another's life and that resulted in a killing, particularly if the something was illegal or immoral. And I suppose Taylor's acts could not be regarded as exemplars of chaste and sober virtue. Grantham gave as an example of this the manslaughter convictions of drunken mothers who unintentionally overlie and kill their infant children.

I latched onto this compromise. It seemed a wonderful way out. Grantham ceased his rumination long enough to urge me to be less confident about it; it would please no one except "uncertain chaps like you."

"Well then," I offered hesitatingly, "why not persuade Taylor to plead temporary insanity? Then, brief treatment in the mental hospital in Rangoon—if it's necessary to commit him at all. After all," I said, struggling for a lighter touch in our burdensome dialogue, "he cured himself by killing her."

Grantham apparently found this distasteful, certainly unamusing; but he did abandon his taciturn mode long enough brusquely to squash my suggestion. "It is typical of you, Blair, another weak compromise. Dr. Veraswami saw Taylor before and after the killing. He diagnosed no mental illness, certainly no psychosis. In the language of the law you must have studied in Mandalay, Taylor did not suffer from a defect of reason from disease of the mind. It won't wash."

Though relentlessly patronising of my ideas, Grantham neither exposed his own nor expressed what must have been his own uncertainties. I tired of this one-sided exchange. He made me feel a fool.

I arranged for Grantham to visit Taylor the next day and left him and his sparkling wit to the care of the few members of the Club who were still

about. They would, I thought, like him about as much as they liked me.
The thought cheered me.

Later in the week, Grantham and I together interviewed Taylor at the
police barracks. Taylor complained of nothing, asked for nothing, replied
when spoken to but volunteered nothing. Grantham urged him to ask that
the preliminary hearing be delayed until he had a lawyer to represent him.
Taylor refused. "I've told you both the truth. No lawyer can make it better.
Can't we get this over and let me be taken to Rangoon?"

Grantham stressed that though he would try to be as fair as possible at
the hearing, and knew I would, there was much a lawyer could do for
Taylor which might be important later at trial, if he were committed for
trial; but Taylor would pay no heed to this. "You know the facts. Whatever
you decide, my life is ruined. Just help me get away from here."

We arranged to hold the preliminary hearing at the barracks. Grantham
began to list those he would call to give evidence. A message came to me
from Veraswami inviting me and Grantham, "if he would be so very kind
as to accompany you," to come to dinner that night. We accepted.

Veraswami had obviously gone to a great deal of trouble. I had never
before dined at his home. His wife and children were nowhere to be seen,
but there seemed to be extra servants, and we were presented with an
excessive and complicated Indian dinner. Veraswami was garrulous
throughout, the overly considerate host, chatting about the food, pressing
the chutneys on us, asking what we might now want, calling for more beer,
pursuing a variety of painfully polite inconsequentialities. Grantham's taci-
turnity became Trappist under this verbal barrage. I did my best to play the
role of a graceful guest. But I was glad when dinner was over and we could
go out to the verandah to discuss what Veraswami obviously didn't want to
discuss at dinner, perhaps because of the servants, perhaps from a misguided sense of politeness.

That day, Veraswami told us, accompanied by Aka Thon to help him as
interpreter, he had gone to the girl's village and had talked to the girl's
mother. There would be a cremation ceremony in the village tomorrow.
Veraswami saw no reason not to release the body—the cause and time of
death were obvious; there was no reason for an autopsy, "an exercise I have
never greatly enjoyed."

Grantham enquired whether the mother would be likely to behave
calmly at the preliminary hearing if he decided to take her deposition and
to call her. Veraswami was unsure but doubted she would be a helpful witness, not because he thought her overcome by grief but because she might

think she ought "to rant, to rave, to scream, to wail about her loss." His reasons for thinking this surprised me: She does not worry at all what happens to Taylor. Like the rest of the village she does not believe he will be punished. But she hopes that she can get compensation from Taylor, or from the company he works for, or from the government. "They took her daughter from her; she should be paid. She wass, I am sure, getting some of the money Taylor gave the girl, and she hoped for much more; the loss of the money and of the hope were grievous, quite grievous to her. She will scream loud and long for that, believe me, and keep wailing on and on and on, Mr. Grantham."

We had dined early, and it was pleasant on the verandah. Having told us of his trip to the village, Veraswami seemed less oppressed by the burdens of hospitality. Grantham had relaxed perceptibly as the evening proceeded and now seemed almost at ease. With the oval bucket of beer and ice beside him, Veraswami beamed at us: "This iss a very delicate matter for you both. I hear it iss much discussed at the Club. Nothing else obtrudes, I am told. If I am not presumptuous, my friends, what should happen?"

"He will be charged with murder, I suppose, and tried at Mandalay or Rangoon Quarter Sessions," Grantham offered, unhelpfully, I thought.

"Oh, that I know, Mr. Grantham, but what do you think iss the correct final result? If I am not again being presumptuous. . . ."

Grantham gave no reply.

Opening both palms in an outward, enquiring gesture, Veraswami turned to me. So I tried: "Well, if we believe everything Taylor told us, and it does seem to hang together and to agree with what you said about fugue states, Dr. Veraswami, then I think Taylor is not a murderer. He, Taylor, awake Taylor, thinking Taylor, did not kill her. It is as if he were possessed, as if he were controlled by someone else; but the someone else, the possessor, is sleeping Taylor. We can't hang him for his dreams or even for acting them out. So I think a suggestion of yours, Grantham, is right: Taylor knew he was unwell, knew he should not drink, did so, and as a result killed the girl. He has been reckless. He should be convicted of manslaughter and given a short prison punishment."

I rarely produced such rounded arguments, and Grantham and Veraswami both looked surprised. But with a smile to one another, a linkage I was pleased to see, they joined in attacking my conclusions, but from different directions.

Grantham thought that on Taylor's story, drinking or not, he could hardly be expected to forsee any risk to the girl. He might see that he was getting himself into a psychologically depressed or disturbed condition, but surely not that this might injure the girl.

I reminded Grantham of Taylor's spider dream, which I had, with Veraswami's permission, previously told him about. "Surely, from that dream, he should have realised there was some risk to the girl." Grantham said that that dream was quite different. Taylor was protecting the girl then.

"So he was, in a way, on Sunday night. Protecting her from the Indian lover," I said.

Grantham thought that was farfetched; while he was awake Taylor could surely not foresee any risk to the girl from his protecting her in a dream he had not then had.

Veraswami had started pacing about on the verandah as our talk turned to the details of Taylor's dreams. He seemed agitated. With an odd gesture, a half-raised left hand like a hesitant policeman stopping an oncoming car, he turned to Grantham and myself: "Perhaps that iss what this iss all about—racial prejudice. May we talk about it?" And, not stopping for our obvious assent, with little steps to and fro before us, the sibilant words began bouncing from him in rapid flow. "Have you thought, my friends" (it astonished me that he had so swiftly thus categorised Grantham), "what enormous trouble European ladies go to in order not to consult me? For minor and imagined medical ailments they make the fatiguing journey to Rangoon rather than come to me. They know I did an English residency, and they know that only inexperienced or alcoholic European doctors will work in Burma. So why iss it? Of course, I am black and likely to leap on them in excessive venery if they reveal their flesh to me. It iss madness; they are mostly quite unattractive. You must understand how deep these feelings run.

"Now suppose it had been Mrs. Taylor that Taylor had killed. All else the same—the same dream, the same Pathan lover on top of her. And suppose Taylor's story were believed, as we believe him. Would not everyone feel the deepest sympathy for him? Would you not hold the preliminary hearing with great circumspection and kindness to him and find that the death was accidental? I think you would. So they would at the Club. In the village they would not care—one less European to put up with." And Veraswami stopped, embarrassed after such an aggressive outburst.

Grantham was quite moved. "Perhaps you're right, Dr. Veraswami. Perhaps we are influenced by some sort of reverse racial sentiment. As I understand you, you are suggesting that we think Taylor should be punished, as a murderer or a manslaughterer, one or the other, because he had a native mistress, drank too much, couldn't behave with the gentlemanly confidentiality such things require, and has had the bad luck, entirely without malice, to kill someone as a part of this complexity of immoral acts."

"Yes, yes, exactly!" Veraswami's hands flew up in agreement. "It must be so. Many Europeans here do not cleave unqualifiedly to their lady wives. Many drink. Many are fond of Burmese girls and vigourously and frequently express their affection. This iss true, too," with a knowing glance at me, "even of the unmarried here. But they are at risk, grave risk, that their crossing the colour line will become a public scandal—even if the event which causes the scandal iss not their fault. They are subject to being blackmailed, like poor Flory—you will remember him, Mr. Blair—and if it becomes a public matter they are lost. Taylor's dream made it a public matter. He iss lost; neither of you can do anything for him. The law does not matter. What I told you, Mr. Blair, about running amok, fugue states, and somnambulism does not matter. Taylor iss lost." And Veraswami's right arm came down like a cleaver on a block, severing head from shoulders.

"It iss strange indeed, my friends, that the respective colours of the penis and its receptacle should be so important."

Later that week, again in the early evening on Dr. Veraswami's veran-dah, but this time without Grantham, Veraswami was struggling with the metal levers holding the rubber-ringed ceramic stopper in the top of a bot-tle of Watney's beer. It was a tight fit, stubborn to move, so that he had to press both black thumbs up and under the ring to release the levers that held the top. I had watched him at minor surgery and remained perplexed how such deftness could reside in the same hands that were wrestling so clumsily with a beer bottle stopper. In the result, the ring gave suddenly, and the bottle, being by now quite shaken, squirted foam onto his pants. He apologised to me and to himself—to me, I don't know what for—and when he had forgiven himself on the ground that it didn't matter, we each settled back with a slightly flat, nearly cool beer.

The Taylor topic would not go away, and soon I was burdening Veraswami with my doubts: "What in Heaven's name led Taylor to make such a fool of himself with the girl? I don't mean so much the shooting—I think I begin to understand that—but the whole mess he was in with her, and with his wife returning, all the servants except Aka Thon sent away, the arguments, all the squalor of an affair with someone he can hardly have admired. I saw her—I suppose you did too—before he shot her; she was no beauty. And this jealousy of the mysterious Pathan. Why didn't he just send her away and let Aka Thon bring him any other village girl, if that's what he wanted?"

Dr. Veraswami seemed in no hurry to reply to my convoluted questions. He mopped some more at his pants, turned to speak, thought better of it apparently, and then drifted off into comments on his own youth. "I wass married when I wass seventeen, before I even thought of becoming a doc-tor. An arranged marriage, I think you call it. I had no other woman until she died. Then I would patronise prostitutes occasionally, but medical school cured me of them, and then I married my present wife. And here I am, a mere child in matters of love and jealousy, though I am very fond of and grateful to my wife. But what your Shakespeare had Othello feel, I don't feel. However, I watch others, particularly your English colleagues here in Moulmein, and I see that many of them get themselves involved beyond their wishes with one another's wives or with Burmese ladies. They surely know better than to ruin their careers, either in government service or in a trading company, but they still risk it. So, I conclude, ass I told you before, that the gonads are verry powerful; and they affect passion and sen-timent ass well ass desire."

I remonstrated with Veraswami. Though a quick flirtation or a passing affair may be slightly risky, if it were kept light and transient everyone understood, and there was rarely any serious threat to anyone. If affairs of passion were so handled, tragedies like the dead girl and Taylor would not happen.

Dr. Veraswami seemed to become—could it be?—annoyed with me. He paced about, settling his ample bottom here, then there, on the balustrade, glancing at me querulously. "Blair, my friend, you tell me important things about yourself which bind our friendship, and I am glad of that, believe me, verry verry glad, but then you talk ass if I didn't know them. You have told me of some occurrences in your own life that should help you understand Taylor's folly, have you not?"

I was unsure of what he referred to—perhaps lasting affairs with Burmese girls; but I had enjoyed no such relationships. Indeed, I could not even remember discussing any such things with Dr. Veraswami, and said so.

His petulance seemed to increase but he controlled it. He would never be openly annoyed with me, though he was also never, so far as I knew, withdrawn or secretive. But communication, as now, often had to be by indirection. "Do you remember the poem you showed me? I remember it. You let me write it down. I will get it now." And he bustled off the verandah towards his study.

I did recall a piece of doggerel I had played with. Dr. Veraswami had insisted it had promise. I doubted it. It was certainly meant in fun and seemed somewhat remote from the Taylor killing.

Waving a paper aloft like a winning race ticket, Dr. Veraswami returned. "Let me read it to you. You will see what I mean." He stopped close to my chair, quite still, and read what a few months earlier I had facetiously called "Romance." In his Indian, sibilant, highly inflected voice, it sounded a great deal better than I thought it would when I had written it:

> When I was young and had no sense
> In far-off Mandalay,
> I lost my heart to a Burmese girl
> As lovely as the day.

> Her skin was gold, her hair was jet,
> Her teeth were ivory;
> I said "For twenty silver pieces,
> Maiden, sleep with me."

> She looked at me, so pure, so sad,
> The loveliest thing alive,
> And in her lisping, virgin voice
> Stood out for twenty-five.

I knew the punch line, of course, but Veraswami had read it with such exaggerated inflection that I laughed out loud. He looked even more disapproving. "My friend, even though you are an eminent police magistrate, do not think your servants are silent about your life. I know you occasionally have Burmese ladies brought to your bungalow, and some more than once." Suddenly I realised he was equating me with Taylor—and I resented it.

"Dr. Veraswami: Occasionally to patronise Burmese prostitutes is one thing; to become involved to the point of murderous jealousy is quite another. Surely Taylor's situation is very far removed from what you say you know about me—and I confess to resenting being spied upon."

Dr. Veraswami did his Indian imitation of a blush, revealed more by jerky arm-waving than by much change in skin colouration. "My friend, I am not saying they are the same. Only that you know the delights of Burmese ladies and also that you have some experience of jealousy, do you not? Did you not tell me of Miss Buddicom and what you called your 'calf love' for her? Surely you must have been jealous of others if you loved her and she felt no more than friendship for you?"

Veraswami was right about the village girls, but wrong about Janice Buddicom. Nevertheless, he had struck home. In Mandalay I had been involved in an affair with the wife of one of our training officers. I am sure I was neither her first extramarital adventure nor her last, but that realisation in no way diminished the hurt that followed. A painful scene came back to me. . . . A monsoon threatened, but I was lurking beside the path to her bungalow, waiting for her husband to leave for the Club. Given the threatening weather, he might stay home. And he might already have guessed that I—or someone—was hanging about outside his house. I did not fancy my jungle skills—one of his servants might well have seen me— and yet I stayed. He held my career in his hands. So did chance. It was absurd. To turn and walk away firmly along the path meant complete safety. To stay, to hide, perhaps to be discovered, could mean years of turbulence and many hidden obstacles to my career. And for what? I didn't even like her. She was open about sex, like the Burmese prostitutes, and no one else had ever wanted me in that way—or at least, I never knew it if they had. I hated her husband—and probably her too—yet I stayed, and he came out. He saw me and shouted at me to come out of hiding, and on the path he angrily told me to clear out and never to hang around his wife again—that he would mistake me for a burglar and shoot me if I did. I cringed away, with nothing sensible to say. . . . Curiously, he treated me fairly, even in the training course, though I hated and feared him. Even more ridiculously, I went back to her on several occasions, until she tired of my snivelling attitude in the whole affair and told me it would be better for her and for me if we did not again meet, except as acquaintances when we had to attend official parties.

So, yes, Veraswami was right in his perception but wrong about the occasions he mentioned—I had indeed known what it was like to make a fool of myself over someone I didn't even like, to be fiercely jealous of the sexual behaviour of one I didn't love but merely wanted. I had been where

Taylor had found himself, I suppose. I hated having been there; perhaps
that was why I hated the whole Taylor case.

When I reached my bungalow that night, a note awaited me from
Grantham. He had been directed to report to regional headquarters at
Mandalay on one aspect of the Taylor case and thought I should see what
he had written. He would send it off the next morning, subject to any suggestions I might have.

His report combined overconfidence with simulated modesty of opinion, it seemed to me, but there was certainly nothing of substance in it to
which I could or did take exception. Grantham had presented it as a
memorandum, with paragraphs numbered as we had been taught to do at
our respective training schools, but I noted that he did not always bother,
as he had been instructed, to confine one paragraph to one topic.
Grantham liked to appear to conform; I increasingly noticed that he often
did not do so in fact.

> 1. You requested an immediate report on one aspect of the Taylor
> matter not mentioned in my earlier memorandum—the question of
> Taylor's mental state at the time of the killing and, in particular, "the
> likelihood of his pleading and being found not guilty by reason of
> insanity."
> 2. Here in Moulmein, the general comment is that "he must have
> been mad to kill the girl," and it seems likely to me that that will
> remain the popular opinion. I cannot assess its validity as a proposition
> of medical science, but I doubt that he was insane at the time of the
> killing as a matter of law.
> 3. There is no alienist in Moulmein. The medical superintendent of
> the local hospital, a Dr. Veraswami, has had some training in England
> as well as in India and also some experience in treating mental illness.
> He tells me, and it accords with everything I have learned about this
> killing, that Taylor suffers from no diagnosable mental illness. Prior to
> the killing, no one had ever thought such a thing of Taylor.
> 4. Some time before he killed the Burmese girl, Taylor had consult-
> ed Dr. Veraswami about being upset, troubled, and anxious, and sleep-
> ing poorly; but Dr. Veraswami tells me that Taylor always had a clear
> and realistic grasp of his circumstances, and, by my own observation,
> he still does.
> 5. If mental illness is to be defined as being out of touch with reali-
> ty, then only during the dream (if one believes his story), concerning
> which I earlier reported, was he so removed from clear understanding
> of the objective facts of his surroundings. Nor did he suffer any sense
> of persecution—no partial insanity, according to Dr. Veraswami; and
> he gives no hint of such now.
> 6. If mental illness is to be defined as a statistical abnormality of

mind and behaviour, then, of course, if one believes his story, Taylor's somnambulist acting out of his dream is a gross abnormality; but that would make nonsense of any defence of insanity. Dr. Veraswami says that such a condition would not be regarded in medicine as "mental illness"; certainly it would be no ground for his compulsory detention in a mental asylum until the "disease" is "cured" under our law on civil commitment to asylums.

7. Despite paragraph 6, it may not be difficult for the defence to find a doctor in Burma who will give evidence at the trial that Taylor was mentally ill and that that is why he dreamed as he did and acted as he did. A jury, because of the popular belief that he would not have done it unless he was mad, may incline to believe such testimony, false though it is. I appreciate that such a result may be extremely convenient, but it seems to me to be our duty to resist it.

8. Taylor resents and repudiates the suggestion that he was or is mad. He insists he has told me the whole truth. I believe him. He says it could happen to anyone who got himself into such a hopeless situation as he did. He rejects any suggestion that a defence of insanity may be advanced on his behalf—he prefers to see himself as wicked and stupid rather than mad. As you know, he has no defence counsel here and reiterates that he does not wish for such assistance; but when he has counsel in Mandalay these attitudes may change.

9. If one believes Taylor's story, then, in my view, as the law stands, he has no defence of insanity to a criminal charge. If he were thought of as responsible for his conduct in his sleep, then on his own statement he knew what he was doing—shooting the man above the Burmese girl. On his own story, that is a crime, a "wrong" in law and morality; at the least, taking his view, he would be guilty of manslaughter. And further, in my view, he was not at the time of the killing "suffering a defect of reason from disease of the mind," as that phrase has been interpreted and applied since its adumbration in the House of Lords in the case of M'Naughten and its adoption into the criminal law we apply in this country.

10. As I suggested in earlier written reports and will develop in detail when I report to you in Mandalay, my present opinion is that though Taylor has no valid defence of insanity in respect of his alleged crime, he cannot—for other reasons—be convicted. I see the disadvantage in this position. If found insane he could be held in an asylum until any public anxiety is assuaged, whereas if he is acquitted he must be released immediately, giving, perhaps, an appearance of the administration's excessive leniency towards crimes against natives by Europeans; but, with some hesitation, I think that is the law.

11. Please advise me if you wish me to expand on any of the points in this memorandum. I shall try to do so, although I suspect that my insecurity in these medicolegal problems is already all too apparent.

Grantham and I seemed equally to dislike the Club, so that for the few days he was in Moulmein we would, apart from the evening Dr. Veraswami invited us to dinner, tend to drift after dinner towards Dr. Veraswami's bungalow for our evening talks. In the small European community of Moulmein this was neither unnoticed nor uncriticised. But, since we were both seen as "stuck-up bores," our preferences for company, if resented, were not regretted.

We both *were* bores; that was another sad similarity between us. We were not, of course, bores of the blustering, verbose, overbearing sub-species—which is the most deadly form—but of the hesitant, unsure, diffi-cult-to-talk-to type. But undeniably bores. To drag an opinion from Grantham on the Taylor matter, which fascinated us both, was far from easy, and I suspect he found me equally taciturn. Like so many others of our class and training, we were often paralysed in word and deed by the fear that we might make fools of ourselves. But in Veraswami's presence, we could talk freely not only to him but also to one another—he unlocked the doors of our reticence.

One evening at Veraswami's bungalow the reason for our openness with one another in his presence struck me—and I was ashamed: colour preju-dice, of course. No matter what we said or did, we were, it seems, sure of our superiority to Veraswami and had no need to protect our precious selves as we thought we did with others present and even when alone with each other. When we were together with Veraswami at his bungalow, we could talk and laugh with one another as well as with Dr. Veraswami, secure in the knowledge of our shared and unfailing inherent advantage. Yet, in every way he was our superior—in education, skill, experience, character, and sensitivity—and we knew it.

So this was why I had found so many reasons to visit his bungalow dur-ing my months in Moulmein! What a swinish motive! No, that is not fair: how weak, vacillating, and unsure of myself I must be—to be able to be open and direct only with one whom I see, for no possibly acceptable rea-son, as an inferior. Perhaps this is why the English lower middle class so relishes India—it is not the servants or the comforts, but rather the per-vading sense of their own greater worth vis-à-vis the lesser coloured breeds around them. At "home" the working class took less and less kindly to condescension, but the natives of the Raj at least pretended to accept it.

Grantham wrenched me back to civility. "Blair, you drift off. What troubles you? You look as if that beef at the Club sits heavily—it wasn't that bad."

I decided to risk my thoughts, even those on colour prejudice, with them both. "Dr. Veraswami, forgive me. I was thinking why Grantham and I can talk so easily to you about Taylor and that poor girl. You know, with others, even with each other, we mumble, are silent, and turn away from our ignorance. But with you . . .," and I opened my palms in a poor imita-tion of his expansive Indian gesture.

Dr. Veraswami seemed pleased, and then the rounded smile left his face as understanding came. "Tell uss why, my young friend."

There seemed no avoidance. "Because you are coloured." I blushed fiercely, could feel it, and Grantham started making throat-clearing noises to signify a verbally crippling mixture of embarrassment and dissent. But it suddenly seemed important to me to press on. "I'm right, aren't I, Dr. Veraswami? You know more than we; you have proved your value to yourself and to others. If you were white we would not dare to talk so freely to you as we do. It would be 'Yes Sir; No Sir.' We might think you either an old fool or a wise and sound man of experience, but in either case we couldn't talk to you as we do. But you are an educated Indian; we can talk openly with you on every topic except this one that I am gassing on about now, and, do forgive me, but I'm right, aren't I?"

Veraswami had begun his pacing about the verandah and his jerky hand-waving, anxious either to interrupt me or certainly to get in on my first pause. Yet when I did stop he was silent and stood immobile for a moment. "Of course, Blair, you are right. It iss most unusual, most unusual indeed, for one of your age and background to see it. I do commend you, my friend. You would think they would let me into the Club to help their conversation by my pigmentation—if what you tell me about the talk there iss true. But I think there iss even more to this ease you and your lawyer friend feel in my company." And he beamed with unaffected joy on Grantham, who seemed to be overcoming the more acute pains of embarrassment he had suffered earlier. "Have you thought that the poor girl may have had the same effect on Taylor, issn't it? In another way, if you take my meaning, do you see?"

I didn't then understand what he was talking about, nor, apparently, did Grantham. But my earlier directness with Veraswami had allowed him to give us another view of Taylor which, the longer I thought about it, and later about myself, made more and more compelling, but deeply troubling, sense.

I cannot recapture most of Veraswami's words, but his theme stayed with me quite clearly. And upsetting it was, since, if he was right, my own chances of a happy marriage seemed to recede even further. I remembered poignantly my own vigour and confidence in the brothels of London and Mandalay as contrasted with those few graceless, wordless gropings with girls of my own age, class, and colour; perhaps it was not their relative inexperience that distinguished the latter encounters, but my own insecurity.

"What do you think Mr. and Mrs. Taylor talked about?" Dr. Veraswami asked, and launched into an almost clinical analysis of their sexual relationship which, if it were true, explained Taylor's preference for the teak estates over Moulmein, his cheerful acceptance of Mary's regular visits "home," and, like most of the other planters, his having "a bit on the side" both upriver on the estates and in Moulmein. The conclusion was that many Europeans could not feel easy, in or out of bed, with anyone "they

could not either venerate or dominate." Their vicious class structure had
impeded sexual freedom between men and women, so that the alleged
joys of the flesh required for them dominance or subservience, and had
even severely complicated friendships between males, which were too
often seen as dependent weaknesses, unless they were of the sporting or
hunting variety.

I must say he went on with some relish about what he called the well-
known English weakness for ladies with whips and black leather, or for
boys, most of which seemed a bit excessive to me. He seemed to lay enormous blame on the English sense of class; I had to interrupt him: "But Dr.
Veraswami, surely you in India have a very rigid caste system, more strict
than ours. We don't have untouchables. Indeed, in England, the lower the
class, the more touchable!"

Veraswami allowed himself a smile at my turn of phrase but hurried to
correct me. "No. No, Magistrate friend. You confuse class and caste. And
in sexual matters we in India are much better instructed than you tell me
you were in England; also, from what you tell me about the girls you met
on the ship coming out and a few young European ladies here, we are
much better practised than you. The young ladies of your class have to sell
themselves whole, you tell me, in marriage. Our young ladies have those
bargains made for them. And they would be troubled indeed to think they
were to marry a virgin. Yes, I know, you will remind me that I have told
you how I cannot discuss matters of my work or of the world with my
wife—of these things she knows nothing, it iss true—but, believe me, on
matters of our family, of this home, and of sex she iss a torrent, a verry torrent, word after word, and sensible and pleasing indeed they are to me."

Veraswami's view of the Taylor marriage was quite different: for Mrs.
Taylor, resentful acceptance, with noble and resigned sacrifice the leitmo-
tif; for him, a growing sense of the infliction of his desire upon her, whisky
at first helping to cloud the consequent sense of his own worthlessness and,
as the years passed, helping to prove that very worthlessness in gathering
impotence. Sex, for Taylor, Dr. Veraswami argued, was to be occasionally
inflicted upon a wife but enjoyed only with a Burmese girl or perhaps a
European prostitute.

Walking back to my bungalow from Dr. Veraswami's place that night,
in the moonlit half-light, Grantham and I carried with us the ease of
Veraswami's companionship. For the first time we talked without anxiety
for ourselves about Taylor and the girl. Our difficulty was that, though
Veraswami was no doubt broadly right about the grim sex lives of the married Europeans in Moulmein, it really did not explain Taylor's killing the
girl. For nearly ten years he had adapted to life in Burma with Mary, as well
as enjoying, according to Veraswami, enthusiastic copulation with more
than one Burmese girl. He knew how to play these games, so why the
change? And such an extraordinary change! We had no very helpful ideas,
but Grantham did produce the thought—probably improper for a potential

prosecutor—that though Taylor was morally guilty for his treatment of the girl, he was, it seemed to Grantham, in law entirely innocent of her death.

Although Grantham had suggested as much before, I had never succeeded in seeing Taylor as innocent. The degree of his guilt had worried me, but that he was innocent, not guilty of any crime at all, had not seemed likely to me. Grantham's argument was really very simple: "In the criminal law, Blair, you are responsible only for conscious, intended acts. There is also some culpability for certain failures to act, certain omissions, but that has nothing to do with Taylor's killing the girl. He is not responsible for what he does in his dreams. Even if he had just killed *her* in his dream—forget all that about the Pathan on top of her—he would not be guilty, even if he was in fact acting out his dream. Have you never dreamt that you were urinating and wakened to find it so, or dreamt that you were copulating and wakened to a differently dampened bed? No, I think Taylor is innocent. But whether I will have the guts to say that in Mandalay and not to prosecute him is another matter."

"There must be more to it than that, Grantham, surely. Can he find another Burmese girl and have another murdering dream about her? And what if his wife forgives him, like you seem to, and returns to what Veraswami sees as their grim bed? He may dispose of her too."

Grantham did not respond to the probably alcoholic lightness of my analysis; that night I had made more than the usual dent in Veraswami's beer supply. He took me seriously. "Yes, of course, if he knew of any risk that he might injure her the matter would be very different. Certainly it would be if he knew of any such risk and yet drank a little or a lot before he went to bed with her. But there is no evidence at all of that in this case. So your idea about his next Burmese girl—I doubt there will be one—does not help here."

Grantham told me of a case in which an attendant in a mental hospital, who was diabetic and had drunk too much and fallen into a fugue state, was wrenched off the chest of a helpless patient he was beating cruelly but of whose existence he wasn't consciously aware. In situations like that, foresight of risk spelt criminal liability if the risk were consciously run. The diabetic hospital attendant knew that his blood sugar concentration went awry with alcohol and that he might—although, in effect, unconsciously—act violently. He may not have known the chemistry, but he knew the risk. Taylor had no such advance warning; how could he be liable?

"They won't like this in Mandalay, Grantham."

"I know, I know," he replied, "but it's the truth. I shall tell them that the third eye is not farsighted; that will surely help." And on that unlikely note we parted, agreeing to meet for breakfast and a further talk with Taylor.

Taylor would not now talk to Dr. Veraswami about the events of the night when he killed the girl or what led up to them. In Veraswami's words, "He thinks I failed him when he came to me about the spiders. He cannot talk about matters of sexual jealousy to me, a nigger as he sees me, and particularly of jealousy of another Indian, however dreamlike. Perhaps he can talk to you about it. He would certainly be helped if he could. You should try, Blair, to talk to him."

But how? How to move from policeman and magistrate to confidant and emotional supporter? And should I? I had no idea. Veraswami said it would not be hard if I were direct with Taylor. So I tried; Veraswami was, as usual, correct.

I told Taylor that I believed his story and, unless something he had not told me came up at the preliminary hearing, Grantham and I would likely send to Mandalay depositions supporting its truth. Taylor did not seem to care; he accepted it as obvious that we would believe his story, but that was not what worried him.

He seemed to need my absolution for his relationship with the girl, rather than for anything to do with her death. The killing was not his fault, so it seemed, but her sharing his bed was. I tried to tell him that I was unlikely to be of much use, but he kept repeating that he had no one else to turn to. And then I saw that it was not my absolution, or even Mary's, he needed, but that of everyone with whom he would in the future form any relationship other than the most transient—and such a blanket for-giveness would not, could not, be given.

"Blair, I hated her, always hanging about. If I went up river to the estates, there she would be. And always whining for money and getting it. If Mary went to Mandalay, the girl would wait until I came home from the Club and put me to bed. And if she didn't come, I would send Aka Thon for her. It was awful. I once even went to her village and her miserable room. I hated her and yet kept her on." In his misery he left unasked the obvious question of why he did these things, knowing, I suppose, the obvious answer. How appalling always to have to live with this!

Words came to me, and I heard myself saying them before I had thought through what a burden they would make for me: "If you want me to, I shall go with you to meet your wife in Mandalay or Rangoon, when-ever you meet."

My last evening with Dr. Veraswami before escorting Taylor to Mandalay—Grantham had gone ahead to arrange for Taylor's detention and trial until Mandalay Quarter Sessions—helped me to understand why I hated the Taylor case and the tension it had caused between Grantham and me.

Dr. Veraswami talked less than usual. He ventured an occasional question, but mainly seemed intent on helping me to talk through what troubled me.

In the end, what it seemed to come to was this: Grantham saw the criminal law as a self-contained system, a pure and complete system—at any rate, that is what he thought it ought to be. Taylor was, according to the logic of that system, innocent; that was all there was to it. He intended neither to kill the girl nor in any way to risk her life, except in a dream, which didn't count. Oh yes, Grantham would admit the existence of other closely similar situations where, if you are doing what is illegal or immoral and things go badly, you may be convicted for the larger harm; but he saw them as errors in the law or, at best, as doctrines that had been allowed to harden into rules of law—and should be changed.

By contrast, it seemed to me that the criminal law is a dependent system, very reliant on culture, moral values, custom, and the texture of all the interwoven rules of law. If you are compromised morally and chance to violate any of those rules, and the dice roll against you, then you may lose badly.

Grantham argued fairly, though often aridly, as if about a game long past. He gave me examples of existing rules of law which helped me make my argument for Taylor's guilt, but he also mocked them with what seemed to me distant arrogance. He reminded me of what I had been taught at the Police Training Academy of the felony-murder and misdemeanor-manslaughter rules, under which acts that would normally incur no conviction for homicide did so if they were performed in the course of a crime. He told me how "malice" in the criminal law originally meant a generalised illegal or evil intent, and how what he called the "growing maturity of our jurisprudence" had shifted its meaning to an intent to do the precisely prohibited harm—or to risk it's occurrence.

In the end I remained unconvinced. It was a strange inversion of roles between us. I sympathised with Taylor, thought I understood something of his torment, but thought he should be convicted of manslaughter. Grantham cordially disliked Taylor, had no patience with his self-indulgence and stupidity, yet thought he should be acquitted.

"It will be a miserable time in Mandalay, Veraswami. I do not look forward to being anywhere with both Taylor and his wife. And Grantham seems so above it all. Yet he is willing to risk his career, certainly to annoy his superiors, by taking what will be a very unpopular position. His superiors would much prefer him to stress the immorality and indeed the illegality of what Taylor did—adultery, after all, remains a legal and moral wrong—and the likely connection between his drinking and his killing the girl. That many of his superiors engage in all of these acts, except killing, will only heighten their resolve to see duty done. And they will expect Grantham to be skeptical of the dream and to say that even if you believe Taylor and his dream, what he said he did in his dream was at least manslaughter.

"It won't be an easy time for Grantham or for me. Grantham will frustrate his superiors; I will annoy them even more. I will be on their side, in

a sense, but they will even more dislike my view that Taylor should be punished for bad luck—for chance selecting him from many of us to help us all
shape our moral and legal values."

Dr. Veraswami waved his head from side to side and patted his ample
hips with pleasure at my analysis. "Eric (he rarely used my Christian
name), you are right, I am sure, about Grantham and yourself. Whether
you are right about what should happen to Taylor I do not know, and it
does not seem verry important to me, I am most sorry to say. You are so
much more important! You are right to be repulsed by the crime—if that
iss what it wass—and also to glimpse Taylor's agony. Grantham may be
right in law. He may even be right about how the law should be. He may
be on the right side, but if you report him accurately, and I am sure you do,
it will not be, ass you say, an easy time for you both in Mandalay."

To the distaste of the Europeans catching the mail train to Mandalay,
Dr. Veraswami came to say farewell to his patient, Taylor, and, I suppose,
to me.

Taylor loathed the increased attention Veraswami attracted. Veraswami
understood and made his farewell brief and formal. But there was a fleeting
chance for us to talk; he took it and managed to implant a parting barb.
"Mr. Blair"—in public he was always punctiliously formal with me—"I
have never heard you use the dead girl's name in our discussion of the case.
Do you remember it?"

The name was, of course, spread all over the depositions: some complex, singsong, Burmese name; but for the moment it escaped me, and I
said so.

"You should, may I most respectfully suggest, be careful to use it often
and precisely in Mandalay. After all, the tragedy wass at least partly hers.
You and I both seem a little insensitive to her—you see, I too have been
searching my conscience." He turned and, with a light tread for his roly-
poly shape, set off to walk back from the railway station to the hospital.

A few months later the *Mandalay Times* reported the last I heard, other
than rumours, of Phillip and Mary Taylor. Under the heading "Moulmein
Killing" it said: "A spokesman for the Burmese Police announced yesterday
that Phillip Taylor was acquitted of the murder of a Burmese girl in
Moulmein. The jury found that her death was accidental and that Mr.
Taylor was in no way criminally responsible."

Rumour in Moulmein had it that Mary had returned to England before
the trial and that Taylor had drunk his way further inland, doing odd jobs
on rubber estates. I had heard nothing of him since the trial. I knew Mary
had left him. When it came to the point, she did not care enough for him

to run the gauntlet of Mandalay, let alone to try to build a new life with him thereafter, possibly after a prison term.

In the end I didn't know whether I felt sorry for Taylor or not. I suppose I did, but it wasn't easy. I think I understand why he kept the girl on—Veraswami had forced me to see that—but I lacked any abiding feeling for the tragedy of Taylor's life. Veraswami and I rarely mention the case nowadays. The last time we spoke of it, he compared Grantham's and my attitudes toward Taylor. Veraswami had not been to Mandalay while we were all there, but I had told him something of the burdensome weeks leading up to the trial, and he guessed the rest. "The trouble iss that Grantham wants men to be saints. You are too sensible, perhaps too humanly weak for that, my friend. But I have long thought that those who aspire to sainthood in themselves or others have not felt much temptation to be human—and you certainly have."

I think he was unfair to Grantham, but I am not sure. At all events, Grantham left the service soon after the trial and returned to a barrister's practice in England. When he and I were last together in Mandalay, before the trial, he had developed something like a contempt for Taylor. Taylor's "innocence," on which Grantham kept insisting to the annoyance of his superiors in the legal section, didn't seem to have much to do with it. Grantham resented that Taylor's existence pushed him to those difficult and career-threatening intercessions. As Grantham said, "It was, after all, just bad luck. He should have taken it like a gentleman. He should have shot himself. He let the side down, really."

I never shared Grantham's view. We have lost touch with one another; he seemed too proper for me. No doubt he will go far.

Commentary to
"THE PLANTER'S DREAM"

"Unreal," you say. "Fictional." "It doesn't happen." Well, it does. The law reports give many instances of lethal and injurious acts done by those in fugue states—assaults by somnambulists, by epileptics in *grand mals*, by those acting while unconscious. Many of those reported cases confirm that not even the most skeptical of prosecutors doubted the truth of the accuseds' versions of what happened.

The particular story of Phillip Taylor is fiction, but it strays not at all from the facts of similar narratives in American and English law reports, a few of which I shall refer to in this commentary.

I was led to this story by professional involvement in a case in the Australian state of Victoria, in which a loving mother killed her daughter with an axe, her story being—which in the end none in the court disbelieved—that when she killed her daughter she was in a dream defending her from being raped by a North Korean soldier. It was at the time of the Korean War; hence the geographic origin of the phantom rapist.

The story of Phillip Taylor has a further surprising link with reality. In 1980 a man named Linscott was convicted of the murder of a woman who lived near his home. He read of the killing in the newspaper and then dreamt that he witnessed the killing. He told his wife of the dream. They discussed whether he should risk derision by telling the police about it. He did. The police interrogated him with increasing diligence and came to the view that only the killer could possibly know all the details of the killing that Linscott had told them—the weapon, the posture of the body, the details of the furnishings of the room, and so on. He was tried by a jury and convicted, but some good citizens and a very good lawyer doubted his guilt and moved to his assistance. An earlier version of "The Planter's Dream" came to the attention of the lawyer and (he is kind enough to say) was of some help in clarifying what had happened. Linscott's conviction was, after many years, reversed. He was not the killer.

The less pejorative explanation of the police role in Linscott's conviction is that they did not understand the process of *confabulation*, by which an interrogator unwittingly and unintentionally conveys information to the person being interrogated.

At all events, it is a pleasure to have a piece of fiction based on one real case contribute to the resolution of another real case, particularly when that resolution is the reversal of the conviction of an innocent man.

"The Planter's Dream" started out to be a story about responsibility for acts done in fugue states, but Blair and Veraswami and Grantham took charge and the story evolved into a study of racial prejudice as well. There is little this commentator can add to their speculations, particularly Veraswami's, about the role that skin colour played in this story, but perhaps a few words on criminal liability for unconscious acts may be of use.

That you do not remember your acts does not insulate you from liability for them. All legal systems bring the amnesiac to trial. Here is a common paradigm: a motorcyclist without a helmet rides dangerously, precipitates an accident in which someone else is injured, and is himself concussed in the accident. Retrospective amnesia is a common consequence: he remembers nothing that occurred from about half an hour before the accident until he recovers consciousness. As a witness he is useless, but if there is other evidence to show that he was driving recklessly and that his carelessness caused the accident, he will be held responsible criminally and also will be liable in damages to the person he injured.

Let me now vary the facts of that typical accident to pose the question addressed in "The Planter's Dream." In this version the motorcyclist went to his dentist for a tooth extraction and received an anaesthetic. Thereafter, not having been warned of this risk by his dentist, while riding home he loses consciousness as a deferred result of the anaesthetic. The bike swerves, mounts the sidewalk, and strikes and injures a pedestrian. Is the motorcyclist liable for reckless driving and in damages to the injured pedestrian?

The answer under most legal systems is: he is liable in damages but is not liable criminally for reckless or dangerous driving unless he had, from his own earlier experience or by other warning, knowledge of the risk he was assuming. That answer seems to me both legally and morally correct; but since it is far from a universally agreed-upon result, I tried to test its viability in "The Planter's Dream."

It is important to note that this is not an example of the defence of insanity to a criminal charge, though the two may shade together. There are many cases in which insanity is not at all an issue. For example, diabetics who, by ingesting alcohol, disturb their blood-sugar-to-insulin balance occasionally suffer hypoglycaemic fugue states in which they act violently towards others. Such was the English case of *Quick*, in which the accused was convicted of a criminal assault because he had knowledge of his propensity for violence when he drank. By contrast, another English case, *Charlson*, the case related by Grantham in which a Londoner suffering from a brain tumor attacked and injured his son, properly resulted in an acquittal.

Epilepsy provides one of the clearest and most frequently occurring examples of the "unconscious" or "somnambulist" defence. An epileptic suffering a *grand mal* often makes rhythmic and violent movements with his hands. Suppose a person going to the aid of the epileptic in a seizure is struck violently by such a movement. Is the epileptic criminally liable for the "assault"? Everyone would, I suspect, correctly answer "No."

So, one is *not* liable for one's somnambulist act (unless one has notice of the risk of that type of act and fails to take appropriate precautions against it), but one *is* liable for acts precipitated by one's subconscious. Where did that last proposition come from, you ask? So far there has been no mention of a subconscious—just of being conscious or not conscious. It is a good criticism, but bear with me for a paragraph or two.

Few psychiatrists since Freud have doubted the power of the subconscious, or that many of our actions are substantially influenced by forces below the level of consciousness, forces that are the product of our earlier experiences, particularly those of the early formative years. Too frequently, the child who suffers parental abuse inflicts similar abuse on his own child. We all know, if we search sincerely, that our own actions are often triggered by stimuli that awaken in us deep-seated and ill-understood aggressions, but few would argue that we should not be responsible for them. Freud himself expressly affirmed that one is responsible for one's subconscious, yet there would seem to be little we can do about it. At what point in the understanding of the etiology of human behaviour is responsibility to society, to the criminal law, to be set?

The law sets that point at the level of consciousness of action, and it is hard to see how a legal system could sensibly do otherwise. Similarly, it is hard to see how a legal system could fail to hold one responsible for acts precipitated by one's subconscious, although lack of conscious volition should properly be taken into account in fixing the quantum of punishment that such conditional responsibility deserves.

So, in my view, Blair got it right. Suppose that you were a member of the appellate court in Rangoon, or a senior officer on the staff at Mandalay— would you agree with Blair or would you reject his recommendation? If the latter, what would you do with Phillip Taylor?

The Servant Girl's Baby

MiYan had been in the goal hospital for the two days since her arrest. I should have interrogated her earlier, but I had no idea of what to ask her or what to say. Yet I knew I could not just leave her sitting there in custody, hospital though it was, until some formal legal processes were pursued. As I rode my bicycle to the hospital, I found myself anxiously trying out sentences in my head. I wanted to gain a sense of MiYan as a person to see if I could begin to understand why she had let her child die.

Dr. Veraswami said that there was no reason why I should not speak to MiYan; she seemed in good enough health. He had put her in a single room for the time being and had seen no point in locking the door. He thought it might be wise to move her to a dormitory since she seemed very withdrawn and, he hoped, the support of some other women, sick though they were, might be of comfort to her. He said we should discuss this after I had talked to her.

I looked into the small, scrubbed, single room to which Veraswami had directed me. The swing door was not latched; the window to the courtyard was open. MiYan, if it was she, was not physically restrained. So far as I could see, she could walk out of the gaol hospital when she chose, unless the removal of her Burmese village clothes and the substitution of a plain, white, loosely tied hospital gown would inhibit such an elopement—and I supposed it would.

There was a hospital bed and a small wooden table—nothing more.

The woman on the bed lay on her side. She faced the wall, and I could not tell whether she was asleep.

"MiYan?"

There was a small movement of her head, but no reply.

"May I come in?"

She twisted upright and turned to sit on the edge of the bed, her gown falling apart well above the knees. Her eyes lifted briefly to mine. I moved beside the table, facing the bed and a little to one side of MiYan. "I would like to talk to you," I said. "Do you understand me?" I knew, of course, that as a servant in an English household she would have some English; but I needed some word from her if I was ever to launch a discussion rather than a monologue.

I achieved minimal success: "Yes, Sir."

Encouraged but embarrassed, both by ignorance and by a realisation of her combined vulnerability and attractiveness—which I had not expected—I ploughed into a lengthy explanation, the words and syntax becoming increasingly complex, of why she had been arrested and what the next legal steps would have to be. I spoke excessively of preliminary enquiries and bail, of assigned briefs, of the fact that she need not answer any questions put to her by me or by anyone else, except in the courtroom, but that she could do so if she wished, though she should know that anything she said "might well be used in evidence against her." It all sounded stilted and silly to me; to her it must have been another demonstration of her helplessness. I finished with an oxymoronic "Do you understand?"

MiYan came immediately to the heart of the matter, repeating, I suppose, what the sergeant who arrested her had told her, unencumbered by my legalistic baggage: "Yes, Sir. You brought me here because my baby died. I am to be punished. You will tell me how."

To my astonishment I found my eyes starting to fill with tears. I moved to the window and looked out to cover my embarrassment, and then turned back to face her: "Do you want to talk now?"

She made a small gesture of helplessness, raising her left hand slightly from the bed and letting it fall.

"Did you think that your baby would die when you left her with your mother at Talaban?"

"Yes."

"But did you not want to help her? Did you not love her?"

MiYan made no answer. She remained immobile, her eyes lowered. And then, unexpectedly, she veered away from my questions and challenged me. "I think my mother may die now. She needs me, and you have brought me here. I think she may walk into the jungle and get lost."

"I will see that she is looked after," I said, though not with any great confidence. Perhaps a communication to the headman of Pakara would help.

I determined not to be put off by MiYan's apparent concern for her mother. "But your mother did not help your baby, MiYan. She hit her, I think. And she did not take her to the hospital when she should have."

MiYan became suddenly engaged by what I was saying. She was puzzled by it, or so it seemed. Looking young and much more in need of my protection than of my continued aggression, she said: "It is best for the baby, what happened, and even also for my mother if she is lost in the jungle. But what about me? Am I to have no one to help me?"

I knew I could not in conscience continue the interrogation. The more I understood, the less my own actions made any sense. I asked if there was anything she needed. She did not answer. I said I would call on her again in a day or two, and left.

On the bicycle ride back to the police station I rehearsed in my mind what I knew of the death of MiYan's baby. Now that it had become a problem for me, I had better get the facts straight and clear.

I recalled the shack where I first saw the baby. It stood, or rather leaned, at the edge of the village, in appearance and situation a compromise between the jungle and a village hut, distinguishable from the other huts by its patched and scabrous walls—and by its smell. Dogs, their ribs protruding, had settled resignedly around it, sharing in adversity rather than seeking sustenance.

I had never seen such a wretched hovel; it repulsed me. But Veraswami had told me I should investigate. After Veraswami's regular sanitation inspection of the village a few days earlier, the headman had asked him to look in one of the huts at a baby girl who lived there with her grandmother. The child was bruised about the face and body. Veraswami had suggested to the grandmother and to the headman that the child be brought to the hospital for attention. The grandmother had been evasive about the cause of the bruises—Veraswami thought the child had been slapped frequently and severely. That was also the opinion of the headman. The child had not been brought to the hospital.

Veraswami had decided to mention his anxiety about the child to me because, he said, of rumours he had later heard from some servants at the Club. Some English ladies were talking there of a baby girl in a nearby village, sick nearly to death and badly attended; they had heard about it from one of their house servants and thought it shocking that I had done nothing about it.

Dr. Veraswami had described this Club chatter to me with some relish. I suppose it was a perverse comfort to him that there were others besides himself who were the butts of prejudice and hostility.

I had learnt that whenever Veraswami offered advice about my police work I should take it seriously. So, the day after he spoke to me, I made an early morning trip to the village of Talaban, where Dr. Veraswami had seen the baby.

As I had walked towards the hut, I was astonished to find Charles Moffat, the regional administrator, also there, accompanied by a native assistant.

The regional administrator did, of course, have to travel widely in his territory, but our paths rarely crossed. On police and judicial matters I reported not to him but directly to regional headquarters in Mandalay. On all other matters—"administration" was the word for everything that was neither "police" nor "judicial"—he was, as regional administrator, my superior officer. There was a required weekly meeting when we discussed any police and judicial activities likely to be of general administrative concern, and we also met occasionally at the Club; but not in a Burmese village early in the morning.

Relations between us were cautious and distant. There was not much objective cause for this; we had always been at arm's length. He had been in Moulmein for two years before my arrival; he had been a friend of Captain Humphreys, my predecessor as district officer, and would often mention Humphreys in our discussions, with apparent approval and a hint that my decisions suffered by comparison with his, despite the alcoholic haze in which he customarily moved. Moffat implied that I was rather a ninny compared to the hard-drinking Humphreys, whose common sense kept the natives in their proper place. Yet Moffat had always been careful to respect the narrow ambit of my authority, and I had no cause to complain.

The tension between us was a matter of atmosphere and personality rather than of substance. He was a bull of a man, heavily muscled and stocky, each of the many hairs on his forearms reminding me of the whiskers on my childhood crystal sets. He was twenty years older than me and far more experienced in the East, indeed on the brink of a reasonably anticipated knighthood; but even the impending "K" surely gave him no right to be quite so condescending towards me.

Why Moffat was at Talaban that morning was a puzzle. It appeared that we might be on the same errand. With his assistant a pace or two to the rear, he advanced from the edge of the village, approaching the same decrepit hut, and was equally surprised to find me there.

Moffat swiftly took the initiative. "What are you doing here, Blair? Is there some crime you are investigating—and alone?"

I told him of Dr. Veraswami's advice.

"Why didn't Veraswami look after the matter himself?" Moffat asked.

I told him I had asked Veraswami the same question and that he had replied that the villagers never asked him to visit them. When, as the sanitation inspector, he visited a village, they would let him inspect their huts without protest; but they did not solicit his medical assistance, then or at any other time. If a Burmese villager were so sick as to risk treatment by an Indian doctor in an English hospital, particularly a hospital near a gaol, rather than trust to the traditional Burmese herbs and Buddhist incantations, he would come or be brought to the hospital. Veraswami was not at all welcome among the villagers. They liked Indians little better than they liked Europeans. Also, they were scared of him, and he could understand their fear, since he was always associated in their minds with pain and often with death. Then, too, there was their calm acceptance of fate, the reality of their *karma*, their certainty that pain, suffering, and death were ordained for their progression towards happier and more enlightened reincarnations. Illness and its consequences were to be accepted, not struggled against.

Moffat's question had distracted me from my own appropriate enquiry. What was he doing here? So often Moffat seemed to preempt me! After all, his presence needed as much explanation as my own—indeed more— but I had let the time of courteous enquiry pass.

As Moffat and I approached the hut, a middle-aged woman, bent and tattered, hair and clothes awry, and in apparent fear, scurried out of the hut and away from us into the jungle. Moffat made "Anyone there?" noises but received no reply. We entered. The smell was appalling—and the filth. A baby girl, seventeen months old I later learned, lay naked on a rough plank-and-hessian cot, her left jaw swollen grossly, a dark red bruise across her temple and angry bruises elsewhere. One of her eyelids was puffed closed; the other was half open but the eye did not move to follow our entrance. Flies gathered at the effluvia from her nostrils and at the corners of her mouth. She was breathing quietly, apparently not in pain, but it was clear she was very ill indeed.

My gorge rose. Somehow I controlled myself, though I saw that Moffat had seen my gulp for air, no doubt confirming his ill-concealed view of my sentimental weakness. How could anyone treat a baby like this? Rage struggled with disgust; I had to do something or I would vomit, and I didn't propose to do that in front of Moffat. So I brushed the flies from the baby's face and looked for something with which to clean the excreta from her face and body, eventually dedicating my handkerchief in perpetuity to that fetid task.

Moffat lit a cigarette. I remember my sudden fury at his mid-length, overfilled, precisely pressed khaki shorts, the neat tabs of office on his shoulders, the calf-length socks, and his air of confronting and overcoming the developing heat by calm determination. He had removed his topee as he entered the hut, as a routine reflex rather than any gesture of courtesy. He stood beside me, glancing at the child, and in growing disgust he gazed about the hut.

As I fussed uncertainly with my handkerchief, Moffat stood immobile, apparently trying to decide what to do or what to order me to do or, more likely, planning how to shift the responsibility for an initial decision to me so as to preserve his calm authority. As I was reflecting on the pettiness of my judgement of him, he dropped his briefly smoked cigarette and with studied care ground it out on the dirt floor of the hut. My eyes followed his twisting, well-polished shoe and the tremor of his plump bum as he pressed the butt into the floor. My distaste must have been evident.

"Oh, don't be such a fool, Blair. Look at the place. They live like pigs. And in any event, these huts are tinder. Perhaps you think it would be better to burn it down?"

I did not reply. Clearly the baby needed help. The smell from her swollen jaw reminded me strongly of an odor I associated with hospitals, but I could not recall precisely what it was. I knew I would have to get the baby to the hospital.

Summoning reserves of courtesy I did not feel, I asked Moffat if he would be kind enough to see that the baby was cared for until I could arrange for her to be moved from the hut.

"By all means, Blair, if you think it necessary. I suppose this is police business. I will tell my boy to stay here until you have the child collected."

I rode my bicycle back to police headquarters and made arrangements for a police sergeant to pick the baby up.

"What shall I tell whoever is looking after the child?" the sergeant asked.

"Give any reason. Just say, police business, or something like that. But take the child to the hospital."

I put the matter out of my mind until late afternoon. I knew the child would be looked after and that I could be of no use. But when what passed for a day's work was done, I decided to go to the hospital.

Dr. Veraswami was bustling about one of the wards in his ill-fitting white coat. He gestured me towards his office and soon joined me there.

"I am verry glad, Mr. Blair, you saw to that child. She had only a bruise or two when I saw her in the village; now she iss quite battered, verry sick, verry sick indeed. Probably she will die, though we will do our best, our verry best, I promise you that. But her condition iss critical, critical," and his head waved repeated doubts.

"Is she Burmese or half-caste, Dr. Veraswami?" I asked.

Dr. Veraswami seemed slightly put out by the question. "I don't really know. Her skin iss somewhat light for a Burmese; I think she had a European father, but her features—her eyes and nose—are not now ass they should be. It iss hard to be sure. Doess it matter? She iss, to me, just a baby to be saved."

I asked what was wrong with her and, in particular, about the sickly-sweet smell I remembered but could not place.

"You have a perceptive nose, my friend. I wish the baby's mother or grandmother had your olfactory sensibility," and he gave a high-pitched giggle. I had no idea what he was laughing about, unless perhaps about the ornate words themselves.

He saw my mild annoyance and hurried to answer my question: "An abscessed tooth. That iss the main malady. The tooth either grew into the gum—that doess happen, you know—or it wass twisted or diverted into the gum by a blow of some sort. The tooth infected the gum and then the jaw. Someone rubbed some herbs on the gums, which reduced the pain, but gangrene developed. That iss what smells. The baby has had a gangrenous jaw for several days. It iss very doubtful we can save her. But there iss a chance, a chance."

The chance came to nothing. The child died the next day. I reported the matter to Mandalay, as was my duty, but since the regional administrator had been involved, if only peripherally, I put in a more detailed report than usual. There seemed nothing more to be done—an unpleasant event but not all that unusual, I thought. But I was wrong. Very wrong.

A week later a memorandum came to me from Mandalay Regional Headquarters marked IMMEDIATE. Its curt purport was that I had reported a homicide by neglect, a grave felony, but had not troubled to investigate who was responsible; indeed, it expressed doubt that I had recognised the likelihood of a crime. My attention was directed to the Indian Criminal Code of 1860, section 304A:

> Whoever causes the death of any person by doing any rash or negligent act not amounting to culpable homicide shall be punished with imprisonment for a term which may extend to two years, or with a fine, or both.

Had I forgotten what I should have learned of the law of homicide in my training? If so, certain specified pages in the manual might refresh my memory of both homicide and infanticide. Prompt action and prompt reporting on that action were expected.

It was a far from gentle memorandum.

I had not for a moment thought of the child's death as a crime. Who would think that? But as I did think, the sickening recognition of my stupidity took hold. I knew that exposure and neglect unto death of female babies was a pervasive practice in the East. I knew that in our training and in regular memoranda from Mandalay we had been told of the Government's determination to rid the administered territories of that evil practice, much mention being made of the Infanticide Act of 1870, which had laid the statutory basis for an attack on child killing in India and Burma. But I had not thought of the child's death in a criminal context. Perhaps if she had been exposed, unattended, or allowed to starve to death I would have, or if I had thought she had died from the blows revealed by the bruises on her body; but I had no reason to think anyone wanted the child dead, and so had considered the death from the gangrenous jaw a sadness, but not a crime. Yet it was, to my hot anxiety, true that as a technical matter I had reported to Mandalay what might well be a felonious homicide without giving the slightest indication that I recognised that fact.

I realised I had better find out promptly everything I could about the baby's death and decide what to do about it. The facts proved easy to discover; it was their moral and legal import that perplexed and threatened me.

Within two days the Indian sergeant who had taken the baby to the hospital gave me the facts. No one knew who the baby's father was; the mother, whose name was MiYan, had never been married and apparently had not lived with anyone in a matrimonial relationship. The same was true of the grandmother, so that all three generations—grandmother, mother, and baby girl—were not seen by the villagers as a family at all and hence were peripheral to the life of the village. They were not treated badly—they were tolerated—but they lived in every sense on the edge of Talaban. A situation like this, a family that was not a family and was barely part of the community, was not rare in a Karen village—the sergeant had seen such cases before.

The sergeant was surprised to discover—I was not—that for the past two years MiYan had worked as a housemaid in the regional administrator's bungalow, that is to say, for Charles and Claire Moffat. She had lived in their servants' quarters, some two miles from Talaban. The baby had been cared for, if that was the appropriate phrase, by her grandmother. MiYan spent one day a week at the village—her day off work—as well as an occasional evening when she walked to and from Talaban to be with her child. The sergeant told me that, when she was in the village, MiYan was reputed to do her best to look after the child.

The grandmother would not talk to the police sergeant—she had hidden in the jungle—but the villagers had told him that apart from when he had visited, and when Moffat and I had visited, she stayed close to the child and would not let anyone else near her. She was thought to treat the child quite severely, slapping the baby to stop her crying. That had been true also, some of the older women said, of her treatment of her own child, MiYan.

MiYan had known of the baby's toothache and did what she thought was proper, rubbing the child's gums with taro root. An evening or two after the baby became ill, MiYan had walked back to Talaban to see how the child was. She found the baby much worse. The baby had been crying a great deal and, it seemed, had been quite vigourously slapped by her grandmother to try to quiet her, so that she was more bruised about the head than MiYan had ever seen before, and her jaw was much more swollen.

MiYan spent the night at Talaban and in the early morning carried the baby back to the Moffats' bungalow. She asked Mrs. Moffat if she might keep the baby in her room in the servants' quarters while she worked. Mrs. Moffat said no, telling her there were luncheon guests who would require her full attention, and that she must immediately take the baby back to the village and return promptly in time to help with the luncheon.

Mrs. Moffat also told her to have her mother take the baby to the hospital: "The baby is very sick, you stupid girl. Can't you see that? She needs medical care. Tell your mother to take her to the hospital immediately."

I began to have some idea then why Charles Moffat and I were together that morning in Talaban.

MiYan passed on to her mother Mrs. Moffat's order to take the baby to the hospital; all it earned her was a screaming refusal.

MiYan had never been examined by a Western doctor herself and must have seen Veraswami as a distant and terrifying figure. The only time grandmother, mother, or child had been seen by a Western-trained doctor was when Dr. Veraswami had been taken to their hut by the head-man. On what were reported to the sergeant to be religious grounds, they both rejected Western medicine entirely and had always refused medical assistance.

These attitudes were, I knew, quite common in the villages, and quite understandable. Village life had changed little for centuries: the same pros-perities and the same sufferings, the same local healers and the same reli-gious beliefs and consolations.

The sergeant did not know how strongly MiYan felt about these mat-ters. She echoed the Buddhist beliefs of her mother, but without much feeling. She was clearly even more scared of her own mother than she was of Mrs. Moffat—and she seemed terrified of Mrs. Moffat. She was a scared person generally, the sergeant thought.

On the death of the baby, MiYan and her mother left Talaban and walked the twenty or so miles south of Moulmein to Pakara, the village where MiYan's mother was born and which she had left when she was pregnant with MiYan.

The sergeant told me he had had no trouble finding these facts for me, apart from his interview with Mrs. Moffat, who had resented his enquiries and told him so: "Why doesn't your Mr. Blair ask me himself? I shall speak to my husband about this." Probably she was right; it would have been bet-ter to talk to her myself rather than to send the sergeant as part of his gen-eral enquiry.

So, I forced myself to call on Moffat. Waiting in his office, I found myself at a loss how to broach the question of the baby's paternity—or whether I should.

"Come in." Moffat called a clipped, perfunctory greeting that did not conceal his dislike of the whole affair and his resentment of my intrusion. "I don't see what those dolts in Mandalay think they're on about, really. They've no idea what it's like down here, not an inkling how these people live." He tossed a stack of papers into the rubbish basket and started to straighten the remaining papers on his desk. "I must say you did what you could, and after all, I knew more about it than you. I remember when MiYan brought her, and Claire told me the poor little wretch was unwell, but really there was nothing to be done."

I tried to turn the discussion away from his hostilities to my superiors in Mandalay. Despite our unease with one another, I wanted to discover whatever I could from him about MiYan and her baby. I said I had been surprised that Mandalay saw the baby's death as a likely homicide by MiYan: "After all, she did not kill the child deliberately, though I suppose she may have neglected it unto death." I tried also to apologise for having the police sergeant interview Claire Moffat rather than going myself. "I should have been more considerate," I said; but even that did not seem to mitigate his anger.

"I don't care if your meddlesome superiors think it is a crime or not. It is ridiculous to test such a question in a case like this," Moffat said, ignoring my apology.

I agreed that I had been surprised by this, and wondered why they had selected the child's mother for my investigation: "Why not the grandmother? After all, she was looking after the child for MiYan."

Why not, indeed?" Moffat replied, seeming to like the idea. "I hear she often struck the baby, and she may thus have caused its death for all we know. But surely we can't start punishing villagers for trying to discipline their children. Surely not even your people in Mandalay would take that position. They must know how hard it is to get these villagers to observe even minimal decencies."

"Maybe," I offered, "they see the matter differently because MiYan and, in a sense, her child were part of your household. Do you know who the father was? Veraswami is unsure whether he was a European or a Burmese; he thinks European."

Understandably, Moffat was furious. Red-faced, he glared at me: "Have those police dolts hinted such things to you, Blair? Or is this your own wild theory? Really, I must say, we've acted perfectly properly, and Claire has gone out of her way for that stupid girl and her baby. What utter rot!" He glared at me and drummed at the desk in his effort to regain control.

I tried to retreat as best I could, though I felt hypocritical in the attempt: "I was not, Sir, for a moment suggesting that you had any particular obligation to the baby, other than as a child of one of your servants."

I remember that even as I said it, I felt weak and gutless. Failing to be direct, I sounded mealymouthed. And Moffat was no fool to be put off by circumlocutions. Cold with anger, directed now at me and not at my "meddlesome superiors," he drew my own behaviour into the equation: "I claim no parentage here, Blair. That's not to say my behaviour has been any better than yours, since I do hear that you entertain village girls at your bungalow regularly enough. But if you suggest in any way or to anyone that I am the father of that child, I shall certainly sue you. It will not only be *my* career that's ruined; rely on that."

I think I made waving, dismissive motions with my hands, hoping to separate myself from my innuendoes. "I repeat, Sir, I was not for a moment suggesting any failure on your part."

"You were referring to my wife, then!"

The retreat was clearly in disarray, but I clung to whatever scraps of mendacious protection I could: "Of course not; I'm just trying to understand what happened. I should have interviewed Mrs. Moffat myself. I do apologise for embarrassing you both in this way."

He accepted my apology, though I am sure he suspected that I had, at one or another level, meant to suggest his and his wife's moral failure. But he was far too provoked to prolong the discussion further. He dismissed me with the advice that there were no more facts to be found—everything that needed to be known was known. "If I were you," he said, "I'd get a stiff note off to Mandalay *tout de suite* telling them there is nothing further to investigate and no crime to be tried."

As I got up to leave, he either relented somewhat or had a self-protective idea. "If you like, Blair, I will discuss your reply memorandum to Mandalay with you when you have it in draft. I know it is within your jurisdiction, not mine, but perhaps I could be of assistance."

I thanked him and left, increasingly disliking Moffat and the Moffats' role in the baby's death.

I knew I had better take Mandalay seriously if this were not to develop into an even worse problem for me than it already was. To have failed to recognise felonious homicide before my very eyes was one thing, but to do nothing, nothing whatsoever, about the likely felon was quite another. MiYan would have to be brought into custody, cruel though that might be. She might then be allowed to return to Pakara, but only after I had decided, as a policeman, whether a charge should be filed against her, and, as a magistrate, if she were charged, whether she should be allowed bail or held in gaol.

To follow Moffat's advice and to try to brush the affair off as inconsequential seemed to me a recipe for disaster. He might be right in the long run, but too much had happened for me, at my level of seniority, to dismiss the affair. His knighthood was at risk, it seemed; but that did not worry me greatly, although it possibly explained a lot about his and his wife's actions. For me, more was at stake; direct orders from superior officers cannot be ignored unless one wants to be cashiered.

So, making out the arrest warrant myself and citing the Indian sergeant and Veraswami as the informants, I sent the sergeant to arrest her. I had told him to tell MiYan she must come because of the death of her baby, but otherwise to avoid conversation entirely about that matter. He should take her to the gaol hospital, where Dr. Veraswami would have arranged for her to be held until the preliminary enquiry or a bail hearing, and he should then report back to me at the police station or at my bungalow.

While I was making these arrangements and completing and signing the arrest warrant, yet another telegraphic bombshell struck me from Mandalay. I was advised that Lieutenant George Brett would be arriving in Moulmein a few days hence. Brett would be in touch with me concerning his travel arrangements, and I was directed to assist him with his accommodations, at either the barracks or the Club, depending on his preference. He would be assisting me in the enquiry into the death of the baby in the village of Talaban and would be pursuing other duties of which I would be advised. I knew exactly what that meant: he had a watching brief, which meant that he was coming less to help than to report on my inadequacies.

So, I was not to be trusted at all in this matter. Another officer would

be peering over my shoulder, reporting to headquarters, having no responsibilities other than those of a critic. It was not at all reassuring. I had not
met Brett. I knew of him, of course, to the extent that I had read the
names and ages and seniorities and postings of all officers in the Burmese
police establishment, but that was all.

It seemed the course both of courtesy and prudence to meet Brett at the
railway station; he had, after all, been sent to Moulmein because my superiors doubted my competence in this matter—there seemed little point in
alienating their emissary.

I was dripping wet after my bicycle ride from my office; I had pedalled
too hard for the time of day. I often forget that the height of the sun governs all our activities in Burma. So I rode home, showered, lay on a towel
under the rotary fan until I thought I might possibly have ceased perspir-
ing, and then put on fresh clothes in which to meet Brett.

The train was, as usual, late. And late at the worst time of day, the
early-afternoon boiling point when all sensible people in Burma took rest
or shade, or preferably both. I had changed into the lightest clothes that
could be defined as a uniform, but already I could feel the patches of sweat
darkly staining the back of my shirt and saturating the inner headband of
my cap. There was nothing to do but wait—sit in the shade of the shabby
station and wait—my only companions a line of vultures, heads hanging
low in the heat, perched on the branch of a nearby leafless tree. I thought
the vultures were wise to be waiting for me, but even that notion did not
amuse me.

I heard the train first through the hum of the rails and walked toward
the rear of the station where the first-class carriages normally came to
rest—as far as possible from the soot of the engine. Brett was immediately
recognisable, the only officer in uniform on the train. But I was unsure for
a moment, since he was not alone. There was a woman with him, a quite
unusually presentable woman at that. I hesitated. He caught sight of me.
"Is that you, Blair?" and, as I moved toward him, he added, "Good of you
to meet us. Let me introduce my wife, Rosemary."

I saluted her, murmured a greeting to them both, and moved to help
with the luggage.

"Oh, leave it, Blair. Let the batman look after it."

I had not expected such luxury. As a lieutenant, he was entitled to a
batman, of course, but it was unusual to travel with such retainers. Indeed
the service did not issue travel orders for the batmen of those of rank less
than major, but let the rest of us pick up such assistance wherever we happened to be stationed. And the presence of his wife had the same odd-
ness—she, too, would not be covered by a travel order. Brett must be paying their fares himself!

I told the Bretts that motors were seldom available and that I had arranged to convey them to the Club in a rather small tonga; I gestured toward the somnolent horse and immobile driver at the other side of the platform.

Mrs. Brett responded with enthusiasm. "I much prefer a tonga to a truck, Mr. Blair, particularly in this heat. But I doubt we can all fit in."

"I can send a vehicle for your luggage and the batman later, Mrs. Brett. The three of us can squeeze into the tonga to the Club, I think, or, if you prefer, I can come along later."

"But there is the Burmese gentleman too, Mr Blair." I had no idea who she was talking about, and her husband also seemed either unsure or annoyed.

"No, dear. He will not be coming with us." Turning to me, he added, "My wife speaks of a Burmese barrister who is also travelling on this train. He will certainly not be staying at the Club."

Turning about, I caught sight of him. There stood U Tin Hlang a few paces off, quietly observing the three of us, amusedly waiting for some sign of recognition by me.

I must have seemed most discourteous to the Bretts. I was entirely delighted to see U Tin Hlang again. He beamed at my obvious pleasure in seeing him; even the scar curving from above the right eye over the bridge of the nose and down under the right eye, which usually gave his face a somewhat sinister air, now melded into an appearance of benevolence. I hurried over to embrace him in a most un-English way.

"How grand to see you again, Mr. Lang," I said, accenting as banter the anglicised version of his name. "What are you doing here?"

"You will learn that soon enough, Your Honour, and I doubt that you will be pleased. But let me not detain you now. You have the Bretts to attend to."

I turned back toward the Bretts and sought to unify the group. George Brett, stiff and unsmiling, the very image of the pukka subaltern on parade, was clearly embarrassed and disapproving; Rosemary Brett, however, was smiling in uncritical amusement at my developing unease.

U Tin Hlang relieved the situation for me. "We three met at Rangoon station, Blair. You see to them now; I'll get over to my hotel, the impeccable Htun Hla, you will recall. I'll call on you later." He turned back to the train and, I assumed, his luggage.

Brett was grumbling about keeping his wife standing in the sun. I moved quickly to tell the batman that I would send a vehicle for him and the luggage as soon as I could, and escorted the Bretts to the tonga. I found myself beginning to play the servant to Brett, which was odd. Though we were of equal military rank, both lieutenants, he was probably older both in years and in the service and therefore senior to me; but there was more to it than that. He had such a confident air—taciturn, privileged, assuming he was to be served and thus attracting service. Though it was indeed very hot, he maintained an air of cool collectedness. By contrast, his wife made no effort to separate herself from the hot realities of Moulmein station.

Fanning herself with a large hat she had removed soon after alighting from the train, she climbed into the back of the tonga, patted the seat beside her to tell me to sit there, and looked around in quick interest. But there was not much to see.

Brett checked that the batman was staying with the luggage and joined us in the tonga. We set off for the Club. To make conversation, I asked them about U Tin Hlang and, risking the obvious, enquired if he, too, had come on the MiYan case.

"Of course he has, Blair. Though how he knew I had been sent to assist you is a puzzle. Nobody I know told him, of that you can be sure. When we were at Rangoon station he came up and introduced himself to Rosemary and me, saying some rot about "where you go I go too." But I made sure we were in separate carriages throughout the whole rotten journey. I don't want to talk to him about the case, and I don't suppose you do, either. I knew of him, of course, a troublemaker if ever there was one, but I had not spoken to him before. You seem to know him well, if I may say so"—and his disapproval of the manner of my greeting U Tin Hlang was clear.

Mrs. Brett changed the subject and began a flow of sensible enquiries about Moulmein and what there was for them to do and see while they were here. I did my best, but the truth was that there was not much for a tourist in Moulmein, and I said so. She bridled. "I am not a tourist, Mr. Blair. I want to find out all I can about life here—for people in the government, for the natives, for everyone. I'm sure there is a lot to learn."

She was right, of course. I had been my usual clumsy self. I am never easy in the presence of young women, particularly attractive young women, and even more particularly attractive young women who know you are attracted to them. She let me down lightly and did not pursue the attack, telling me instead that she would be grateful for any help I could give her husband and herself while they were in Moulmein.

Brett interrupted, curtly I thought. "Blair and I will be fully occupied, Rosemary, with the MiYan case. And he also has the district to look after. You must not expect him to be a Cook's tour guide to us."

She made no response.

I left them on the balcony of the Club where the Club steward was, to my surprise, waiting to welcome them. Brett asked if I would meet him for lunch at the Club tomorrow and take him to his office. They were weary from the journey, he said, and the MiYan case could well wait until tomorrow. Mrs. Brett waved a friendly farewell and said she hoped they would see me soon.

I had the tonga take me to the police station and told the driver to go back to the railway station for the Bretts' batman and their luggage. I arranged accommodation for the batman at the police barracks and turned to an afternoon of routine office work.

By mid-afternoon my work was done. The duty sergeant did not need any guidance from me; I decided to call on U Tin Hlang. It seemed proper that we should consult, and anyhow I enjoyed his company.

Nothing had changed in the lobby of the Htun Hla since U Tin Hlang and Veraswami and I had dined there to discuss the case of Ake Dah, except that this time, having ridden my bike to the hotel rather than being driven in a tonga, I was even hotter and sweatier, and the premises seemed at first more tawdry. But on calmer assessment I had to admit that the hotel seemed clean, the ceilings were high, the fans worked, and I was courteously received.

There was no need to ask for U Tin Hlang. The staff knew I must be calling on him. As I arrived, an Indian servant scuttled up the stairs. A few moments later, the same servant hurried up to me obsequiously to enquire if I would be good enough to follow him to Dr. Hlang's room. Dr. Hlang, he said, "would be honoured if I would join him for a chat in his room." I wondered where U Tin Hlang had acquired his medical education, but sympathised with the servant's desire to do honour to the hotel's increasingly famous guest. Since we had last met—on the Ake Dah matter—I had noticed more frequent and critical reference to U Tin Hlang in the English press, which must mean a surge of influence among the indigenous peoples of Burma, that is, among all other than the Europeans and particularly the British, who never could be said to suffer a taint of indigenousness no matter how long their suzerainty of a tropical country.

I followed the Indian servant to the room, which was in the center of the floor above the entrance to the hotel, the only room with a balcony. Before the servant could knock, U Tin Hlang opened the door. He was dressed simply but elegantly, in a full, soft, off-white garment hanging loosely to the calves like a modified nightgown, short-sleeved, with an open, round neck—comfortable and sensible. His greeting was warm beyond courtesy, and I tried to express my pleasure in seeing him again.

The Ake Dah case had cut itself deeply into my memory and my feelings. Apart from its innate interest and my continuing occasional contact with Ake Dah himself, it was a matter in which I had outwitted the redoubtable U Tin Hlang, outwitted him politically, denying him an increment of political advancement by another victory for the Burmese lawyer over the Raj. And what pleased me further was that Ake Dah had not been injured in the process. I suppose I was a little puffed up, and perhaps that is why I felt so warmly towards U Tin Hlang. Anyhow, self-satisfaction apart, it was a delight again to be with such an urbane and amusing companion as the newly medically qualified Dr. Hlang.

"Your man suggests you are now a member of Veraswami's profession. How you have found the time for such demanding studies, while leading the Burmese revolution and appearing bewigged in the Superior Court whenever it sits, astonishes me."

"He is not my man, Blair. He works for this hotel, and you know it. My 'man,' and another servant or two, will be coming tomorrow and travelling back and forth to Rangoon quite frequently, and at costs that I hesitate to load onto my employer, the General Council of Buddhist Associations— but I will. And it is graceless of you to mock my doctorate. A university in Delhi needed a non-Indian for its annual commencement ceremonies and thought my efforts in the law and on behalf of my countrymen, downtrod- den mercilessly by your countrymen, merited an honourary doctorate. We negotiated whether it should be in law or letters; I preferred the former, they the latter; we settled for philosophy since they lacked a faculty of pol- itics. So don't mock my academic distinction, Blair; obviously jealousy moves you."

I offered excessive congratulations on his doctorate and expressed the hope that it would not remove him too far from his circle of erstwhile friends, amongst whom I hoped he numbered the district officer of Moulmein.

Suddenly serious, the scar on his face reddening, his voice hesitant rather than orotund as usual, U Tin Hlang said: "Thank you for the oppor- tunity to say so, Blair. I was touched, deeply touched, by the manner of your greeting me this morning. It was in the presence of an officer of rank equal to yours, but a man of more influence than you. I know such things are not easy. You must know his opinion of me. You must know what will be reported to your superiors. Yet you expressed yourself in that wonderful- ly warm way. I am, as I say, deeply touched." And he glowered at me as if he were angry.

I was, I knew, receiving credit I did not deserve. None of the calcula- tions he suggested had passed through my mind at the railway station when I caught sight of him. I had simply seen him, and my body had rejoiced for me. I am glad it did. I am glad I embraced him. But certainly no merit attached to the gesture. It took no courage; it was almost reflex- ive. But there seemed no point in saying all this to U Tin Hlang. Indeed, I doubt that I understood it enough at the time to have said anything sensi- ble, and the moment passed. I found myself, blushing I suspect, accepting his offer of some chilled barley water and looking around the room for a chair.

It was a clean and spacious room, with wooden slats for windows, wick- er furniture, and a large and comfortable-looking bed crowned by spotless mosquito netting, neatly folded. U Tin Hlang's suitcases were of dark leather, and there were several small wooden trunks. One was open beside a desk and had obviously been the center of U Tin Hlang's interest before I arrived; I could see several papers, folded lengthwise in the fashion of lawyers' briefs, tied with single, red ribbon bows. It struck me that U Tin Hlang must in fact work hard and long, that his air of effortless superiority was an affectation to cover extreme diligence. He had not come to Moulmein only to work on my case, to keep a watching eye on Brett while Brett kept a watching eye on me: there must be many other matters, legal and political, that currently burdened him.

I sat on a wicker couch while U Tin Hlang went out to the top of the stairs above the lobby and shouted down for barley water. I had no particular agenda of topics to discuss, though I supposed the case of MiYan's baby should not be avoided. Otherwise, I was there because I wanted to see him.

"Is it MiYan that brings you here?" I asked.

"Of course. Again your superiors have given me a cause I cannot lose. You punish her: you are insensitive brutes, uncaring for the cruel lives of your village servants. You don't punish her: you are insensitive brutes, uncaring for the lives of Burmese infants."

I could not resist a jab. "You said something like that about the Ake Dah case, as I recall, but it didn't work out that way."

"I thought you wouldn't soon forget that victory, Blair. Yes, you won that, I admit, though whether you won it fairly I am not sure. Still, I would have been pleased to win as fairly as you did. But I don't see how you can win this one, particularly with me and George Brett and Charles Moffat and your superiors in Mandalay all peering over your shoulder. Those young shoulders are wide and they may even support a sensible enough head; but what with the haughty and selfish Moffats, the strangely matched Bretts, and the rest of us. . . ." His voice trailed away in artfully contrived doubt.

I asked him how he had heard about the baby's death. His answer revealed that very little passed through official police or military channels, or over the telephone line or by telegraph, that did not find its way to the political planners of the General Council of Buddhist Associations. But he was not boasting, just admitting realities I had suspected; and he made the contrary point, which I had not suspected, that the military and police authorities gave the same attention to all his communications. Hence his need for servants from Rangoon to travel back and forth should they be needed as messengers—with some hope of confidentiality. And he reminded me that when secrecy mattered, my superiors directed me by documents hand-carried and delivered by members of the Corps of Signals who, in these cases, used no signals whatsoever, which amused him: "They should be called the Corps of No Signals, don't you think?"

"I hope we may talk to one another about the MiYan case, Dr. Lang, as we usually do, rather than trying to avoid it," I said, finding myself giving him his academic honourific. "It seems to work out better that way."

"There is no need for the doctorate in our conversation, Blair, you have teased me quite enough with that to satisfy your envy. Yes, by all means, let us share our views on this case, though you must not count on any complete disclosure—nor will I. I well remember that you kept your plan for Ake Dah entirely to yourself until you sprang it on me as a piece of immediate blackmail in his presence. So don't be too sure I will be open as the fields to you—I will try to dig a secret ditch or two for you to fall into. But let us at least pretend to play it all openly."

The barley water arrived in a tall jug covered by a round crocheted cover weighted around the edges by coloured glass beads. Remarkably, there was a substantial piece of ice floating in it. U Tin Hlang poured for us both, handed me a glass, and wandered towards his desk and its attendant trunk of papers. I found myself more at ease than I usually am in another's presence. The game of pretended disclosure between us amused me, even though people's lives were at stake. I knew that in a deeper sense, beyond the politics, our views tended to match. But I was in no hurry to come to a discussion of the death of MiYan's baby. I would have to know more and to have thought more before I could continue to play this game with my friend. And I had the secure sense that he was a friend.

"When would you like to see your client?" I asked.

"She is not yet my client, Blair. I will have to offer my services, paid for by the admirable General Council of Buddhist Associations. They are, as you know, a generous and selfless group, seeking nothing other than to demonstrate the iniquity of the Raj. MiYan may as well be a beneficiary of that noble sentiment, don't you think?"

I told him I did not so think, but suggested that he call on MiYan soon and then advise me if he were representing her so that we could arrange a bail hearing, if she should want it. He was ahead of me, of course. He had already arranged with Veraswami to see MiYan first thing the next morning. He told me he would call on me to discuss bail and the arrangements for the preliminary enquiry later in the morning, if it suited me. I said it did.

These preliminaries out of the way, I turned to what also troubled me about the day's events. "Tell me about the Bretts, would you?" I asked. "They seem to travel in some style."

"I know a little about them, not much," Hlang replied. "They do indeed spend freely, far beyond his military pay and allowances. But it is not his money; it is hers, I am told. Indeed, the lawyer who told me, an English Silk, put it rather well, I thought. He said that though Brett is a soldier, he earns more by his prick than by his sword."

I found I was annoyed. Annoyed that Hlang should speak of her like that—it seemed demeaning, unmerited by her. I said that I had found her a charming and intelligent person.

"What has that to do with it, Blair?" and then he saw my annoyance and smiled happily. "I apologise for my vulgarity, Blair. I meant no disrespect of her. She is indeed a most attractive lady. I wish you well. As I said, they are a mismatched pair."

"Do you know why she came here?" I asked. "Surely the MiYan case won't take that long. Can't she bear to be separated from him at all?"

"You keep worrying about their love life, Blair. I have no idea as to her erotic needs. But before you fly at me in a rage, let me say that I do think there is more than one reason for his being here, which may explain why she came too. Was the previous district officer at Moulmein not a captain? Are not district officers normally captains? And you are not really yet due for promotion, Lieutenant Blair, despite your wonderful service to us poor Southern Burmese. Brett is, like you, a lieutenant; but I am told he is about due for a captaincy. He is not without influence in Mandalay and

Rangoon. Nor is she. Perhaps they are surveying your fiefdom, wondering if it would suit them. I thought of this on the train. It makes sense, but I don't know if it is so. His watching brief in the MiYan case was easy to arrange, I should think—a word or two in the Club when he heard of your myopia towards baby killing, and your need for assistance in the matter. And here they both are."

I felt hollow. I did not wish for indeterminate service in Moulmein, but this was certainly not the way to leave. And she had seemed so pleasant, so outgoing, so genuinely interested to learn everything she could about Moulmein and all who lived there. Of course she was interested! She was deciding whether she wanted it for herself. How utterly mean of her, to be dissimulating in this way. And how cunning of him, to use a minor oversight of mine both as a means to see whether he wished to take over my job and as a lever to arrange it if the case came out badly. Heaven knows where I might be sent.

I was slow to reply to U Tin Hlang. He sat, his hand beside the glass of barley water, looking at me speculatively. I said that I was troubled how all the cases we were involved in together seemed to threaten me in one way or another. "They become so autobiographical, don't you think? Anyhow they do for me; perhaps less for you, though they all run close to your political ambitions. I thought judges and lawyers were meant to be immune from these personal concerns in their cases, but it doesn't work out that way for me."

I found myself troubled by the increasing unpleasantness of this whole case. It had been a long day. I was detaining U Tin Hlang. I had exceeded my welcome. It was time to go to my bungalow and try to think. I told Hlang that I hoped he would spare me time for a talk soon at my bungalow, and asked if tomorrow night, after dinner, would be convenient. Perhaps he and I and Dr. Veraswami could together bring some sense to this case. I said I was sure Dr. Veraswami would be willing to join us.

He was nodding in amused agreement throughout this long and circuitous invitation. "I will try, Blair, but like the full disclosure between us, don't count on it. Still, it would be good to be with you two again. I'll try."

Since U Tin Hlang had told me that he would interview MiYan the next morning, I had an early breakfast and rode my bicycle to the barracks and the police station in the cool of the morning. It promised to be a busy day: George Brett and I were to lunch at the Club and work through the early afternoon. Then, in the evening, after dinner, I hoped that Veraswami and U Tin Hlang would come for a talk; and now I probably faced a bail hearing in the morning, as well as the usual small pile of official and largely formal reports.

I fell to the paper work and completed a surprising amount before an

Indian runner brought a handwritten message from U Tin Hlang, asking me to come to the gaol hospital immediately if I were free to do so.

U Tin Hlang was waiting for me at the entrance to the hospital as I leaned my bicycle against the wall. "Blair, she says she does not want my help. Have you already poisoned the air? Did you warn her against me when you brought her here?"

"I certainly did not," I said. "I would prefer that she be represented by someone, and I know no one here of your ability. I am not at all clear what should be done about her, whether she should be sent to trial at the Rangoon Assizes or tried summarily here, or whether she should be put on trial at all. No, I did not get in your way."

"Well then, Blair, talk to her. Tell her she needs my help—or that of someone else, if she dislikes the scar on my face."

I suggested we go together to see MiYan immediately. U Tin Hlang declined: "I can't keep pushing myself on her. You will have to persuade her. If not, we shall save some money for the G.C.B.A. and I can return to Rangoon."

I said I would do my best and added the hope that I would see him that night after dinner at my bungalow. We parted at the entrance to the hospital.

Dr. Veraswami was not in his room. I did not need his permission to see a gaoled inmate of his hospital, though as a courtesy I normally sought it. But I wanted to see MiYan promptly. I went to her room.

The half-door to her room was swung closed, but I could see someone sitting on her bed talking to MiYan as I approached. I knocked and entered without waiting for a reply. To my astonishment, there sat Rosemary Brett smiling warmly in greeting. Even MiYan looked up in apparent amusement at my surprise.

"What are you doing here, Mrs. Brett?" I asked, too curtly I suppose.

"I always first visit the hospital at any new station, Mr. Blair. It is a good spot to begin to find out what a place is like. And I do have some experience of these matters. Dr. Veraswami has been called to a patient; he suggested I talk to this lady while he was away. Is there something wrong?"

"No. Not at all. I'm sorry I barged in on you. But I do have to talk to MiYan," I said, gesturing toward MiYan.

"Very well. I shall wait in Dr. Veraswami's office until he is free." And she stood down from the edge of the bed, ready to leave if I got out of her way.

"Oh, I didn't mean that, Mrs. Brett. Please stay. You can perhaps help me."

She looked about, uncertain. There seemed little space for the three of us in the tiny room. "All right, if you say so. Perhaps you could sidle past us and park your bottom on the table there." She seemed to be taking charge. MiYan still had not spoken, but her physical attitude seemed less strained than when I had first seen her. I brushed past them both to the table beside the window and half-sat, half-leaned there. It really was close quarters. If I relaxed, our knees touched. It seemed too intimate for the type of legalistic conversation I must pursue with MiYan, but I was certainly not about to ask Mrs. Brett to leave, even if she and her husband were after my job.

I found I was still wearing my cap. Good heavens, I should have saluted! But that would have looked absurd. I took it off and put it on the windowsill. "You look hot," Mrs. Brett said.

I said I was, and mopped at my head with a fortunately clean handkerchief. I found I constantly wanted Mrs. Brett to see me in a good light. But it was not easy now; I felt so awkward interrogating MiYan. Yet here was Rosemary Brett chatting lightly with MiYan, or so it seemed—certainly not at all ill at ease. And then the suspicion came to me that perhaps he had been sent to interview MiYan, sent by George Brett; perhaps he thought a woman was in a better position to wheedle facts out of another woman, facts that might further underline my inefficiency in the whole matter. Within me, resentment fought with attraction.

I turned to MiYan. "The Burmese lawyer who came to see you this morning tells me that you do not want him to help you. Is that right?"

She nodded assent.

"I think it would be a good idea to let him help you, MiYan. You will not have to pay him. He is an excellent lawyer. If you go to trial for the death of your baby, and you might, you will have to have a lawyer. You might as well get a good one."

MiYan managed to say, "You know what happened, Sir. You will do what is right. He cannot help me."

"You are wrong, MiYan," I said. "I am sure he can help you. He knows much more about the law than I do. And he wants to help you."

Rosemary Brett obviously could no longer contain herself: "Surely, Mr. Blair, you should not be badgering her like this. If she doesn't want U Tin Hlang, that is the end of it. And I can't say I blame her. He will simply turn it all into a political circus to serve his own ends. Why should you be pushing him upon her?"

I said that I had had some experience of U Tin Hlang and his work before, as she probably knew, and that I had always found that though he did indeed seek political ends embarrassing to the administration in the cases he took, he also was a considerate and forceful advocate for his clients. "MiYan can hardly do better," I concluded.

Rosemary Brett raised a very graceful eyebrow, and turned her head slightly to signify her disengagement from this issue: "Well, it's up to her, of course," and then added, with a smile of understanding towards me, "but I do believe you really are worrying about what is best for MiYan here," and she laid a hand on MiYan's arm. "I think it would be a good idea for me to leave you both now. I will wait for you, Mr. Blair, in Dr. Veraswami's office."

I stood up, occupying even more space, and unintentionally made her exit quite difficult.

MiYan appeared sorry to see Rosemary leave. I continued to argue the case for her being represented by U Tin Hlang, after a while making the point that I could do my job better if Hlang helped her. It seemed an odd inversion, but it persuaded her: "If you say so, Sir, I will trust him." Relieved, I hurried off to Veraswami's office, hoping that Rosemary had not left.

She was talking, happily and easily, with Veraswami. He waved me to a chair. "Would you like tea, Blair? Nurse Brett won't join me." I declined the tea. "Did you not know that she iss an RN, Blair? If you get sick enough, perhaps she will help me save you." Veraswami was right that any intact male would like Rosemary Brett for a nurse, but it was indelicate of him to carry on in this bantering way, though she didn't seem to mind.

Veraswami said that he would have to get back to work and suggested I stay in his office with Mrs. Brett until a tonga could be brought for her. He bustled out.

Words deserted me. They often do when I most want them. Appropriate and clever words flood forth unsolicited when I am alone, but Rosemary Brett completely dried up the flow. After an uneasy silence while she looked at me expectantly, she said: "I am sorry I argued with you in front of that poor girl."

"No. Not at all. You were right. No you weren't; she should have counsel. But you were right to say what you thought, though you were wrong." I must have sounded mystifying to her. It was not clear what I was saying. But there seemed a thread of truth in it somewhere; at least, I hoped so.

She laughed lightly, a sound I found I greatly enjoyed. "I suppose you persuaded her to have that dreadful Burmese Silk as her counsel." I nodded agreement. "What persuaded her?"

"To help me," I replied. And now she laughed out loud. "You seem dangerous, Mr. Blair. No one told me that. I shall have to warn my husband."

I decided to go directly to the point: "You know the broad facts, I assume. What do you think should be done about MiYan?"

"Why, nothing, of course."

"But surely, Mrs. Brett, we should try to protect village babies. MiYan's baby does seem to have been very badly treated."

"Help them, protect them, yes; but policemen and lawyers are not the people for that. You and George seem to agree: make an example of MiYan to save other babies. I've told him you won't improve maternal care in that way, but he thinks it will help. I suppose you agree with him," and, in self mockery, she glared at me balefully.

I found I disliked being linked in her mind with her husband; to hold the same opinions on any topic seemed a mistake, though on this topic the course of bureaucratic caution was to be in agreement with my silent overseer, Lieutenant George Brett.

"I am unsure what I think, Mrs. Brett. I find it very difficult. The law may not help much, but it may help a little; it may protect some babies who would otherwise be neglected—perhaps die. It may be worthwhile."

"Do you really think, Eric, that anything the law does can strengthen a mother's love? And how can you know about that? I don't think a parliament of women would pass a law to punish a mother like MiYan. You and George and other men make the laws and the punishments; you mean well, I know, but you seem so insensitive."

I increasingly disliked the way the conversation was going. To oppose her in anything seemed an incongruity; to be thought unfeeling and punitive, a disaster. "I'm sorry you think so. May we talk about it together sometime later?" I added, as I saw her tonga arriving outside the entrance to the hospital. She had seen it too, and rising said, "I should enjoy that. I think you will be seeing my husband for lunch. Perhaps we can meet soon and talk. I shall ask him to arrange it."

This time, even though capless, I made a sort of saluting gesture to say good-bye. It seemed to amuse her.

Veraswami accepted my invitation for the evening, and I set out for the Club for lunch with George Brett.

Brett went by the rules. He dressed, spoke, and acted precisely and primly. Worst of all, he insisted on telling me at length, and with reflective deliberation, what I already knew about the law pertaining—yes, he did use the word "pertaining"—to the death of MiYan's baby. I found myself thinking of many other things while we lunched and talked. Did he think I had not boned up on the law? Did he think that my police training manual and the notes I had taken on omissions and duties to act during that year at the Mandalay police training course had remained undisturbed over the past few days? He was relentless. He insisted on our wading through it.

It seemed to him, he averred, that MiYan was under a legal as well as a moral duty to take better care of her child, at least to sustain her life; and since medical care was readily available, her failure to fulfill that legal duty might well be criminal homicide. So he averred, and averred and averred. How could Rosemary stand him?

Yet I had to admit he looked the part of the young officer on his way to staff rank: every blond hair in rigid place, square-jawed, squarer-shouldered, his face a mask of severity and sincerity never to be erased by any lightness of feeling. He was of my age, yet he seemed to me of an earlier, mid-Victorian era, clinging to appearances as all. I struggled to pay at least minimal attention to what he was saying; after all, he was my Inspector General as far as the MiYan case was concerned.

He said he thought there was no problem of causation in the case. The child had died from the neglected abscessed tooth and from nothing else. If there was criminal responsibility for failure to provide medical or dental care for the abscessed tooth, there must also be criminal responsibility for the child's death, did I not agree?

I said I thought the cause of the baby's death was obvious enough, as a matter of medical fact, but thought there was much more to consider before MiYan could be convicted and punished. He most seriously concurred—again, his word—but offered the opinion that it was desirable for us to get all these things straight, did I not agree?

I had little choice; I "concurred." And then, in revolt, I decided, despite the likelihood of alienating him, that I should make this harangue more difficult for him by raising a few obstacles in his grimly dull path— concur less and probe more.

"What about the grandmother, Brett? It seems she hit the baby quite hard in the face. Perhaps those blows, and not just the neglect of the tooth, helped kill the baby."

Brett was astonished. "But Mandalay isn't interested in her. Surely you know that. Obviously babies should not be struck, but every villager knows that. What they don't know, some of them, is that they must provide proper medical care for their babies, particularly their girl babies, whom they don't seem to care about so much. That is what the case is about, not violent grandmothers. Anyhow, it would be enormously difficult to prove that her blows hastened the baby's death. And in that case both MiYan and her mother might escape punishment."

I allowed that this did not seem too bad an idea to me. Brett, troubled, decided I must be joking. "Surely, Blair, we must put an end to this infanticide. The Government could hardly have made it more clear."

I was beginning to enjoy myself, though I felt I might well pay a heavy cost. Still, he was too tempting a target. So I agreed, indeed several times vigourously concurred, that the central problem in the case was the failure to provide needed medical care for the baby, once her serious, life-threatening condition was apparent. Was I right? Yes, I was right. "Well, then, what about Mrs. Moffat? She knew how sick the baby was, yet she did nothing to help."

Brett was appalled. "She does not have to take care of sick Burmese babies. She did what she should have; she told MiYan to get medical help for the baby."

"First her luncheon party, then the baby; those were her priorities. Wasn't that neglectful of the baby's life?" I asked.

"You cannot mean to involve her, Blair. I know U Tin Hlang will try to, but you must not let him. She had no duty of care for the baby—you know that. You are not called "The Rickshaw Wallah" for nothing! You know you should not volunteer in such matters. Mrs. Moffat behaved sensibly; it would be dreadful to involve her and her husband in this. And I know, for certain, that Mandalay would not like it at all if you did." And his precisely shaped mouth clamped shut.

I did not share with Brett my suspicions about the paternity of the child. I don't think it was fear of any action by Moffat that stilled my tongue; it was rather a recognition of the frailty of the allegation and of the turmoil that would follow if the facts were as I suspected. Also, my suspicions, true or false, didn't make much difference in the issue of MiYan's duty to care for her baby.

Brett was probably right, and my obstacles to his analysis were gaining me nothing other than his increased dislike. They were probably also increasing the likelihood of my losing this district office. Claire Moffat had no duty at law to care for the baby; MiYan did. The common law of England had found that duty to exist for centuries, and had backed it up occasionally with criminal punishments in egregious cases. And the section of the Indian Penal Code that had been set out in the memorandum from Mandalay, section 304A, had also made such conduct punishable. "Neglect" was the operant word in the section—she did seem to have neglected the child's care. But even that idea had a certain imprecision to it: would it include consideration of all the pressures bearing on MiYan— her own violent mother, her views of the better future life for the baby if she did die now, her wish to keep her employment with the Moffats—in general, her own miserable circumstances? Under those circumstances, was her failure to take the child to Dr. Veraswami, whom, anyhow, she mistrusted, really "neglect"? I didn't know.

I yielded to Brett the accuracy of his analysis of MiYan's duty of care for the baby and her failure to provide adequate care, but I fear that I did not concur as energetically as he apparently expected. My doubts were poorly concealed. The law might be clear enough, and I thought he was right about that, but it seemed so wickedly cruel and pointless to punish MiYan further. I could not see myself pronouncing judgement on her—the scene was abhorrent to me—and if, as I suspected he would, U Tin Hlang elected to put her on trial summarily before me instead of having her face a jury at Assizes, I would have to confront that abhorrent moment. The law seemed clear, but it also seemed nonsense. MiYan and her mother had suffered enough already, and every villager would share my view. My error was in reporting the story at all, but I suppose that since Moffat was there I had had no real choice.

I dealt with the remainder of the lunch with Brett as best I could, calling again on such reserves of courtesy as I could summon. I tried not to alienate him further. I think he saw my enquiries as to the guilt of Claire Moffatt and MiYan's mother as the troubles of an overtaxed mind. In the end, he invited me to dine with his wife and himself two nights hence. It was not the joy of *his* company that led me promptly and with gratitude to accept.

I had a new object of self-indulgence to show off to my guests: an upright, oaken ice chest, with a zinc-lined container for a block of ice in the upper half, and a well-insulated bottom half with front-opening doors and brass fittings where bottles could be stored in surprising coolness. To the touch, the beer bottles felt quite cold, colder than Veraswami achieved with a block of ice resting in a large open bucket surrounded by a garland of beer bottles.

My bungalow was set in less built-up surroundings than Veraswami's, more a part of a jungle clearing than of a township. I left the verandah unlit so that the insects of the night would not intrude. It was not oppressively hot; I counted myself very fortunate. With a full moon, as tonight, and occasional scudding clouds to move shadows across the heavy foliage overhanging the verandah, it was a dramatic and luminous setting for an after-dinner talk.

Close to the magnificence of the ice chest, I placed three high-backed wicker chairs facing out toward the jungle, each chair having a convenient recess in its right armrest to hold a glass. The chairs were also recent acquisitions, products of local craftsmanship, so much cooler and more comfortable than the severe, stuffed, government-issue armchairs of the Club. Veraswami and U Tin Hlang would be ideal guests to appreciate my splendid appointments. I would insist that they admire the ice chest and the chairs before we talked of anything else. Civilisation had come to Moulmein, and I was its embodiment.

Veraswami arrived bursting with jollity. His greeting was effusive. He admired my ice chest as if it were the achievement of a cultivated and precise taste; he gasped in delight at the coldness of the beer, the comfort of the chairs, the charm of the surroundings. I began to believe him.

He had visited me rarely at my bungalow and I tried to express my pleasure that "my only friend in Moulmein" was visiting me and my hope that it would not be so long before he came again. "You are very kind to me, Dr. Veraswami. I seem to spend most of my leisure hours on your verandah—anyhow, the hours I most enjoy."

He was pleased by my reference to him as my only friend in Moulmein. I am not sure, but I think he blushed; it is hard to be sure with one of Veraswami's Dravidian colouration.

To cover his embarrassment, I hurried on, "But we have another friend coming tonight—U Tin Hlang. He said he would try to drop in. I think he will. He knows you are here. And I think he will be interested to learn of my talk with MiYan today."

Veraswami plunged into the MiYan case, pressing me on the relevant law. I told him I had done my best to brush up my understanding of the law over the past few days and that, although George Brett had given me an exquisitely dull refresher course, I was no authority on its subtleties.

He waved this disclaimer aside as excessive modesty, but added, "In any case, if U Tin Hlang joins uss, he will be able to advise precisely, issn't it?"

"I'm not too sure how much we can rely on Lang's commentaries on the law," I said. "After all, he will slant what he says in favour of his client. He will not quite lie, but he will be parsimonious of the truth. He is quite open about it. That's one of the things I like about him."

We were hardly into our first beer when loud and repeated noises from the jungle, which at first I thought came from a large animal in pain, heralded the arrival of U Tin Hlang, tooting vigourously on the horn of his bull-nosed Fiat. He pulled up briskly at the front steps of my bungalow; he must have had the car driven down from Rangoon by the "man" of whom we had spoken. But he had driven himself to my bungalow this evening.

U Tin Hlang and Veraswami made *eyebong* to one another; U Tin Hlang shook my hand in both of his. "It is good to be with you two again. I like it in this peaceful backwater. Though I must say, Blair, you do manage to attract to yourself an undue proportion of politically disturbing cases—no doubt in the hope of seeing me."

I got him seated and equipped with a cold beer. He asked immediately about MiYan. "Tell me, Blair, shall I head for Rangoon in the morning in this chariot," gesturing toward the car parked beside the verandah, "or will MiYan deign to allow me to serve her?"

I told him of her decision and, on his enquiry, of the grounds on which she had made it.

"You really must give up being a policeman, Blair, and join me at the Bar; don't you think so, Veraswami?"

Veraswami waved his head about somewhat wildly in the manner of an Indian who does not wish to give an opinion but wishes also not to be thought unsympathetic—it is a peculiarly rounded and effective gesture, I thought, demanding much of the neck muscles and shoulders.

"So. I stay," Hlang said. "Let us talk about the case then. Blair and I agreed, Veraswami, that we should fence with one another in this way; and you know more about the case than either of us, I imagine. I'll tell you what puzzles me: The baby is dead. Blair's superiors are on his tail to punish MiYan for the death as a warning to others. Why doesn't he just go ahead and commit my new client for trial? What is he fussing about? He needn't decide. Just commit her for trial at Rangoon Assizes. I shall be happy to defend her there and find a way to persuade a jury to acquit her. I won't trouble him further with it. Why must he act the moral hero, a hero uncertain of the path of heroism but sure that if he searches, it will be somewhere for him to follow?" And lowering his voice conspiratorially and leaning towards Veraswami, in a stage whisper of surprising resonance Hlang offered his answer to his rhetorical question: "Could it be that our district officer is racially prejudiced? Burmese babies don't matter!"

I knew he was baiting me, not really attacking me, but I confess I was hard put to keep my temper. I turned to Veraswami: "Is that what you think, too, Dr. Veraswami?"

Veraswami was silent for a moment. "I have watched you for some time, Eric, and I know you mean well by the natives here. But let me press you in the same way. Suppose it wass a member of one of the European families who had mistreated a baby unto death, would you be hesitating? Would you not then think that it wass a jolly good thing to punish whoever had killed the baby? Your duty to let the law take its course, and so on, issn't it?"

The question troubled me. I had to admit that I thought the criminal law would have a more deterrent, educative effect in such a case than when a dominant culture, here the British, tried to impose its values on another culture, here that of a Burmese village, by means of criminal punishments. Anyhow, it seemed a harsh, pedagogical method, even worse than those corporal methods pursued at St. Cyprian's and Eton.

"I don't think it is racial prejudice that moves me, Doctor," I said. "I think I would feel the same way about a European baby."

U Tin Hlang was upon me before the sentence was out: "You deceive yourself, Blair. You don't even know the baby's name, or that of MiYan's mother. I can hear you if they were English—such solicitude, on a first-name basis, I'm sure."

And now I felt beleaguered, angry. Of course one identified with one's own more than with others. But neither in this case nor in my few years in Moulmein had I been neglectful of the villagers. Yet, . . . it was true what they said. I didn't know the baby's name and I would have known it had she been English. I had not seen a possible crime before my nose, and I would have had those involved been European. My anger abated in a sigh.

And then the realisation of a sharp threat struck me: The baby might well have been part European. A phrase of U Tin Hlang's came back to me: "I will try to dig a secret ditch or two for you to fall into." Perhaps this was such a ditch, and a deep one, too. At trial he might spring on me the suggestion that it was *because* the baby was half-caste (with a strong hint that Moffat was the father) that MiYan was being tried for the baby's death. He would be protected from an action in slander by the courtroom setting; my ruling in court that such a suggestion, unsupported by evidence, was both improper and irrelevant would not for a moment diminish its devastating political effect. His employers of the General Council of Buddhist Associations would be well pleased with U Tin Hlang. I certainly must avoid this ditch if I could. I wondered whether MiYan would help him with the digging; surely not, unless it was true.

Dragging my mind back to the verandah, I tried to turn discussion in a less threatening direction: to MiYan's ethnicity rather than her baby's. "Perhaps I would think European parents more deserved punishment. After all, it is easier for them to look after their babies. But MiYan is Burmese, not European. I don't think punishing her will help other Burmese babies. And I am not at all sure that she deserves to be punished; I find it hard to think of her as wicked. But you both seem to be attacking me, although you are supposed to be helping me. Tell me what you would do. Do you wish her to be convicted of child killing, Veraswami?"

"I had hoped you would not ask me that, Eric, but I suspected you would. Walking over here tonight I knew I must make up my mind about that. If I have to answer you now, I must say, yes; on what I now know she should be tried and convicted. I think I am a reluctant protagonist of putting her to trial. I think you are a reluctant opponent. We are both reluctant, we vacillate, we are unsure, we both hesitate too much. And when I am with MiYan, I must admit, I do not think of her as a criminal; in that you are right, she doess not seem to be deserving of further punishment."

"Well, then, how in conscience can you punish her? You say she doesn't deserve punishment, but you would punish her."

"I have watched what happened in India with suttee and with infanticide, Eric. Many who followed village ways, good people, were punished. Many widows have thuss been saved from the fire, many babies thuss saved from painful deaths. It iss worth it, I think, and what they did wass wrong, absolutely wrong, even if their culture said it wass not."

U Tin Hlang, who had been watching me carefully as Veraswami declared himself, interjected: "So you don't believe in cultural neutrality, Veraswami? Most interesting, most interesting. It is a difficult question for a Burmese politician."

"I don't know what you are talking about, Lang," I said; "I don't know what cultural neutrality is."

Veraswami seemed appalled, not at my ignorance but at his causing me what he thought was embarrassment. He decided that a high-pitched giggle would best meet the occasion, culminating in a "Ha Ha, how verry funny. Yes, I reject cultural neutrality; some things are bad even in those cultures that think them good—culture cannot entirely define virtue. Suttee iss bad, though many Indians hold it to be part of their religion. Infanticide, letting baby girls die, or exposing them to die, because of the caste system and the need for dowries for daughters, iss bad. We must stamp them out." And he tried to do so, pounding his foot on the verandah.

U Tin Hlang moved uninvited toward the ice chest. I was glad he felt at home. But I began to resent his role of spectator of the disagreement between Veraswami and me. "Is Veraswami right about that, Lang? Do you wish your people to be educated by the English criminal law?"

"Oh, you do it to yourselves too, Blair. Whenever you English lost a battle at sea—not often enough for my taste—you executed an admiral or two to encourage the others, so the history books tell me. It made the fleet, I'm told."

"I thought you were defending MiYan, Lang. You talk more like a prosecutor."

"No doubt, when we get the Raj out of Burma, if I am not Prime Minister I will be the chief government prosecutor. But don't confuse what I say and do for a client with what I believe. You hit the right jurisprudential note to defend MiYan, stick to it: only the wicked deserve criminal punishment, no matter what good such a punishment may do for others, and I will drub you with that at the preliminary hearing and drub your superiors with it in Rangoon if you put her to trial. But still our good doctor is right. What MiYan did is bad, absolutely bad, whatever the local customs. It is, how should I say it, species bad, in a real sense, inhuman. And at one level or another MiYan knew it."

The vision of U Tin Hlang years hence as a leader of his government came clearly to me. And I began to see, too, why successful defence counsel often become aggressive prosecutors—they have heard and used all the excuses. U Tin Hlang had not committed himself about MiYan, but it seemed clear that, as a personal view, he inclined toward her prosecution. I wondered how he would approach the prosecution of others in the case.

"Tell me, Lang, as a prosecutor, is MiYan the only one you would pursue in this case?"

"Of course not, Blair. My name must constantly be in the news. I would prosecute them all. Dr. Veraswami, an Indian you know, doesn't give a damn for Burmese babies. Sees them sick in the village and does nothing about them except talk to a young district officer. What a villain! Let us prosecute him. And the Moffats, oh the Moffats: slave owners neglectful of their slaves. Let us prosecute them. You are right, Blair, the life of a prosecutor will be a wondrous joy."

"Stop it, Lang, please," I said; "I have enough difficulty with this case without your mocking me. Seriously, what about Claire Moffat? I'm sure you agree with me, Veraswami, she should have seen that the baby got to the hospital, or called you to her bungalow to see the baby when MiYan brought her from the village. Surely giving precedence to her inconsequential luncheon party over the life of the baby is both wicked and criminal."

U Tin Hlang was delighted. Prancing about the verandah in front of us, waving his glass but managing not to spill a drop, he was a picture of joy. "Do please charge her with the baby's death, Blair. It will be wonderful fun! Of course, the master owes a duty of care to the servant, and presumably to the servant's baby if it is on the master's premises, though I am not so sure about that. But yes, do it, Blair. What wonderful fun! I'm sure Rangoon and Mandalay and Charles Moffat will approve of your moral diligence and express their approval. As will I." And beaming at me, he added, "Believe me, I will dwell on it in court, Mr. Rickshaw Wallah, how you, the district officer, have appreciated that the typical behaviour, no, the paradigmatic behaviour, of English memsahibs is morally grotesque, meriting criminal punishment. Perhaps I could act as Crown Counsel for the occasion. It would get me elected, appointed, anointed—I know not what honours—by a grateful Raj anxious to make amends for its earlier moral myopia, and by very grateful Burmese nationalists anxious to be rid of the Raj."

"If you go on like this, Lang, we shall have to talk about something else," I said. "Try to be serious for a moment. So far you think only your client should be tried for the baby's death. What about MiYan's mother?"

"Another name you don't know, Blair. But put that aside." And turning to Dr. Veraswami as if he were an expert witness in court, Hlang asked if it was his view that the baby had died from blows struck by her grandmother.

Veraswami said that his examination of the baby's jaw and teeth both before and after her death did not reveal, so large was the swelling and so advanced the gangrene, whether the abscessed tooth was a result of a blow to her face or had occurred independently of any trauma. "It wass impossible to tell, impossible both when she reached the hospital and later. But her hitting the baby probably contributed to the death."

U Tin Hlang held his finger to the side of his nose in the posture of the cunning negotiator. "Beware, Blair. There is more to it than that. Apart from striking the child and thus hastening her death, MiYan's mother had undertaken to care for the baby. She might be just as responsible in law for a failure of care as MiYan. There was no express contract between MiYan and her mother, of course, but it was clear to both that caring for the baby was her job while MiYan earned what she could for the three of them from the generous-hearted Moffats. So, beware, Blair: if you put MiYan on trial *without* the mother also being charged, I shall have a great deal, a very great deal indeed, to say in court about the behaviour of MiYan's mother. *She* was the true villain."

But U Tin Hlang was not finished with the theme. The prancing and gesturing continued. "And was MiYan's mother not instructed by MiYan herself to take the baby to hospital? And she failed to do so. Is it not very likely, Dr. Veraswami, I say likely and certainly quite possible, that had the baby reached you earlier she would have lived? You can give only one answer to that; it is the only type of question I like to ask. So, I urge upon this honourable if slightly inebriated court the guilt of MiYan's mother for the death of her grandchild. She must be executed forthwith as a warning to other Burmese grandmothers and English admirals."

Then, even more dramatically, U Tin Hlang posed, left hand to brow, right hand and glass extended laterally: "And if you *do* put her to trial I shall have even more wonderful fun. Oh, flint-hearted Raj, bringing this good woman to this sad state of penury and madness, so that she loses the only two people she loves, and now seeking to punish her further and cruelly for what you have done to her. Your hearts are as empty as . . . this glass," which he handed to me.

Veraswami applauded, looking for a moment like a young Indian urchin, the rotundities of age and prosperity falling away. "Magnificent. What doess it all mean?"

I got a beer for Hlang, who had stopped his theatrics and was back in his wicker chair.

"It means very little," I said, "other than that Lang greatly enjoys opposing whatever I do. And he does it rather well, if a little on the melodramatic side, don't you think?"

Veraswami and U Tin Hlang both ignored my question. It was hard to be sure what U Tin Hlang really believed, but I had the sense that everyone I had consulted, except Rosemary, thought MiYan should be punished. Perhaps the support of Rosemary was enough. My mind drifted far away, far away with Rosemary, not on the verandah at all. A change in the tone of Veraswami's voice wrenched me back. "So, if that is good law—that MiYan owed a legal duty of care to her baby which she broke and which caused the baby's death and that she iss therefore guilty—what, if anything, other than those distractions about the failures of others, can you say in her defence, Mr. Lang?"

"Don't underestimate the effect of such distractions on a jury," Hlang said, "but there is another line of defence that does seem to me to be persuasive. Tell me what you think of it. The Raj said it would respect the freedom of religious beliefs in India and Burma. Let us put them to the test. Perhaps I can make a convincing argument along those lines."

The thrust of his argument went beyond the belief in *karma* that the Indian sergeant who investigated the case had told me about, according to which the baby would move on to another and a happier life. U Tin Hlang spoke of the religious obligation not to interfere with the mystical workings of this *karma*. "Nothing happens by chance. You are responsible for yourself; you make life for yourself, life after life. In a previous existence, the baby made its miserable life in Moulmein; it remains responsible. You are not punished *for* sins, you are punished *by* sins; they are the punishment, they influence this life now and the next life, so that it is more than futile for others to interfere with the baby's condition. The baby is making its own *karma*. Its sickness could be made more comfortable, that is all. She will be happier thus, and her next life cannot fail to be preferable to this one. You see the idea, Blair? It is by no means stupid—difficult to swallow, perhaps, but so are most religious ideas, and no less believable than some ideas about God that were drummed into your head at Eton."

"So the baby committed *karma* suicide. Is that it?" I asked. "Have I invented a new crime?"

"Don't be frivolous, Blair," U Tin Hlang replied. "Let me tell you a Burmese folktale that may drive the matter home despite the superiority of your British beliefs to those of us lesser breeds without the law."

And he told the story of Ma Pa Da, a young woman from Thawati who, in the time of the Buddha, in most poignant circumstances witnessed the deaths of her husband and two children, and then—because of her unwillingness to accept her *karma*—even the deaths of her parents, so that she was alone in the world. She went mad; her troubles were more than she could bear. She threw off all her clothes, let down her long hair and wrapped it about her naked body, and walked about raving. She came, after a time, to where the Buddha was teaching, seated under a fig tree. She told her troubles to the Buddha, who tried to console her, but she would not be comforted and demanded of the Buddha the return of her dead. The Buddha replied: "You must go, my daughter, and get some mustard seed, a pinch of mustard seed. Bring it to me and I can bring back their lives. Only you must get this seed from the garden of him near whom death has never come. Get this, and all will be well."

"You already see the moral of this, I'm sure," U Tin Hlang continued. "Her lightness of heart at the Buddha's promise restored her sanity. She dressed and searched diligently and long for the pinch of mustard seed in such a garden. You know what happened. There is no such seed. She learned that death and life are one. So that, as the Buddha said, "There is nothing that can happen to us, however terrible, however miserable, that can justify tears and lamentations and make them aught but a weakness." MiYan did what was right. She suffered quietly, knowing the unity of life and death. Is she to be punished for her devout religious beliefs? As you see, Blair, it is not only for political purposes that I put on my Buddhist face; I really do know the stuff."

Veraswami had been silent through U Tin Hlang's talk of religion, silent but apparently interested. Still, I felt that Hlang and I had perhaps not included him enough. And there was one question on which I wanted his guidance. "Let me ask you a medical question, Doctor, which may not matter in law but seems important to me. How much pain did the baby feel? Do babies feel pain as we do?"

"That iss most interesting, Eric. Some research colleagues in London say that a baby's nervous system, in the first few months of life, iss not completely formed, and that it iss much less sensitive to pain. Like fish, I suppose, though how we know fish don't feel pain, I don't know. And people act on that belief about babies, boy babies in particular, when they cut bits off their little penises without anaesthetic, the penises of commoners' babies and princes' babies alike. It iss very strange. But I have listened carefully to babies crying when they are complaining, whining, uncomfortable; that crying iss quite different from when they cry in pain. I think they feel pain precisely ass an adult doess. What iss different iss that they cannot tell you about it—like fish. We are untroubled by pain in animals that cannot express pain—fish, insects, smaller animals. And even the largest animal, the whale, iss cruelly tortured, partly, I believe, because it cannot communicate its pain to uss. What a huge and terrifying noise it would make if it could! I think MiYan's baby endured a lot of pain, but I don't think MiYan knew that she did."

There was a booming sound from U Tin Hlang's chair. "I am a large animal that feels pain now. Too much beer. Too much of Blair's agonizing. Even the ice in Blair's oaken chest grows weary. I'm going back to the delights of the Htun Hla. Can I give you a lift, Veraswami?"

They thanked me for my hospitality, of which there had been little enough, and I spoke of my pleasure in their company. Veraswami said he would walk home: "It will clear my head." They left together, Veraswami silently with a wave to me, U Tin Hlang loudly with tooted farewells.

I doubt that the Club had ever contained the like; certainly I had seen no dress like it in Burma. A simple, sleeveless dress of raw silk, almost aged ivory in tone—the silk's original colour, I suppose. The dress set off the brighter tints of her long blonde hair, and a blue sash, tied at her left side and hanging to the hemline, precisely caught the vibrant colour of her eyes. I was not the only one who stared. And I suppose I must admit that with Brett in his dress uniform they made a strikingly handsome couple.

The Moulmein Club was not at all accustomed to such style. My own freshly pressed uniform—tidy enough but not designed to conceal, as if that were possible, my angular awkwardness, protruding wrists, and too-large hands—better matched the local style.

I did not think I was late, but there they were at a table in the corner of the bar waiting for me, looking like mannequins in a window at Harrod's—precisely how the young officer and his wife should appear to such of the native servants of the Raj who might be privileged to observe them about to dine.

I must have stopped and stared. His eyes lifted, not coldly, but neutrally. One can never tell much from a greeting when one is expected. It is only when you come upon people by surprise, when they do not expect to see you, that their first reaction tells you something of their feelings for you.

Rosemary spared me any embarrassment. "Hello, Mr. Blair. How nice to see you."

I made my apologies for lateness, hoping I had not kept them waiting—though I was sure I was not late.

"Don't worry, Blair," Brett said, "there's not much to do here anyhow. But join us, do."

I filled in a chit for a beer and signalled the "boy." We drifted into small talk about Moulmein.

Though it was clearly against my own interests, if U Tin Hlang's suspicion was correct and the Bretts were exploring whether Brett would like mine as his first district, I found myself acting the enthusiast for Moulmein and its peoples, struggling to add touches of grace and interest to even the dullest of realities about my district. I understood what moved me—enthusiasm for her. She was so absolutely stunning—I had seen nothing like her since London. No, I had never seen anything like her! Such a combination of simple loveliness and genuine solicitude. And she seemed so unqualifiedly interested in what I was saying, while he evinced a slightly condescending tolerance of my excesses of praise.

I found Brett's constant reference to Rosemary as "my wife" rather than as "Mrs. Brett" or "Rosemary" quite annoying. Here I was, "Mrs. Brett"-ing her in sentence after sentence, and he "my wife"-ing her as if she were a proprietary interest of his, when, according to U Tin Hlang's intelligence, their financial relationship, at any rate, was quite the contrary. Brett seemed to think she thought and spoke only within the ambit of his permission. When our dinner-table conversation drifted towards the Moffats, he advised me crisply that "my wife doesn't wish to discuss the Moffats; it's sort of *sub judice*, don't you think, Blair?"

Annoyed, I said I didn't think so at all. We could talk about them without discussing MiYan and her baby, surely. And if he were in Moulmein to assist me and not merely to observe and report what happened, he and I would have to talk about all these matters. "And I assume you will discuss such things with Mrs. Brett. It seems to me that a woman's perspective may be very helpful indeed." Recalling Rosemary's earlier comments, I added, "Women carry the burden of care for babies; perhaps what will influence them is different from what you and I think."

"Don't be sentimental, Blair. Your only authority here is the authority of law. You're not some sort of social worker. But in any case, even though my wife has already talked about the case with the woman MiYan and with you and with some Indian doctor—though without my approval, I must confess—I still think it inappropriate for the three of us to discuss the matter further."

What a pompous ass! Did he think we were witness, counsel, and judge in the Royal Courts of Justice in the Strand, holding bench conferences about a pending case, rather than minor functionaries of the Raj trying to serve Burmese villagers? It seemed silly to me. Obviously I would have to make up my own mind as a magistrate, but their opinions could be useful, and there seemed no point in avoiding the topic. But what astonished me was that Rosemary put up with this disrespectful verbal dominance. Indeed, she seemed more interested in calming me than in confronting him. Why, in heaven's name, shouldn't she be entirely capable of discussing the Moffats without trespassing into his apparent task?—whether it was to see that I handled the case sensibly or to report on how badly I handled it, I began not to care which.

"Have it your own way, Brett. As yet I don't entirely understand your rules and I don't feel at all bound by them; you talked to me long enough about the case at lunch two days ago and gave your advice without much hesitation, not at all troubled by the case being mine to decide. Why not now? Still, have it your way."

I had clearly upset Rosemary, and, by so doing, had even more clearly upset myself. My hands wrestled with each other beneath the tablecloth.

"It's simple enough, Blair. I'm sure my wife understands, if you don't. We three should not talk at all about the death of MiYan's baby. You and I can talk as much as you like—but on duty. I'm happy to help you then, and I think you need help. But it is none of my wife's business whatsoever, and you should spare her your uncertainties."

What a cad he was, despite his dress uniform, square jaw, and neat head with every short blond hair in place. I did not reply, and Rosemary had apparently decided that the topic was exhausted. We managed to get through the dinner without further reference to MiYan or even to Moulmein. Rosemary did her best and I tried, too, for her sake; but we were condemned to an awkward dinner. Despite my swiftly increasing pleasure in Rosemary's company, I found my eyes wandering to the clock on the wall of the Club's dining room.

The tension was alleviated by a general move from the dining room toward the bridge and billiards tables. Brett seemed to welcome the idea; I hated it. I had no idea of Rosemary's preference. To my relief, I heard her saving me, and more: "George, don't let us stop you. I know you would enjoy a game. I would prefer to sit here and talk to Mr. Blair about whatever he wishes to talk about and," with a smile to me, "I don't think Mr. Blair will mind. Play a few rubbers. We will be alright here."

The daft man was obviously pleased to be released, and with a reiterated "if you are sure" he joined the bridge players, and we were alone. That is to say, we were not alone, but we could talk to one another as if we were alone. The chairs in the Club lounge suddenly seemed near to paradise for me.

My joy must have been apparent to Rosemary: "You suddenly seem happy, Mr. Blair."

"Of course I am. To be talking to you alone—no MiYan, no Veraswami, no . . . , no one else." I had nearly said "no Brett." By her smile I saw that she knew it. It astonished me to be talking like this; I never had before, to any woman, to anyone. And what was both surprising and delightful was that Rosemary seemed to understand and to be both lightly amused and friendly. She didn't seem to mind at all.

I had talked in terms of frank sexuality with those ladies who visited me from the village, but they had little idea of what I was saying. Anyhow, this was entirely different, and it was crude of me even to have thought of those others at this time. My attraction to her was of a higher order. Yet she must know how I felt or she would not be reacting so kindly—not angry at all, not moving to join her husband, just smiling gently at me.

For a time she did not speak. Her hand reached out and touched my arm lightly. There was warmth in her glance. I felt ill at ease, but not embarrassed. I knew I was in no way troubling her, but the silence between us was beginning to oppress me.

"Perhaps you should not be so obviously happy about such things here, Mr. Blair. Later, perhaps; not now. Let us talk of other things for a while, not of ourselves. And surely your coffee must be quite cold by now."

I gulped the demitasse of lukewarm brew that passed for coffee at the Club: "I like it chilly in this climate." She was amused, so I launched without anxiety into the topic forbidden by her husband. "What did you think of MiYan? If you don't mind my asking, M . . . Mrs. Brett."

I had tried to say "Rosemary" but the word had stuck. She had seen my hesitancy. She glanced toward the bridge tables and made no immediate reply.

"I hope you do not mind my asking, . . . 'Rosemary,' if I may?"

"Of course you may. I hope you often will."

Astonishment upon astonishment. She seemed genuinely pleased by my now open attraction to her. It was quite unbelievable, but it was indeed happening.

"Really, Eric, I think we had better do what you say—start talking about something. You seem excellent at discussing what should be discussed, and disagreeing with George about it. He is not my censor. So let me say what I think: I found MiYan a most troubled and troubling per-

son. I found it impossible to put myself in her place. That is my fault, not
hers. I have no idea what her life must have been like. You have seen
where she lived. Do you have any idea of how she lived? What a day was
like for her?"

"Not very much, I fear. I once lived in a fishing village for a few days,
and I have some idea of the pattern of their lives. I suppose the inland villagers live much the same, but I don't really know. I do know that MiYan,
her mother, and her daughter lived in a ramshackle sort of hovel on the
edge of the village, but with what MiYan earned from the Moffats they
would have had enough to eat even if the other villagers had not been reasonably helpful to them, which the headman tells me they were. But why
does it matter? Her life in Talaban did not stop her getting medical help for
her baby."

Rosemary leaned toward me, her hand most distractingly brushing some
wisps of hair back from her brow. "You may be right. It may not matter. But
if you and George are to punish her as a criminal I would like to have some
idea of what it must have been like for her with an unreliable mother caring for her very sick child."

I tried to tell Rosemary of the condition of the baby and of the hut
when I found her. I did not do very well. It sounded so bland. No smells.
No flies at her nostrils and lips. No urine and excreta on her legs. It was
hardly a fit subject for an after-dinner talk at the Club. Perhaps Brett had
been right. And then an unlikely and wild thought struck me and
expressed itself before I could judge its wisdom: "U Tin Hlang is driving me
to Talaban tomorrow, about mid-morning. We both want to talk to the
headman and perhaps to others. We plan a picnic lunch by the river afterwards. He does these things well. I wonder, would you come? I know he
would be pleased, and I . . . ," and I left the sentence unfinished, for it was
all too obvious how I felt.

Unhesitatingly, crisply, with no apparent thought of her husband's certain displeasure or of my discourtesy in not inviting him, Rosemary
responded: "Of course. Yes. You are sure Mr. Hlang won't mind?"

"Lang will be delighted. But what about your husband?"

She bridled slightly at my enquiry, but quickly relaxed. "You must not
worry about that, Eric. He is less authoritative in private. He knows I dislike scenes in public, so he goes on with those orders he issues to me and
about me, knowing I will let them pass. But don't worry. When will you
pick me up? I will be ready."

"Lang told me he would pick me up about ten. We shall come straight
over here if that is convenient. I will let you know if there is any change."

Brett returned from the bridge tables too soon for my taste. Rosemary
rose as he approached. "I am on the weary side, George. I think I shall go
to bed. And I have a busy day tomorrow. Mr. Blair and Mr. Hlang are taking me to the village where the baby died."

"But, really, Rosemary. I thought you had agreed not to meddle," he
said.

She made no reply, but turning to me, held out her hand. "Good night, Eric. I look forward to seeing you tomorrow."

I think I took her hand. I think I thanked them both for a pleasant evening. I am not sure. My purpose was a swift retreat. I was getting out of my depth.

There it was again, a full-scale production, a noisy U Tin Hlang arrival in his green, bull-nosed Fiat tourer. The car was more appropriate to a Sunday morning in Chelsea than to the ribbed and dusty roads of Moulmein, and so was U Tin Hlang's dress—khaki slacks, open-necked white shirt and matching leather driving cap and gloves, the scar curving across his cheek adding a rakish touch. I am sure he enjoyed the attention he attracted, but I am also sure that he was not insensible to the political advantage he gained. No one, either townsman or villager, native, Indian, Chinese, or European, could possibly fail to enquire who he was, if they didn't already know. I wondered whether he would have been prepared to substitute a top hat for the cap if he thought that necessary to achieve universal recognition throughout Burma.

My staff—cook, houseboy, and gardener—were assembled, open-mouthed, to observe his arrival. He did not disappoint them. Making his usual swift approach and vigourous stop at the steps of my bungalow, he shouted, "Come along, Blair," over the still running engine.

I was ready, of course; one tended to be ready for U Tin Hlang.

I tried to turn the handle of the door on the passenger's side. It was stiff. "Leave it, Blair," U Tin Hlang said. "Climb over like everyone else. Don't be so militaristic."

It was an easy vault, with U Tin Hlang patting the seat to signal the rather obvious spot for my bottom. He beamed at me joyously. "I hope we are not rained out this time. You remember our last trip, to the pagodas?"

Of course I did, and as Hlang, waving to my staff, launched us from my bungalow, I had the sense of chucking away all anxiety for the welfare of my district—a youth on a spree.

"We head for the Club, do we not? I assume your inamorata has not changed her mind about this trip."

I was astonished. I had not thought it necessary to send a message to U Tin Hlang about Mrs. Brett's acceptance of my invitation. And I had not even asked U Tin Hlang if I might invite her, since I knew the general lavishness of his catering for lunch and was sure he would be pleased if she came too. But how did he know? My mouth had been opening to ask his consent to her coming with us to Talaban—it stayed open.

"Don't look so bewildered, Blair. There is not much that happens at the Club that I am not advised about if I enquire. The little scene last night between Rosemary and the two officers of our constabulary did not go unnoticed. It wasn't difficult to guess the rest."

"Yes, if you don't mind. She said she would last night. I thought you would enjoy her company and I know you always overfill luncheon hampers."

He nodded his agreement, while I added: "But I do wish you would not call her my inamorata, or anything like that—things are difficult enough with George Brett without your adding to it. I think they are looking over Moulmein, as you suspected, to see if they would like it here. So, please, be gentle with her and with me; it's not easy."

"Have no fear, Blair. I will not embarrass you, anyhow while she is with us, but I must tell you now that I have thought of the perfect solution—he stays in Mandalay, or preferably further away, and she comes to Moulmein to comfort the district officer. Right?"

I thought it best not to reply. It was a lovely day, and it was a joy to be rushing along, the air whistling over the windshield and tugging at my cap, for I had worn my uniform, but mercifully the version with baggy shorts and long socks, Sam Browne belt, and officer's cap. It was too hot for more formal dress, yet I had to be in duty dress for what was obviously an official call on the headman of Talaban.

Hlang asked, in mock seriousness: "Do you think they will let this chariot enter the sacred precincts of the Club? I suppose they will think I am your chauffeur, Blair. Perhaps you would climb over into the back seat, look as haughty as you can manage, I will crouch in servility, and we will make an entrance."

I stayed where I was. Rosemary was on the verandah of the Club as we arrived, slightly ahead of time. I suppose she wanted no further public scene. U Tin Hlang was quiet and circumspect, as he had promised. I climbed out of the car and took Rosemary's offered hand as she came down the front steps of the Club. U Tin Hlang remained at the wheel. The three of us performed the Anglo-Saxon rituals of repeated "good mornings."

Rosemary seemed entirely at ease, not at all troubled by what I assumed must have been a conflict-ridden time with her husband. She was dressed in clothes startlingly like those U Tin Hlang was wearing: an open-necked shirt of a lighter material than his, but of a very similar soft white, khaki slacks which seemed to suit her admirably, though I had not before seen a woman so sensibly dressed for a jungle path, sensible stout boots, and (quite unlike U Tin Hlang's leather cap) a soft, wide-brimmed hat of the style worn by Australian soldiers—again a dress I had not before seen on a woman, but it certainly looked stunning on her.

"I am so glad you decided to come with us, . . ." I tried for the "Rosemary," but it would not come.

"You seem surprised, Eric. I told you I would."

I insisted that she sit in the front beside Hlang, and I managed to wrench open the little, curved side door to ease her entrance.

It took us fifteen or twenty minutes, and a rather bumpy fifteen or twenty minutes, to reach Talaban. Hlang drove well but not at all timorously, and the road was more suited to a bullock wagon or an elephant carrying a howdah than to a rakish Fiat tourer. Rosemary removed her hat—fearing it would be blown off if she didn't, I suppose—and her hair blew back toward me as I leaned forward hoping to talk between the two in the front. My earlier juvenile joy in an escapade had changed to some anxiety about what I was doing here with these two. It seemed to fall out-side military regulations. I did not know what rules I was breaking, but I had the sense there must be some. I remembered my housemaster at St. Cyprian's telling me, "There are no rules here, Blair, and if you break them you will be sent down." I knew precisely what he meant. Now I again had that childhood sense of free-floating guilt. Everything seemed so fine—there must be something wrong with it.

The journey passed too swiftly. I knew this schoolboy joy in an outing would fade with the realities of Talaban and the baby's death. It was obvi-ous that we were expected—anyhow, that U Tin Hlang was expected. I might be the official representative of the Raj, but U Tin Hlang was of much more interest as the official representative of nationalistic opposition to the Raj—entirely apart from the compelling attraction of his automo-bile to the children of the village.

He performed his usual dust-scattering arrival, and we stopped in front of the headman's hut.

It was all rather formal and contrived, like an official inspection. The hut MiYan and her family had occupied had been cleaned up, the dogs scattered, the smell reduced. The hessian cot on which the baby had lain in her excrement had been removed. I did my best to tell Rosemary what it had been like, but sounded to myself somewhat precious, as if exaggerating the squalor by contrast to my own fine sensibilities. She listened, enquired occasionally, but did not talk much.

U Tin Hlang barely glanced at the hut before having the headman take him around the village in the manner of a politician, U Tin Hlang pressing him for swift details of each family in the village, making *eyebong* to as many villagers as he could draw into his vicinity, patting any passing chil-dren on the head, and generally enjoying himself.

As Rosemary and I left the hut, I found myself wondering how MiYan must have felt when she did what Claire Moffat had ordered her to do and left her obviously very sick baby with her mother. Did she feel rage? Was she really helpless? Why did she comply? She could have got a job with some other Europeans, I supposed. Or could she, if the baby was half-caste? An unmarried planter would certainly not mind that. Perhaps she thought the Moffats could stop her. I really had no idea. I put my doubts to Rosemary.

Rosemary seemed equally perplexed: "I tried to feel what the hut and the baby must have looked like when you first saw her, Eric, and I cannot understand at all how a mother could let that happen . . . it is very wicked . . . somehow we should try to prevent it. Yet MiYan seems such a sensible and kind girl. She must have been torn apart. Perhaps all her life she has been helpless, doing only what others tell her. Yet think of the pain and misery of that baby."

While Rosemary and I were standing outside MiYan's hut, one of my policemen rode up on a bicycle. I had, of course, told my staff where I was going, but his arrival surprised me.

He handed me a message from Dr. Veraswami which, apparently, Veraswami had sent over to the police station earlier in the morning. The envelope was unsealed; the duty sergeant had had the sense to read it to see if it was urgent enough to send on to me. It was brief: "Dear Mr. Blair: A man from Pakara came to the hospital this morning to tell MiYan that her mother has been missing for two days. They have been searching for her in the jungle. MiYan wishes to go to the village to try to find her. I am not empowered, I think, to let her do this unless you authorise it. I shall wait to hear from you." It was signed, "With sympathy, V."

Rosemary saw my distress: "Is it bad news?" I handed the note to her.

I did not see how I could release MiYan at this stage. Mandalay had surely impressed upon me that I was dealing with a felony, a homicide. If it was proper to have MiYan arrested, it could hardly be proper to let her go to help search for her wandering mother.

The policeman had his message pad with him. I asked him for it and wrote a note to the duty sergeant telling him to advise Dr. Veraswami that I would call on him in the late afternoon and that in the meantime he should not release MiYan. I instructed the duty sergeant to send two men immediately, by lorry, to Pakara to help in the search.

Rosemary waited quietly while all this was going on. When the policeman left, she handed Veraswami's note back to me, took my arm, and said, "Let's leave now. It's time for our picnic, don't you think? I am finding this a sad little visit. I suppose that is what I should have expected, but we're not doing much good here now. Should you go straight back to Moulmein to see about MiYan, or can we have our picnic?"

Since it seemed wrong to release MiYan, there was no urgency in our return. "No, there's no point in my hurrying back. Let's see if we can drag Lang away from his state visit."

Hlang made no protest. He could, apparently, adjust the time of his gracious condescension to the villagers to whatever period was available. "Yes, Blair, your chauffeur is ready if you are."

I managed again to wrench open the little door on the passenger's side for Rosemary, while Hlang and I climbed over the side into the car, he to drive, me to ride in the back seat.

A comet's tail of naked children rushed behind us as Hlang performed his usual impressive circling of the open spaces between the huts, revving the engine but moving quite slowly, before setting off on the narrow road from Talaban.

He drove with one hand on the wheel, the other waving an ordinance map on which he had marked the bend in the Salween River he said was perfect for lunch. Soon he turned onto what could hardly be described as a road—more a jungle path, but wide enough for the car—and we bumped and edged our way to the river.

It was indeed lovely. The Salween widened into a lazy curve. The jungle stood slightly back from the banks, which, on our side, were shady and cool. We had hardly stopped before Hlang was at the hamper, strapped on the back, removing two large rugs which he ceremoniously spread as "dining room, sitting room, buttery, kitchen and all, armchairs, dining chairs, couches and all."

I carried the hamper to the edge of the rugs. Rosemary started to unpack it, Hlang advising with glee on the impossibly extensive lunch that faced us. And then, feeling behind the spare wheel strapped on the driver's side on the running board, he produced a paper-wrapped parcel whose shape told me immediately its contents: two bottles of wine, wrapped when chilled in paper and towels. Stripping one bare and carefully rewrapping the other, Hlang said: "Hardly chambré, but potable, I believe."

It was a feast, and we feasted. What we talked about during lunch I do not recall, but I do remember that it was Rosemary who first turned us from chatter to the business of the day. And she was kind to me in doing so, asking Hlang, not me, what he thought should be done about MiYan and her mother.

"Blair can't do much about the mother except hope that she will be found. As to MiYan: I think Eric has to prosecute her. On the face of it, she seems to have broken the law. I will find a way to get her acquitted at trial in Rangoon. But his superiors haven't given our district officer much choice."

Rosemary pressed Hlang on what might be done to give infant girls in the village better protection from cruelty and neglect. Hlang said he did not think the law would help much: "After all, it doesn't do much good in England. The babies of the poor die there at least as frequently as here—anyhow, there's not much difference—and what our district officer should do is help the villagers attain health and prosperity, and help me to give them independence from their English masters. Though I don't suppose he can be too open about the latter."

Of a sudden the events of the morning struck home. A parallel hit me that turned the joy of the picnic into queasy misery. In my heart I had been blaming the Moffats more than anyone else for the death of MiYan's baby. But now . . . now . . . I saw clearly that if MiYan's mother died, as well she might, I would have behaved towards her exactly as Mrs. Moffat had behaved towards the baby, denied her the care of the one person who gave her a chance of life and protection. No one cared for the baby except MiYan. No one cared for the mother except MiYan. She did her poor best for them, and given a chance she might have succoured them both. But hindered as MiYan was, the baby had died, and the mother might now have. Mrs. Moffat had allowed the first death, I the second. The mother was as helpless, without MiYan, as the baby, or very nearly so. Was I a felon also? Should I report myself to Mandalay? What crazy wickedness it all was.

Rosemary saw my distress. "What is wrong? Do please tell us."

She and Hlang were sitting well apart on each side of the rugs. I had propped myself against the hamper between them before getting up and wandering about. I shut the hamper, and sat down on it, facing my friends, from whom it was unnecessary to conceal my feelings, except perhaps a few about Rosemary. I told them the parallel I saw between the Moffats and myself.

Hlang tried by satire to jolly me out of it: "Of course you had a great deal of freedom of decision once Mandalay told you to treat her as a child killer. You've got to be a king, not a lieutenant, to play Lear."

"That's true," I replied, "I had to arrest her. But I could have arranged for her mother to be better cared for, and I didn't give it a thought."

Rosemary seemed moved by my self-criticism, moved more than it merited, I thought: "Poor Eric, you do punish yourself a lot, don't you," and she stretched out her hand to me.

U Tin Hlang got up briskly for one of his bulk. "I'm going for a digestive walk along the river, you two, and I don't want company. You had better talk to one another, I think. I mean talk, not chatter. Good luck." And he was off.

I took Rosemary's hand and sat down beside her. She was blushing as U Tin Hlang left.

It might have been the wine, but I think not. It might have been her reference to caring for others. More likely it was the utter novelty for me of being with a lovely woman of my own age who openly and warmly expressed affection for me. Whatever the causes, I found myself for the first time in my life capable of being both loving and direct.

I put my arm around her, leaned towards her, kissed her lightly on the cheek, and said, "Thank you, Rosemary, for worrying about me." It sounded most unlike me—but that seemed a most desirable change.

She made neither resistance nor further approach, but sat there, still holding my hand: "You must not further punish that girl; it would be punishing her for the sins of all of us. She cannot purge all our uncaring. You must find a way."

Every instinct told me she was right. But I could not banish the doubt that it was nothing more than that: my instinct telling me she was right and not my judgement. Her humane, unlegalistic directness appealed to me deeply. But did it appeal because I was falling in love with her, or was I falling in love with her, at least partly, because I found such comfort in what she said? I smiled at such a silly confusion. Rosemary was watching my face. "What are you amused about, Eric? I meant what I said. You must find a way to save that poor girl."

"I was amused at me, Rosemary, not at you. I am moved by what you said, but I think that is because I begin to love you. MiYan has a powerful champion in you if I am to decide her fate. But at the moment I think I would agree with most anything you said."

Rosemary seemed resentful. She moved slightly away from me. "You must not humour me, Eric. Treat me as an equal. Don't agree with what I say because you like me." And then she relented, moved closer again, and added, "Though I do know the feeling."

We were silent for a moment, and then it was clear to me. She was right. I was no longer prepared to sacrifice MiYan on the altar of deterring others from neglecting their babies. How I would square that decision with Mandalay's obviously contrary wishes, and indeed orders—as well as with Brett's watchful eye—was not clear to me; but even if it cost me my posting, I would not further punish MiYan.

"It may mean my leaving here, but I agree she has suffered enough," I said, and, letting my thoughts run free, added: "It probably also means that you and George will come here in my place. That's what U Tin Hlang thinks."

She sat a bit more stiffly but did not move away: "No, it doesn't. We had talked about that on the way here, but once I got to know you and thought what it would be like here with George, I knew it wasn't for me. Which means it isn't for him. He may order me about in public, as you have seen; but when things matter he does what I want. He doesn't have much choice if he wants to stay with me. Mandalay or Rangoon with George are sufferable; a small district would not be."

I was astonished, not by what she was telling me about her relations with her husband, but by her rejection of Moulmein. I could imagine nothing more perfect than the life of a district officer here with her as a wife. And—I don't regret it—I said so.

"It sounds lovely, Eric, but that is not what it would be like. George never in any way involves me in his work, never tells me what he is doing, never talks to me about anything that matters. I have tried hard, but he is beyond changing. He has an unalterably fixed view of a woman's place. He knows I have a swifter mind than his, but he is adamant that my interests are a woman's interests and none other. The prolific Mr. Mill and his dear friend Harriet Taylor will never change George Brett's opinion on this— women are a subject race, they are happy only that way. I am useful to him, we enjoy one another in many ways, together we make it possible for each of us to lead the lives we lead. But a small district with him would provide a very dull life for me—though it would be fine for him, perhaps. We will not be coming here, that I promise you. George in the end has to do what I want if we are to stay together, and he wants that."

Empowered by her frankness I asked the probably unforgivable question: "Do you love him?"

She looked me directly in the eyes as she hesitated and then replied, "He makes life possible for me."

I was at a loss as to what she meant. "But Lang tells me that you are wealthy. That you keep him. How can he behave as he does?"

She moved closer. I could feel her breast against my side. She was clear-ly not at all troubled by my interrogation. "You two go in for tittle tattle, I see. Yes, my father had good sense in such matters, even if the law doesn't. The dowry means that I can travel with George and live as we do, but the real money is safely in a trust for me only and not available at all to George, except through me. Daddy explained that with effort even the English law governing married women can be overcome."

"Why did you marry him? It sounds like a business enterprise."

"You have no idea how awful life is for an unmarried woman in London who detests the round of parties and the futility of the social scene. You are treated as a fool; you become a fool. There is so little you may do. Brett set me free, and I am grateful to him. And we were attracted to one another in a physical way, and still are—I hope I do not shock you. No, why should it shock you? I'm sure you do not live all that solitary a life here. George tells me that he is informed otherwise. See, I hear things too. Why should it be any different for me? So George has many valuable purposes, you see."

I knew it would take me time to understand all that she was saying, but broadly, it sounded as if U Tin Hlang was right—Brett did earn more by his prick than by his sword! But what an awful thought that was. No, it wasn't—there was more to it than that—I could see how useful they were to one another. And why should I feel so proper, so censorious about such matters? I should rejoice in her openness, not be troubled by it. And yet, and yet, my feelings for her were surely not only sexual; apart from that it was a delight to be with her, though her shirt did cling wonderfully to her body and those pants were incredibly fetching.

"Will you leave Moulmein soon?" I asked.

She knew I spoke with regret. She understood and replied to more than I had asked. "I don't think we can be together here, Eric. It is too awkward. Perhaps we can meet again somewhere else. Before too long, I hope. But you do so very well here. And my father was not able to rearrange English law sufficiently so that a married woman could transform her life as you and I would both like. You arrived too late for me." And, smilingly, she added, "Though even if you had been on time I cannot really see you fit-ting into the London society which gave me George. You would be even worse than I was."

"So there's nothing for me—for us, I mean?"

"That's right. Not now. Perhaps when you come to Mandalay. Perhaps when we meet again somewhere else. But not here. I won't do that to George." And she leaned against me and returned my earlier kiss, equally lightly, with at least equal affection.

A noise of exaggerated tramping could be heard. U Tin Hlang was apparently trying to emulate the stamp of an elephant. Rosemary did not move away from me, but held me beside her as he arrived. He beamed down at us. "Time to be going, or must I go for another walk? It's nice to be wanted."

She was as direct with him as she had been with me: "Eric and I have gone as far as we can go for the time being. You don't need to keep walking. May I drive back to the Club?"

U Tin Hlang looked shocked. "Drive? Can you? Have you ever driven a Fiat? It's a heavy car, you know," and he looked around as if there might be a way of escape in the jungle.

Before he was finished Rosemary was on her feet and we were packing the hamper and loading it onto the car.

Our talk had left her joyous, me sad. She drove with less panache than U Tin Hlang, but carefully and well. When she had traversed the track and reached the road to Moulmein, U Tin Hlang insisted that we change places, and that I ride beside her in the front while he sat in the back. "I have always wanted to be driven to the Club by a female chauffeur and a military postillion" he said, and folding his arms in the style of a pasha, he prepared for his grand entrance.

At the steps to the Club, Rosemary thanked us warmly but briskly for the outing and the lunch. She did not invite us in. U Tin Hlang resumed his place at the wheel, and we left. No one seemed to have noticed our arrival or departure.

I asked U Tin Hlang to take me to the police station. We did not talk much, and not at all about the case or about Rosemary or myself. Hlang was a dear chap; he respected my need to try to think it all through.

At the police station the news I had feared awaited me. The two policemen were on their way back from Pakara. MiYan's mother had been found before they arrived—dead, fallen a day or two ago into an animal trap in the jungle.

It was a wretched night. By her visit Rosemary had made the stark loneliness of my life in Moulmein more than clear to me. And having listened to Veraswami and U Tin Hlang and George Brett urging me to prosecute MiYan, and to Rosemary urging me not to (and my then agreeing), I found I was still unsure whether I was being led astray by loneliness and affection to do that which I ought not to do, and which, incidentally, would likely not help my career in the Civil Service. I was tired, depressed, sorry for myself. My bungalow seemed desolate without my guests of two nights before. The beer was poor consolation, though I vigourously tested its adequacy to that end. Miserable, I crawled early and unsteadily to bed.

For once the beer helped; I slept soundly. I went to bed confused and uncertain, but I awoke clear-headed and without doubts. I must draft a brief memorandum to Mandalay and get it off today. Copies must be sent to Moffat and and to Brett, and this must be noted on the memorandum; a blind copy must be sent to Dr. Veraswami and its confidentiality marked on it. I must not consult further with anyone—if I could not rely on my own judgement now I would never develop that capacity in the future. I should no longer wrestle with the question of whether I was moved by heart or head; in this case they came together, to my larger comfort. In the memorandum I would not struggle to give closely reasoned explanations of what I had done—it would state my decisions and the broad reasons for them. The keys were confidence and brevity. That is how they had told us to conduct ourselves towards others in our districts; let me now so conduct myself towards my superiors.

I found the memorandum easy to write. Its thrust was that there had been no provable failure in law by anyone concerned with the death of the baby, that this was not a suitable case for deterrent efforts directed to improving infant care in the villages, that I had been in error in not noting these facts in my previous report, and that I appreciated the opportunity to do so now. I added that further enquiries would, I thought, cause embarrassment to the administration in my district and urged that I be called on the telephone to explain these likely embarrassments if this were thought necessary.

In good bureaucratic style I numbered the paragraphs of the memorandum, confined each paragraph to one topic, and kept each paragraph short. In the second to the last paragraph I undertook, as I visited each village in my district in the future, to speak to each headman about the desirability of advising me of any cases of infant or child neglect or cruelty he might suspect in his village—I would tell them that such matters would be dealt with kindly and discreetly, and that the parents would be helped by a benevolent Raj to care for their children better. In the last paragraph I reported my intention to arrange immediate and extra instruction for my men to be on the lookout for such cases and to bring them promptly to my attention.

It read crisply. I sent it off to Mandalay, with copies to Brett and Moffat delivered by a policeman on a bicycle.

I saw Moffat the next day when I had to report to him for our weekly meeting. He made only passing reference to the memorandum: "A pity you didn't let me help you with that memorandum, Blair—I could have helped you shape it up a bit—but all in all it did no harm. Let's see what they say." I gained the impression that he was well satisfied with what I had done— and greatly relieved.

I asked Moffat if MiYan would be returning to work for him. "I mentioned this to Claire," he said; "I doubt she will have her back—too unreliable." I thought there was more than a gleam of relief in his eyes.

Veraswami read my memorandum carefully when I gave it to him. "It iss verry good, verry wise. You were right to be conclusionary and not argumentative. These questions are too close for exegesis, issn't it? You are learning the ways of power, I see. I hope you have done the right thing; it iss difficult." And for reasons which at first I found elusive he told me that he thought there were only two good professions: his, medicine, because with some effort you can persuade yourself you are doing good, and astronomy, because you can be fairly certain you are doing no harm. "Primum non nocere, Blair, that's the great thing, isn't it?" His joke, if that is what it was, caused him glee; it depressed me.

Nevertheless, I felt that Veraswami thought I had chosen the right path, but that he was unsure about it; that he hoped it had not corrupted me in any way, and didn't think it had, but was not sure of that either.

I asked him what he thought should be done about MiYan. As usual he had anticipated me. "She tells me she wishes to work in the hospital. She will be most helpful, most helpful. Though you arrested her ass a neglectful killer, Eric, I think she hass a talent for caring for others; it iss most unexpected."

I was anxious about Brett's reaction. By now he must detest me cordially; my handling of the MiYan case certainly had given him ample room for the insertion into my fledgling career of some professionally damaging knives. Mandalay had not sent him to Moulmein to cheer me on.

He came to the police station the next morning. I had hoped to avoid him until I had heard from Mandalay, but there was no escape. He was not cordial, nor was he hostile: "My wife and I plan to leave Moulmein tomorrow, Blair. Could we requisition a vehicle to take us to the station?"

I said that would be done, and enquired if he had decided to leave now that MiYan was not to be prosecuted.

"Well, yes, I'm glad that's over; but my wife and I want to get back to Rangoon. The new C.O. Burma Police has just arrived in Rangoon. I met him in London and my wife knows him well. He hasn't yet appointed an A.D.C. It carries a captaincy. I'm about due and there is a chance, so he says. The MiYan matter can wait."

My heart leapt for Rosemary: that would suit her perfectly. But the thought of her leaving was misery—perhaps he would die before the morrow, but the odds of that seemed long. Not a word from him about my memorandum; not a criticism, not a compliment. How could she stand him?

Later that afternoon, to my surprise, I heard the unmistakable sound of U Tin Hlang's Fiat performing its ritual of arrival at the police station. I went to the entrance to greet him. He seemed furious. "Blair, may I see you in private?"

I stood aside at the entrance to my office to show him in. He brushed past me, glaring ahead. My sergeant looked at me enquiringly. I waved my hand to reassure him and followed Hlang into the office, closing the door behind me.

Hlang came to the point. "You've wasted my time again, Blair. You arrest her and then release her. Why don't you make up your mind before having me dragged here? And that poppycock you wrote to Mandalay. . . ."

Now I, too, was furious: "How do you know what was in my memorandum? I'm sure neither Moffat nor Brett nor Veraswami would have shown it to you."

"Don't be so simple, Blair." And waving to my outer office, he added,

"With Burmese and Indian policemen here you can't think that your official correspondence escapes me."

Suddenly the tone changed. The fierce demeanour fell away. I realised his eyes had been shining with insincerity, not anger. Throwing wide his arms, Hlang said, "You're a beamish boy, Blair. I enjoy these visits—the G.C.B.A. can afford them. I'm on my way to Rangoon, so I came to invite you to breakfast the next time you are there. I have a bungalow on the beach that you would enjoy. Breakfast is the best meal; we have it on the beach with my elephants, my horses, and my mistresses. You will enjoy it." He wrapped his arms around me, embracing me as I had embraced him at the railway station. Then, reassuming his mock rage, he stormed through the outer office, and the Fiat roared to life.

I stayed in my office. One has to have dramatic skills to be with U Tin Hlang in public.

As to Mandalay: a telephone call came a few days later from a staff captain. I mentioned the Moffats' role in the case, not in detail, not with any criticism, merely that MiYan had worked for the Moffats and that they had known of the baby's illness so that some care was required in handling the case. No senior officer mentioned the matter to me until, during a routine inspection some months later, I was advised almost jovially that I should avoid including uninvestigated killings in my regular reports—better they not be a matter of record, more circumspection perhaps, if in doubt a private note to a senior English policeman, or a telephone call, not through channels, you understand. Still, all in all, considering the delicacy of the matter, which was now understood, I had done very well indeed.

I was pleased with my decision—until I was commended for it.

Commentary to
"THE SERVANT GIRL'S BABY"

The death of William Joseph Tabafunda in 1969 in the State of Washington, and his parents' subsequent conviction for manslaughter, which was upheld on appeal, led me to write this story about MiYan and her baby. Here, in brief, are the facts of the *Tabafunda* case.

William Joseph Tabafunda, an infant seventeen months old, died when an abscessed tooth became gangrenous and prevented him from eating, leaving his weakened body susceptible to pneumonia. William's mother, a twenty-year-old part Indian with an eleventh grade education, and her husband, a twenty-four-year-old full-blooded Sheshont Indian with a sixth grade education, did not understand how sick the baby really was; they thought that William merely suffered a toothache and treated him with aspirin. William's parents feared, they said, that if they took the child to a doctor, the welfare department would take him away—a somewhat similar situation had led to a relative's loss of a child. Both of William's parents worked during the day; on working days William was cared for by his paternal grandmother, age eighty-five.

The appellate court upheld the parents' conviction of manslaughter, finding that the parental duty to provide medical care for William was both a statutory duty and "a natural duty existing independently of statutes." For a conviction of manslaughter at common law, recklessness or gross negligence would have been required; a Washington statute provided that simple negligence would suffice. William had been sick for twelve days and might have been saved if he had received medical attention during the first five days. Hence manslaughter.

I found this a deeply distressing story, and so did my class. I noticed in reading the appellate report that I knew the district attorney whose office had prosecuted the Tabafundas. So, some five or six years after the case had been decided, I called him on the telephone to ask him about it and to find out what punishment had been imposed on the Tabafundas. He had no memory of the case but directed me to the lawyer, now in private practice, who had actually prosecuted the Tabafundas. The lawyer had a faint memory of the case, but not of any of the details; he thought the parents had been put on probation, but he was not sure. Nobody remembered the case; it had passed without impact, except on the Tabafundas. And yet here the majesty of the law had been invoked to convict loving parents of the death of their infant child, cruel punishment heaped upon deep grief. To what end?

So I shifted the story to a different time and place, softened it (since fiction cannot with comfort encompass the realities of such uncaring facts as were displayed in the Tabafunda case), and used it to raise two legal and moral issues for your consideration. First, should MiYan be held criminally responsible for the death of her baby? And second, if the first question is answered in the affirmative, should her cultural background and religious beliefs, both different from those of the framers of the law, provide a defence?

On the basic responsibility question, let us set aside cases where the parent intentionally neglects the child unto death, or intentionally causes the child's death. They raise no problems other than problems of proof. Difficult questions arise only when it is the unintentional neglect of the child that leads to its death, and when that neglect is in part a product of other pressures on the parent.

It is true, of course, that the criminal law cannot confine itself to acts of commission; parents who deliberately fail to provide food for their infant child, when food is available, would properly be held liable though their inaction rather than action had caused the death. So the question is one of intent, and not of the form of the lethal act or omission. At this point different jurisdictions and different systems of law part company. All will convict of murder or infanticide if the parent intends the death; most will convict of manslaughter if the parent foresees the likelihood of the death but takes no action reasonably within his or her power to prevent it; and some, like the State of Washington, will convict if the parent fails to live up to the standard of care for the child expected of a reasonable person in the parent's situation. In the language of the law: intention will always suffice for a conviction, recklessness or gross negligence will usually suffice, and simple negligence will sometimes suffice.

Simple negligence was the standard applied in the *Tabafunda* case. The difficulty with that standard is this: who is the reasonable person against whose hypothetical behaviour the accused parent is to be compared? Is it a person with the education of MiYan, in need of retaining employment if she and her child are not to starve, and who is thus compelled to leave the child's care to a dotty grandmother who strikes the child? Consider the realities of her life and her background, her personal qualities of intelligence and education, if any, in sufficient detail and you will find that you are not comparing her conduct with that of a hypothetical reasonable person in her situation, but rather, are comparing her conduct with her conduct—which is nonsense. This is part of the reason why the simple negligence standard is widely rejected as a basis for a conviction of manslaughter.

To most people it seems proper that before a parent may be convicted of this grave felony, that parent must have foreseen the likelihood of the child's death and also must have been in a situation where an alternative life-saving course of action was reasonably available.

This question of the definition of manslaughter by neglect shades into the second main problem in the story of MiYan. Should her cultural background and religious beliefs provide a defence for her, even if she has not lived up to whatever standard of care the law imposes?

Blair, Veraswami, and U Tin Hlang spend a lot of time on this question of the cultural neutrality of the law in their discussion on Blair's verandah, and there is little I can add to their views except to risk the opinion that the law should sometimes override religious and cultural values. This was surely the case with suttee, the immolation of Hindu widows. It should, however, do so only when it is utterly necessary and when there is good reason to believe that the overriding law can have a beneficial effect.

MiYan and the Tabafundas embody primarily a cultural rather than a religious defence against those who would impose the will of the State with complete impartiality. The thread of religion that connects MiYan with her "crime" is hardly more than an enervating fatalism—certainly not the "flamboyant" religious challenge that suttee posed to the Raj. It should be noted that, in the United States, distinctly cultural practices or values are not afforded the constitutional protection that religious expression routinely enjoys. For that reason, the Tabafundas were punished and forgotten with little evidence of moral agonizing, while prosecutions for criminal acts cloaked in the mantle of religious doctrine often fail.

The clash of law and religion is particularly wrenching for those who, like Christian Scientists, reject medical assistance on grounds of firm religious conviction. The courts have not found this an easy question to answer. The current formula is something like this: the State should respect religious beliefs in all its legislation, and should not interfere with them unless there is a compelling State interest in doing so. Translating that to MiYan's case: Was there such a compelling State interest? I suppose the protection of its citizens is a leading duty of the State, and MiYan's baby was a citizen. Hence, by this line of analysis, a line which has allowed the conviction of Christian Scientist parents in similar cases, a conviction of manslaughter is not an injustice. But is it the path of wisdom?

Too often legal analysis marches on relentlessly, heedless of what it is achieving, heedless of social consequences and human suffering. It seems to me, and here you may well disagree, that in the Tabafunda and MiYan situations and in the situation of the Christian Scientist parent not seeking medical assistance for the child who, as a consequence, dies, there is little utility in the intervention of the law. I doubt the educative effect of the law in such cases; the true believer may well only be confirmed in rejecting the law and cleaving to the religion, and it is only on the true believers that there will be any effect since, in these cases, we are positing parents who love their child and wish for the child's health and safety.

For your criticism: I much prefer Eric Blair's decision in the case of MiYan to the decisions of the trial and appellate courts of Washington State in the case of Tabafunda.

What is it that leads Departments of Welfare to such excesses of "Badfare"? And how do they manage to influence the prosecutors and the courts to go along with them! Do they believe that they are saving lives, or is their purpose rather a bureaucratic affirmation of the virtue of their profession?

The Veraswami Story

I told the story of the accident, if it was an accident, as starkly as I could. I suppose I hoped I could unburden myself to Dr. Veraswami and yet not allow him to see immediately what a fool I had been.

The jungle in Burma can be very dense, particularly in areas close to rivers and streams, where there is never what passes for a dry season to reduce the bursting luxuriance. None of us had seen the cliff beside the overgrown path. We were aware only of the unbroken ceiling of trees above us, the taller trees at the foot of the precipice reaching to share the tropical sun equally with their shorter brethren beside the path. I was day-dreaming when I heard the Burmese policeman's cry, the noise of branches breaking, and then a thud as he struck the ground some thirty feet below.

We had been making a routine visit to an outlying village, the regular duty of every district officer throughout the vast territories of the Raj. Burdensome though some of these journeys were, they did force one to have some sense of the concerns of the villagers.

The last few miles of this trip had to be made on foot, the rains having made the path impassable by truck. I was walking ahead, followed by the driver, who had decided to come with us rather than wait at the truck. The Burmese policeman-interpreter was in the rear. He, too, must have been daydreaming, paying too little attention to the path, so that he stepped on the wrong side of a tree, slipped off the path, and plunged to pain.

I told the driver to stay where he was and found a nearby palm tree to climb down to the policeman.

He had fallen heavily. His head had struck a substantial branch near the ground, knocking him out. He lay twisted awkwardly, his left leg grotesquely skewed underneath him. My guess was that he had broken his hip and possibly his collarbone. I knew we would have to get him to medical help as quickly as possible.

I shouted to the driver to hurry the mile or so to the truck and to bring back the first-aid kit and the two blankets it carried, and the ropes which were to be found in all trucks in Burma to help pull them out from their frequent boggings. He took an eternity, or so it seemed.

I made the policeman as comfortable as I could, but even unconscious he jerked in pain as I moved his arm and leg. I found a reasonably straight branch of a tree and then another, and with my jungle knife, a kris—sharpened at both edges and slightly curved, which the training school had recommended for patrol duty—I trimmed them for the blanket-and-pole makeshift stretcher I planned. The driver had not returned. All I could do was fume.

I must make a stretcher, perhaps one pole with a blanket hung like a sack under it. Then, on the path, I could fashion a better stretcher with both of the poles, so that the driver and I could carry the policeman to the truck. At last I heard the driver's returning trot.

With difficulty I climbed a tree to the path and took stock. The ropes were new and strong. The blankets seemed in good condition. I tied a rope to a tree on the other side of the path and climbed down the cliff again, carrying the blankets. The driver followed.

When I had recovered from my unjustified rage at the driver for his slowness—he had in fact been swift and sensible—I found him a great help. Together we fashioned a sling from the blankets, eased the policeman into it, and attached it firmly to the stronger of the two poles.

Near the bottom, the cliff jutted out over the fallen policeman. I could not at first see how I could lift him to the path without injuring him further by bashing him against the cliff face. So I told the driver to stay below and ease the sling away from the rough edges of the cliff as I pulled the rope from above to haul the policeman up. I then clambered back to the path.

All went well at first. I looped the rope around another tree near the edge of the cliff so that I could take in the slack as I dragged him up. The driver helped from below with the first lift, but then the strain was on me.

"And it was a great strain, Dr. Veraswami, believe me. I did try. As I gained a few feet I took in the slack as I recalled mountaineers do. But then it was too much. The policeman was within feet of the edge of the cliff. The rope slipped. I stumbled. The policeman fell—this time to his death."

Dr. Veraswami had been quite still during my narrative. Now he wandered about the verandah, looking out toward the hospital.

I broke the silence. "May I have a beer, Dr. Veraswami?"

"Of course, Mr. Blair. Please help yourself." This was unusual—he usually liked playing the fussy host. He must have been wondering how to let me down as lightly as honesty would permit. When he did speak I could not at first follow the drift of what he was saying, but it was clear that he recognised what I had done wrong.

"In medical school, Mr. Blair, the instruction iss that in a crisis you first take your own pulse, not that of the patient. But I do verry well understand how your solicitude for your policeman led you astray. Many of us make errors like that. It iss so easy to err under the pressure of anxiety for a patient; I did so many times in France during the war."

I doubted that this was true, and I was annoyed at him for saying so— but also grateful. "Both of us know, Dr. Veraswami, that I killed the policeman. If it were not for my stupidity, it is almost certain that he would be alive now. He might have been injured a bit more while in the sling, hitting the face of the cliff, but had the two of us been on the path above to pull the rope, we could have got him up and back alive to you."

Veraswami was again silent. After a moment or two I added: "I have reported it in detail to Mandalay. I wonder what they will do?"

"They will think of it only as an accident—no more—you can be sure. And you must try to do so also, though I know it will not be easy. It iss painful, I am sure, but you must try to avoid self-flagellation. It iss too pleasurable."

Veraswami was right about Mandalay. My report on the policeman's death was noted. I was directed to convey sympathy to his family and was advised that a replacement would soon be on his way. My stupidity was apparently ignored, though I am sure it had been noticed.

I found that one effect of this death was to lessen my inclination to visit Veraswami. I felt I had diminished myself greatly in his eyes, and I did not relish the sentiment. And then an event occurred that forced me back to an even closer relationship with him—one that for different reasons gave me more anxiety.

It had never happened before: a dusty, leather-helmeted military motorcyclist roared up to the Moulmein police station, stamped into the office, saluted in all directions, and announced a message for the district officer. On the opened page of a substantial book he pulled from his haversack and held out to me, I signed for a brown, heavily sealed envelope marked DISTRICT OFFICER ONLY. The saluting and stamping were repeated, and I stood, slightly bewildered, and watched him roar off.

I retired to my office, anxiety beginning to churn within me. And when I saw that the message was from Burma Army Headquarters in

Rangoon, rather than from regional headquarters in Mandalay, my anxiety intensified.

It was a brief message:

TO: District Officer, Moulmein.
FROM: OIC, Imperial Forces Burma.
DATE: 26/6/1927.
COPY: OIC, His Majesty's Military Forces, Moulmein.
CLASSIFICATION: CONFIDENTIAL   READ AND DESTROY.

RE: Prohibited Drugs.

It has been reported to this headquarters that quantities of heroin have been distributed through Moulmein Hospital in the past three months.

The informant is Kau Reng, a male nurse working at that hospital. He is attached to the Intelligence Section of this Staff. He must not be exposed. He will establish contact with you.

The possibility that prohibited drugs are being distributed through an Army Hospital is of particular concern. This investigation will require sound judgement and the utmost confidentiality.

You are to assist Kau Reng and to keep this headquarters advised directly, not through regional channels. You are to use military communications for this purpose. Telephonic communication should not be made except in emergency. End of message.

I had the immediate and overwhelming sense that I was already involved beyond my competence. To bypass Mandalay in this way and reach down directly to a fledgling district officer for a task that might challenge a trained detective—what must they be thinking of? Why not send someone of experience to help me in such a matter? Unless, of course, they thought to do so would increase the risk of exposure of their agent, Kau Reng.

I read and reread the memorandum and then burned it in my wastepaper basket, which caused quite a conflagration and brought the duty NCO into my office—I suppose to ensure that the message had not precipitated my self-immolation.

I returned to my bungalow with what materials and notes I had from my training course dealing with illegal drugs.

I learned that the Shans, in the far east corner of Burma, live in a region more hospitable to the Eurasian poppy than any other on earth. They, and the other hill tribes of the area where China, Siam, Laos, and Burma intersect, had for centuries grown the poppy as their staple crop. I had always thought of poppies as the "Flanders field" variety—narrow-stemmed, spindly flowers with small red petals and black stamens. But the opium poppies of the Burmese hills were quite unlike their decadent European relatives. These were grossly luxuriant, thick-stemmed, with many standing to eye height, and blossoms larger than a man's hand.

Until 1906, the cultivation of these larger-than-life poppies and the consequent trade in opium had been encouraged by the colonial powers, but in that year the House of Commons suffered one of its occasional bouts of self-denying virtue and declared the opium trade "immoral." Inexorably, "illegal" soon followed "immoral." As a result, steadily increasing efforts were made to reduce cultivation of the poppy, to limit the opium trade, and to prohibit the sale or purchase of its refined derivative, heroin.

But even the Raj had to recognise the limits of the possible. For centuries there had been many Burmans, many Indians, many Chinese, and very many Shans who were habitual consumers of opium; to enforce absolute prohibition would have required armies of detectives. Hence, in Lower Burma, where I served, the law entirely prohibited heroin but allowed registered consumers to purchase and possess opium for their own use. The latter provision, even my generally idealistic teachers at Mandalay admitted, was unevenly enforced; many used opium without bothering to be registered. Indeed, few Burmans even knew of these registration provisions, the ways of the Raj in such matters being a mystery to them.

I wondered how many registered consumers there were in my district. That seemed easy enough to find out, since it was the district officer's task to keep the register—and the somewhat depressing thought came to me that since I had been in Moulmein I had never looked at the register. I did hope it was to be found in the files and cabinets that Captain Humphreys had left me.

I rode my bicycle to work early the next morning, meaning to try to find the opium register before anyone other than the duty NCO was present. I thought I might be able to conceal from him, if he were alone, the direction of my search and thus avoid revealing anything of what was in the message from Rangoon—for I knew my police would be consumed with interest in what it contained.

I checked the index to our files and found the register, which contained very few names. Apparently Humphreys had at first made some effort to keep it up-to-date, hoping to have some sense of the extent of opium use in the Moulmein area, but he had gradually relaxed his efforts. The name Kau Reng did not appear—I don't know why I thought it should—nor did the name of anyone I knew to be working at the hospital.

What to do next eluded me. It would be helpful for me to be better informed than I was about illegal drugs and their distribution in my district before Kau Reng contacted me, but such knowledge was not entirely easy to obtain without compromising the confidentiality Rangoon and Kau Reng expected of me. If I asked any of my police about drugs in Moulmein they would immediately guess more than I should reveal—I had never made such an enquiry before. Perhaps my best course would be to start with Dr. Veraswami. Maybe I could lead a conversation with him to the subject of illegal drugs and their control, without having to disclose my hand. It seemed an uneasy course, but none other appeared. I would call on him in the late afternoon—a social call, just for a beer and conversation; he would not be suspicious. There was the difficulty, however, that since telling Veraswami of my failure to save the fallen policeman, I had not visited his verandah. I would just have to do the best I could when I got there.

The day passed slowly. I felt so ill-informed; I didn't even know if we had an opium den in Moulmein—presumably the Chinese community knew, but now I couldn't enquire about it for a few days.

In mid-afternoon I decided to walk around the market area to fill in time before calling on Veraswami. The market was always colourful and sometimes amusing. I enjoyed hearing and watching the high-pitched and apparently acrimonious haggling culminating in warm and laughing settlements. Negotiation seemed more a sport than a business.

As I left the market, I saw a procession approaching, a straggling, uneven group, shepherded by one of my policemen, who saluted me. It was really less than a procession: about eighteen or twenty men, ranging in age from the early twenties to the mid-fifties, wandering along in loose congruence, with a boy ahead beating a drum to an imprecise rhythm and another boy behind wheeling what looked like the base and wheels of a cheap English pram on which was perched a tawdry, over-decorated statue. Whether procession or wandering group, they certainly caught and held my shocked attention.

All the men had skewered or pierced themselves in some obvious and, one would think, painful way: through the lips, in a fleshy part of the stomach, or on the biceps, thighs, upper legs, or back. The pin industries of the English Midlands, about which Adam Smith had written to such effect, provided the adornments of the celebrants. The large safety-pin was much in use, though for a purpose its manufacturers could not have anticipated. Pins made patterns down chests and backs, the skin being pinched up enough for the incision and exit of the pointed end but not too much to preclude locking the safety catch. They were also used to seal lips and to attach short chains to chests and backs. Bits of wire went through from front to back of several hands; other pieces of metal ran through cheeks and mouths. There was some blood around all these penetrations but not much; mostly the blood had congealed earlier in apparently small amounts around the wounds. Three or four of the men also carried short, knotted-string whips with which they vigourously struck their backs over their shoulders.

The policeman saw my surprise and volunteered that the sufferers were

Malays on their annual parade to install one of their gods in a temple—
which god and which temple he did not know. Yet there was hardly the
atmosphere of a real parade: the participants wandered along unemotionally,
seeking no response from the onlookers in the street and getting none.

Though the piercings looked most painful, the men's facial expressions
were of resignation, of duty being done. This was true even of the man
with a skewer through the front of his protruding tongue, braced at an
awkward angle against his chin and upper lip, the mouth snarling agape.
And I saw one of the celebrants with a whip, his lips pin-sealed together,
scratch at his crotch with the handle of the whip. What an extraordinary
conjunction! Did pain not block minor discomforts? How could such tor-
tures and such customary relief coexist?

Distaste and incredulity moved me equally. Old Burma hands had told
me that coolies feel pain less than we do. "Look how they squat for hours
on their haunches. Have you ever seen a white man do that, Blair?"

Of course I had. And so had they. Every photograph of an English army
unit, if it is not on parade, shows scattered groups of squatters, often
clutching their rifles either as balances or as supports; but at the Club such
things are not seen or, if seen, are not remembered or, if remembered, are
not to be mentioned.

So, I suspect, those Malay stoics felt pain as I do, but custom and experience had trained them to minimise its force and to endure, dull-faced and
uncomplaining, their mortifications of the flesh as did the hair-shirted
Christians of the Middle Ages.

One of my NCOs must have given a permit for this parade without
bothering to bring it to my attention. He must have known that self-injury
and self-flagellation would be displayed. And infection and death were
thus risked, to no apparent benefit—although one cannot easily weigh religious benefits. Yet he had not thought even to discuss with me whether it
should be prohibited. Surely a permit for such a parade would not be given
in London. Disturbing the peace, offensive or obscene behaviour, or some
such misdemeanour would be the excuse to prohibit the parade or to arrest
those who punctured and displayed themselves in this way. Did this mean
that the law in London was less tolerant of religious beliefs and practices
than the law in Burma? It was obviously different in Burma, but why this
was so seemed unclear to me.

So speculating, walking a few paces beside the procession and paying
insufficient attention to my path, I bumped quite firmly into Dr.
Veraswami, who was standing in the street, also watching the procession.

He apologised as if the fault had been his: "Oh, I'm so sorry, Blair, so
sorry. Clumsy of me." And he started dusting at my coat with his hands.

I stepped back and made a duet of our apologies, adding "But what an
extraordinary sight this is."

"Yess, yess indeed. I have seen many such, but they still amaze me. It
seems so . . ."—and there was a long pause while he grasped at the air with
his pudgy hands for the right word—". . . so unnecessary."

He told me that he had also witnessed men walking on burning coals in Burma and in India, and mentioned the fakirs who in the name of religion had publicly inflicted severe pain on themselves for centuries in India.

We stood talking while the procession moved away. It became awkward, standing in the street, carrying on a ranging conversation—hot and awkward.

"It iss very steamy here, Blair, issn't it? Would you do me the honour of coming to my bungalow for a beer so that we might talk more about thiss?"

Indeed I would. I had not even had to make up an excuse to call again on Dr. Veraswami after my recent absence. I began to fancy myself a detective.

It was eerie. No sooner was I settled with a beer in my usual rattan chair on Veraswami's balcony than he started in about the message from Rangoon. "I hear the military might of the Governors of Burma is in close, mechanised, and swift communication with you, Blair. They send men on machines; they do not trust the mails or the telephone."

I must have blushed. Could Veraswami possibly know the content of the message? I certainly was at a loss as to a reply. Veraswami hurried on, seeing my unease, "Oh, I am sorry. It iss none of my business. But you must know that such things cause some stir in our little town—and, for me, memories of the heroic motorcycle messengers of the War cling to such events. I hope it iss not a matter to cause you anxiety." And he waved the subject away, with his left hand, balancing his beer carefully with his right. Still, he seemed ill at ease, even defensive. I thought he might return to the subject, but he dropped it as suddenly as he had brought it up: "Let uss talk about that strange procession. You have seen nothing like it before?"

I asked him if people felt pain differently. Were pinpricks, a toothache, a skewer through the tongue, similar sensations to all?

Veraswami thought that, broadly speaking, people feel the same sensations, that the nervous systems of humans—black, white, and brown; men and women; adults and children—transmit the signals of pain in much the same way but that people could train themselves to different responses, to a degree, and to different tolerances without complaint, also to a degree. His reason for believing in the similarity of sensations of pain was that most people subjected to similar "painful" stimuli winced, sweated, jerked, cried, or screamed at about the same time. People might express pain quite differently, but they usually expressed it at a similar stage in relation to any given stimulus. The drilling of a tooth might cause one to cry out, another's face to blanch, but the crying out or the whitening of the visage would occur at about the same time in response to the same intensity of drilling. It was a subject central to medicine: expressing pain was one way—sometimes the most reliable way—the patient communicated to the doctor. And drugs could be used with some precision to vary the thresholds and intensities of pain.

With the mention of drugs, the discussion seemed to be on track for my Rangoon enquiry: my detective work was going almost too well. I pressed Veraswami with a vigourous interrogation, hoping somehow to approach the topic of heroin. But there was only so much to be said about pinpricks and pierced tongues. I recalled that Veraswami had told me that Ake Dah suffered pain when he understood, at one level or another, that he was mentally ill. "Surely physical pain and psychological pain are different, Doctor."

Veraswami paused reflectively. "I am not sure that it iss proper to call that sort of pain 'pain.' I know I did; it iss common usage. What I think I mean iss that the mentally ill clearly suffer, feel anguish. I do not think it iss pain like that of a pinprick or a dentist's drill. But it iss very real—yet it iss not obvious, and it iss often hard to talk about, ass you and I both find." Smiling, almost beaming at me, he continued: "Hass not thiss kind of pain being keeping you from visiting me recently?"

It took me a moment or two to understand what he was talking about, but then I did: "You mean my pain at my own stupidity in the death of my policeman."

"Precisely, Blair, and your further pain in telling me about it. Such things are not easy. Emotional wounds can be lastingly painful."

I nodded my head in embarrassed recognition. But suddenly, the ease and confidence of his conversation, his Socratic joy in leading a student to answer his own question, changed to a silent immobility; the shaking leg, so favoured by the Indian middle class, became still. When he spoke again his voice was quiet, his eyes averted. "Blair, have you ever heard a brave but torture-ridden patient cry out in an agonised plea for relief from pain? I think it must be even harder for me to endure than for most. Perhaps there iss a reason for that. Let me tell you, my friend, something of myself which I think you should know—why I am so troubled by pain."

Not wanting to interrupt, I poured myself another beer without asking his permission and sat back to listen. He hurried on with his story: "I must be one of the very few boys from a privileged Indian family who hass been beaten ass a child, I mean beaten severely, not just spanked. It could never have happened in India—my extended family in the Punjab was large; I would never have been so isolated. It wass when my father and mother took me with them on my father's first protracted business trip to England. It wass a nurse. She had the verry best references, my mother told me, the verry best English manners and condescending voice.

"I do not mean to malign them, Blair; I loved them dearly, but my parents were well on the snobbish side, copying English ways, critical of Indian customs, fiercely emulative of the Raj. Many privileged Indians are like that—the school tie, the pipe, the grey slacks and suede shoes. And they spent too little time with me in England, always out and about, he on business, she on social occasions—even a French cooking school in London, issn't it! No wonder you laugh at me. But, of course, Miss Hutchins, as a nanny, seemed perfect to them. Those were the days, Blair, when Mrs. Beaton, of cookbook fame, would urge her female readers that it was not an excessive burden on them to have nanny bring the children to afternoon tea with their mother. My mother was never that aloof, but she would leave me with Miss Hutchins and travel about England on business with my father, and leave me even for her cooking school or any silly social invitation. And she never did learn to cook, except Indian food, as her mother had taught her."

Dr. Veraswami fell silent, filled my beer, walked about the verandah fiddling with the fronds of palm rimming the roof. "I have told no one other than my wife about this, Blair, but I want to tell you.

"Miss Hutchins always used her open hand, never anything else to beat me with. But she wass verry strong, or so she seemed to me then, aged four or five. There were never any marks of the beating—I would search diligently for them later—but they hurt, that I knew, and there seemed no limit to what she would do in her rage. And her rage was justified, I felt sure, for there was always some error of mine, some failure, some clumsiness that precipitated these punishments. It wass always my fault; I knew that.

"Though it seemed to make the punishments worse, I always cried out. But my high-pitched 'Oh please, Miss Hutchins,' over and over again in tearful wails, only led to a handkerchief being forced between my teeth, held in place by one hot and damp hand while the other rose and struck, rose and struck."

He did not look at me as he told this sad story, walking up and down the verandah in front of me, his hands clenched in front of his chest. Yet for all his movement, he seemed more calmed than agitated by the narration. It must have relieved him to unburden himself to me. Finally, he settled on the edge of his chair, facing me.

"I know now that a child in that situation iss not helpless. If a child habitually prattles to his parents about whatever comes into his head, and the parents—or any other adults—are at all sensible, the torture will be put to an end. But I also know that a child in that situation really iss helpless. You see, fear iss verry powerful, and it wass clear to me then that the punishments I had so far received would be ass nothing, nothing at all, compared to what I would receive if I told my parents what Miss Hutchins sometimes did to me when they went out and left me with her."

I had to interrupt him. What he was now saying didn't make sense to me. "But all you had to do was to tell your parents. You know they would have protected you from further beatings."

Dr. Veraswami's head waved gently from side to side in his usual indication of qualified agreement. "A child's world iss not like ours, Blair. I remember that well. What I wass trying to say iss that the child may never be strong enough to tell his parents what has happened in so many words. My parents knew how I hated to be left with Miss Hutchins. I clung and cried till it annoyed them. But it iss like the doctor and his patient, Blair— the patient always expresses pain, but the doctor must be trained to listen.

My parents did not listen carefully enough. And for me, the trouble wass that, though I loved my parents, and they me, ours wass not a relationship in which they customarily heard my childish prattle. They thought it wass enough to tell me that Miss Hutchins would take good care of me and not to worry.

"Miss Hutchins was my confidant; there wass the rub, ass your poet would say. Hers wass a world of duty, obligation, discipline, and deserved punishment, but also a world in which much of the time I could play and talk like a child, in which she listened to me and understood me, unless I did something that wass wrong, verry wrong. If the only adult in the child's world with whom the child feels free to talk without constraint iss hiss assaulter, the child iss lost, quite lost.

"And there was another reason I could never tell my parents. They were gentle and loving, but in my childish mind I believed they must also have intended the disciplinary world of Miss Hutchins for me for my own good. And it had always been my wrongdoing, ass I saw it, that brought on the punishments. To resist the correction my parents had set out for me would only have compounded my guilt. No, Blair, logical or not, I know I am speaking the truth of that young child's situation.

"But let me go on with the story, Blair. I don't know how or why it grew worse, but I know it did. I know my fears intensified, but a kind forgetful-ness has veiled the details—though some remain, enough for me to know I wish to recall no more. It was not only on the buttocks she would strike me, but everywhere, most painfully. But there wass always something that foreshadowed the wild bouts of violence; something led to the torture, though less frequently anything I could recognise as a wicked act of mine.

"I remember her coming once into the nursery with a small glass of orange juice in her hand. I was playing in a section of the room concealed by the door she had opened ass she entered. I spoke to her. I have no mem-ory of what I said. But it startled her. To my astonishment her forearm jerked forward, and the orange juice, glass and all, whistled above my head into a broken and streaky mess on the wall. Her punishment of me wass particularly brutal that night, and my whimpering efforts, later, to try to help clean up the mess on the wall earned me no show of forgiveness.

"The end came, for perfectly sensible reasons, after another terrible bout. I wass to pour milk into a glass to put on a tray on which she would serve dinner in the nursery. I wass allowed to help in thiss way when things were calm between uss. The milk wass in a narrow-necked bottle. My childish hands poured too quickly. The bottle made funny gurgling noises and too much milk burbled out into the glass, some spilling onto the neat tray she had set. The gurgling noise wass in my ears as the first blow fell on the side of my head. Thiss time she did not worry about the handkerchief nor, I think, about any informative bruises. It went on and on, continuing until a woman, a neighbour, could stand it no longer and burst in to find me on the floor sobbing and Miss Hutchins collapsed in a chair also crying in fury and striking at the table, mercifully no longer at me. I remember ass if it were a photograph how she looked: her hair in wild disorder, torn loose from the tight grey bun at the base of her skull where before it had been neatly pinned; her face a dark red, sweaty, ass were her flabby under-arms with the black hair showing under her blouse.

"My parents seemed soon to be back with me. I never saw Miss Hutchins again. I wass told much later that she died soon after in what wass then called a lunatic asylum. I have survived, damaged no doubt in ways I cannot know, nor particularly want to. Perhaps I am a little more scared of women, a little more distrustful, than most Indian men of my age, but I don't know if Miss Hutchins had much to do with that. And I have never since much cared for the gurgling noise some bottles make when the liquid iss poured from them rapidly—it still causes my stomach muscles to tighten in anticipation of pain."

Veraswami fell silent. It had obviously been a strain. He had not looked at me when he resumed telling about his childhood agony. But now he turned to me, smiling, yet still more subdued than his normal self, and said, "I am glad I told you about that, Blair. Perhaps you understand now why I was so anxious to discuss those self-injuring Malays and your pain in the death of your policeman—why pain worries me so much, perhaps more than it worries others. It iss with me so much, ass a doctor and ass a person; I experienced it first ass a child, then in war, and I see it always in my daily work. A doctor should grow inured to pain; I haven't."

I was glad Dr. Veraswami was treating me as a trusted friend, sharing much of himself with me—though I was embarrassed by his confidences and had little to say. I could see why he might think it could have lastingly weakened his character. He seemed to feel guilt, much as I had felt when I had confessed to him my stupid failure to save the policeman who had fallen in the jungle. But I did not wish to return to my own failings.

I remained annoyed, I must admit, that my efforts to lead our discussion to the topic of drugs had failed so miserably. It would seem callous to return to that topic now, but equally callous to let our conversation end on such an unsettled note.

Veraswami had spoken of pain in the War. I had not heard him talk of the War before. So I asked him, "You mentioned pain in the War; were you wounded?"

"Yess, a few pieces of shrapnel now and then. Quite painful but not dangerous. Of course, the suffering of the soldiers wass verry great, verry great, and I came to bless morphine for them, and even for me."

Veraswami had finally mentioned drugs, indeed, his own use of drugs. But it was growing late; by now we were both too exhausted to pursue it. The stumbling detective had taken too long to get to the point. Veraswami had never confided in me in this way before. On reflection, it seemed that he had been leading the conversation, not I. Why had he confessed to me in this way?—if confession it was. Perhaps it was a result of my telling him about the jungle accident—and that was a confession. And why did he mention his use of morphine during the War? Perhaps he had guessed the contents of the message from Rangoon? In any event, I had found his confidences about the childhood beatings quite troubling, like the confidences from a parent to a child which embarrass the child; but I was glad he had trusted me, though I had made little headway as a detective on the heroin trail.

We parted in slight embarrassment, our relationship changed in ways I did not understand.

A voice came from the moon shadow of a palm tree as I approached my bungalow, my mind full of Veraswami's stories: "May I talk with you, Sir? I am Kau Reng." I was startled. I don't know how I had expected Kau Reng to contact me, but his waylaying me at night near my bungalow surprised me. Also, I had expected him, from his name, to be a Burmese, but this man was Chinese, a short, rather fat, Chinese, in long uncreased white pants, an open-necked white shirt, and neat sandals—the dress of a hospital orderly.

Recovering from my surprise, I asked if we should talk here or at my bungalow. He had apparently reconnoitered carefully: he said that since only my houseboy was at my bungalow, and asleep, he thought, it seemed safe to go inside.

He was courteous—perhaps too courteous—clear, and incisive in what he told me. He knew I had been visiting Veraswami that night and frequently referred to him as "your friend, Dr. Veraswami."

As we walked towards my bungalow, he told me what to say if we were interrupted by anyone, though I assured him that I had few uninvited guests and was expecting no one to call that night. Nevertheless, if that did occur, or if my houseboy awoke and came to us, I was to say that he had brought an urgent message from the hospital to which I was drafting a reply.

We sat at the table in my dining room, a badly trimmed kerosene lamp smoking between us, a blank sheet of paper for the hypothetical message in front of me. I did not offer him a drink; it seemed out of place to do so. He did not act as if he were in a hurry, but he came straight to the point. "We have two tasks tonight, Sir: to arrange how we should communicate, so far as that is necessary, and for me to give you some information about this enquiry so that you can assist me in it as headquarters has ordered."

His manner was not brusque. He treated me with deference as his superior in military hierarchy. But he wasted no words.

The arrangements for future communication were simple enough. If he wanted to talk to me he would come to my bungalow exactly as he had tonight; if a message would suffice he would have his brother, who kept a wood-carving stall in the Chinese market, arrange for someone to bring it to the police station. It would be marked "Confidential—Mr. Blair Only." If I wished to get a message to him, I should give it to his brother at the market. His brother knew me and would be at his stall every morning; perhaps I should buy one of the carvings, "to preserve our secret, Sir." If I needed to talk to Kau Reng, a note delivered through his brother telling him when to come to my bungalow would suffice. He seemed confident that we needed no more contrivance than this fraternal intermediary to protect his position in the hospital.

He was less precise concerning the background information. Apparently he had been on the staff of the Moulmein Hospital for some time, well before either Dr. Veraswami or I had come to Moulmein. His work for the army involved general intelligence in the region: what the army needed to know about attitudes to the Raj and any political rhetoric or action hostile to the administration.

He had, he said, stumbled unexpectedly upon the illegal traffic in heroin. "As you know, Sir, some opium comes through our markets to registered users, and of course to many others. It comes from the hills and is sold in all our markets and at some of our pagodas. My brother does not deal in opium, but he knows many who do—my countrymen as well as the Burmese have long been smokers of opium. Those who deal in betel nut and spices often also sell opium."

I began to find his manner patronising and interrupted to ask what all this had to do with heroin being distributed from the hospital. He came straight to the point. "It was reported to my brother that your friend, Dr. Veraswami, tried to buy heroin from one of the opium dealers. He had none. He sent Veraswami to another stall where heroin could be bought. My brother tells me that Veraswami bought heroin at that other stall."

Kau Reng had recounted these rumours in his next report to Rangoon Headquarters. He had immediately been directed by Rangoon to give his full attention to discovering whether his report had been accurate and, if it was, the extent of Veraswami's involvement. He judged that the fact that the hospital administrator—"your friend, Dr. Veraswami, Sir"—seemed to be involved made the affair a matter of serious concern to Rangoon. The order to me, with a copy to him, had followed soon after.

It shook me to think of my being so deeply and, it seemed, inexorably involved in investigating my only friend in Moulmein. Kau Reng knew this and quietly enjoyed it.

I was unsure whether the responsibility to carry the investigation further, to confirm or disprove the rumours, was mine or Kau Reng's. On reflection it was clear that I had been directed by an authority senior to police authority—though what was being discussed was a crime and therefore within my jurisdiction—to be of assistance but not to take the initiative myself. If the army authorities in Rangoon had wanted me to lead the investigation, they would have passed orders to me through the proper channels, rather than over the heads of my immediate superiors.

"Do you want my help in this investigation, or the help of any of my police officers?" I enquired.

"No, Sir, except of course that you should say nothing about this to anyone, particularly anyone at the hospital. I think I know how to find evidence of your friend's dealing in illegal drugs. I will keep you informed."

I made no response to his obvious suggestion that I should not prejudice his investigation. To have made the suggestion was an insult; it merited no reply. There seemed nothing more to discuss. I was silent, looking at him somewhat angrily, I suppose.

"Have you any questions, Sir?"

"No."

As he left, Kau Reng saluted. I made a vague waving acknowledgement. It all seemed so incongruous; I did not feel at all like a detective, more like a traitor to my friend.

My inclination was to stay away from Dr. Veraswami until Kau Reng had found out more about the heroin. On the other hand, after Veraswami's telling me so much about himself when we were last together, making such an open overture to a closer friendship, it would be discourteous for me to separate myself from him for any substantial period without explanation. I felt torn.

And I felt torn, too, by Kau Reng's and Rangoon's suspicions of Dr. Veraswami. I found it hard to believe that Veraswami was engaged in anything illegal or unethical—it seemed so out of character. But then there were the hints in Veraswami's confidences at our last meeting: the extreme sensitivity to pain in himself and others, and his use of morphine in the War. He might well have found himself addicted to the drug after the War; he must have thought each day his last during the War, and the anodyne of morphine would have been a huge temptation for both the physical pain of shrapnel and the psychological pain of being unable sufficiently to reduce the sufferings of others. I could well understand how he might have been trapped. And then after the War came heroin, medically supported and publicised as a cure for morphine addiction, its own fiercer addictive penalties not yet recognised. It all made sense. And that must be why such a well-trained doctor as Veraswami found himself in this Burmese backwater. Yes, he must be as guilty as those investigating him thought. But guilty of what? Veraswami was suspected of distributing the drug. Why deal in heroin? To support a political movement perhaps. Or, of course, it may be simply greed—government doctors don't accumulate fortunes; drug dealers do.

But it seemed incredible—the phrase kept pressing itself upon me—so out of character. Perhaps I should turn my suspicions towards Kau Reng and his conveniently well-informed brother. But I had to recognise that I had little more than sentiment to go on.

I let a few boring days pass, swinging from certainty of Veraswami's guilt to certainty of his innocence, unable to do anything about either. No word

came from Kau Reng and there was nothing else in the routine of the days
to interest me.

The sergeant told me that the letter marked "Confidential —Mr. Blair
Only" had been brought to the police station by a Chinese youth late the
night before. The youth knew nothing of what the letter was about or
from whom it had come; he had been paid by a stranger in the market to
deliver it. The sergeant had not thought it necessary to disturb me at my
bungalow.

I opened it in my office. Unsigned, in rough print, its "provenance and
intendment" were nevertheless obvious: "Buy a wood carving for
Rangoon."

I found Kau Reng's brother's stall easily enough. Of finished wood and
fitted canvas, it stood out from the light bamboo and palm-fronded stalls
characteristic of these transient markets. I was clearly expected. Kau
Reng's brother, larger than Kau Reng and of unkempt peasant dress and
appearance, immediately engaged me in haggling about various wood carvings, forcing one after another on me and exaggerating their value. I
played the game for a while, eventually agreeing to buy a small piece, representing oxen pulling a plow, which I paid for and never received; Kau
Reng's brother apparently did not wish to serve the Raj gratuitously. He
said he would wrap the carving carefully for me and disappeared behind
the stall, emerging with a neat parcel wrapped in a colourful piece of cloth.

On examining it at the police station, I saw that the parcel was
addressed in clear, precise print, quite unlike the note to me, to "The
Officer in Charge, Intelligence Division, Burma Army Headquarters,
Rangoon" and was marked "Urgent."

My duty was obvious: get it as quickly as possible to Rangoon. There
was no problem in gaining access to the senior army officer in Moulmein;
the parcel was on its perilous, motorcycled way around the Gulf of
Martaban within an hour of my masquerade at the market.

I remained troubled by my role; I felt deceitful toward Veraswami. Of
course I could see why military intelligence would be concerned if a hospital administrator were dealing in illegal drugs. It would be an ideal cover
for a black market operation, linked possibly to anti-Raj political, even ter-
rorist, activities. What was Veraswami doing in Moulmein? He was so
obviously over-qualified for his position.

In breach of the spirit of the orders to me, if not of their letter, since I
was clearly intended to follow and not to lead, I returned to Kau Reng's
brother's stall in the market and asked him to tell Kau Reng that I would
be alone at my bungalow that night.

Kau Reng came. I did not hear him approaching the bungalow, though I was on the balcony waiting for him. We went inside, back to the dining table, the smoking lantern, and the blank sheet of paper for the hypothetical note. I told him I felt in need of more information than he had given me: "After all, it is a crime you are investigating and in my district. I have duties independent of serving as the army's messenger for you."

He took no umbrage but told me what he had found out. "My brother has confirmed that your friend, Dr. Veraswami, has made another purchase of heroin—he has given me the name of the man who sold it to him. Also, I have kept close to Dr. Veraswami at the hospital and managed to be given the task of sterilising several of the syringes and needles he uses in the hospital and keeps in his medical bag. They are what you sent to Rangoon. I think, when chemically analysed, one at least will show traces of heroin in the solution. There is nothing more to do now. We must wait for instructions."

I began to feel like a fool. I should have been told how far along the investigation had come—I really was only Kau Reng's messenger boy. Annoyance made me abandon caution. Unwisely, but the words gushed out, I found myself telling Kau Reng that I intended to call on Dr. Veraswami, that my staying away from him now might itself make him suspicious, since we normally met so regularly, that I would not in any way reveal what was going on. I sounded excessively defensive, even to myself.

Kau Reng made no great protest, saying only that he hoped I understood that he could be in some danger if it became known that he was a spy for the British: "Even army headquarters would not like you to inform on me, Sir." He managed to infuse the "Sir" with some antagonism. This time he did not salute as he left.

I slept well. It was a relief that I could resume my visits to Dr. Veraswami's verandah. I would have to use some duplicity when we met to avoid endangering Kau Reng and frustrating his investigation, but that was certainly preferable to continued absence after being trusted with Veraswami's personal confidences.

The next afternoon, I made my usual pre-tiffin way to his verandah. He was there before me and was obviously pleased by my arrival: "It hass been too long, Blair. High affairs of state, no doubt, many burdensome duties," and he kept chattering on in this fashion, waving aside any apologies on my part.

I did not often find myself rehearsing in advance the words I would use to Veraswami, though that is a habit of mine, which does me no good, when I am thinking about discussing something of importance with those who make me ill at ease. But on this occasion I had rehearsed an enquiry of Veraswami, and when we were settled, our beers in hand, I asked my planned question.

I told him that I remembered that once he had been somewhat annoyed with me for not wondering why he was in Moulmein. So I asked: "How does a doctor with your qualifications and skill find himself in this Burmese backwater?"

It had seemed to me a cunning ploy—an apparently innocent and genuine enough question, yet if Kau Reng's suspicions of his guilt were correct, it was a question that would surely lead Veraswami into difficulty. But he took a quite different tack, far different from what I had expected. "I am verry glad that you are interested to ask about this, my friend, but I fear it will be a long and egoistic story, such ass I inflicted cruelly on you quite a few evenings ago. Let me try to answer you with less wind than I usually blow about myself."

London had palled for him after the War. He felt alien there and decided that for a few years at least he would serve as a doctor in the Imperial Army Medical Services. Then he would decide whether to return to his native Punjab or become a permanent resident in England.

Since he had served with the army medical corps during the War, his return to service in the British administration in India and Burma was welcomed. His first posting was to the Rangoon General Hospital, on Strand Street just west of Khelly Street, a large, white, wooden edifice, with deep balconies, towers, spires, and cornices, "a verry colonial building" in Veraswami's phrase—where, I found myself thinking, his syringes were now being tested.

The early months in Rangoon were not particularly pleasant. He was the only Indian among the senior doctors. He was not excluded from their company, but he remained somewhat outside the warmth of their associations. And then a railway accident removed him entirely from any affection the Raj could form for an Indian doctor.

He had been the only medical officer on duty at the hospital one Saturday evening, there being a dance at the Club which all the English doctors and most of the English nurses were desperate to attend. A police call came to the hospital: south of Pegu, the train from Rangoon had collided with a bus, overloaded as usual, at an unguarded level crossing. Two carriages of the train had derailed and overturned. Immediate medical assistance was required. The doctors and nurses at the dance would be notified, but Veraswami and any other doctors and nurses who could leave the hospital were asked to come immediately on the first rescue train, which would be leaving in a few minutes—going by rail was the quickest way to get there.

Veraswami and a few nurses, Burmese and English, collected some emergency supplies and, since all motorised transport was dedicated to the dance, hurried in tongas to the railway station, a little over a mile away, opposite Shwedagon Pagoda Road, where a special train took them on to the carnage of the accident, some twelve miles up the line.

Part of the reason for the speed and relative efficiency of the mobilisation of help was that the injured probably included a senior local army officer, a colonel returning to Mandalay from home leave who was a friend of the medical superintendent of Rangoon General Hospital. The railway telegraph had suggested that the colonel was in one of the overturned carriages, and this had added urgency to all responses. Veraswami and the nurses were at the scene within an hour of the accident, which, all things considered, was prompt indeed—though the suffering of many of the injured must have made the hour long for them.

Having been a doctor on the Western Front in 1917 and 1918, Veraswami was no stranger to mass injury. But this accident, he said, was in its bloody way as sickening as anything he had seen in France, with severed limbs and crushed and trapped bodies pressed under the carriages and the bus.

There was much noise and futile confusion, with no one in charge until the rescue party arrived. The military officers on the rescue train with Veraswami fixed lights and organised the uninjured into gangs with axes and levers to cut and lift, and generally brought some order to the rescue efforts. But noise, screams, cries for help, pain, and death were pervasive.

Veraswami was taken immediately to the colonel, whose lower torso and legs had been badly crushed, but who now lay clear of the train. A morphine injection reduced the colonel's pain. Turning to the officer in charge of the rescue operation, Veraswami said, "He requires immediate abdominal surgery. Get him into the rescue train. I will come soon." And with that Veraswami scurried off to do his best for the surrounding sufferers.

Within minutes sharp conflict developed. Veraswami, according to the military officers who later reported on these events, would give brief attention to some who, like the colonel, were suffering grievously, limiting himself to an injection to reduce pain, while he gave others, less severely injured than the colonel, what seemed to his now furious critics to be excessively protracted care.

The officer in charge of the operation eventually gave a direct order to Dr. Veraswami to board the colonel and those who most needed hospital attention onto the rescue train for an immediate return to Rangoon. Veraswami told him it would take time to treat and select those who should be on the train for the hospital. Asked if the delay would risk the colonel's life, Veraswami replied curtly: "Yes, of course it will."

It was that admission more than any other evidence that injured Veraswami at the subsequent hearing before the regional administrator. The hearing was not, of course, into the link between Veraswami's behaviour and the colonel's death; it was into the accident itself and the rescue operations generally, but Veraswami's conduct became a focus of criticism. It was hard to pinpoint anything he did wrong, but everyone knew that "Indian doctors are not really balanced, you know. No standards under pressure. Cut corners. Can't be trusted."

As Veraswami told me this story, I remembered the death of my Burmese policeman; the authorities seemed quite willing to overlook my error of judgement then. By contrast, these same authorities had gone to some trouble to misinterpret Veraswami's conduct after the railway accident. Was it because in my case the victim was Burmese and in Veraswami's case the victim was a colonel of the Raj?

Dr. Veraswami did his best to explain his triage decisions; to explain the need to select neither the most severely injured, who would probably die whatever was done for them, nor those who would probably survive without hospitalisation, but rather the middle group—those for whom hospital care and surgical intervention other than in the field would be likely to make the largest difference to saving life and minimising lasting incapacities. But he had to admit that in situations of crisis these classifications are chancy and imprecise, and that one can never be sure of one's true motives. His repeated affirmations of the cold, professional calculations that guided him hardly refuted the steadily advanced innuendo that racial prejudice had led him to tilt his judgement against the obviously desperate need of the colonel.

What Veraswami had done sounded so "un-British," so vacillating and unsure, when described at the hearing. The regional administrator kept enquiring of the degree of danger to the colonel and several times asked if Veraswami thought the colonel's life could have been saved had Veraswami not imposed nearly an hour's delay on the return of the rescue train. Veraswami said the colonel might have lived if he had got to surgery earlier, or even if Veraswami had risked an abdominal operation in the field; he could not be sure, but it seemed quite possible.

It was never said, but all of Veraswami's talk of triage was seen as evasive; his actions were viewed as a failure to recognise sensible priorities, probably the result of panic. Veraswami's claim that he had treated equally all patients, white and coloured, sounded spurious since it was clear that Veraswami had spent more time treating natives than Europeans.

I asked Veraswami if there were not many more seriously injured natives than seriously injured Europeans on the train, and if that "might not sufficiently account for the inequality of your treatment?" He bristled at the word "inequality" but admitted that his talk of equality, guided only by professional ethics, was thought by many to be typical of his devious ways. Clearly I had hit a sore spot.

The enquiry made no finding critical specifically of Veraswami, but a series of recommendations were made for handling such emergencies in the future, the tenor of several being that Veraswami and the officers in charge of the rescue had acted without prompt decision and sufficient clarity of purpose. And it was specifically recommended that, because of the possibility of large-scale emergencies, there should always be a European doctor on duty at Rangoon Hospital.

It was not difficult to understand why Veraswami soon thereafter had accepted the opportunity of a posting to Moulmein. Nor was it difficult to understand that the military authorities in Rangoon would welcome—indeed, eagerly seek—proof of his criminal conduct.

The crisis was now upon me. The same beleathered cyclist returned with orders to investigate Dr. Veraswami's dealings in heroin. Reports of two purchases of heroin by him were set out, as well as the fact that one of the syringes I had sent for analysis had contained the residue of a solution of heroin. I was directed to interrogate Dr. Veraswami and to charge him with dealing in prohibited drugs unless an entirely satisfactory explanation for his conduct appeared.

The order added that this was no longer a matter for military authorities, that my civilian superiors in Mandalay had been informed of prior military intelligence actions in this matter, and that I should telephone Mandalay Regional Headquarters if further orders were thought necessary.

I doubted that a telephone call to Mandalay would help me much. I had better take some time to think—as Veraswami had advised, first take my own pulse.

"Bar Chit, Bar Chit," "Chit Boy, Chit Boy," the brusque cries of the thirsty—indigenous as far as I know to the European clubs of the Indian subcontinent—served as a background to my anxious reflections. It seemed too lonely to go to my bungalow; there was no one with whom I could discuss my problem. A few drinks at the Club, sitting away from the bar so that I could see the two billiards tables and pretend to be watching, would probably provide the safest haven.

I filled in my chit for a cold beer; the "boy," in his mid-forties, collected the chit and delivered the beer, while the chit remained at the bar to define my bill, the assumption of the lack of memory and trustworthiness of all "boys" thus reaffirmed.

There were occasional brief interruptions while those who knew me nodded in my direction or called out a greeting, but I was otherwise undisturbed. "Would you care for a game of billiards, Blair?" "Later perhaps, thank you."

My mind pursued a debate within itself, serving both prosecution and defence: How can Veraswami be innocent? It's impossible. Either he is using the drug himself, injecting himself—I could not bring the scene of such an injection to mind—or he is selling it. No, that would not explain the syringe and needle, and anyhow it is a ridiculous thought.

Veraswami, an addict? With such sense and kindliness! I suppose it is not impossible after a childhood like his, with the pain and loneliness he told me about, and the spur and constant temptation of the ready avail-

ability of drugs in his profession—it is not impossible. And the agonies of
War and the constant use of morphine on the Western Front, as well as the
treatment of his own wounds, might have pressed him to that escape.
Could that have been when his addiction began, and he then moved on to
heroin? Yet it still seems impossible. He is so direct, so open, so gently
interested in others, so wise—how could such qualities be those of an
addict? But he purchased heroin in the marketplace on at least two occasions; why act clandestinely if he is not an addict? And what should I do if
he is using heroin? Arrest him? Punish him for his own good?

I could not call to mind the scene of my arresting Veraswami. And, if I
did arrest him, what should I do with him? Lock him up in the gaol of
which he was the medical officer? It all seemed so senseless. But the realities forced me back to my internal debate—clearly something had to be
done and, equally clearly, I had to decide what it was.

The law must be obeyed. He must be arrested. But why are we British
so sanctimonious—so sure of our right, some would say our duty, to punish
addicts? Why do we insist on meddling in local customs? I suppose we may
have had some effect on suttee, or something equally offensive, but opium
and betel nut and, I suppose, other drugs have been used here for centuries
without any apparent harm. And not that long ago, our policy in the East
was vigourously to support the opium trade, even to fight a war to preserve
it. Is my friend to be sacrificed to our changes of policy, which do not seem
to have much effect anyhow on the use of drugs—readily available in every
marketplace in Burma?

"Bar Chit, Chit Boy."

But then my heroic resistance began to fail. These thoughts are well
and good for after-dinner discussion, but as a police magistrate and district
officer my job is to apply the law as it is written. I should leave to others
the policy questions. And how can I really know the long-term effects of
registering opium users and entirely prohibiting the sale or purchase of
heroin? My simple duty is to arrest Veraswami; he will understand my duty.
Then I should help him personally as much as I properly can, but I should
not fail in my duty under the law from some misguided sense of friendship.

"Oh yes, Bar Chit please."

What if he is not using the heroin himself? What if I am wrong about
that, and he is using it in the treatment of a patient? If he is just supporting
an addict, I suppose he is clearly guilty; but what if he is using it to treat an
addict, slowly withdrawing him from the drug? Or what if he is giving it to
a patient who is in great pain so as to minimise his suffering? Are these acts
illegal? I suppose not, though they may be. I will have to learn more about
the law. But even if they are legal, it is clear that his buying the heroin in
the market is a crime. Yet that seems crazy. If that were so, he could administer it legally but could not buy it legally—that would make no sense, but
the law may come to that.

I suppose that would not be as daft as it first seems. Perhaps that is the
only way the hospital authorities and the government could keep control

of the supply of dangerous drugs —to prohibit any purchases and then themselves carefully to control the supply for legitimate medical use. If that is so, why did not Veraswami get the heroin through the proper channels? Why, instead, in the marketplace?

"Of course, Bar Chit."

And here I am, like the rest, using my own drug, alcohol, to diminish the pain and loneliness of this place. What hypocrisy, Mr. District Officer! A sozzled child arresting a fine doctor because his habits are different. Have we all got to be peas in a legal pod, conforming even in our vices, our little deaths?

"Bar Chit, Boy."

Eventually I had the sense to realise that this maudlin self-flagellation, lubricated by too many beers, was doing good neither to me nor to Veraswami. My gloom was deep, but at the nadir one sensible thought at last came through: there was now no reason at all why I should not openly discuss all this with Dr. Veraswami. I need not mention Kau Reng—just tell Veraswami everything I knew, refuse to hint at how I knew it, and ask him to explain. Until now, that would have been contrary to my orders; now, to my awakening satisfaction, I realised it was not only the decent thing to do but even the proper thing to do from a police perspective—interrogate the suspect.

I left the bar and its trail of chits much happier than when I had arrived; the point was that Dr. Veraswami could help me, as he always did, with one of my more difficult problems—that it concerned him made his help even more likely to be wise. What a sensible fellow I am!

I had the sense, despite the multiplicity of beers I had consumed, to delay calling on Dr. Veraswami until the next day. It seemed to be underhand, cheating, to confront him with his criminality on his own verandah, so I sent a note to him in the morning, as soon as I arrived at the police station, asking if he could spare me an hour during the day. I added that I was not wishing to consult him professionally (which was not literally true, since I was pursuing my profession of the law, if not his of medicine).

The policeman returned with the message that Dr. Veraswami thought his hospital rounds would be completed by eleven o'clock and that he would be very pleased to see me then.

I was shown into his office, a scene of barely controlled chaos, with periodicals and papers, books and notepads, everywhere. A few minutes later he bustled in, his doctor's gown fanning out, batlike.

I had no idea how to begin. How to interrogate a friend with a view to his arrest and prosecution baffled me. And I had become accustomed to relying on Veraswami, to remembering what he said and later thinking about its implications. I relied on him as a sounding board for my own difficulties, but as more than a sounding board, as a surrogate for the guidance and wisdom of the father I had not earlier known—my own father having spent the period of my childhood and youth serving in India.

The balance of our relationship was changing. It was like those first occasions when one's parents actually appear to listen to, and to consider seriously, an opinion one has offered. Veraswami's telling me of his brutal nurse, of the pain of the War, and of the railway accident near Rangoon had altered the flow of emotions between us. That my mentor and adviser should be reaching out to share his problems with me was flattering; but it was also unsettling. That the child had been encouraged to grow from dependence to fraternity was one thing, but that the child should become the stern parent to the father was quite another.

And Veraswami seemed, if anything, more strained than I. His usual teasing, light friendliness was gone. I cannot say he looked pale, but had he not been black that is how he would have looked.

"You wish to see me, Mr. Blair?"

"Yes, Dr. Veraswami," and I sat like a dummy without anything at all coming to my mind or tongue.

He took pity on me: "What iss it about? I was told it wass not because you are unwell, though you do not look verry well—quite tense, in fact."

And it burst from me, a flood of words. I told him that I had been ordered to investigate heroin distribution from his hospital and to find out why he himself had bought it illegally. I managed, I feel sure, not to give any hint of the role of Kau Reng or his brother, but all the rest, including that there were witnesses to his having twice bought heroin in the Chinese market, poured out of me.

Veraswami took off his white coat slowly as I spoke, placed it carefully on the couch beside the wall, and sat down on the chair beside mine in the posture of a doctor listening attentively to a patient's description of his symptoms.

I ended with: "Tell me what you think I should do, Dr. Veraswami," which, when I thought about it, was an absurd way to interrogate a criminal. But it was right for Dr. Veraswami.

"I cannot tell you, Eric. It iss your job, and a difficult one. But I will tell you everything I know about all thiss, everything, and then you can decide what to do. And I don't know what I shall do with myself. But I will not deceive you."

I knew without possibility of doubt that he would speak the truth and that my task of fact-finding as a detective was over; but I hated his uncertainty about what he would do, or rather, what he would do "with himself." Could he possibly be hinting at suicide?

"It iss not ass it must seem, Eric," and again he was using my Christian name which, until recently, he rarely did. "I have an Indian patient here, Mr. Chanduri, who iss in the last stages of cancer of the pancreas, a cruelly painful form of that horrible disease. Nothing can be done to cure him. In his now emaciated condition, orally administered drugs are completely ineffective, and the pain-reducing drugs we have, all except heroin, have to be injected in massive doses, doses so large ass to cause severe nausea and vomiting, and to be painful in themselves. I am not sure of the chemistry—there may be little difference chemically between morphine and heroin—but I am sure that for a few patients like Mr. Chanduri, who do not get relief from morphine, heroin iss a blessing. I have observed it carefully. I am sure of thiss no matter what the chemists may say. No, Eric, morphine will not do it, and I cannot let him die in agony. Mr. Chanduri tolerates heroin well—indeed, it gives him peace, even pleasure. Ass your doctors do in England, I have been reducing hiss pain these past few weeks by intramuscular injections of a solution of heroin. He hass probably become addicted, and needs increasingly substantial doses; does it matter?"

I did not reply. Clearly he had more to tell me. "No, I do not use drugs myself. I do not like them. I am too unsure of my brain, even when it iss at its best. A few beers only, ass you know. I have treated other dying patients the same way and will again if it be necessary, though I have not decided on thiss easily. From what I have told you, you must know that I am perhaps too sensitive to pain. But I will not let my patient suffer. Yess, I know it iss a crime to buy heroin, and I do not like to break the law. But there iss no other way to help him, since those who supply our drugs in this country do not trust uss—they think we will sell the heroin or use it ourselves."

I interrupted him: "Why did you not come to me about this? Why buy it yourself? Surely together we could have avoided all this trouble."

"I thought of that, Eric. But I decided that I should not burden you with thiss problem. There are only so many times that one district officer can be asked to save the Raj from itself. It iss fake heroism, I admit, but I am angry that those who govern uss are so stupidly cruel."

We sat in silence. I did not know what to do.

Was I to arrest Veraswami for doing what he thought was right? If I had learned anything from the jungle death of my policeman it was that we creatures of folly often make mistakes of judgement when emotions run high—and they certainly ran high with me now. As Veraswami had said when we discussed that death, "It iss so easy to err under the pressure of anxiety for a patient." In a sense I saw Veraswami as my patient now. I found it impossible to condemn his breach of the law, yet my obligation to that law and to my superiors seemed clear. I decided I had better follow my mentor-patient's advice and think as clearly as I could before I did anything, not just leap down the cliff myself—first take my own pulse. "May I call on you for a beer before tiffin this afternoon, Dr. Veraswami?"

For the first time at this meeting, Veraswami smiled at me: "Of course, Eric. Then or at any time it will be an entire pleasure to see you, whether I am in or out of gaol. I will expect you thiss evening. Do not be late; I do not think I will find it easy to work today."

I walked to Veraswami's bungalow by the longer route beside the Salween; I needed to have some idea in my mind of what I wanted to happen before the pressure of decision was upon me.

I started off toward the river in mid-afternoon, the heat of the day abating under a light breeze, the seductive ring of the temple bells calming my anxieties. The scene was more peaceful, the river lovelier, and the greens of the foliage more varied than I had recalled. It was hard to shift my mind to the pain of investigating Veraswami. The wandering and uneven path, and the glimpses of the river through the thick foliage, distracted me —I had never before been so aware of surrounding beauty. But if I were to be of any use to Veraswami and also do my duty as a district officer, I would have to turn my mind to it.

So far, all I seemed to be worrying about was how not to prosecute Veraswami. If I were to be effective, I would have to make myself consider seriously the other side of the argument, the reasons why he should be charged. Perhaps the law I was supposed to enforce did have some sense; it was no good railing against it in my mind as if that would achieve anything.

Opium had been used for centuries in Burma without ill effects. Already I was deceiving myself—how did I know there had been no ill effects? There must have been. Quite apart from the tyranny of addiction, controlling and warping many lives, the regular use of opium must have had a debilitating effect on the Burmese, individually and collectively. So, how could I know that it was not worthwhile to try to stamp it out?

But what if the law tried to stamp out alcohol in England? The English worker would not easily renounce his beer—it would be revolution, a bloody revolution. And it was unthinkable that the Anglo-Indian would give up his stengah. So there were bad customs in both cultures which were not easily eradicated.

But (again a "but," there always seemed to be "buts" in the law) some customs could and should be eradicated by the law and its vigourous enforcement. Suttee, thuggee, and infanticide had all been attacked in this way in India by the Raj, and with success—suttee and thuggee eliminated, infanticide greatly reduced. In Sind it had been objected that suttee was a national custom that should be respected by the British. The reply of the Raj had been succinct: "It is your custom to burn widows. It is our custom to hang murderers. Let us both follow our customs!"

But—again—to agree that the use of opium could properly be controlled did not suggest that any means to that end were sensible. There had had to be concessions so that the poppy growers in the hills would not be ruined and so that some users could register and get opium for themselves.

So why the ban on heroin for the hospitals? There was only one possible reason: it was thought too difficult, too troublesome, to control that line of supply. It was easier to prohibit heroin altogether than to risk some misuse. In other words, Veraswami was to be sacrificed to the unwillingness of the authorities to make sensible arrangements for the proper medical use of this drug. No, that was wrong; it was not Veraswami who was being sacrificed. There might be only a very few of the terminally ill for whom heroin was the drug of choice, or even the only effective painkiller; but there were some, and the balance was between their pain and the difficulty of controlling a limited supply of heroin through hospital channels.

And then it struck me. As usual I was being childishly simple in my approach. The order to me to investigate Veraswami and to arrest him if he had bought heroin probably had little to do with any policy concerning drugs; it related back to his behaviour at the railway accident! It was precisely the excuse the Rangoon army authorities needed to get rid of Veraswami—not for dealing in prohibited drugs but for failing in his duty to save the lives of British soldiers when he could have done so, and then, in their view, finding a politically effective but morally unsound excuse to escape responsibility. Had any other doctor been involved, Rangoon would have turned a blind eye. I became utterly convinced: It was not the word "heroin" in Kau Reng's report that had caught Rangoon's attention, but the name "Veraswami."

Was I to be co-opted into this persecution? And, if not, was there a way out that would preserve my own position in the service of the Raj? The excuse my masters had found to get rid of their distasteful doctor was, after all, of some powerful legal force; it did appear that Veraswami had broken the law. It would not be easy to get behind the excuse to the reality.

For once my thoughts seemed to have followed a reasonably logical path, but my feet had not. I found I had walked well past the turnoff to Veraswami's bungalow. I hurried back; he had asked me to come in the early evening—I could imagine how troubled he must be.

To my surprise, Dr. Veraswami was not at his bungalow when I arrived, yet he had asked me to come early. It was quite out of character. I asked a servant where he was; the servant was unsure—Dr. Veraswami had never left like this before, without a word. Growing unease became hot anxiety. Veraswami had hinted to me, and I had pretended not to notice: "What shall I do with myself?" He had tried to tell me of his fragility, and I had been too obtuse to respond. His stories of his childhood and of the War were also intended to give me a sense of his personal pains and difficulties. And I had left him to go off on my own, when I should have stayed with him. I had let him down, failed to understand his pain. Why did I always let my immediate selfish needs take precedence?

At this moment of panic my fears were disabused. Veraswami, wearing sandals, a long white dhoti, and an open-necked white shirt, came happily bouncing up the path and onto the verandah.

"Thank you for coming, Eric. It iss good to see you," and then he caught sight of my face and stopped his ritualistic greetings. "Oh goodness me, you have been troubled. I am so sorry. It iss thoughtless of me. But all iss well now, I think. Let uss talk. Will you have a beer?"

He seemed to be going on meaninglessly. I found my anxiety for him turned to annoyance, as when a child has caused you to fear for his safety and you discover him safe and ignorant of your fear. How could all be well now? I was coming to investigate a crime, and he was the suspected criminal. But, yes, I would have a beer.

Veraswami beamed at my obvious annoyance, taking it for the caring compliment which I suppose it was. He made more than the usual fuss of having the oval bucket of ice and wire-stoppered bottles of Watney's ale brought onto the verandah, and of seeing me served and settled.

For my part, I was anxious to get on with our discussion. I found this bouncy bonhomie and his odd dress—a dhoti with a shirt seemed a wild confusion—quite unsettling. His troubles had not caused him to kill himself; they'd driven him daft. And I found myself, too, smiling in bewilderment.

"Good, Mr. Policeman—and now you really are the policeman—let uss talk. But let me tell you that I have come to a firm decision about all thiss and I am not upset and worried ass I wass earlier today. And my wife and daughters seem verry happy about it and so, I find, am I."

"You mean you have told your family about this, Veraswami! Why did you do that? I still hope we can find a way out."

"Of course you will find a way out for me as far as the law goes. I am sure of it. I have watched you over these years we have been together in Moulmein, and you have become verry skillful, verry devious with the law. No, you misunderstand; I am not clear with you. For some time, my wife has urged me to return to the Punjab when my present contract with your government is ended—and quite soon it iss, only a few months. I have been putting off submitting my resignation. I suppose I had lingering doubts—perhaps I still do not trust the judgement of women. But these events have helped me to put aside my uncertainty. My wife, who doess not often say such things, tells me that I must now stop lusting after strange gods. I wonder where she read it? But she iss right."

It was happening too quickly; I found it hard to follow. But as his words penetrated, I too came to share his sense of relief. It must have been very hard for my friend as a medical student and young doctor in London, very hard to bear the loneliness of isolation in a foreign city while eschewing the comfort of the enclave of Indian students that would negate the value of exposure to English customs. And these pressures must have intensified during his service in Rangoon, especially after the crisis of the railway accident. Moulmein must have been an oasis of peace for him. But here, too, he was isolated; I am sure I was his only friend in Burma.

"So because of this damned heroin and Mr. Chanduri you're going to leave me friendless here, Dr. Veraswami?"

"You are right, Eric; it did force my decision. But I am glad, verry glad, that the matter of the heroin for poor Mr. Chanduri hass brought the boil to a head, so to speak. It hass made me realise that I should be with my people. I have learned what London and the War and Rangoon and Moulmein have to teach me; now I will go home. If I had been able to become a great doctor, or a creative surgeon, or a great teacher of medicine —and I have dreamed of all those things—or even a great medical administrator, I would have stayed with your countrymen. But I am never going to be more than a competent and considerate doctor. That, I now find, and to my surprise, iss enough, quite enough. And ass a good doctor I shall go home."

His mood turned jovial: "Bhatinda is not Siberia, Eric. My family lives well there, believe me; we are not starving peasants. Bhatinda has a seventeenth century fort, with walls over a hundred feet high, much admired by English military men, and there iss also a famous shrine to a Muslim saint, Baba Ratan, who iss supposed to have lived to the jolly old age of fourteen hundred years, a feat my wife hopes I shall not try to emulate."

I realised that his ebullience was in no way a shelter for anxiety about the charge against him. He was genuinely pleased. That was well and good for him, but I still had orders from Rangoon—or were they now from Mandalay?—to arrest Veraswami and charge him with a serious crime. He might not care about this, but I did.

I tried to lead the conversation back to the heroin, and kept trying. He was almost impatient with me. "You tell me what to say and do, Eric. It would be better if you can avoid convicting me of a crime, but I do not think even that would stop my being a good doctor in Bhatinda. I will do and say what you tell me to do and say, provided I do not have to pretend I am sorry to have helped Mr. Chanduri." And suddenly he was serious and firmly direct with me: "And you should know, Mr. Policeman, that unless you have me locked up I will continue to care for Mr. Chanduri in the same way. It would be verry cruel to increase hiss pain now."

We talked long, through the downpour of the late-afternoon rain and ensuing gaudy sunset into the first dark of night. The metaphor of bringing the boil to a head changed to that of two fishes out of water, an Indian doctor and a somewhat lost young Englishman. I found that we were talking more about me than about Dr. Veraswami and his family—for him all problems seemed to have been resolved.

"I have watched you over these years, Eric, with growing affection, if I may be so bold. You too, I think, should soon go back to your people. Neither of us iss comfortable at the Club; at one time I thought it right to try to join, ass you know, but it wass a silly pretension.

"You have been clever in softening the law for the people of Moulmein, but you have had to be devious and scheming. Too much, and you may grow to like manipulating power in thiss way. At one time I thought you might become a lawyer, a barrister, a judge. I imagined you eating all those dinners in London—I believe they are verry bad—but now I do not think so. You do not like executions and prisons; you worry about Ake Dah in my mental hospital; you constantly question the rules of the Raj and try to adapt them to Moulmein rather than just apply them in Moulmein ass iss expected of you. I think about why you do thiss; perhaps you wish to write about uss. I do not know, but I watch you becoming subtle and manipulative of power, even pulling the wool over the eyes of our friend U Tin Hlang. You do it well, Eric, but it iss not a life for you."

We parted with nothing further resolved in the matter of Veraswami's purchase and administration of heroin. As far as he was concerned, that was my affair; he would, within the limits he had defined, do and say whatever I suggested. I suppose he had to trust in my manipulative powers, of which he was otherwise so critical—no, that was not fair, it was rather that he feared their effects on me.

I walked on the road back to my bungalow; the path by the Salween was difficult by night.

I awoke clear-headed, knowing exactly what I must do. Dr. Veraswami had irked me by calling me "manipulative" and "devious." I would do my best to live up to his worst expectations. I thought I saw how to persuade Rangoon to leave Veraswami alone by a mixed argument of politics and law. If I should make an error or two in the law, that would not matter. They knew I was not a lawyer; but neither were the senior officers who would make the decision, though they would be advised by lawyers. I would do precisely what I was told to do when in doubt: set out an "appreciation of the situation"—it had a euphonious lilt which pleased me. But this "appreciation" would be different; it would be for Rangoon rather than for me, and it would be stronger on politics than on the law. And if they sensed a tinge of dissimulation, so much the better.

TO: OIC, Regional Headquarters, Burma Police.
FROM: District Officer, Moulmein.
DATE: 6/7/1927.
COPY: OIC, Imperial Forces Burma.
CLASSIFICATION: CONFIDENTIAL.

RE: Prohibited Drugs.

I have completed the investigation of the purchase of heroin by the superintendent of the Moulmein Hospital, Dr. Veraswami, as directed by the Commanding Officer of the Burma Imperial Forces.

Dr. Veraswami has confessed to having made two purchases of heroin in the Chinese market in Moulmein. He advises me that the heroin was used—and will continue to be used while he is medical superintendent—to alleviate the agony of a patient, a Mr. Chanduri, who is terminally ill with cancer of the pancreas. I have no reason to doubt the truth of Dr. Veraswami's story. I am satisfied that Dr. Veraswami neither uses heroin himself nor sells it.

Despite this apparently clear breach of the criminal law, it is my advice that Dr. Veraswami should not be prosecuted. Contrary to orders, I did not arrest him. Two considerations led me to this decision: one legal, one prudential.

First, I believe Dr. Veraswami has a more than colourable argument that his purchase of the heroin was not illegal. As I understand it, otherwise illegal actions may be justified under Section 81 of the Penal Code if the evil of the accused's act is less than the evil sought to be prevented by the law, and there was no less injurious method of reaching that result—the doctrine of lesser evils or of necessity. I do not pretend, of course, to be well versed in the details of this doctrine or of the cases applying it, but if the matter came before me as a magistrate, as I now understand the facts and the law, I would hold that Dr. Veraswami's otherwise illegal act was justified by that section of the Code. I believe that his buying and using the heroin was a lesser evil than letting Mr. Chanduri suffer avoidable agony and, further, that there were no otherwise legal means of achieving that end.

Though far from skilled in the law, I have not reached these conclusions lightly. I enclose with this message an "appreciation" I have prepared for myself (as instructed in my training course at Mandalay) of the considerations which would lead me to allow a defence of necessity to Dr. Veraswami if it were advanced before me as a magistrate. I believe the same considerations would allow a spirited defence of this nature by Dr. Veraswami were he put on trial before the Superior Court.

I appreciate that I may well be wrong in law, but I have become sufficiently convinced of the appropriateness of the defence that it would be better that Dr. Veraswami should not be tried before me in Moulmein Magistrate's Court should you decide to prosecute him. I therefore await your order to arrest him with a view to his indictment for trial before the Superior Court in Mandalay or Rangoon.

Dr. Veraswami tells me that it is his intention vigourously to press the defence of necessity if he is charged with this crime; he believes that it is a scandal, a grave reflection on the administration's medical services in Burma and India, that merciful treatments used in England are in effect prohibited in this country. He intends to seek the assistance of leading counsel to present this argument if he is charged with a crime. His attorney is Mr. U Tin Hlang, who may be counted upon to recognise the damage to the administration that would result from a necessity defence, whether successful or not.

My other reason is prudential. Dr. Veraswami advises me that he intends to offer his resignation from government service to take effect at the end of his present tour of duty four months hence. He plans to return to his home at Bhatinda in the Punjab and to enter private practice there. He has discussed his reasons for this with me. Quite apart from his present difficulties, they seem to me to reflect a firm intention. The four months may be a desirable period in which to arrange for a successor to Dr. Veraswami as the medical superintendent of Moulmein Hospital. Further, if he changes his mind and does not resign, the present charges could then be brought against him should you so direct; the evidence is adequate and is unlikely to dissipate within four months, and we would be well within the limitations period.

I therefore urge that it would be unwise now to precipitate a public trial of a contentious and sensitive issue. I shall take no further action in this matter unless directed to do so.

I did what my grandmother had told me always to do with such missives; I kept it overnight and read it carefully the next day before sending it. I sent it off, not by leather-helmeted speedster, but through ordinary channels. This too would probably be thought indiscreet, but I felt indiscreet, indeed outraged—outraged and smug.

It was clearly time that I, too, should take Mrs. Veraswami's advice, and stop lusting after strange gods.

APPENDIX

Appreciation: Heroin Charges against Dr. Veraswami

At the Mandalay Police Training College we were instructed that in our judicial work in the Districts we should be chary of expressing in the courtroom our reasons for a decision; but, by contrast, we were urged—if the time allowed or if the issue we faced was sufficiently important or difficult—to try to set out in writing for ourselves what weighed, and how it weighed, in our decision. I find Dr. Veraswami's purchase of heroin and his injection of a solution of heroin into Mr. Chanduri of sufficient difficulty that I will try to write such an "appreciation" of the law in order to guide myself on the question of Dr. Veraswami's culpability.

The facts I assume for purposes of this document are these: on two occasions Dr. Veraswami bought heroin in the Moulmein market. On one occasion he injected a solution of heroin into a terminally ill patient to reduce that patient's suffering.

Dr. Veraswami knew these actions were prohibited by statute.

Unless he has a valid defence, he has committed three felonies. I must determine if he has such a defence.

Having consulted by telephone with his attorney in Rangoon, Mr. U Tin Hlang, Dr. Veraswami tells me that justification of what he has done is to be found in Section 81 of the Indian Penal Code, which, he is advised, provides that an otherwise criminal action is not an offence if it is done to avoid a harm greater than the harm the statute seeks to prevent. Section 81 is inartfully drawn, but I believe Veraswami's summary is an accurate representation of how the section is interpreted and applied.

Of course, the accused cannot become the lawmaker, and Section 81 or any necessity defence is unavailable if the legislature has already made the choice of evils faced by the accused. The citizen cannot find justified what the legislature has determined to be unjustified.

The central issue, then, is whether the legislature has spoken on the use of heroin for terminally ill cancer patients. If it has, Veraswami's justification defence should be rejected as a matter of law. If not, it becomes a jury question.

There are some indications that the legislature may have spoken. The statute prohibiting heroin in India and Burma is absolute in its terms, making no exception for the medical administration of heroin, either as an analgesic for the terminally ill or as a treatment for heroin addiction, though at the time of the passage of the relevant legislation both these problems were understood. The lack of exceptions may therefore be due to a legislative intent to disallow such use. Parallel English legislation allows for the medical administration of heroin in both situations. It was perhaps thought unwise to extend these medical exemptions to the different circumstances of medical practice in India and Burma. If this was the intent of the legislature, then Veraswami's contrary belief that his act was justified can have no legal effect. But on the other hand, the lack of exceptions may mean nothing more than that the legislature failed to address this issue.

It is no use my straining further at this question of whether the legislature has spoken; I have to do my best with it, inadequately trained and advised as I am. I have come to the conclusion that the decision Veraswami made, involving the rare patient not responsive to alternative and legal means of reducing pain, was too unusual to have attracted the attention of and to have been rejected by the legislature.

Dr. Veraswami, therefore, seems to have a right to have his defence of necessity put to a jury. After all, when the legislature has been silent on an issue, a defendant can argue that society should give him a chance to have his choice ratified by a jury—next to the legislature, the body most representative of society.

This is not to argue that what Veraswami did was right. It is to suggest, however, that Veraswami probably has the right to have his choice of evils considered by a jury of his peers. And I think it probable that Veraswami will win his case if he can get it to the jury. Asian jurymen—some of whom may well be antagonistic to our administration—will likely view Dr. Veraswami as protecting one of their own, Mr. Chanduri, from the tyranny of our hypocrisy.

And even if at trial this defence of necessity is withdrawn from the jury, many of the same issues could be aired at sentencing, since Veraswami's purposes and motives are then clearly relevant.

I am confident that, either way, U Tin Hlang will insure that the trial will be much publicised, and I fear embarrassment for the administration.

Commentary to
"THE VERASWAMI STORY"

The ethics of triage and the defence of necessity are the central problems in "The Veraswami Story," both explored in the context of making decisions in situations of crisis.

Veraswami speaks of the need in emergencies first to take your own pulse. A friend of mine who led Australia's first Antarctic settlement phrased the same point differently: "Unless the spear is about to hit, don't immediately act in crises; sit down for a few moments and think." Because he failed to do this, Blair's policeman died when Blair could have saved him—solicitude, anxiety to minimise the fallen man's injuries by protecting him from being bashed against the cliff face, caused his death.

Veraswami's story of the train accident and of his behaviour at the accident, which probably prevented the colonel from being saved, is also a tale of decisionmaking in a medical emergency. However, there is this important difference: From his training and from his experience on the Western Front, Veraswami had learned to guide his actions by the principle of triage, treating all lives as of equal value and concentrating his immediate efforts not on the most seriously injured (like the colonel), nor on the least seriously injured, but on the middle group to whom immediate medical attention would make the greatest life- and health-saving difference. It is understandable that that decision could be misinterpreted in the Mess. The colonel's life would there be seen as of more value than the lives of many others injured in the train crash, and Veraswami's conduct would be deeply resented.

From the perspective of a colonial power, entrusting these decisions to an English doctor might well have made more sense than relying upon Dr. Veraswami, despite his superior medical competence. And, from a utilitarian point of view, surely the Mess is right and Veraswami wrong. At all events, triage raises a number of difficult moral issues, some of which are explored in this story, and it is no surprise that after the train accident Dr. Veraswami would remain profoundly unpopular with his military superiors. They would be anxious to be rid of him and delighted to find an excellent excuse in his criminal conduct—buying and using heroin, a prohibited drug—which leads us to the main problem in this story, the defence of necessity to a criminal charge.

The problem Veraswami faced in treating Mr. Chanduri is a serious issue in this country today. Heroin is the drug of choice to relieve pain for some terminally ill cancer patients; morphine works equally well for all but a few, but for those few there is nowhere else to turn but to heroin, whose administration is, on the face of the law, a criminal offence. This is not so in the United Kingdom or in Canada, so that a very few wealthy patients in this country have been able to leave their families and their country to relieve their sharpest agonies prior to death.

Veraswami instructed Blair in some aspects of pain and its endurance when they discussed the religious procession of self-mutilators and self-flagel-lants they both witnessed (I observed something similar years ago in Malaysia); he also confessed to Blair his own possibly hypersensitive response to pain as a result of the beatings by his nurse in his young childhood. Nevertheless, he comes firmly to the view that, law or no law, he will not let Mr. Chanduri suffer needlessly, and he trusts to Blair to find a way out from the law through the law.

The defence of necessity—the choice of evils defence—is Blair's solution. The moral and legal issue is: does Blair get it right?

It seems proper for me to add that it is now much more difficult to reach Blair's decision in the United States than it was for Blair in Burma half a cen-tury ago—we have regressed, not advanced. Blair could argue that no legisla-tive decision on this question had been reached in Burma; that could not now be argued effectively in this country, since it seems clear that Congress has indeed expressly decided that there are no occasions, none whatsoever, when heroin or marijuana can be used as medical treatments—surely the ultimate victory of moral posturing over medical necessity.

Necessity as a defence remains a great moral issue in a variety of contexts. May the shipwrecked, airwrecked, or marooned, or starving castaways, resort *in extremis* to cannibalism so that some may survive? Does the convicted pris-oner commit a crime when he "escapes" from the burning gaol, or when he "escapes" from threats of immediate rape by other prisoners? (The Supreme Court has held that he does unless he immediately turns himself in to the authorities; happily, there were vigourous dissents.) Statutory pronouncements on this aside, is abortion a crime when it terminates the life of the fetus to save the life or health of the mother?

The typical formula to answer these questions, drawn from the Common Law, requires that three conditions be fulfilled. First, the person pleading this defence must not himself have created the crisis which precipitates this choice between evils. Second, the evil avoided by the otherwise criminal act must be greater than the evil committed. And third, the legislature must not have spo-ken to this choice (the actor's view of the relative gravity of the two evils is subservient to the legislature's decision on that issue).

These are sensible enough ideas, but they are far from easy to apply in practice. So-called "political necessity" has been of recent prominence: burn-ing draft cards to protest what is seen as an illegal war, giving sanctuary to prohibited refugees who are seen as escaping from political tyranny, blocking the entrance to military installations believed to contain nuclear weaponry, destroying the records of abortion clinics or threatening their personnel and their patients. From the political left and the political right there are men and women of good conscience who, in the above circumstances, see their moral duty to be a breach of the law. Should the law allow such a defence? Generally speaking, the answer, pursuant to the three principles I have stated, is "No." But that is not really the end of the matter, since often those making such claims are more interested in the public airing of their position in the media than in the result of the case. The issue thus becomes whether the judge should allow evidence of a claim of necessity as a defence to a criminal charge in such matters. If he allows it, the media will serve the dissenters well. And on this the courts are deeply divided, so you will not get much comfort from the case law. But it remains a difficult and interesting question.

One last comment: it is important sharply to distinguish the defence of necessity from conscientious objection as practised by Gandhi and Martin Luther King, Jr. The conscientious objector says: I break the law and accept punishment so as to heighten the community's perception of a grave injustice and to shame them to change the law. Dr. Veraswami made no such claim. His purchasing and administering the heroin to Mr. Chanduri was a private— not a public—action, an act of private conscience and not of public persuasion. Further, he claimed, the law already permitted this. Blair agreed. Do you?

The Tropical Bedroom

The telegram read:

> LT. ERIC BLAIR
> MOULMEIN DISTRICT OFFICE
>
>
> TOP SECRET SOURCES REVEAL SUBSTANTIAL LOCAL
> LEAVE DUE MOULMEIN'S DISTINGUISHED DISTRICT OFFI-
> CER STOP PLEASE VISIT RANGOON FOR A WEEK AT LEAST
> AS MY GUEST EXCEPT SUGGEST YOU RESIDE OFFICERS
> CLUB STOP COME TO MY BUNGALOW MONDAY MORNING
> TWELFTH FOR BREAKFAST STOP CAR WILL COLLECT YOU
> SEVEN THIRTY STOP EVEN MORE DETAILED PLANS IN FOL-
> LOWING LETTER STOP NO EXCUSE ACCEPTABLE STOP
> CORDIAL REGARDS
>
>
> U TIN HLANG
>
> RANGOON

My chagrin at his boasted access to confidential police files did not long delay my accepting his invitation. Lang interested me. He amused me. I had much to learn from him, and I could easily persuade myself that what I learned would help me to do my job better in Moulmein. He was, after all, a leading Silk and prominent in an important Burmese political group. And, I must confess, the resonance of his earlier invitation to "breakfast with my elephants, my horses, and my mistresses" had rung insistently and alluringly in my lonely ears for some weeks.

I heard a trumpeting and some neighing, and there they were on a path through the trees on the other side of the beach, just as he had promised: two elephants and their mahouts, a few horses and their handlers, a few dogs (he hadn't mentioned the dogs — took them for granted, I suppose), and several young sari-wrapped women, rather portly for mistresses, I thought. U Tin Hlang hurried ahead towards me, a largish dog bounding around him. He clasped me in a brief, warm hug. He had never done that before, though I did recall that I had behaved similarly when I had once come across him unexpectedly at Moulmein Station.

He looked wonderful. Energy flowed from him, and fueled my joy in his friendship. Even the sometimes sinister-looking curved scar on his cheek seemed to have faded in the exuberance of the morning. He wore native garments, but of a quality no villager could afford: a soft, blue, loose-fitting, round-necked, silk shirt above a calf-length dhoti of off-white linen, and simple, shining leather sandals. I felt overdressed in my military cap, shirt and shorts, Sam Browne belt, long socks and shoes, and carrying in my hand, wrapped neatly in a towel, my neck-to-knee swimming costume, which is the appropriate attire for a European who might be observed bathing by a native — or so I had been instructed.

He led me immediately to a promontory of rocks and stones that curved out above the light surf some fifty yards from the left of the beach. The rocks and stones had been collected from the waters in front of the beach — and it must have been a huge task — so that pale yellow sand and only pale yellow sand formed its floor, giving the water a translucent blue-green clarity, perfect for swimmers and for U Tin Hlang's elephants, dogs, and horses in their pre-breakfast ablutions. We picked our way to the end of the stony promontory and looked back on the scene.

The horses high-stepped in the shallows and plunged as they were taken into deeper waters; the elephants rolled on their sides close to the beach while their mahouts scrambled about on them, splashing water on them to rub them down with their hands, and receiving an occasional playful squirt from their trunks. The dogs barked and snapped at the wavelets on the shore. The mistresses seemed less enchanted by the occasion, huddling together under the palm trees close to where the breakfast tables were being laid, showing no inclination to join the other mammals in the water.

"Aren't you going in, Blair?"

"Of course; let me change into my costume."

"Costume. Costume. You sound like the West End, Blair. Change here." And he gave me a vigourous push off the rocks into the gentle surf.

I came up determined to return the compliment, but he forestalled me. His clothing was already suited to the water and, kicking off his elegant sandals, he dived off the end of the rocks before I could move to seek revenge for my own unexpected inundation.

Fortunately it was not deep where he had pushed me in and I had kept a grip on my now soggy towel and swimming costume. I waded toward the shore and a clump of palms that seemed a suitable screen behind which to change out of my dripping military attire. The clothes would dry; once I was properly costumed, a swim would be a joy.

When I emerged, U Tin Hlang had swum to shore and was greeting a European lady on horseback at the waterline. I walked toward them. He spoke and her head turned sharply. Rosemary! She did not seem surprised to see me, but she did seem pleased. "Blair, how jolly to see you here. I had no idea. What a schemer Lang is!"

I knew she was teasing me, but I had no reply other than what I suppose was an inane grin. I think I made as if to salute her by way of greeting, but my hand stopped, elevated only a few inches — a full bathing costume is entirely inappropriate get-up for a salute.

She did not prolong my embarrassment. "I'm going for a swim. Come in with me. I won't be a moment." And horse and rider set off toward the back of the beach.

I called to U Tin Hlang, "Why didn't you tell me Rosemary would be here? Is George Brett coming?"

"I'm sorry to disappoint you, Blair. George is most unfortunately in Upper Burma for a few days, possibly a week or two, accompanying what he calls 'his General' on an inspection tour I learned about some time ago. I should have told you. We could have deferred your visit until his return. Stupid of me."

I ignored his efforts at badinage: "Do you see them often?"

"I find him heavy going, but I'm glad to say that Rosemary quite often joins me here at these breakfasts."

I felt stirrings of jealousy. What a ridiculous thought, Rosemary and U Tin Hlang. She never would. But I did not let myself pursue the analysis.

Rosemary joined us, leading the horse. "Will you have one of your men wash and rub him down for me please, Lang?" She passed the bridle to U Tin Hlang's outstretched hand and then, to my delight, took my hand and, child-like, pulled me toward the surf.

My memories of that morning are scattered but strong; I shall never lose them.

U Tin Hlang persuaded me to let myself be picked up by one of the elephants. Had Rosemary not been there I should most certainly have refused. It is an extraordinary feeling. The trunk is so strong, yet gentle, as it wraps itself over your shoulder and around your waist; the lift is steady but inexorable—and there you are, swung over, upright after being canted left en route, seated astride the hump, surprised by the gently moving, huge head in front of you.

I remember too that I never have eaten a larger breakfast, even as a youth returning home for school holidays. First, a typical Burmese breakfast of fruit and fried plankton; then we celebrated U Tin Hlang's London barrister period with chops and sausages, eggs and toast, and marmalade and tea. At last, prostrate and happy, we lay silent on the sand as the sun gradually took on its tropical fire.

Later, we went back to what U Tin Hlang called his bungalow, though its size and complexity belied the term. It seemed to have grown rather than to have been built, hewn from the jungle, of polished wood, with sweeping balconies, thatched roof, and carved shutters—orderly, comfortable, and spacious, yet still a part of the jungle.

U Tin Hlang had been testy with one of the mahouts for not bringing the baby elephant to the beach along with its mother; the man had resisted his criticism, saying it was better to let the baby rest longer that morning. Lang had yielded to the wisdom of his decision. Now Rosemary insisted that we visit the baby. Baby, indeed. It pushed up to me, eye to eye, trunk waving about under no apparent control: a threatening playfulness, a potent inquisitiveness. I rubbed it behind the ear, as instructed, which it seemed to enjoy.

"May I feed him?" Rosemary asked.

The mahout found a large bottle with a very substantial nipple, and while I stood on one side of the animal rubbing behind its ear as self-protection, Rosemary stood on the other side and held the bottle in the baby's mouth, tucked in behind its trunk, while we smiled in delight at one another across its huge baby head.

The mahout handed me a banana, indicating it was for the elephant. "Should I peel it?" I asked.

"He prefers it that way, I should think," Lang replied, rolling his eyes at the absurdity of my question. "Don't they keep elephants at Eton?"

So I peeled it—one-handed, awkwardly, since I was determined to continue the self-protective behind-the-ear rubbing—and then, handing the peel to the mahout, speculated how to give the banana to the small-large beast. I held the banana in my left hand, waving it in front of the elephant's eyes, my right hand continuing the self-preserving ear-rubbing. The delicate pink end of the trunk curved up, sniffed at my hand, and then eased the banana from me, waving it uncertainly in front of our two heads. Clearly the small giant had no intention of abandoning the bottle, and this made it difficult for him to ingest the banana. The trunk waving continued, the banana clutched firmly, and then the trunk curled down and around toward the side of the mouth that was not fastened on the bottle. It missed. The banana squashed on the elephant's cheek. With a slight squeal of surprise, the animal reared backwards, abandoning the bottle, and began cleaning its cheek with its trunk, this time safely conveying the remains of the banana to its now available mouth.

The mahout pushed at it and stroked it with his hands, delighting in the fuss that was being made of his pet.

U Tin Hlang said, "Now everyone has had breakfast, though I must admit this little one eats a lot less than we did—certainly than Blair did."

"What's his name?" Rosemary asked.

"He hasn't been named, yet," Lang said. "Have you a suggestion?"

"Let's not call him Eric," Rosemary said. "He doesn't eat nearly as neatly as Eric. I'll think of something and let you know."

U Tin Hlang said he had to be off—litigants awaited. But we could stay as long as we liked. Would we be free to have dinner with him that night? I certainly was, and not to my surprise by now, so was Rosemary.

I found myself shy in Rosemary's presence after U Tin Hlang left. It was all too obvious, too contrived. She, too, seemed somewhat strained. We walked to where her horse was stabled and she left to ride back to her bungalow, arrangements having been made for U Tin Hlang's Fiat, in which I had been driven out that morning, to collect us for dinner that night.

The drive to dinner, the three of us together through the evening (for U Tin Hlang had come himself to pick us up), our conversation—all fade in my memory into the reality that that was the night Rosemary and I became lovers. U Tin Hlang made no effort to conceal the role he was playing, but it was performed in such warm friendship that embarrassment left me after a while. Dinner was served on the verandah of a small bungalow near the beach where we had bathed that morning, a bungalow U Tin Hlang said he "kept for house guests he did not particularly want in his house." And he managed to leave us there later in the evening in circumstances that could have but one end.

I had not known that there could be such easy and light sensuality. Certainly it seemed far from my character and far, far distant from any prior experience of mine. Rosemary stayed the night. U Tin Hlang joined us for a swim in the morning, coming alone, without his usual retinue. Presumably he had had a servant watch our bungalow through the early morning to alert him when we were up. To my surprise, this did not trouble me at all.

When we were sitting on the beach after our swim, Rosemary asked me why I had not come to Rangoon on the previous Monday when U Tin Hlang had invited me. She said it cut our time together and this was a pity. I had never before been so openly admired and I still found it hard to accept. But it was certainly true that I had had to defer my holiday for three days because of the Seymour affair in Moulmein.

"The Seymour affair?" U Tin Hlang asked.

"My near neighbours, Brian and Jean Seymour; you must have met them when you were in Moulmein." But neither Rosemary nor U Tin Hlang could call them to mind.

"Anyhow," Rosemary said, "what about them?"

"He beat her up rather badly a few nights ago. Dr. Veraswami and I tried to bring some peace to their marital relationship. I couldn't leave until some semblance of order was restored."

U Tin Hlang looked serious, for once. "The tropics are hard on Englishmen like you, Blair," he said, "more than on other Europeans. You do better, I think, in the daytime; but in the evenings and nights you drink too much—more even than the Dutch—and you treat our Burmese women only as whores. It has something to do, I think, with the pedestals you erect for your wives and girlfriends in England. You divide women into two groups: wives or potential wives to be respected, and others not to be respected at all—to be used, if possible, but only to be used. And, of course, that is how you see all of our women. It is sad."

U Tin Hlang may have been talking sense, but it didn't seem to me a suitable occasion for such animadversions, considering Rosemary's and my present situation; nor did he seem to me to be in the best position to offer this type of sagacity. The night before he had been boasting to us that his name had been prominent in a competition run by the *Rangoon Times* to compose epitaphs of well-known Burmese. U Tin Hlang had been the subject of the winning epitaph: "At last. He sleeps alone." The energetic pattern of his bachelor life was well known; it seemed to help his career, and not only among the wealthy Burmese. The Europeans did not seem to find this aspect of his life an impediment to their purchasing his skills as an advocate. But he was probably right about most middle-class Englishmen; for me the idea of love—I had never experienced the reality—pertained to, and only to, English women. I did not think of it as possibly applying to a Burmese.

"But Rosemary is right, Blair," U Tin Hlang continued. "Don't be so mysterious. Tell us precisely what did detain you." So I told them. It was probably a breach of professional confidence, but I'm glad I did.

I couldn't expect Brian Seymour to believe it, but I had to give some excuse, devise some way of protecting his houseboy. I could hardly have heard screams at that distance. True, the Seymours lived just three doors down the track, but three bungalows' distance in Moulmein often exceeded a quarter of a mile. So I said I was out for a walk before retiring and had heard a shout as I passed by his bungalow and thought somebody might be in trouble. "Could I be of help in any way?"

"Yes. Get the hell out of here, Blair. It's none of your damned business. Just clear out." And he made to slam the screen door in my face.

But I could see through the screen door from their verandah into the lit interior, and there was no doubt that Mrs. Seymour was on the floor, her clothes dishevelled, blood about the corner of her mouth, and what looked like a substantial swelling above her left eyebrow. And Seymour was obviously in a rage and far from sober.

I put my foot forward to stop the screen door and, as calmly as I could, said: "Your wife seems unwell. Should I call a doctor?"

He kicked at the door, trying to move my foot, and continued to shout at me and then at his wife. "Get out of here, Jean. Let me deal with this idiot."

She struggled to her feet and it became apparent to me that though she was not badly injured she had been beaten more than lightly. I had no choice in the matter. I could not leave. I remembered what I had been taught at the Mandalay Police Training College, at least the part that said that domestic disputes were both difficult to handle (I could have guessed that) and often the cause of injury to the police. The fact that both parties to the dispute sometimes inflicted injuries on the police seemed to me grossly unfair but, on reflection, also not surprising.

Seymour was a largish man, overweight and too full of alcohol to be a serious threat to me in a fight unless he were armed, but I had no inclination whatsoever to struggle with him. Nevertheless, I did push the door open when he turned his head to shout at his wife. I shoved my way past him to assist her. She seemed dazed and grateful, but as he rounded on us both she jerked away from me and tried to grab his upraised arm. He shook her off.

The three of us stood there bewildered, as in a tableau vivant, for what seemed an appreciable time. I broke the strain by doing what I remembered had been suggested by one of our teachers in Mandalay. "If you want to avoid a fight, and think you can get away with it, take off your cap and sit down. It's very hard for anyone to hit a man when he's sitting down. Goes against the grain of most everyone." I had no cap to take off, but I pursued the rest of the advice, pulled a chair from the table in the centre of the room, and sat down.

I thought I had better try to interrupt Seymour's continued shouts for me to get out and mind my own business. I was getting tired of the repetition, even if he did vary the imprecations surrounding his central message. "Shut up for a moment, Seymour, and listen to me. It's clear you've assaulted your wife and I should arrest you, but I don't want to do that. But I can't just do nothing and leave."

"Arrest me. Arrest me! You miserable prick. You can't arrest me. It's you who ought to be arrested for bursting in here and meddling in what doesn't concern you."

My effort to get him to come to his senses had merely raised the decibel level of his fury; but after a while he did seem to become a little more controlled and, turning to his wife, ordered her to tell me what had happened. "Tell the fool how you fell and hit your face. Help me to get him out of here."

Poor Jean Seymour was sobbing quietly in a chair in the corner. She nodded her head in agreement. Triumphantly Seymour turned to me: "Now will you get the hell out of here?"

The general advice given in Mandalay on such matters was that family disputes in the villages should be left to the headman, unless someone was in danger of death or lasting injury, and that if European spouses fought, as they occasionally did, it was best not to take any official action unless the injured party wanted to swear out a formal complaint, and even then only if considerable injury had been inflicted. Yet I could not just leave Jean Seymour to the mercies of this brute.

"Alright, Seymour, if you will just go out on the verandah for a few minutes while I talk to your wife, I will go if she then wants me to."

He hesitated for a while and then walked onto the verandah. "You'd better be sensible about this, Jean," he shouted as he left the room.

I took my chair over beside hers and offered her my handkerchief—surprisingly clean, I noted. She took it and mopped at her face and tried to rearrange her hair.

"He hit you, of course. What do you want me to do about it? Would you like me to take you to the Club for the night? I could arrange it quietly, if you wanted."

She gave no answer, the sobs becoming sniffles.

"Should I arrest him for assault? I will if you want, but you will have to come to the police station in the morning and sign an information against him."

The sniffles turned back to sobs and then to words, at least a few words: "No. No. Don't do that. Please don't." And then, grabbing at my hand, she said, "Stay for a little while. He will calm down. He always does after he has been drinking. He comes to his senses quite quickly. Then leave us."

Perhaps it was good advice, but I remained unsure. "Does he hit you often?"

"Oh, no. Never. Never before. He gets angry, but this is the first time he has hit me." Her previous sentence had tended to contradict what she was now saying, and, that apart, she was a poor liar. I knew this was not the first beating she had received. So I decided what to do, and did it. I sat with her for a few minutes, until she seemed more in control, and then called to Seymour to come in. He was obviously still furious but in better control. I told him I would go but only on condition that Dr. Veraswami be allowed to call on his wife the next morning to be sure she had no lasting injury. I was sure she didn't, but it seemed one way to give her some protection through the night.

"You really are a meddling fool, Blair, but if you insist, I assume that your pet Indian doctor won't do her any harm. But I'm not going to pay for it. You can be sure of that."

I told him there would be no charge to him—I would see that Dr. Veraswami's fee was otherwise met—and, leaving my handkerchief with Jean Seymour, as a tribute to my safe retreat, I made my way back to my bungalow and, I had better confess, felt quite pleased with myself. I thought I had handled it rather well.

I had hoped to leave for Rangoon the next day as I had arranged with U Tin Hlang, but I decided to await Dr. Veraswami's report on Jean Seymour in case I had to take any action in the matter—I certainly didn't want to leave that to the Indian sergeant who would be in charge during my absence. After all, Seymour had been a major in the Burmese Rifles in the War and was now a quite successful rubber planter. Any police action against a European gave Mandalay anxiety. So, the next day I tried to telephone U Tin Hlang, but finding him away from his office, I left a message deferring my trip to Rangoon and expressing the hope that it would not inconvenience him if I came a day or two later. I then called on Dr. Veraswami at the hospital.

Dr. Veraswami listened quietly to my story of the events of the night before and said he would call on Jean Seymour immediately; there seemed no need for him to make an appointment with her since I felt sure she would not show herself out of her bungalow with the facial bruises she must still have.

Veraswami suggested I come to his bungalow for a beer in the early evening and I accepted. Perhaps I would soon be able to get away to Rangoon.

"First, Eric," he said, as he fussed over me and my Watney's Pale Ale on the verandah of his bungalow that evening, "there iss a problem of medical confidences, ethics, keeping mum. When I got to the Seymours, Brian was there also and tried to insist on being present while I examined Jean. I refused, of course, and told him I had come not ass her doctor but representing you, Mr. District Officer Blair. I told him if he didn't want me to examine hiss wife and if she didn't want to be examined, I could do nothing except report that to you and, of course, to a court if it should come to that. I have no idea, Eric, if that makes any sense, but that iss what I said. And I did even more." Here Veraswami rubbed his palms together in self-satisfaction, bouncing about the verandah. "I gave her a paper to sign, saying she was not my patient and that thiss examination and whatever I should learn from it could be told to you." Veraswami paused and beamed at me, producing a slip of paper from his hip pocket and waving it high, anticipating applause.

I gave it: "What a wonderfully astute, legally acute, medical officer the Raj has in Moulmein," I allowed, earning his high-pitched giggle. But it did not really seem a subject for hilarity to me and I said, "Surely, after such an introduction, you cannot have got much information from her."

"No. No. Not at all. Once we got rid of Mr. Seymour I performed a quiet, complete, and verry leisurely medical examination of Mrs. Seymour, paying close and friendly attention to her medical history, which becomes, issn't it, a life history. She spoke to me verry freely, yess, freely indeed. I don't think many people have ever taken an interest in her. Here iss what I found out." And with sudden seriousness of purpose and precision of language he told me how matters stood between Jean and Brian Seymour.

The gist of it was that when Brian drank he became both aggressive and suspicious of his wife, though she had given no cause for suspicion. She would protest, whimper, become fearful of him, and this would feed his anger. Quite often he struck her, never doing serious damage but bruising and hurting her greatly. Sobriety would bring repentance and contrition, followed by a period of gentle affection, which she regarded as the "real" Brian. Then the slow cycle would repeat itself.

Though the drinking and violence seemed to have been growing over recent months, Jean Seymour refused to consider either leaving him or taking any legal action to have him bound over to keep the peace—which she knew could be done. Such action would ruin his career; his firm would likely sack him, and their work together over the years would be for naught. She thought the events of last night had brought him to his senses. He had been solicitous and loving when Mr. Blair had left them alone last night. She said she was grateful to Dr. Veraswami for coming but asked him to do nothing further, and asked him to say the same thing to me.

I confess that I felt relief. I was looking forward to the Rangoon holiday, and Seymour's squalid attacks on his wife were an unpleasant distraction. I said as much to Veraswami, who did not disagree, but who did give me the uncomfortable feeling that he thought I should perhaps have a talk with Brian Seymour.

"But what am I to say to him? We both know what happened. He knows I know. He knows I won't do anything unless his wife wants me to."

Veraswami waved his head in a circular motion indicating neither agreement nor disagreement.

"These are verry difficult matters, Eric. Ass some men's potency declines, they drink more, and their potency further declines, and they blame their wives, and they drink more, and they look elsewhere, and they blame their wives for that too, and on and on. . . ." His sentence trailed off into his beer glass, his free hand making circular motions away from his body.

I drew him back to one aspect of my talk that night with Jean Seymour. "I remember, Dr. Veraswami, that Jean Seymour seemed worried for her husband rather than for herself, even when she knew that I was not going to arrest him and make their problems public. It seemed to me more than just some queer sort of affection for the brute. She said something about him not being able to help it, about him having been often beaten by his father as a child. Did she say anything like that to you?"

"Yess, indeed. Indeed she did. I tried to tell her that wass no excuse for hiss beating her, that he had been beaten. And I don't think it iss, but she kept on about it."

"Well, it does help to explain his behaviour, don't you think?"

"Explain, yess. Excuse, no no no," and his head-waving became vigourous."

The distinction seemed elusive; surely it did help to explain, and therefore to excuse, his conduct, and I recall that I pursued that line of argument with Dr. Veraswami. He would have none of it and drifted to what seemed to me very unreal comparisons. "Eric, we are all of uss responsible for what we are. Some are born verry intelligent, like you, but that iss not at all to their credit; they couldn't help it. Some are born with wonderful, caring parents and they find it easier to become loving husbands and true friends; some are born retarded; some are born to brutal, neglectful parents and they find life verry cold and verry hard; some are born to the rich, some to the poor. There iss no less virtue in inheriting money than in inheriting brains, and no more. There iss no more virtue in having loving parents than in having brutal parents, and no less. We are all of uss responsible for what we do with what we are given, whatever it iss or wass."

It seemed to me a most unfair doctrine, and I said so. Veraswami stopped his head-waving and glared at me in mock indignation: "Unfair, you say. Of course it iss unfair. Who ever thought that life wass fair? Look about you, Eric my friend. How fortunate we are; how sad the lives of some around us, and no fault of theirs. All you can do, ass I say, iss hold people responsible for their actions, whatever caused them, and then try to alter your own response to what they have done, in accordance with your best understanding of all that caused them to do it—and you will never be sure, so you had best be kind. But don't pretend they are not responsible; it iss a maudlin and dangerous way to think. Brian Seymour wass responsible for hiss drunkenness and for hiss brutality to hiss wife even though we believe he wass heavily pushed to drunkenness and brutality by hiss own parents."

I forget how that discussion ended. I think I lost track of it after a while. But I remember that at the time I doubted that it had much to do with the likelihood of Seymour again beating his wife—and anyhow, I was most anxious to be on my way to Rangoon. I found it easy to persuade myself that it was proper for me to leave Mandalay for a few days. I have always found it easy to persuade myself of the wisdom of doing what I want to do—perhaps that is what Veraswami meant by being responsible, or should I say, irresponsible.

Rosemary and U Tin Hlang had listened to my narrative without interruption, but it was clear that Rosemary was troubled by it. "And you have done nothing about it, Eric? He can just go on hitting her and apologising?"

"What should I do? Arrest him, try and convict him, bind him over to keep the peace? Get him sacked? That won't be much help to her. Surely it is best to consider her needs first."

"It depends on what sort of world you want to live in, Eric. I want one where it is a crime for a husband to strike a wife or a wife to strike a husband. A few like your Seymours may suffer in the process, but I think there should be no tolerance at all for such domestic tyranny. I'm not talking about a rare drunken quarrel that turns violent; what you describe is a regular pattern, a predictable pattern, of oppression and violence."

I felt beleaguered, and U Tin Hlang did not seem inclined to help. His offering the observation that, at early common law, it was an offence for a man to strike his wife with a stick thicker than his little finger, was no help at all. Rosemary turned away from us both in annoyance.

Shattered by her disapproval, I promised that my first task on returning to Moulmein would be to call on the Seymours and make clear to them both that I proposed to take a continuing interest in the prevention of any repetition of violence in their household, and if there was a recurrence that I would initiate the prosecution of Brian Seymour whether his wife wished it or not.

This somewhat mollified Rosemary, and we turned to more pleasant topics, and after that, when U Tin Hlang again quietly left us, we entered on another relaxed, joyful, and intimate day and night.

U Tin Hlang had told us that he would have his driver take him to his chambers each morning while we were his guests and bring the Fiat back to us; we should make use of the car as we wished. If we were out when he wanted to come home he could easily get a tonga. It seemed overly generous but he insisted.

Rosemary decided, on the third day of our idyll by the beach, that she had better go to Rangoon to check that all was in order at her bungalow; we might then go a drive down to the mouth of the Irrawaddy, which was said to be a most fertile and lovely delta.

Rosemary liked to drive; she drove well, if slightly flamboyantly; there were no punctures for me to repair; and the day should have been a joy for me. But it wasn't, and it was clear that my resulting reticence was beginning to annoy Rosemary.

I did my best to be bright and cheerful, but it was no good. And it made no sense to me. Here I was on leave with a lovely and affectionate lady, with no obligations, no expectations of me except to do what came so easily—to adore her; I was free to chatter about myself, which she seemed particularly to enjoy, and also about her, which with some reservations seemed acceptable to her and certainly engrossing for me. And yet I felt a knot of sadness below my rib cage. I was morose.

Rosemary did not exactly show me off when we called in at her bunga-low; she asked me to wait in the car, but she certainly took no pains to hide my presence. And the same was true as we drove south through Rangoon. Indeed, she drove to the Officers' Club and waited while I went in to check if there was mail for me. In Rangoon, as she must have known, the word would get back to her husband that she and I were driving about in U Tin Hlang's very recognisable Fiat tourer, and that I had both been staying and not staying at the Officers' Club for a few days. That she essayed no concealment whatsoever troubled me.

I knew I was being childish and did my best to cast off the spell of gloom. I think I largely succeeded; at least I don't think it spoiled her day. But that night, after perhaps too much wine at dinner, the dam of conceal-ment broke.

It was such a trivial occurrence. We were in bed. One of the shutters outside a window of a neighbouring room had come loose and was flap-ping. I favoured letting it flap. Rosemary thought it would keep us awake. I said that the way we were behaving, before long nothing would keep us awake. She persisted. I said I would try to fix it and asked if she thought there was a torch in the bungalow.

She got up—scrambling out from under the mosquito netting and tucking it in behind her—and walked into the second bedroom, not bothering to put on any lights. I heard a drawer being opened and then she was back with a torch. I, too, pushed the mosquito netting aside, got up and pulled on some shorts, stuffed my feet into my shoes, and, taking the torch from the still naked and lovely Rosemary, made my way out of the bungalow and around to the shutter, guided by its squeaking and clumping.

All that was required was a finger-tightening of the attachment that held the open shutter back to the wall. It would have been just as easy to close the shutters from inside and leave the repair, such as it was, to the morning. But since I was there I fixed it.

By the time I returned, Rosemary was asleep and I was furious, wildly enraged. How the hell did she know precisely where that torch was? She must have been here often before, probably with U Tin Hlang and God knows how many others. This wasn't love, this wasn't affection; I was sim-ply being used.

I wrenched the mosquito netting aside and shook her awake. "How did you know where that bloody torch was? Tell me! Go on, tell me!"

She was sleepily bewildered. I found I was still shaking her quite vigourously. "You must have been here with others. Even with Lang?" And now she was very awake and entirely perceptive.

"Eric, Eric, do be still. Sit down. Stop shaking me." She seemed warmly affectionate despite my fury, and her calm did nothing to cool my rage. But

I did let go of her and sat down on the edge of the bed, fists clenched and banging on my knees.

She knelt in front of me, straight-backed, and wrapped her arms around me, pinning my arms to my side, and made noises of comfort and encouragement. "Dear Eric. Don't be jealous. There's no one else. Of course I have not been here with Lang. The torch was in the second bedroom. I have slept there occasionally when George has been away, but never with anyone else. Please don't be angry and spoil it all."

But I knew she was dissimulating. I knew she was not speaking the whole truth. Part of the truth, perhaps, but not the whole truth. I knew for a certainty I was not her only adulterous lover. And in fury I wrenched my arms free. My clenched right fist struck her sharply on the cheek. I felt the impact and heard the thud.

Did I mean to hit her? I certainly meant to escape what then felt like a deceitful embrace—and to escape vigourously. Did I intend my clenched fist to hit her? I must at least have realised that possibility, but did I intend it? I still don't know. Perhaps I meant to hit her, perhaps not. Does it make a difference?

Her knees bent and she knelt backwards on her heels, her hands clutching at her face where I had struck her. She made a faint "Oh" noise.

Misery engulfed me, and I had her in my arms in the deepest contrition.

She forgave me.

Thereafter, it was a wonderful night, and before long I doubt that a house full of banging shutters could have kept us awake.

But the bruise was there in the morning, a deep embarrassment to us both.

We were lying in the shade beside the beach when a houseboy came running from U Tin Hlang's bungalow calling me to the telephone. There was no telephone at Lang's "guest house" but there was at his bungalow. When I got to it, Lang's secretary was holding the line; Lang came on: "Sorry to disturb you, Old Boy, but you had better hurry back to Moulmein. You're needed there. Apparently your Seymours had a bout more vigourous than their usual fisticuffs. Dr. Veraswami tells me that Brian is dead and that he has Jean hidden away in his hospital. He seems a little unclear what to do, needs your help."

I thanked U Tin Hlang for his hospitality, asked when the next train left for Moulmein, and got his permission for his driver to take me to it. There was just time to pick up my things at the Officers' Club and catch the afternoon train.

U Tin Hlang agreed, of course, and added that, if she cared to, Rosemary could drive me to the train and then leave the car at his chambers, or he could drive her home. Again I felt the stirrings of jealousy; I hope my voice did not reveal them. U Tin Hlang added, "And, by the way, Veraswami sent his best regards to Rosemary and yourself and expressed his deep regret at disturbing your honeymoon."

We might as well have hired a hall for our affair!

I arrived in Moulmein early the next morning, blaming myself throughout a long and miserable night for my failure to have taken the Seymour matter more seriously—such selfishness, such neglect of obvious duty—and went straight from the station to the hospital. Dr. Veraswami was on his rounds but interrupted them to join me.

"What a pity to terminate your holiday, Mr. Blair. I am so sorry, so verry sorry." One would have thought he had killed Seymour, such was the intensity of his apology.

"It's not your fault, Dr. Veraswami. I'm glad you were able to find me so quickly. Can you tell me now what happened, or would you rather I called back later?"

"Perhaps you should speak first to your duty sergeant. He iss anxious and doess not know what to do. He tells me he hass not yet reported Seymour's death to Mandalay. Mrs. Seymour iss safe here. Perhaps you would be kind enough to return to uss here ass soon ass everything iss in control with your police."

As usual, he was right and I did what he suggested. The duty sergeant was certainly glad to see me. Apparently it had been a call from the hospital that had brought him to the Seymours' bungalow. Dr. Veraswami was there when he arrived. Seymour was obviously dead, naked on the bed with a sheet thrown over him, shot in the temple at close quarters. Dr. Veraswami had not—as the sergeant said he should have—left the scene of the death untouched, but had moved the body from the couch in the living room to the Seymours' bedroom and had to a degree cleaned up the mess on the couch, where many bloodstains revealed the site of the killing. He had also given an injection to Mrs. Seymour before the sergeant arrived, and had suggested to the sergeant that she was in no fit state to be interrogated. He further told the sergeant that he would take Mrs. Seymour to the hospital and would call me on the telephone to return to Moulmein.

The sergeant had then arranged to have the body taken to the hospital in case an autopsy was thought necessary.

All of Dr. Veraswami's advice had appealed to the sergeant, though he seemed to resent Dr. Veraswami having taken charge so forcefully; but he did precisely as Veraswami had advised. When Dr. Veraswami later told him that I would be back the next day, he decided not to report to Mandalay, but to leave that to me.

I sent a telegram, marked IMMEDIATE, to Mandalay advising them of the death of Brian Seymour and that I would report details as soon as I knew them. I did not think it necessary to give the date or time of his death.

Dr. Veraswami was waiting for me when I got back to his untidy room in the hospital. His electric fan kept the air moving, but it was a typical hot and humid Moulmein noon of the rainy season, and we were both sweating miserably.

"It wass the Seymour houseboy that came for me. The same one, I assume, that came for you a few days ago. He could not call me on the telephone; it had been torn from the wall. Thiss wass, it seems, a much worse fight than we knew of before. Jean Seymour says so and I think she speaks the truth."

When he got there, Veraswami found Brian Seymour naked and dead on the couch in the same room where I had found them battling before. Mrs. Seymour lay wailing on the bed in the bedroom, where Brian's rifle rested against the foot of the bed. There was no blood in the bedroom, but the couch and the carpet in the front room were saturated. Veraswami cleaned up the mess as best he could before the sergeant arrived.

I asked why he did this. He said he was not sure, but perhaps it would be better, he then thought, if the story of that night were not so obvious.

"Have you pieced together what happened, Dr. Veraswami?"

"Well, I have talked several times to Jean Seymour and I think I know, but, of course, I know only her story. Still, it doess not vary and it iss a sad, sad story."

What had happened was, he thought, this—though the details had been beyond her narration and he did not wish to imagine them: Brian had come home late—from the Club, he said, though she doubted this because he did not seem to have been drinking and he always did drink at the Club. He was late for dinner and she expressed her annoyance. He became quite angry, but the meal passed in relative peace, though he did, over her objections, have several whiskys with dinner, which was unusual for him. For reasons she cannot recall, she became convinced he had not been to the Club that evening and suggested that he had visited a native girl. Words progressed to deeds, blows and tears followed, and she rushed into the bedroom. He followed her in a rage, but in a rage which had amorous overtones—"sexual relations between them were often thuss initiated, Eric, I think"—and despite her protestations he struggled with her, made her undress, and tried to force her to intercourse, "but it wass not her strength so much ass hiss weakness" that made this impossible.

His impotence enraged him further. He began to beat her more. His fury took a different but predictable turn: "It's your fault. You've always been cold as a fish unless you've been pushed around a bit first. You never do what I want, and you know what it is. Of course I look elsewhere."

She did not know what he was talking about, and then suddenly, and clearly, she did. His impotence was not only alcohol driven, he was sleeping with anyone who would have him, exciting him as he wanted to be excited—paying them, no doubt. A rage deeper than she had ever known supplanted her usual cringing terror. She challenged him with what she believed: that he was impotent unless he could hurt someone first, or unless it was a girl paid to do disgusting things to him. She would leave him the next day.

He made no denial, merely continued drinking and promising her that if she left or told anyone about this, he would kill her. And there were blows to prove it, more brutal than ever before. She tried to hide from him, but he dragged her back into the front room and held her there, terrorised. She believed herself in danger of death.

Veraswami said that her physical condition was powerful evidence of the truth of her story, at least as far as the protracted beating was concerned. She was bruised badly, heavily in the breasts and torso, and about her thighs. She may well have feared for her life.

Eventually he fell asleep on the couch.

"And then the story becomes quite strange, Blair, but I think I know it. It's hard to be sure, of course; one who knew what happened iss dead and the other is verry, verry upset and now quite heavily sedated. But I think she spoke truth to me, truth about what happened, not why it happened. I am sure she doesn't understand that, nor do I, though I may guess. But what happened, yess, she iss mercilessly honest about that. And it matches hiss injuries. Yess, she speaks the truth ass best she can. . . ." And he was silent for a while; then, bringing his palms together and turning the fingers towards me for emphasis, he said: "She tried to kill herself. She feared for her life if he should wake. She knew she had to do something. Naked and injured, she saw only one course—to kill herself."

I could not help interrupting. "Tried to kill herself and managed to shoot him in the head? You can't believe *that*?"

"I am sure of it."

"Simply because she told you so—you believe her?"

"Eric, you become angry with me. Pleass stop it. Thiss iss a matter I have thought a lot about these past hours and there iss more than her words to tell the tale of that night. I have examined her physically, and the corpse too. They both tell a lot."

I gestured an apology and managed to control myself.

"When I got to the Seymour bungalow that night I noticed she wass bleeding slightly from the mouth. I assumed he had struck her. Well, he had, frequently, ass I told you, but not, so it happens, on the mouth or jaw. He attacked her thighs and body, not her face. It wass not until later that I understood."

I had no idea what he was talking about, but thought it better to hold my tongue.

"Well, you see, he wass killed by hiss own rifle but that rifle had also injured her. You know that little bit of metal that sticks up at the end of the barrel of rifles with which you British aim at uss natives when you want to shoot uss? The front sight, I think it iss called."

"Dr. Veraswami, I still don't understand what you are talking about. Please tell me briefly what you think happened and then let us try to tease out its details. You are losing me with blood here and blood there, and bits of metal and sights, the relevance of which I am sure you know, but I don't."

"Yess, yess . . . it iss so. I do drag out these things . . . let me try to be curt . . . brusque like a British, issn't it?" He was quiet for a moment, and then it burst out staccato and even more sibilant than before. "After her severe beating and with her husband drunkenly asleep, naked on the couch, Mrs. Seymour decided it must end. Her disgust and hopelessness turned towards herself, not her husband. She knew he kept a Lee-Enfield 303 rifle on top of the wardrobe. She took it down, pulled back the bolt ass she had been shown, and loaded the rifle. She then tried to shoot herself in the mouth. Why thus, I suspect, because of the particular humiliations to which he had forced her that night. But obviously, she could not reach the trigger. I can imagine her tortured, despairing wrestlings with the rifle. Her disgust with herself built on her hatred of her husband, and, furious with the rifle, ass if it too had betrayed her, she put it to hiss temple and then the trigger wass within easy reach."

Dr. Veraswami surmised that the houseboy had heard the earlier shouting but knew better than to interfere, certainly after the treatment he had received when he had previously called me to the Seymour bungalow; but the noise of the shot and then the utter silence compelled him to seek her, and she managed to pull herself together enough to send him for Dr. Veraswami.

The facts seemed clear enough; even my duty seemed clear enough. Jean Seymour had murdered her husband; that was all there was to it. I must arrest her, hold a preliminary enquiry, and unless some extraordinary further facts emerged, and I could not imagine what they might be, commit her to the Assizes on a charge of murder. Her husband's brutality might persuade a jury, exercising its prerogative of mercy, to convict her of manslaughter rather than of murder so that a more lenient sentence might be imposed; but that she was guilty of homicide seemed clear enough.

And yet, knowing the depth of her suffering, I could not but be deeply sorry for her.

I told Dr. Veraswami that I would have to arrest her but that if he would hold her in a locked ward for the time being, I would not further trouble her today. She had enough to put up with without a callow district officer arresting her in her misery.

Veraswami took a less clear-cut view of the matter when we met for our pre-prandial Watney's on his verandah that evening. "Much of the fault iss ours, Eric. Yours and mine. We knew her peril a few days ago and we did nothing about it. It iss not really surprising, abandoned ass she wass, with no one to help her, far from any friends and fearful of that nasty man, that she finally broke. We should have helped her more."

I was impatient with him. It was so easy to be wise after the event, and I said so, though I did not pretend that I did not share his sense of guilt. "Surely, Dr. Veraswami, you wrap a hair shirt around both of us needlessly. I don't think it fits me. From what I knew—and we talked about this, you will recall—we had given Jean Seymour what little protection we could in the light of her insistent wish to do nothing that might embarrass her husband in the Moulmein community and in his work. And she certainly did not wish to leave him. In fact, she seemed more sorry for him than for herself. I offered to have her put up at the Club and to keep him away from her until she could make other arrangements, but she would have none of it."

"Ass a doctor I should have seen her danger more clearly and tried better to protect her, and, if I may, Mr. District Officer, perhaps you too could have done more for her on the night you saw her being attacked. You say, and I know it iss true, that she told you she did not want you to do any more. But surely you saw her impossible situation. If she wanted protection that night, perhaps she wanted you to impose it on her—at least in the eyes of her husband. You see, Eric," and his tone softened with the affection I knew he felt for me, "you could have given her some of your authority, strengthened her then and for the future in the eyes of her husband by giving her the sure knowledge that—regardless of what she says she wants—you will not leave her helpless. I am unsure, but perhaps you should have arrested him and then later let him go when she took no further action—not put her to election then and there after a beating, with her husband lurking on the balcony."

It seemed most unfair, and I said so. It would have been an illegal arrest if I knew there would be no subsequent prosecution. But still, was I sure? What harm would an illegal arrest do in such a situation, and if no one could bring an action suggesting that the arrest was illegal—and Brian Seymour certainly wouldn't have—then what does "illegal" mean in such circumstances? Blast Veraswami, he does upset me sometimes! I tried not to show my annoyance: "You may be right, Dr. Veraswami, but we both did what we thought was right at the time. It's all one can do."

Veraswami would not be completely mollified, though he did soften his criticism: "Yess, Eric, I am perhaps too hard on you, but not on myself. I recognised the pattern of hiss behaviour. I saw its regularities, the cycle of violence, repentance, and sex which he needed to escape impotence with hiss wife—though not perhaps with others. I knew how they both were trapped. I should have taken it more seriously, provided more help and protection for her, insisted on talking with her husband and explaining matters to him, not just left it, hoping for the best, as I did."

For once I thought Veraswami was in maudlin error and said so: "We could have arrested him, taken her into protective custody if she agreed, or done what we did. We could not further force ourselves on them against their wishes. It was their lives; we could not run them. You blame yourself without reason, Dr. Veraswami. And anyhow, all this is spilled milk—spilled blood rather—and we had better talk about what is now to be done rather than what perhaps then should have been done, but was not."

Veraswami held up both arms in front of his head as if to ward off my blows. "Be less severe with me, I beg you, my young friend. I merely regretted my own lack of foresight. But you are right, it iss spilled blood about which we can now do nothing. So now we must worry about the lady that did the spilling."

"Not only her, Dr. Veraswami. As the representative of the law in Moulmein, I suppose I must also enforce that law. Killing unfaithful husbands would decimate the European population—more than decimate, few would be left standing—and it is my duty to restrict such carnage by punishing those who do the killing."

"Surely she wass pushed beyond all endurance, Eric. Must she be further punished? Few European husbands are ass brutal ass Brian Seymour. It wasn't just hiss infidelities that made her kill him; it wass the regular and increasingly violent beatings. Iss she not free to defend herself?"

I told Dr. Veraswami that I well remembered this part of the law I had been taught at the Mandalay Police Training School. A killing by one attacked could be justified or excused, or could amount to the felony of either murder or manslaughter. But, to be justified or excused, there must be "imminent" danger to life or serious danger of personal injury at the time of the killing, the person killed posing the imminent threat. This just was not so in the story we now believed of Jean Seymour's killing of her husband. He was asleep at the time, a deep, alcoholic sleep; he was an imminent threat to no one. She could have left the bungalow and sought safety at the Club. She could have sent her houseboy for me. (He wouldn't have found me since I was in Rangoon, but that seemed irrelevant to my argument.) She could have gone to a neighbour. She certainly had no need whatsoever to protect herself from a then-helpless man by shooting him in the head. It was not as if she had had children to protect and was thus tied to the house; she could just have left.

It was a rather long harangue, which I did not interrupt when Dr. Veraswami hand waved his desire for me to pause so that he could comment.

When I stopped, he looked pained, and asked, "Do you really think she iss a murderer, Eric? Think of the pressures on her. She had no one she wass close to in Moulmein; am I not right that at the Club she wass seen ass, would you say, declassée? I don't know what family she hass in England but I doubt there iss much to support her there. Brian Seymour wass not only her master and her trainer in violence and love ass she came to know it, he wass also all she had by way of a meal-ticket and a protector against poverty and exposure to hardship. Do you think she would give all that up if she could see any other way out? True, there were no children to bind her to the house, which iss the situation too often in these miserable wife-beating cases, but she may well have thought that wherever she went in Moulmein he would follow her and that the beating would be worse for the departure. She wass terrified for her life; you see that, I know; can she not defend herself? In her beaten condition she could hardly have been thinking verry clearly. But it iss quite possible, issn't it, that she thought she would be killed when he stirred from hiss drunken sleep—and so she tried to kill herself, failed, and seeing no other way, killed him. And there iss another matter which iss perhaps relevant, I am not sure, and it iss hard to talk about. . . ." And his voice trailed off amid meditative head wavings. "What will become of her now? How will she live?"

"Well, she won't have much to live on now," I pointed out. "Whether or not he left a will she can inherit nothing from him. On that, at least, the law is clear, if her killing him was a crime. But what is the other matter you hint at?"

"You speak of crime, Eric. Did he not force her to crime?"

"What do you mean?"

"Iss not what iss technically called fellatio still a criminal offence under your law, Eric? I am sure he thus compelled her. I know it iss a verry common matter, and not seen ass a crime, but ass your law stands it iss a crime, a felony, iss it not? Can that help her?"

I surmised that if her case could be brought before a jury it would certainly help her, and I then saw more clearly the double relevance of her self-injured mouth. But it was also quite obvious that it gave no justification for her killing him.

"If she goes to trial the jury could bring in a verdict of manslaughter rather than murder, or even find her not guilty—against the evidence, it seems to me, but within its prerogative of mercy nevertheless. Our juries, however, generally follow the judge's directions on the law, and I think it very unlikely that she could do better than a manslaughter verdict with a light sentence. And, if that happened, whatever Brian had saved would not go to her."

"Eric, I don't think you understand how Mrs. Seymour wass forced to do what she did. You speak ass if it were planned, thought out. You must understand, there's more to it than that, much more, and it issn't quite so obvious, not at all well understood, but certainly more than you might think."

I gathered I was being obtuse and suggested I would do my best to follow what he would tell me if he would make it very simple. I laid it on a bit thick.

"Oh pleass no, Eric. I wass trying to shape it for myself. Of course you will understand, better than me no doubt, no doubt at all. . . ." And his head jerkily waved dissent and encouragement in contradictory circles.

I smiled and gestured for him to continue. He began the verandah-pacing that always accompanied his more formal presentations. "It iss called, I believe, a syndrome, a regular pattern of behaviour, a psychological condition, if you follow me as you undoubtedly do, a pattern that occurs in many people. And, if I am right, Mrs. Seymour's syndrome wass that of a woman who hass become accustomed to, built her life around, regular beatings by her husband, followed by repentance, contrition, and affection for a time . . . and then around and around and around again. She became dependent on and under the control of thiss pattern. Just ass it controlled him, so it controlled her. It seems strange but I believe it happens in such cases. And you must remember there wass no easy escape for her, no way to go that did not threaten entirely to upset the course of her life. So the acceptance of the pattern, the beating syndrome, develops. But it also contains seeds of explosion. Too great an increase in violence, some other brutal complication, and desperation iss there. No way out. And now the usual pattern iss broken. So, self-destruction. And if that for one or another reason iss impossible, destruction of the brute that creates the pattern. It iss, in short, a compulsion, an inexorable psychological pressure. It would be cruel to punish her further; she iss not responsible for what she did that night. Perhaps she wass responsible when months or years ago she accepted that pattern of dependence on the ritual of violence and forgiveness, but not when she shot him. She was then entirely helpless, entirely. . . ." Dr. Veraswami stopped his pacing and turned to me, full face and expectant.

Possibly he was right, and, if he was, what should I do? It didn't help me much. "They'd never accept all that in Mandalay. She shot him when he was helpless, that's all they'd say, though they may add that he was a rotten bastard who deserved it. But then they'd also add that we can't have wives shooting husbands; it would never do. No, Veraswami, your syndrome would never wash in Mandalay."

"Perhaps not, but it iss so."

There was a period of silence and then Veraswami changed the direction of our conversation. "You have not talked to her since her husband's death. Don't you think you should?"

"Yes, I suppose I must see her; but really there is not much to talk about in such cases, knowing what we know, nor even much to do. Anyhow, it sounds easy: notify the next of kin, determine the cause of death, and if it might be the result of a crime, hold a preliminary inquiry. In this case I didn't think there was much point in notifying the next of kin—she already knew."

Veraswami glared at me in mock fury. "You are becoming light in the head, frivolous, between the Seymours and the Bretts. It iss unlike you, Eric, to feel no sympathy for Jean Seymour. I am quite troubled for her, quite. . . ." And his enigmatic head-waving was clearly intended to drive home to me my own churlishness.

He was right. I did not feel much sympathy for the self-made widow. I knew, of course, I had to give her the opportunity to tell me her side of the story before I held the preliminary inquiry. After all, it might have been so clearly an accident, say while he was naked cleaning his gun (I did find it hard to avoid gallows humor in this case and still did not know why), that I might not face the need for any magisterial inquiry; but I had kept putting it off until Veraswami pressed my duty upon me.

When I went to her cell in the prison hospital the next morning, Jean looked even more mouse-like than when I had last seen her. She was curled in the bed, thin-faced and scraggly-haired, covered only by the light hospital gown, for it was steamy hot in the ward. Three other women were there, all Burmese, sitting close together on one of the beds. Dr. Veraswami had told me that he had put her in with others because he still thought there was a risk of suicide and she was safer if others were nearby at all times. But it did not make a congenial ambience for a heart-to-heart conversation.

She was polite, withdrawn, almost servile, answering me in monosyllables. It seemed to me it would be a good idea to shake her vigorously and tell her to talk openly, but that was hardly my role.

I told her she did not have to talk to me at all about her husband's death if she didn't want to, and I told her further that what she said might be used in evidence against her.

She replied that she had told everything to Dr. Veraswami and had agreed that he could tell it to me or to a court—whatever the law required. She glanced nervously at the others in the room: "It is hard to talk here."

I said that they could not understand our conversation and repeated that she need not talk to me at all if she didn't want to. I think I hoped she would turn me out; I certainly found the situation distasteful.

She said she did want to, and I had the feeling that she did; but then she never managed anything except brief replies to enquiries that retraced what Veraswami and the sergeant had told me. All I gained were her nodded or one-word assents. "What it amounts to, then," I tried to sum up, "was that again he had beaten you, violently, that you believed he would carry out his promise to kill you if you left him or spoke to anyone else about it, and that you did not know anything else to do except to kill yourself. You tried to shoot yourself but did not know how and turned your anger on your husband and shot him."

She nodded tearfully.

"And that's all there is to it? No more? That's it?" And again the tearful, curt agreement, the crying nod. Yet I had the sense that I still did not understand all that had happened. I had not been willing to enquire about the sexual indignities that had been hinted at. I had enquired about Brian Seymour's confession to having slept with someone else on the afternoon of his death, but this did not seem to have figured in her killing him as much as his brutalities to her. She seemed quite disinterested in other than appearances. Perhaps she was grieving for her husband. Perhaps she was deeply anxious for herself. But it was hard to tell; only when issues arose of others knowing that she had killed him did she manifest any emotion.

I decided I had better try to ask her about the forced fellatio that Veraswami said had precipitated her self-disgust and then her murderous rage—or was it murderous? I suppose that was the central question. At any rate, her lethal rage. "Dr. Veraswami tells me your husband made you do disgusting things to him, and that is why you killed him. Was that so?"

She buried her face in her hands. "Does all that have to come out? Poor Brian. What a terrible thing for people to know. He so hated himself when these fits occurred." And, to my astonishment, she went on with sympathy for her late husband, even avowing that he was a wonderful man and that life without him had no meaning for her. She was a great one for melodramatic clichés, but I gained the impression that she meant them. I found her appallingly unattractive.

Getting nowhere, realising that she was telling me nothing I did not already know, and not even giving me any sense of what it must be like to be in her situation, I became aggressive. I am usually too much of a Milquetoast, certainly in my dealings with women, but she seemed so excessively meek, so tremulous, that I found my voice rising and my anger too. "You know, Mrs. Seymour, you are helping neither yourself nor me. No one wants to see you locked up for years and years, but if you keep on whimpering like this and saying nothing about why you shot Brian, you might just manage it."

She made no reply. Trying to get something out of her, I asked, "Has he any relatives I should notify?"

And now she was suddenly impassioned. "Oh, please don't. Let me write to her. Not you."

"Write to whom?"

"His mother, of course. It will kill her if she knows all these horrible things. She has no one else. Do you have to tell her everything?"

I made no reply.

She reached a hand out to me. "Please don't. We write only once a fortnight. Let me tell her. I'll make something up, an accident or something. I promise to show it to you," and the crying intensified.

After a period of silence, to my surprise she asked, "What have you done about Brian's burial, Mr. Blair? Can we not have a very private service, perhaps just you and me and Dr. Veraswami if he wishes to come?"

It was clear she had no idea of what was to happen. Apparently she thought that the central though absent figure in a trial, the corpse, was to be quietly buried before even a preliminary hearing into the probably felonious death, while the killer mourned quietly and then, grieving, left to get on with her quiet life. The desire to shake her increased.

"Mrs. Seymour, you must understand your situation. There will have to be a formal preliminary hearing into the cause of Brian's death and that had best be before his burial. These things cannot be hushed up. Then you are likely to go to trial for killing him—a public trial—in Rangoon or Mandalay. The papers will be full of it. Of course his mother will know. The only question is how to break it to her now."

"But I loved him. I loved him," she wailed. "All of this is cruel to him, to his memory. He didn't mean to do those dreadful things. He got sick out here. We should never have come here. It would be cruel for his mother to know. We were so happy, so happy. . . ." Her body curved away from me toward the wall, and the wails became sobs and the sobs tears; it was clear there was no use my struggling on with this interview.

I left with a sense of dissatisfaction, with irritation towards her, clear as to my duty but annoyed by it.

I felt the need for advice and guidance. It all seemed too pat. Commit her to the Assizes. But nobody would gain, except the disembodied Law. Seymour's company would detest the public revelations of his brutality to his wife, for that would surely come out at the trial; the British community would perhaps enjoy the salacious aspects but would resent being lowered in the estimation of the Burmese; and it could do no good, no good at all, for Jean Seymour. And I doubted it would have any influence on the incidence of husband-killing in Burma, a rare event in any case. Yet there seemed no other course for me to follow except that of the letter of the law, for there certainly had been no "imminent" need for her to kill Seymour in order to protect herself, which is what the law required to justify lethal self-defence.

However, could "imminent" be differently interpreted to mean something like "necessary at this time"? Even if it could, it was not easy to see how that would help Jean Seymour—after all, she did not have to stay there until he roused himself. She said she had no choice, that there was no one she could turn to; but that was plainly untrue, even if she thought it true. She well may have thought that if she left him he would inevitably follow her and that the eventual beating would be even more violent, more life-endangering. Could Veraswami's idea of a syndrome, a psychological compulsion, be used to turn her response into one of an "imminent, i.e., necessary and unavoidable at the time" automatic reaction? In any case, such legal niceties were not for a district officer, whose duty was clear; they were for His Majesty's judges and their juries. My duty: if there is evidence to support a conviction of a felony, arrest the felon, confirm the evidence at a preliminary inquiry and, if it stands up, commit for trial.

Yet I remained dissatisfied. And then a wonderful idea came to mind, an idea formed of a sweet combination of self-interest and a desire to do my job better. I needed independent advice. Who better than Burma's leading barrister and an independent-minded, thoughtful, and loving woman, a trained nurse, excellently able to advise me on the wife's viewpoint in such a difficult matter. How I went on embellishing this thought! Of course, I could catch the night train on Friday to Rangoon, consult with U Tin Hlang and Rosemary on Saturday and Sunday, and be back at work in Moulmein on Monday morning. I would not even have to dig into my stock of accrued local leave for such a two-day, weekend absence. It was obviously the best course—duty and delight combined.

I telephoned U Tin Hlang. It was arranged. I managed to convey my preference that my being in Rangoon not be known, except of course to Rosemary. U Tin Hlang said he thought his Fiat was a bit too well-known and that he would send another car and driver for me who would meet me at the station and take me to his guest house. U Tin Hlang seemed pleased by my plan. I told Dr. Veraswami about it. He thought it "a not too unwise indulgence" which, for encouragement of what at one level I knew to be an impropriety, was about as far as I could reasonably expect him to go.

"A telephone call for you, Sir. Someone called Brett."

It must be Rosemary confirming the arrangements for the weekend. My "hello" was more suited to the boudoir than to the barracks. George Brett sounded nonplussed: "Is that you, Blair?" It was indeed, and my tone of voice changed with remarkable alacrity. I made some noise about a bad connection.

Courtesies were not Brett's long suit. He plunged into the purpose of his call, and I was glad I did not have to make small talk with my cuckolded acquaintance.

"It's about Seymour's death. He worked for quite a big company, you know. They have been talking to my General. There has been talk of your preparing to wash some very dirty linen in public. Wouldn't help the company; wouldn't help the Raj. Couldn't it be an accident? Both playing with the gun, cleaning it, or something? Do your best, Blair."

It did no good, of course, but I could not stand being demeaned by him in this way. "His" General, indeed! And the expectation that I would lie about the facts, even find facts I knew to be false. I must have sounded unusually stuffy; I sounded so even to myself: "I shall have to do what I have been trained to do, Captain Brett. My police and magisterial duties are quite clear. I am sure you would not wish me to do otherwise."

"Of course not, Blair. The General is not suggesting that at all. Just handle it as quietly as you can. Call me if you think I can be of any use." And he rang off.

Friday saw me up earlier than usual. A swim before breakfast and the day seemed exciting to me. The train through the night would be wearisome, but I would recover quickly from it—a shower would wash tiredness aside. And then a weekend with Rosemary, for surely she would be able to escape for a few hours from her dull husband. And, probably to comfort my conscience, I told myself what a help Lang and Rosemary would be in the Seymour matter that now seemed to be of interest even to the Rangoon authorities. What a wonderful world!

I worked diligently at my office at the police station. Not a memorandum would remain unwritten, not an enquiry unanswered, before my weekend away—I would be the very model of an administratively correct district officer, every file filed, every return returned, every deadline slain.

As my euphoria reached its peak, about an hour before the Rangoon train was due to depart, Dr. Veraswami came unannounced to the police station. He had never done this before. Normally he telephoned or sent a messenger asking if he might call on me or asking me to call on him. But there he was, sweating freely, the tonga which had brought him standing outside.

"I am so sorry to burst in on you like this, Mr. Blair, but there iss something I must tell you before you go to Rangoon."

I waved him to a seat and brought my chair around from behind my desk. I glanced at my watch.

"I shall not detain you long, Mr. Blair; you will catch your train. Perhaps the tonga I brought could take you to the station; perhaps we could ride there together."

I thanked him and accepted his suggestion. His news did add to the difficulty of my decision of what to do about Jean Seymour. I found myself on the edge of testiness with him; it is very hard not to be annoyed with the messenger bringing bad news. Or was it bad news? It certainly complicated my task emotionally, if not in law.

As we bounced about in the tonga Veraswami told me that a cable had come for Brian and Jean Seymour in the morning. It had been addressed and delivered to the Seymour bungalow and the houseboy had had the sense to bring it on to the gaol hospital. "I took it to her myself," Veraswami said. "I thought I should keep an eye on her; there iss still the risk of a further suicide attempt."

I found myself most improperly wishing that Veraswami would, in effect, give her her suicidal head. I could hardly say so, even to Veraswami, but I knew I would not much regret her bringing off the trick this time. Fortunately, I risked none of this with Veraswami and he pressed on: "At the first glance at the text of the cable she wass in tears, and she thrust it at me to read. It wass from Brian Seymour's mother in a Southampton hospital. She says she hass been diagnosed terminally ill—cancer, she says—a few weeks only to live. She hopes Brian and Jean can get leave and come to her before she dies. Apparently she does not know of her son's death."

I made no reply. It did not seem to alter matters, yet surely it must. Was there possibly some way that I could make use of this to sidestep the whole mess and get the maddening Jean Seymour out of the country? I found myself increasingly annoyed with her, as if it were all her fault, which of course it wasn't. She seemed such a nuisance and so useless, a punching bag for the fates—and for aggressive males, like Brian and me, I supposed.

I dragged myself back to the moment and asked Veraswami how he had left matters with Jean Seymour.

"Eric, I did not disabuse her. Just promised to talk to you, and here I am." And he bounced excessively to the trot of the weary horse dragging the tonga. "I think she thinks you will now send her home to England. That if her late husband's mother iss dying you would not be so cruel as to let her know of her son and daughter's troubles. You would let her invent an innocent story of Brian's death so that she can comfort the declining days of her mother-in-law's life. Apparently, Brian's mother and Jean were verry close; Jean says she iss the only person in the world who cares for her, and that the affection iss mutual. She really iss rather a fool. She kept saying that it would kill hiss mother if she knew how Brian had died, which, given that mother's present situation, iss a macabre turn of phrase. Anyhow it iss another matter for you to think about ass you pursue your ascetic consultations in Rangoon."

U Tin Hlang's driver met me at the station and took me to his master's chambers, not to the guest house and to Rosemary, as I had hoped.

The antechamber was vast, sweatily crowded, noisy and untidy. Clients and potential clients were sitting on benches, squatting on the floor, shaking their legs in the anxious Indian fashion. Most seemed to be Indian, though there were a few prosperous-looking Burmese, and those that were not arguing with one another were either remonstrating with or trying to catch the eyes of the two male clerks sitting at desks on each side of what I deduced to be the entrance to Lang's inner chamber.

To shouts of annoyance, I was waved through.

Double doors silenced the noise of the antechamber. Quiet, book-lined comfort replaced the outside chaos.

Lang looked up from his desk, gestured for me to wait a moment, briskly concluded his business with a client, waved him out, and grasped my hand. I felt ill at ease. This was no time to interrupt him. I said as much. He agreed, but said he was interested to talk to me for a while—"a break from all that," motioning toward the antechamber—and led me to a couch and chairs set for comfortable conversation (for his more prosperous clients, I found myself thinking).

"Tell me about the Seymour case, Blair. We can talk about it this evening, but it will help me to have some idea of what happened before we talk. I find my later reflections much more reliable than my first reactions."

I could not help myself: "Will Rosemary be coming this evening to talk about the case?"

U Tin Hlang smiled kindly: "To talk about the case? I am not sure. She knows you are here for the weekend, but she is doubtful that it will be easy to get away. She told me to tell you that she will try but that you should not count on it."

I made no reply. After a pause, U Tin Hlang leaned back and raised his eyebrows at me: "Go on, tell me about the case. Don't just sit there gloomily."

I did my best, but gloom had indeed descended. I tried to shake it off and to tell him what I knew about Seymour's death. He listened without interrupting me, and when I had finished stood up and said: "And now you will have to excuse me, Eric. I begin to hear rage growing outside. I will get away as soon as I can and join you at the beach."

I tried to persuade myself that it was good to be back at U Tin Hlang's guest house. I swam. I lay on the beach. I even visited the baby elephant. But the day dragged on endlessly and my solitary presence, hiding in Rangoon, seemed both contrived and childish. Surely Rosemary could have sent word—a note, a telephone call to U Tin Hlang's house. She must know they would fetch me. The day dragged. It had been a stupid mistake to make this rushed and unplanned trip.

U Tin Hlang arrived home in the late afternoon, joined me for a swim, and suggested I come to dinner at his bungalow later in the evening. Still no word from Rosemary. Had he heard from her? "No." Was she expected for dinner? "No, but if she comes she will be most welcome."

Rosemary did not appear for dinner. U Tin Hlang was a generous and amusing host, trying openly to shake me at least to a more lively participation in the evening. And his comments on the Seymour case did finally stir me from my jealous preoccupation with myself.

He quizzed me on the details of what I had outlined in his chambers earlier in the day and, when he had them straight to his satisfaction, asked what I wanted of him.

"Advise me what is the right thing to do, of course," I said.

"What a quaint idea, Eric. I am not yet a judge, just a Silk. Tell me who my client is in this case. Am I the prosecutor or do I represent Mrs. Seymour? I am trained in the adversarial process, not in the role of a saint in the wilderness. Tell me my client and I shall swiftly marshal powerful arguments for him or her; ask me for a balanced and conclusionary opinion and I shall hem and haw, become verbose, talk about 'on the one hand and then on the other,' and so on and on."

"You mean: Tell you who pays you and it all comes clear," I said, and, as I said it, regretted it.

U Tin Hlang did not bristle as I expected; rather, he shook his head sadly at me: "You make the common mistake, Eric. You miss the point. The good advocate is moved by the chase more than by the refresher. We really do quite quickly and genuinely persuade ourselves of the virtue of our client's case, whatever virtue it may have."

He repeated his original question: "Well then, Eric, whom do I represent in the Seymour matter?"

Since I was coming to the view that Jean would have to be prosecuted and would probably be convicted of manslaughter at least, I thought it best to have him argue for her: "It seems clear enough to me. She was in no danger when she shot him. It cannot be justified. I must send her to the Assizes."

He was on his feet, moving out to the verandah, brandy balloon waving in his right hand. I followed and found a cane chair while he paraded back and forth before me. "You are quite wrong, your honour. She should not be sent to trial and if you do send her to trial she will be acquitted. Totally acquitted; I will see to that since it will gravely embarrass your employers. What you have failed to do is to put together three quite distinct defences. This is perhaps pardonable in the light of your lack of legal training, but my client must not suffer because of that. And it is also true that no case has as yet put these lines of defence together and formed the greater whole; but the conclusion is clear: she is not a criminal."

I was not really following him. "What defences? She told me she shot him because she feared he would kill her when he awoke and the battle recommenced. But he was not *then* doing anything and that is what matters."

"Hornbook law, hornbook law, your honour, missing much. First, repeated beatings of a wife create a situation where the *only* time she can safely defend herself against death or serious bodily injury is when she is *not* being attacked. I will persuade the court that she had no real alternative in the light of the long history of brutality at his hands and the impossibility for her—conditioned as she was by him, made to respond like an obedient and mistreated animal—to do anything else. But that is only one line of defence, though a powerful line, you will agree. It alone, vigourously presented, will produce a manslaughter verdict if not a complete acquittal."

I indicated some doubt in the matter. He ceased his pacing and confronted me face on, looking down at me with warm intensity. "Well then, add this defence: What could be more outrageous than to be told by a brutal and faithless husband, one you know has had intercourse with a prostitute that very afternoon, that you must take his hateful private parts into your mouth—to be forced to do that in fear of your life—forced to commit a crime of such loathsomeness that for many decades it was punished capitally. Oh, I will have the jury in an outrage; I won't be surprised if they attack the wicked police prosecutor who persecutes such a tortured woman. No court would find that less than adequate provocation for a lethal attack, and though this alone may lead only to a manslaughter conviction, when you combine the self-defence and the provocation surely you have something larger than either" (and here there was a long pause while he found his chair beside mine)—"an acquittal."

He seemed to relish the silence after his mock forensics. It was true that Jean Seymour had been cruelly abused and intensely provoked, but there still remained the fact that she could do much to protect herself other than shooting at her husband's head. Apart from anything else, with him asleep, she could scrabble together a few clothes and leave him. True, she could not call for help on the telephone—he had seen to that—but she could just go. It struck me that U Tin Hlang had said there were three lines of defence but had offered me only two—self-defence and provocation, each insufficient for an acquittal as the law stood but, he argued, together reaching that result. It seemed doubtful. And if I was not of the view that she would be acquitted under a proper application of the law, it was my duty to send her for trial, no matter what my sympathy for her.

"You said three defences, Lang. Your powerful, though wordy, oration mentioned only two."

"Your honour, don't protest my words. They are the coinage of my profession. Do you prefer grunted insinuations, hints, nods, and winks? Words are my coinage."

"But you spend so freely," I said, and urged him on: "What is this mysterious third defence? Or has it slipped your mind?"

"This, your honour," he said, rising again to resume his forensic pacing. "Brian Seymour must have known that his wife was not consenting to intercourse: he was raping her. But, you say, a husband can't rape a wife." And here he struck an exaggerated pose, right arm outflung: "I will challenge that. I shall marshal the many arguments for you, if you like, but you will find it hard to stop me at the preliminary enquiry since there is no direct Burmese case holding that the husband is immune, even though his immunity has been assumed by you parochial British, who believe every culture suffers from the defects of your own while none matches its virtues. And, you see, I will win this argument even if I lose it."

His pause for dramatic effect went on for what seemed to me an absurd length of time. "Do press on, Lang. I am listening. Stop prancing about on a stage. You lose, you win, how?"

"That the jury will be impressed must be obvious even to an English judge, but I will win in another way, for it will allow me to develop a subsidiary argument. If, in law, he cannot rape her (which I doubt), he most certainly can assault her. And if he assaults her violently, either to overcome her resistance or simply because that is the way he behaves, it will be an assault occasioning grievous bodily harm, which is a felony. Seymour thus, at some earlier time, committed a felony of violence against his wife when he had intercourse with her, which in fact caused her grievous bodily harm; it was an assault to which she had not consented—and all this he knew. Do you follow me so far, your honour?"

I nodded a somewhat desperate assent.

"Well, then. On the night she shot him she had suffered that felony and he had told her it would be inflicted again. His drunken sleep would not last long. She knew he would renew his sexually purposive violence against her. He might not kill her, I grant you that, but he would, she knew, succeed in forcing himself sexually upon her, renewing serious injury, committing a crime of violence. She clearly had a right to defend herself against this crime. There was no other way to avoid this further cruel crime against her. So, at least three defences: self-defence, provocation, and preventing the commission of a crime of violence. They blend, I agree, which gives me even greater room for the forensic eloquence that Burma thirsts for." And U Tin Hlang subsided again beside me, reaching to replenish his brandy balloon and mine.

It seemed contrived, but I had to admit that if one could get all three lines of argument to a jury they would be powerfully inclined to acquit her. But was that my business? Surely that was the jury's prerogative of extra-legal mercy; was not my duty merely to follow the routine procedures of the law and if there were a prima facie case of homicide to commit her for trial?

I tried another tack to lure U Tin Hlang to my assistance. "Suppose you were briefed by the prosecution—and I understand that does happen occasionally—what theory would you follow?"

"That's easy, my magisterial friend. I would bang away over and over and over at one theme: she was not a self-protector, she was a punisher. He deserved the punishment, but that is for the law to impose, not the wife. Hers was lynch law, not law. She was an executioner, she appointed herself to that role, and that is criminal homicide. You, the jury, are not trying him; you are trying her, and any sympathy you have for her must be left to the judge in sentencing and to the executive thereafter, who may pardon her if he wishes. You are the law. She was an unauthorised executioner. You must carry out your oath as jurors."

Rosemary didn't come to U Tin Hlang's bungalow or to the guest house.

I spent a lonely and, at first, sleepless night. Eventually I tossed and turned into sleep. A dream beset my sleep, troubling me deeply in ways I did not understand, leaving me uncertain, lacking confidence in myself, and regretting even more that I had sneaked off from Moulmein for this ill-contrived weekend.

It started quite innocently, in black and white, though I often dream in colour. I was talking to Rosemary and for some reason explaining the five senses to her. Touching my eyes I looked at her, then my ears, my nose, my lips and tongue, and the tips of my fingers, gesturing appropriately with each to convey their respective sensory roles. She made no response, just sat there demurely, distant, and proper. And then suddenly she was naked and not sitting at all, but lying alluringly on our bed behind a mosquito curtain at U Tin Hlang's guest bungalow, in the bed I now in fact occupied, though not in my dream, beckoning me to join her.

But instead of moving towards her, I stood still, shouting at her, "There are only five, only five, only five!" She held up one hand, fingers and thumb extended, five digits uplifted, and then the other hand rose with the index finger pointing at me. "Six" she said, "six, six, six." And then it seemed she was saying "sick, sick," while she counted the fingers—one, two, three, four, five, six. And then "six" and "sick" became indistinguishable.

I gestured at her angrily to be quiet. And then it became clear what she was telling me—that making love to her involved more than each of our five senses. They were involved, all of them, true; but there was more to it than their confluence. A different sense emerged out of the unity, not all five together but something more than all five together, a separate and compellingly quite different experience—a sixth sense, a real one, not the fictitious sixth sense of intuition that people deceive themselves about. It seemed to me a desperately important discovery, an insight that would bring me fame.

Until this point it had been merely a dream—a dream telling me something true that my conscious mind had not previously understood, the most useful type of dream. But then it changed, into garish colour and into a nightmare.

She was still on the bed. The mosquito net had disappeared; she was cringing in anguish and I was crouched above her trying, trying, trying to strike her, but my right arm, uplifted to strike her, would not move no matter how I tried. And I was helpless in another way: I was not ready to enter her. I desperately wanted to, but I couldn't. And I knew that if I could hit her my other disability would be cured. And the horror of it was that she was taunting me in both directions, suggesting that I was inept in two ways, and mocking my inability to cast off both weaknesses. I tried and tried to hit her, but my arm would not move; just as when you are trying to run away in a dream and your legs won't work, so it was with my arm. And, still struggling, I awoke shaking and sweating.

It was the noise of a horse outside the guest house that awakened me rather than my efforts to escape the nightmare, and when I realised this my troubles vanished. She had come, and early in the new day!

As usual in the tropics, I had slept naked under the mosquito netting and since it had been such a miserable, tossing, turning, and humid night I had put a towel under me. Pulling the towel around me as a loincloth, I rushed out to the verandah. And there she was, dismounted, tying the reins to a verandah post.

We kissed, somewhat briefly I thought, and she held me back with her two hands at arms' length: "Eric, my sweet. It's good to see you. I'm sorry I couldn't get away last night but we had a dinner at our place. And I fear I can't stay long now. I promised George to go to something at the barracks with him this morning; I only managed to get away now for my usual early-morning ride."

"Surely you can stay for a little while. Come on inside." And I tried to lead her onto the verandah and into the guest house.

Glancing pointedly at my attire she said, "You're not dressed to receive company. Better not. Let's talk out here."

And so it went. My erotic imaginings were to be frustrated. I did not try to conceal my disappointment.

"Eric, I'm too fond of you for that sort of a quickie," and there was more than a hint of annoyance in her voice.

"You didn't always take that view of it," I said.

"It's different when George is about. Surely you must see that. I made it plain enough, I would have thought."

I struggled for composure. The last thing I wanted was to waste time with her in argument. "Why don't you sit out here for a moment or two. I'll pull on some shorts and a shirt and we can talk."

Her response was immediate and affirmative. I would at least have a few minutes with her, and I had best not talk about our relationship or we would be biting at one another, I felt sure.

But in the event, no topic was much use that morning. Rosemary was ill at ease; so was I. We struggled along for five or ten minutes, though it felt much longer, and she said she had better be getting back. I said that I had wanted to talk to her about Jean Seymour, that I really did need her advice. She would, she said, try to get away for an hour or so in the afternoon, go for another ride perhaps. She would try but could not promise. "But it really is for a talk, Eric. I can't handle these affairs as lightly as you seem to think. I'll try, and if you are here we can talk, but no more than that."

I nodded a bleak assent. We kissed perfunctorily. I helped her mount. "I promise I'll try to make it," she said, and then added, after a pause and somewhat angrily, "but Eric, if I don't, you mustn't let that poor woman be further punished just because you failed to enforce the law."

She did manage a wave to me before she disappeared into the trees beside the beach, but it was little comfort. It was not only George's proximity that stood between us—"these affairs" indeed!

Of course, Rosemary didn't return, and I took the night train back to the duties I should not have abandoned. I had come to hate that train and rather to dislike myself. I determined that I would spend the journey coming to a firm decision about what to do, firm other than in the sense that I would not do anything until I had consulted with Veraswami. At the very least, I must have a plan to put to him, not just meander around my own insecurities.

The plan came to me in the miseries of that night. I recalled that there are two paths to a criminal trial: an indictment by a magistrate, in this case by me, or an information that can be laid by a senior officer of the Crown before an Assize Court. I would hear the preliminary case, refuse to indict her, and give my reasons in some detail, making the most I could of the possible lines of justification of Jean's actions in her appalling situation.

With the record of the preliminary enquiry and my statement of the reasons for my decision, I would send to Mandalay a confidential report pointing out that I lacked sufficient training in the law to be secure in such a difficult case, and I would suggest to my senior officers in Mandalay that, if they disagreed, my error could easily be rectified by their pursuing the path of laying an information of murder or manslaughter against Jean Seymour. I would add that there seemed no risk of her fleeing the jurisdiction if they wished to proceed further in the matter.

I thought I knew what Mandalay and Rangoon would do—nothing. They would be delighted to be rid of the embarrassment of the public airing of the soiled home life of the Seymours and, if they were criticised for failing to uphold the law, would slough it off as the usual inefficiency of that Rickshaw Wallah district officer in Moulmein. I felt quite pleased with myself as I contemplated telling Veraswami of my plan. I would reach the result I desired without deliberately contravening my duty to the law—for, if truth be told, I still thought that Jean Seymour should be charged with homicide. And, like a disgruntled and petulant child, I also thought that Rosemary had been grossly unfair in blaming it all on what she had called my failure to enforce the law. Oh yes, Veraswami would surely be pleased with me.

But, as I approached Veraswami's bungalow for our evening chat, doubts began to stir. The words did not rehearse themselves easily. I felt I would have to explain and explain. And so it was. I talked too much. Veraswami nodded and smiled—somewhat weakly, I thought. The more I talked the less I was sure whether I was a principled magistrate, a man of mature judgement, or a simpering lover who cowardly avoided doing what should be done. Was I Solomon or Pilate? Surely Solomon. Everyone would be pleased with me—Rosemary, U Tin Hlang, Jean Seymour, my senior officers in their private conversations, even opinion at the Club as the details leaked out, which they surely would. And Veraswami . . . ?

"It iss not easy, Eric. I give you that. But Mr. Eliot, the American-English poet, you know, somewhat full of God ass he sees him, did he not say that the greatest sin wass to do the right thing for the wrong reasons? If what you really think the law says iss that she should go to trial for the jury to decide her guilt or innocence (and you hope they will acquit her), are you not, by declining to charge her, doing what Mr. Eliot says you should not?"

"That's not quite fair, Dr. Veraswami. I will give my reasons in detail why I think her actions can be justified in law and why she should not go to trial. I know doing this stretches the law a bit, but I think it the right decision, and I believe that is where the law should go. And if I'm wrong, no harm done." But as I spoke, I knew I was dodging.

I found I wanted to tell Veraswami of my having hit Rosemary, but I could not bring myself to it. Yet the need to take him further into my confidence was very strong. Perhaps it was the Watney's that liberated my tongue. I told him instead of my dream of a few nights earlier in Rangoon, the dream from which Rosemary and her horse had awakened me. It seemed to me necessary to discuss the dream with someone in order better to understand myself.

Bouncy and peripatetic as a talker, Veraswami was still and intent as a listener; he didn't fiddle or look about, nor did he stare at you unblinkingly in excessive concentration, but he did persist in the usual Indian leg shaking. Still, I was used to it, and managed not to be distracted.

When I had finished a somewhat long and detailed recounting of the dream-nightmare, Veraswami made no immediate comment. I reached for more beer and he pushed the oval tin with its load of ice and Watney's towards me. And when he did speak he seemed to have skipped several steps in our conversation: "So you think Jean and Brian Seymour are equally guilty, that they did it to themselves, that they did what they both wanted?"

I was baffled. I had not been talking about the Seymours; I had been talking about a dream, or perhaps at another level about Rosemary and that miserable time I hit her—and, I suppose also, of our reactions to it, hers as well as mine. It had been an incredibly wonderful sixth . . . sick . . . oh hell, wonderful loving! I struggled to turn my mind to the Seymours and to follow Veraswami's train of thought.

"Surely that cannot be so, Dr. Veraswami. Surely Jean Seymour did not want to be beaten by that husband of hers."

"Eric, you use 'surely' to mean something else, issn't it? You often say 'surely' when you are verry doubtful; many people do. You are wondering whether she did or not, issn't it? Well, I am never sure in such matters, but I have no doubt she dreaded the beating even if she had come to accept this whole pattern of beating and loving, ass you call it."

"But even if that is right, and we all have some understanding of both—the beating and the loving—if we think about it, does that alter anything? Does it help me to know what to do about her?"

"Perhaps not, my admirable District Officer friend," and he was now beaming at me in approval—why, I knew not. "But you will be a better person for doing whatever you decide you have to do, if you have some understanding of what you are about—unlike your friends at the Club, I think." And his usual derogatory head waving, which accompanied his every reference to the Club, began its insistent rhythm.

"Eric, with your six senses you have me all at sixes and sevens—or iss it sixers or sickers and sevens—verry bewildering; but I see what you are driving at. For your age and your vast Rangoon sexual experience, you seem perceptive, issn't it, in these matters. Oh dear . . . let uss stop talking about such things, most un-British. It would never do at the Club; let uss talk about something else."

And we did. One more Watney's, some light banter, and I made a somewhat relieved withdrawal to my bungalow.

On reflection I understood that Veraswami had been gentle with me, but he had offered no solution to my dilemma other than a conditional approval of the course I had hoped he would applaud. I had consumed more than my usual share of his Watney's that evening and headed toward my bungalow determined to proceed with my plan but unsure whether I was guided by a larger sense of justice or merely succumbing to Rosemary's

admonition, "You must not punish that poor woman further for your failure." And constantly with me, insistent in my mind, was the thought that
I had hit her.

Why it was so, I am unclear, but the next morning I woke in the confident and not regretful knowledge that Rosemary was a part of my past—an
important part—but not of my future. I also felt clear and less anxious
about what I planned to do in the Seymour case.

As my first task on arriving at the police station, I instructed the
sergeant to advise Jean Seymour that there would be a preliminary hearing
into her case a week hence and that I would be calling on her at the hospital that evening to see how she could be helped and cared for in the
interim. I instructed him to tell her that if she so wished, I would arrange
for legal counsel to represent her at the preliminary hearing without cost
to her and that I would discuss this with her. But as to an immediate trip to
England to comfort her dying mother-in-law, no, that was not possible; a
person charged with murder can't become an international traveller, no
matter what the circumstances, until that matter is disposed of.

I would certainly be helped in my efforts to spell out a satisfactory legal
theory to justify Jean Seymour's actions if I could persuade U Tin Hlang to
come to Moulmein for a day or two to represent her. I knew he would
enjoy it—he always enjoyed mock-teasing me—and after our last meeting
I could tell him truthfully how much I wanted to see him without the complicating circumstances of my transient affair in which he had so readily
cooperated.

Commentary to
"The Tropical Bedroom"

The tropical bedroom of this story is not much different, I fear, from bedrooms
all over the world: the violence of spouse against spouse does not seem to be
confined to any one branch of the human species. Recently, in the Western
world, and especially in the United States, spousal violence has become a
focus of increasing concern. I doubt that this attention represents any increase
in the incidence of wife beating; rather it reflects a change in the status of
women and a change in social attitudes: physical violence is to be tolerated
only in the clearest cases of self-defence.

There are two main issues in "The Tropical Bedroom": the policeman's
duty when he confronts spousal violence and finds that the injured party does
not wish the other spouse to be prosecuted, and the troubling question of
whether the criminal law should develop a special defence, "the battered wife
syndrome," either to excuse the killing of a brutally abusive husband or to mit-

igate the punishment of the killer, possibly by reducing the crime from murder to manslaughter. On neither issue are the prudential and legal decisions clear.

It seemed to me important, as a background to considering these difficult issues, that my hero should recognise that he too may have intentionally struck a woman in anger, so that he might better understand the power of the emotions, particularly sexual jealousy, which play in these conflicts. The pride and passion of man, and of woman, are not easily controlled by the silken threads of the law; but that does not mean that the law should not have an educative purpose, a purpose to affirm minimum acceptable standards of conduct, and, one hopes, to have a deterrent effect on spousal violence.

The Policeman's Duty

When Blair pushed his way into the Seymours' bungalow, he had three courses of action open to him. First, he could have arrested Brian Seymour and charged him with battery, whether or not Jean Seymour wanted him to. He had seen that she was quite severely injured; he had probable cause to believe that Brian Seymour had inflicted that injury. No more is necessary for a valid arrest. But the trouble with this course of conduct is that Jean Seymour may refuse to testify or may become a hostile witness. The case in court will then be likely to evaporate, and little good will have been done, either for the cause of deterring wife beating or for the Seymour marriage.

The second course open to him was really an aspect of the first: he could try to bring immediate calm to the conflict, which his presence had apparently achieved, and then take further action against Brian Seymour only if Jean Seymour wished to prosecute the crime. If, as in this story, he confirms for himself that she really does not so wish, and that this decision is not the product of immediate fear, he then moves to his third course of action, to try to mediate the situation, act the counsellor, take off his cap and sit down and have a cup of tea.

With variations to suit different times and different places, the choice between those courses of action still confronts the modern policeman. There will be glosses of difference—walking the man around the block for a time, talking to him in the police car for a time, and so on—but the difficult choice between official action (unsupported by a complaining witness) and acting the social worker still remains.

There has been one further action favoured by some police departments, though it is probably illegal: arrest the man, hold him in gaol overnight, and release him before he can confront a judge. I say, probably illegal, because an arrest with an intention to prosecute is a legal arrest if there is "probable cause," and it remains a legal arrest even if the police or the prosecutor later decides not to go forward with the case. But an arrest with no intention to prosecute is, in my view, an abuse of police power and is an illegal arrest.

Over the past decade there has been extensive experimentation with these alternatives, particularly in the common situation where it is clear to the policeman that some injury short of a life- or health-threatening one has been inflicted on the woman and that she does not wish her husband (or cohabitor) to be prosecuted. Some police forces have favoured psychological training for the police to assist them in being good counsellors in those situations; others have favoured an arrest.

The empirical data on which alternative is to be preferred are far from clear. Blair favoured the avoidance of official action, though he added to his pacifying role the idea of Veraswami's visit to inhibit any further violence by Brian Seymour that night. Later, however, he regretted that he had not done more. It is a question worthy of discussion.

Feminist activist groups strongly argue for an immediate arrest in all these situations and suggest that when this happens there are fewer subsequent complaints of further beatings by the arrested husband or boyfriend. The data support them in this. But what is far from understood is *why* there are fewer subsequent complaints. Is it because the arrested male has learned his lesson, or is it because the arrest has terminated the relationship (which might not have been terminated had there not been an arrest), or is it because the woman fears further to complain, believing that another arrest will indeed terminate the relationship? On this question the available data are inconclusive.

Finally, it must also be appreciated that the conflict between the Seymours did not have the complicating factor of children. When young children are part of the family, the woman's position is rendered even more miserable and the complications for the police even more difficult.

Here, as elsewhere in these stories, we face the problem of ensuring that official legal action under the aegis of the criminal law does more good than harm.

The Battered Wife Syndrome

On page 265 Dr. Veraswami summarises the "syndrome" of "the battered wife"—accurately, in my view. Of recent years the reality of that psychological condition has been accepted by some courts and allowed either as a defence to a charge of homicide or as what is called an "imperfect defence."

To lay bare the central questions surrounding this defence, it is necessary to state a few basic principles of the law of homicide.

All common law systems grade criminal homicides. The most common grading division is between murder and manslaughter. Many states of the United States go further than this, classifying some homicides as capital and others as first and second degrees of murder; sometimes there are also degrees of manslaughter. Let us disregard capital murder and set the executioner aside—we dealt with him in "The Brothel Boy" and its commentary—and confine our attention to the three possible results of a charge of homicide in the case of a battered wife who kills her batterer: conviction of murder, conviction of manslaughter, or an acquittal.

Murder is essentially an unjustified and unexcused intentional killing; there is much more to it than this, but that is all we now need. Murder is the most severely punished criminal offence.

Manslaughter is either a criminally reckless unjustified killing or an intentional killing excused by reason of provocation or some similar personal excuse. Manslaughter is traditionally punishable by a wide range of sanctions, varying in harshness with the gravity of the particular crime.

The third category is, of course, those killings that are not criminal at all, for our purposes those intentional killings in which the actor was justified in what he did. At present, proportional self-defence that leads to the killing of an aggressor is a justified homicide, attracting no criminal sanction.

Self-defence is, of course, a justification of the killing that leads to an acquittal, but jurisdictions are divided on what is required for such a defence to succeed. Some require the accused to *reasonably* believe her actions to be immediately necessary; others allow the defence if the accused's actions were *honestly* believed to be immediately necessary.

Further complicating the matter, there is a gloss to the reasonable belief criterion: some of the jurisdictions that require the belief to be reasonable will allow a reduction of the grading of the crime from murder to manslaughter if the belief were honest even if it were not reasonable—that is the "imperfect defence."

Conceding for the moment that there is a diagnosable psychological condition, "battered wife syndrome," should it lead to an acquittal on a murder charge, or to the reduction of the crime to manslaughter, or should it leave the murder verdict intact but mitigate the punishment to be imposed?

I believe the discussions between Blair and Veraswami and U Tin Hlang present most of the information necessary to answer this question, but I should like to add a comment in defence of the prevailing view among lawyers that the "battered wife syndrome" defence should be rejected, other than as relevant to the sentence to be imposed. This view of what the law is, and should be, is not reflective of an anti-feminist position; it addresses the general theory of self-defence, by which it is required that if lethal or potentially lethal self-defencive measures are taken there must be an immediate necessity for their use. This view pervades the law of homicide and has much to recommend it. The prototypical battered wife homicide case is like that of the Seymours, one in which at the time of the killing the previously battering male is helpless, not threatening any immediate harm. If the requirement of immediacy of need to use lethal force is abandoned here, why not elsewhere?

There is another reason why lawyers are suspicious of allowing too wide a latitude to this defence: the person claiming it has killed the very witness who might best offer a different view of the facts; she has, in effect, destroyed the evidence.

The Curve of Pearls

For five years as District Officer in Moulmein, in Southern Burma, I had been both policeman and magistrate, interrogator and judge, for nearly one hundred thousand Burmese, Indians, and Chinese, and a few hundred Europeans. It felt strange now to be the subject of an enquiry—to be interrogated and judged. I remember that I had often complained to Dr. Veraswami about the strain of interrogating and judging—I now knew which role I preferred.

I had expected something like a court, with my three interrogators and judges—from the Foreign Office, the India Office, and the Burma Police Command—dressed in judicial finery, peering down at me from the bench while I was relentlessly cross-examined by an all-knowing prosecutor.

The reality, of course, was quite different. The mood was one of circumspect assessment, not high drama. English judges dress splendidly for public ceremonials: they dress to impress. But when a judicial issue is not thought to be appropriate for public concern, the well-cut business suit and private club-like surroundings create the preferred ambience.

Why at such a time snippets of trivia like this should concern me seemed a puzzle; perhaps they helped me not to take myself too seriously. Whatever the cause, I found myself reflecting on dress and plumage in the courts, wigs and gowns, high benches and elevated docks, as I waited for my professional fate to be decided.

The sharpest contrast I could call to mind was that between the House of Lords, with the deep-wigged Chancellor resplendent on the Woolsack in the Great Chamber, the Law Lords red-gowned, throne-seated around; and the very same men sitting as the Privy Council disposing of matters equally important but of no immediate concern to the local citizenry, this time dressed in the best products of Saville Row, and seated around a plain but highly polished table with not a wig or a gown in sight.

I should have known that the enquiry into my role in the future service of His Majesty would be a quiet and hidden affair, with mandarins of the civil service, knights only in title, aided by a military man in mufti, politely but insidiously settling my fate. And it had taken not much over half an hour, though it seemed to me there was revealed in that half hour more failure by me as an English gentleman (which was apparently the form of behaviour required) than one would have thought possible.

I had given brief responses to their every question, and each reply had been met with silence and subtle movements of the faces and bodies of my inquisitors, pursings of the lips, slight rearrangements of posture, raisings of the hands to adjust spectacles, brushings back of hair from forehead, all indicative of the poor regard in which they held my conduct. They repeatedly stressed that the findings of the coroner's enquiry absolved me from any criminal liability, either by commission or omission; and by thus repeating the obvious made me understand beyond cavil their doubt of its wisdom. But it was their duty, they made equally and repeatedly clear, despite the coroner's decision, to recommend whether or not, in the light of the whole affair, I should return to the service of His Majesty in Burma or be considered for another post in Ceylon about which enquiries had been made.

I waited and waited, furious with myself for the situation in which I was entangled, but puzzled where it had all gone wrong. Even my three judges— anyhow, one or two of them—must surely have strayed at some time from the path of monogamous virtue. Where, then, did I commit the sin or sins that merited my present censure? And, anyhow, what did I really want to come from this morning's enquiry? I could have avoided the enquiry by resigning; indeed, that had been suggested as the right thing to do. Did I now really want to return to Moulmein or take on a long and difficult task in the Southern Region of Ceylon? I was unsure. But I did know that I did not want those three stiff-backed mandarins to hold me in the sort of contempt that I judged they had implied in the enquiry. Why had I not tried to defend myself rather than to rely on the tight-lipped responses I had given to difficult and testing questions, questions which were full of ambiguities and imprecisions, which hinted at guilt and left no room for wordy justifications, and which were yet in no way capable of effective dismissal by my curt affirmative or negative replies?

And then the door from the enquiry room opened and Geoffrey Pollit came to join me in the anteroom. So he was the other witness. What in hell could he tell them that I hadn't? His evidence at the coroner's enquiry had supported my story. And he hadn't had much to tell.

We exchanged brief greetings and sat in silence, not looking at one another. Time passed even more slowly. Again, what did I want to come from this enquiry? Did I really want to go back to Moulmein? Was it only egotism—the thought of being uniquely wanted by someone, somewhere— that attracted me to the task in Ceylon? I did not rejoice in the opinion of me and of my behaviour that my three inquisitors had seemed to express in their interrogation, but did that really matter if I believed I had done what was right? I did not value their collective opinion as much as a raised eye- brow of Dr. Veraswami. And I knew what those three would think of him. Yet, I must confess, I was deeply, deeply hurt by their criticism; it seemed so unfair, so unjust.

And then the door opened and the beak-nosed, bespectacled man from the India Office dismissed Geoffrey Pollit with a "Thank you, Mr. Pollit, for your invaluable assistance" and gestured for me to follow him back into the enquiry room.

They left it to the Colonel, my directly senior officer in the room, to deliver their judgment. It was an opinion of subtlety and ambiguity, clear as to its intendment but evasive as to its basis, so that it was both irrefutable and irresistible.

They were agreed that I was not at fault in the whole matter, but it was their view that I had displayed poor judgement, very poor judgement. They did not propose to particularise this error or these errors of judgment; it was just plain to them that such existed. Nevertheless, there was no reason why I should not return to my posting in Moulmein when my leave had elapsed, should I wish to, nor any reason why I should not apply for the position in Ceylon about which enquiries had been made from that coun- try. That decision would be noted in my record. They thought it proper to add, however, that having considered my file, and taking into account the notations that would be made on it after this enquiry, they thought it most unlikely that my application for the Ceylon posting would be successful.

On all this, the Colonel said, all three were in agreement, and that is all that his colleagues wished him to say. And the other two nodded and grunt- ed their "Quite so"s. But for his part, the Colonel added, he wished to go further and to say that it was his view that I now would be unwise to antici- pate a distinguished career in the Burma Police, or indeed in any branch of government service, and he would urge me to look around so as to turn my undoubted administrative capacities in another direction. The fact of the enquiry, even with its formal finding in my favour, would be a substantial impediment to rapid promotion. It was for my own good, I must understand, that he added these words; they would form no part of the official record— and he, for one, he confessed, had some sympathy for my misfortune.

I said a formal "Thank you" to all three collectively, stood up and gave a sort of half bow, since being out of uniform I could not salute, left the enquiry room, and made my way down to the large entrance hall to the India Office where those soliciting or awaiting interviews sat in serried ranks. I joined them. It was a quiet place to sit unnoticed. I needed time to calm down.

Unexpectedly, I was happy. Veraswami had told me often that I must leave Burma. So now I would. But it was a graceless way to go, captured myself by one of the moral ambiguities in the behaviour of others that had fascinated me through much of my police and judicial work in Burma.

Facts are so very difficult, guilt so very elusive—or is it that guilt is so all-pervasive that measuring its extent is a challenge beyond man's competence though necessarily within his moral obligation? Well, I had tried, for others, perhaps succeeded occasionally for them, even if for myself I seemed to have failed. And yet I was happy sitting there quietly, exactly where I had sat before I had been first interviewed for the Burma job.

My mind drifted back to a discussion with Dr. Veraswami a few weeks before I came home here to England on leave, which seemed to be the origin of the entire bloody mess.

"Iss it not strange, Eric, that the more prosperous people become the more they are likely to kill themselves? You would think it would be otherwise."

I did not know whether it was strange or not. Dr. Veraswami's question had come from nowhere; certainly it had nothing to do with our previous desultory conversation about cricket and the unlikelihood of getting a game going involving the Indian policemen and those at the Club still capable of bowling a ball or wielding a bat. He saw my puzzlement and shook his head in mock annoyance. "Oh, I am a silly fellow, jumping about all over the place. Why should I think you have been with me all day, and therefore know what is troubling me, when we have just met for our evening Watney's and you have, no doubt, had many police and military and judicial and I know not what other important matters to attend to?"

I urged Veraswami to spare me the mockery and to tell me what had precipitated these gloomy thoughts of suicide.

"A patient, of course, a patient. And I suppose I should have reported the matter to you formally, Mr. Policeman—I don't know. I suppose your busybody of a law takes an interest in such matters." And he fell into a reflective silence.

"Dr. Veraswami, you become more elusive by the moment. Please tell me what this is all about."

Veraswami's conversational style often shifted from these opaque rambling musings to swift, direct, and precise summations, as it now did: "A patient in the psychiatric section of our hospital—you know it, you have been there often—cut his own throat with a knife he had managed to acquire. He did a bad job of it. An awful mess. I have sewn him up and he will live for the time being, which iss all you can say for any of uss. But it upset me. I felt ill at ease, issn't it, when I wass patching him up. He wass in no pain then; he very nearly died; perhaps I should have let him." And then Veraswami seemed to become angry with himself: "No, no, that iss not right. I could not let him die. I am becoming a maudlin, self-indulgent fool. You must speak severely to me, my friend."

"I would not risk that, Dr. Veraswami; you seem to be chastising your-self vigourously enough without my help. But if I understand correctly what you are saying, the man was mad, so he couldn't make a rational choice to kill himself, and so there was no doubt that you should try to save him."

Veraswami wandered about the verandah, clutching his beer mug, not quite muttering to himself, but looking as if he well might.

The thought struck me: Would it make any difference to a doctor's duty if he thought someone who had tried to kill himself was entirely rational, had thought the matter through carefully, had quietly determined that death was to be preferred to life, and if the doctor knew this was the patient's considered opinion? After all, a patient can refuse medical assis-tance even if the refusal will lead to his imminent death. Why not then regard a genuine attempted suicide as such a refusal? The intent could hardly be more clearly expressed.

I tried to phrase this idea to Veraswami. He stopped his pacing, listened intently, and replied promptly. "Verry interesting, Eric, verry. Let uss think about it. Socrates, it iss said, was a verry rational chappie, and he killed himself. Of course, for reasons I have never properly understood, hiss suicide iss regarded ass a fine, noble gesture. But let uss put him in a different situ-ation, but keep it him, if you see what I drive at. And not hemlock, but rather wrists cut and bleeding to death. I see him sitting there, quietly bleeding to death, and I say to him: 'Come along with me, Sir. Let me sew you up.' He replies: 'No. Leave me alone. I know precisely what I am doing and why, and if you have the time and I live so long I can in a most com-plicated and circuitous dialogue prove that to you—I am famous for such contrived dialogues. But believe me now: I want to die.' And I do believe him. What am I to do and what should I say to him?" And Veraswami beamed at me joyfully as he felt about in the ice in the oval bucket for the means of replenishing my glass.

"I suppose, if you believe the rationality of his decision and also that a patient may refuse medical attention, you leave him alone and enquire only if he would like something to ease the pain of his departure."

Veraswami rounded on me as if I had fallen into a trap. "Perhaps you are right, though I did not think district officers, distinguished defenders of the law ass they must be, said such things; but what if, instead of doing what you suggest, I replied to Mr. Socrates something like this: 'Wise man though I know you to be, I have this difficulty. The facts are against you. It iss well established that when we patch up attempted suicides, bring them back from the banks of the river Styx, ass it were, fewer than half of them subsequently even try to kill themselves. So half didn't really mean it, in the sense that given a chance for further thought they change their minds. And . . . and . . ." Here Veraswami paused and extended his open palm towards me as if I were the object of his oratory. "I do not know to which half you belong, Mr. Socrates, those who prove their determination to kill themselves by trying again, or those who come to accept this life, vale of tears or not. So . . . I must patch you up, whatever you say."

And then Veraswami thanked me for clearing up his doubts about his treatment of his suicidal patient that day. "It iss very acute of you, Eric, to help me in that subtle way."

I accepted the compliment though it was quite clear that he had helped himself to clarity, if clarity it was—I had had very little to do with it.

There seemed a weakness in Veraswami's logic. Why should not Socrates be allowed to make the decision as to which half of those who attempted suicide he belonged, those determined to succeed or those moved by a transient depression? Surely he knew better than anyone else, even if he was not entirely certain. If it were a fifty-fifty choice, why should not he rather than the doctor make it? Why should the doctor be allowed to deny all attempted suicides that choice? In other situations, in ordinary medical and psychiatric treatments, the patient's wishes govern; the patient can refuse treatment even if later he comes to wish he had accepted it. Why the difference here? Why should the doctor govern this decision and not other, equally life-threatening decisions? But in the circumstances I did not wish to pursue the matter further, and we drifted to other topics.

Veraswami's talk of suicide left me depressed as I made my way home to my bungalow for a solitary dinner. I felt lonely and lost, increasingly burdened by the thought that my life was going to waste here in Moulmein. True, I was reading more than I ever had before—there was little else to do—but if I was to become a writer I had better know more about life and art and politics than I could experience in this Asian backwater. I can't say that the thought of my own death oppressed me—in one's mid-twenties such a thought is transient at best—but I did have the strong feeling that my life was slowly wasting away and that it was time I did something about it. But these depressing reflections did not survive my arrival at my bungalow.

A cable awaited me. My houseboy had put it on the dining room table. It was from the GOC Burma Command. I had never had a direct communication from such a remote power before. The text read:

DEEPLY REGRET TO INFORM YOU THAT CAPTAIN GEORGE BRETT DIED HEROICALLY IN ACTION AGAINST DISSIDENT FORCES ON NORTH EAST FRONTIER STOP LEAVE GRANTED TO ATTEND FUNERAL RANGOON TUESDAY SEVENTEENTH.

It certainly took my mind off myself. Rosemary a widow! And why had such an eminence as the GOC Burma Command granted me unsolicited leave to attend a funeral of someone whom, for all he knew—and such was in fact the case—I cordially disliked? To celebrate his demise! The answer seemed obvious enough: it must be Rosemary's doing. But why had she not telephoned or written or cabled herself? Perhaps I was just one of a batch of officers who had served with Brett that headquarters thought should be invited to the funeral to put on an appropriate show. Yes, that seemed more likely than any scheming by Rosemary. And she had told me that she was quite fond of George: "quite fond" were her precise words. He was in her eyes a "silly but predictable fellow," so she might be mourning him, or at least mourning the effects of his death on her life. She would probably return to England, and with her looks and her money she would not be long for widowhood.

I took a deep breath, poured myself a whisky despite the earlier beers with Veraswami, and settled down in considerable satisfaction for a last drink before dinner. I could not in conscience pretend to regret Brett's demise nor, if truth be told, Rosemary's imminent return to England.

I telephoned U Tin Hlang at work and told him I had been ordered to Rangoon to the funeral. There was no need to explain. As usual, he delighted in demonstrating that he was vastly better informed than I would ever be on all military and police matters, the more confidential the better. "Of course you will visit my modest bungalow. We shall drown our sorrows and struggle together to devise how to confront a world without George Brett. The baby elephant grows and is trumpeting for you—she needs another squashed banana." And then, uncharacteristically, U Tin Hlang abandoned his bantering tone and in a firm, quiet voice urged me to caution: "You must know that you are welcome to stay at my guest house should you wish to, but for this occasion don't you think the Officers' Club more appropriate? Your previous visits to my place and the contemporaneous visits by Rosemary did not go unnoticed—you must know that. Better avoid associating with the natives this time, Eric, particularly barrister natives like me who are known to grow too big for their London-made shoes."

It was obviously sensible advice, and I took it. During the three days I was in Rangoon, I did go to U Tin Hlang's magnificent bungalow for a swim and an inspection of his horses and elephants, including the now much larger and even more threatening baby elephant; but I did not visit the guest bungalow of joyous and turbulent memories of Rosemary. Lang was busy, the two rehearsals for the funeral ceremony were time-occupying and boring, and so was the funeral itself. It had become a political ceremony; there was hardly a true note sounded, though the drill and military pomp were superb. I saw nothing of Rosemary, except at the funeral itself, and she made no attempt to contact me. I knew she was staying at the home of the GOC Southern Command—no place for an inconsequential district officer of police.

After the funeral there was a reception at the Officers' Club. Rosemary stood to the left of the GOC Southern Command. Well-cut, shapely widow's weeds contrasted crisply with her light complexion and blonde hair. She certainly looked the part of the beautiful military widow grieving bravely the fall of her warrior husband. A half veil frustrated my attempt to decide whether she was emotionally in mourning or whether relaxed relief more accurately described her state of mind, and the few words she said to me as my turn in the line led me to her gave little enlightenment. "This is all dreadful, Eric. I will write to you as soon as I can get away from Rangoon."

She did write, a few weeks later, to tell me that she had decided to return to England and that, as much as she would have liked to visit Moulmein, it now seemed impossible with everyone fussing to help a poor suffering widow, thus precluding any sort of life for her here in Burma. She would, she thought, be more free in England. And she looked forward, or so she alleged, to seeing me just as soon as I could make my way there. Was I not due for leave before long? And the letter closed with expressions of affection far beyond the formal, though there did seem some strain and contrivance in them.

My own letter in reply and our subsequent occasional correspondence was even duller. I told her of such events in my life in Moulmein as seemed worthy of report, or rather as seemed capable of being shaped into not uninteresting stories, and also did my best to express love for her—yes, I used that word, but not without effort and reflection, which must mean that I used it falsely; but I did use it, and given our prior relationship there seemed no way to avoid it. And as the time for home leave approached I even began, on occasion, to believe it myself.

The *Chitral* was a vessel of some twelve thousand tons, quite well appointed. I had a first-class passage, sharing a cabin with another junior officer, circumstances appropriate to our rank. But since boarding school I have greatly disliked having to share sleeping digs—it is so cramping, so unrelaxing, so inhibiting. Still, I had no choice; that is all the Raj would pay for and I certainly had no funds to splurge on private and posh (port out, starboard home) accommodation. So it was a double cabin, port home; "soph," not "posh."

As cabin companions go, Mathew Links was acceptable: neat, clean, circumspect, his devoutness apparent from his unconcealed prayers before bedding down. He made the usual polite enquiries about my postings and I about his, about school, family, and so on. But in a key respect he proved to be the most admirable of cabin mates; certainly no male could have matched his excellence: he still had his appendix. And better yet, midway between Rangoon and Colombo it became inflamed and the ship's doctor ordered an immediate operation if Mathew Links' life were not to be at serious risk.

During the voyage I had several times talked with the ship's doctor, Major Gorse. Like me he was a servant of the Raj travelling on leave, but he was supplementing his military stipend by serving as the ship's doctor, a customary practice enriching both the shipping line and military medicos. I had no way of assessing his competence, but he had seemed sensible enough. However, my appraisal of Gorse seemed less certain when he requested my assistance in Links' operation. We had talked about the hospital at Moulmein and about Dr. Veraswami, and I had mentioned my occasional attendance at operations performed by Dr. Veraswami. Major Gorse based his request (more like an order, considering his rank) on those conversations and the fact, compelling to him, that Mathew Links was my cabin mate, a phrase I found increasingly unacceptable. I suppose the real reason he wanted my help was that, because I had previously attended surgical operations, I was less likely to faint away entirely and leave him destitute of an anaesthetist. I had little choice, and I was bolstered by the likelihood that, even if Links survived our attentions, he would be in the ship's hospital for the rest of the journey, and I would have the cabin to myself. As I said, Links had proved to me that he was entirely fitted to share a cabin with me.

Major Gorse instructed me in my duties. There was a registered nurse aboard and she would assist him in all aspects of the operation other than the anaesthetic; she would look after the instruments, asepsis, and a host of similar operating theatre duties. Under his control I would be responsible for administering the ether, though he would take care of a sedative injection to quiet the patient prior to my anaesthetising him. Thereafter, by observing the patient and also listening for the doctor's or the nurse's advice in the matter, I would administer more or less ether as the case may be. "Administer?" I enquired. "Yes. You know. Shake it out of the tin onto the mask you will hold across his nose and mouth. And, of course, you must watch his tongue carefully; perhaps you will have to hold it. He must not swallow it. Some patients do, you know, if the anaesthetist is careless."

At this, my confidence in the entire enterprise, but particularly in my role in it, evaporated entirely. I didn't particularly like Mathew Links, but neither did I dislike him; I certainly wished for no role in his demise. Major Gorse seemed to be launching us both on a perilous course. I said as much. He waved aside my anxieties and took me to the dispensary to give me what he called "a dry run." It wasn't dry at all; liquid ether is damp, very damp, and he spread it around generously. It came in metal cans, which Gorse punctured with what looked like an ordinary tin opener. I was to hold a piece of cotton muslin clamped in a metal ring over the patient's nose and mouth, not pressing it on his face, but just off so that most of what he would breathe would have to come through the cloth, which I would keep soaked to the proper degree with ether. "How will I know how much?" I enquired. Again the confident brush-off, "Stop worrying about that, Blair. I'll tell you, more or less." I began to have sympathy for Links, which was deepened when Major Gorse reminded me that my most difficult task was to ensure that the patient did not swallow his tongue. "How, in God's name?" I blurted out. "With this," he replied, handing me a teaspoon, indicating that if I used the back of the teaspoon to keep the tongue depressed behind the teeth there would be no risk. This I deduced rather than understood since the Major gave me this advice at the same time that he demonstrated on himself how the teaspoon was to be wielded.

The Bay of Bengal did not cooperate: a substantial swell, winds gusting to thirty knots, and a quite heavy sea. Gorse insisted that the operation must nevertheless go ahead. The ship was turned into the wind and I retired to my cabin to prepare for my medical ordeal, choosing as dress an open-necked white shirt, shorts, long socks, and plimsolls. Gorse had also instructed me how to tie knots in the four corners of a handkerchief so that it could be formed into a clean head-covering to assist in keeping my hair out of the way and the operating theatre germ free. I remembered making hats like this as a child, and felt quite distinguished in my surgical apparel.

Gorse had indeed heavily sedated Links. Nevertheless, Links recognised me when he was wheeled in by the nurse to the Engineers' Mess, where the operation was to be performed. It was early afternoon and that location had been chosen since it had a glass ceiling and provided excellent light on the operating table, which had been contrived from two square tables lashed together and placed centrally under the glass ceiling. Despite the sedation, Links saw my anxiety and murmured encouragements to me as the nurse, Gorse, and I half-lifted him onto the sheet-covered table. He also clutched at his side with what I thought was despair.

Gorse said to him, "Now, breathe evenly, and start counting from one hundred backwards when I tell you to." And then he snapped at me, "Go ahead. Go ahead. What are you standing there for?"

I clutched my ring of cloth, my teaspoon, and my can of ether with holes punched in its top, and stepped forward to do my desperate duty when the door to the Engineers' Mess opened and an extraordinary figure entered: the ship's captain, Captain Walsingham, a presence I had distantly seen at lunch that very day dining with senior officers and a few privileged civilians, but had certainly not expected to meet in these circumstances. Normally he was a quite distinguished-looking ship's captain, trimmed beard, neat cap, blue eyes, the usual rig; but on this occasion seafaring trim had deserted him. He wore an open-necked shirt, like mine, and loose-fitting long white shorts known to other ranks as Bombay Bloomers, and he had taken his dentures out, giving his face an extremely flaccid appearance. He had moved from the trim to the grotesque in the interval of lunch to early afternoon.

I stopped in my tracks. Gorse raised an enquiring "Sir?" and an eyebrow. Captain Walsingham muttered something—his diction being far from clear for reasons that required no deduction—about "Thought I had better be present . . . going down with the ship . . ." and gesturing toward his mouth, "might throw up, you know."

Gorse behaved splendidly under this trial. "If you'll mind the door, Sir, we'll get ahead with the operation," and he gestured peremptorily at me to begin my ministrations. Links began to moan at the very thought. I moved to action with can and cloth, holding the teaspoon in reserve as instructed

for later use if required. Links kicked. "More, more . . ." said Gorse. I saturated the cloth. Links kicked more. The nurse, previously standing back
minding the aseptic instruments, lent her weight on his feet. "More,
more," Gorse repeated, and I obliged, though I was beginning to feel
squiffy myself. "Start counting, Links" Gorse commanded.

A muffled "Counting?" came from Links and then, after a pause, apparently in midstream with my ether, "87, 86, . . . 83, 82, 81 . . . 70. . . .," and
then silence.

"Ease up there, Blair; you'll have us all under." And I did, and, brushing
the tears from my eyes, peered into the patient's mouth to be sure his
tongue was still there, which it was.

"So far, so good" from Gorse did not greatly reassure me. His "Let's get
on with it" did.

The nurse busied herself by untying Links' pajama pants and pulling
them off.

I heard the sound of cheering and some clapping. Looking up I saw a
considerable number of the ship's company formed up around the glass
covers above the Engineers' Mess peering down approvingly. The site carefully chosen for the operation had its drawbacks. But now Captain
Walsingham showed his mettle. Mouth working furiously, he stepped close
to the operating table and shouted imprecations up at his crew massed
above. Precisely what he said neither I nor they could have been sure of,
but its general intendment was unmistakable and they indeed removed
themselves from their observation posts promptly.

I began to feel confident in my task; perhaps this would be a better
career than that of a district officer. The patient semed to be breathing
evenly and lying calmly. Gorse and the nurse moved to their tasks. She
cleaned his lower stomach with ether—the entire Engineers' Mess was
becoming ether malodorous, but I preferred that to any risk that my
patient, as he now was, should feel pain. Then, at his request, the nurse
handed Gorse a scalpel and we were at the starter's gate.

For reasons I did not then understand, Gorse looked up at me as he
made a very small incision. Links jerked slightly. I understood. "More, just
a little bit more, and keep dripping it on very slowly." I did, and the anaesthetic procedure began in earnest.

There is not much to report about that operation. It went well
enough—quite interesting, really. There was only one interruption. When
the blood flowed from the large incision Gorse made to get the operation
under way, Captain Walsingham had had enough. Clutching his mouth
and retching vigourously, he made a fast exit, and we three, we brave and
competent three, did our duty. At one stage, in an excess of medical caution, I judged the need to hold the tongue down with the back of the teaspoon; but I think it was a pretension of mine rather than a need of Links'
I have kept that spoon as a memento.

Gorse and the nurse obviously knew what they were about. Links lived—indeed there was even the threat that in the Mediterranean he could leave the ship's hospital and return to our cabin.

The captain made amends for his rapid departure by inviting the successful surgical team to his lavish quarters after the operation to celebrate the continued existence of Lieutenant Links.

I weaved back to my solitary cabin some time later, belching, laughing, and scratching myself in ways previously prohibited by the presence of my still living but happily removed patient.

The silence wakened me. The ship was at anchor, the engines stopped. My cabin was just above the waterline and I could hear the waves lapping gently close to my head. At the shout of a boatman I was fully awake, scrambling into my clothes for an early morning view of Colombo harbor.

We were anchored about two hundred yards from the shore. A few small boats were clustered around the stern of our ship, their native occupants involved in dealings with members of our crew who were leaning out over the railings. And more boats were on their way with what must be articles of trade—fruit, coconuts, baskets, hats, curved knives, carved model boats, a collection of bric-a-brac, a motley of colours.

A rope with a basket on its end was thrown up to me from one of the small boats and I was directed to loop it over the railing and lower it down again. Trade could now begin. But I didn't want anything. This did not seem to faze the aspiring vendor. I kept telling him I didn't want anything; but he persisted, holding up one article after another. I would shake my head at each. Eventually he plunged deep into his tattered cornucopia and produced a midsized envelope, put it in the basket, and started to pull it up. I raised my hands in rejection. He would have none of it, shouting that he knew what young sahibs wanted. A glance at the contents of the envelope confirmed my suspicion: it contained what were then known as "French postcards," though these had a distinctly Asian flavor. If truth be told, I would have liked to buy them, but by now there were other passengers on deck and our dealings had been the focus of too many eyes. I regretfully lowered the photographs of the ornate couplings back to the boat and managed to lure other passengers to my side to distract my persistent vendor's attentions. He had clearly had more than enough of me.

At breakfast a note was delivered to me from the purser's office. It had come aboard with the mail, which had not yet been sorted. It was from a Mr. Lindhausen. A mutual friend, U Tin Hlang, Q.C., had suggested that he should offer all courtesies to me for the period the *Chitral* was in Colombo. A rickshaw would pick me up dockside when I disembarked. It would be convenient if I would leave the ship shortly after 9 A.M. If this were not convenient, would I please notify the purser, who would get a message to Mr. Lindhausen?

How very kind of Lang. I had been a bit lost as to what to do in Colombo, other than to accompany Major Gorse, who told me he planned to visit the main public hospital, which did not particularly attract me. Since we had left Rangoon I had formed no shipboard acquaintance with whom I would wish to explore Colombo, and solitary tourism is to me no joy. Lang's friend was likely to be interesting and helpful.

There was a *Chitral* motorboat plying back and forth to the shore, which was the most sensible and popular conveyance; but there was also a diversity of native boats desperately soliciting patronage, including one fishing boat of the type I had come to know in Chinaka, with the rower standing at the rear, long oars crossed in front of him as, upright, he swayed forward and backward to propel the boat. Thoughts of Chinaka led me to wonder how JayJay was doing with his prosperous parents. These memories led me in turn to select that boat to take me to the dockside.

I am neurotic about time, always fearful of being late no matter how unimportant the appointment, and in the result always arriving too early. This often means meandering about waiting for the hands of my watch to move. And this morning was no exception; I was too early for the Lindhausen rickshaw.

On my landing dockside, a gaggle of rickshaw wallahs grabbed at my hands trying to lure me to their rickshaws. I waved them off and stood back to wonder how I would know which one came from Mr. Lindhausen. I called out "Is anyone from Mr. Lindhausen?" without any effect.

I stood about for a few minutes, passing the time by looking back at the *Chitral* and its surrounding entourage of trading boats. Shortly before nine, a spotless white rickshaw, with highly coloured seat and cushions, an ornate wicker front, and a crisp, white-fringed canopy, came whisking up behind the line of rickshaws. It was embarrassingly distinct, not only in its smart furnishings, but more tellingly because it was drawn not by one but by two strapping young men trotting together almost as one—Tamils, I thought, by the darkness of their skins and their tall stature—startlingly similar in appearance.

How demeaning! To use men as animals! And to make such a show of it. Who would use such a rickshaw? And then the appalling thought came, as the twin human horses looked around enquiringly, that "they," "it," the whole flamboyance, had come for me.

I gestured in their direction. As one the two Tamils made *eyebong* to me, attracting the attention of many on the wharf. There was no help for it; I would have to use their conveyance. I hurried through the scruffy line of rickshaws for hire to their elegant equipage. My rickshaw men handed me into the luxury of their chariot, carefully adjusted the canopy to shield me from the morning sun, and first with long paces and then at a steady trot, shoulder to shoulder, took me in style away from the small knot of passengers from the *Chitral* watching my embarrassed departure.

What an extraordinary change! In me, I mean. When I had first ridden in a rickshaw here in Colombo on the voyage out I had hated it; it seemed so unnatural, so inhumane. And later in Rangoon I had acquired an unfriendly nickname by my efforts to help a dying or dead rickshaw wallah. And now, only a few years later, I was allowing myself to be pulled along by what was, in effect, a rickshaw "matched pair." I wondered would they step in unison, as their equine counterparts had been trained to do? Would they lift their knees high and arch their necks? Surely they would not snort in unison.

I was puzzled how to address either or both of my matched pair. Communication so far between us had been confined to gestures and an occasional "Sir." I took refuge in the Englishman's convenient "I say" and shouted into the breeze created by their even progress, "I say! Could you tell me where we are going?"

They did not break step. I think it was the man on the left who shouted back, "The Galle Face, Sir. Mr. Lindhausen will meet you there."

I knew that hotel. I had visited its pinkish ostentation on my trip out. It was, I recalled, on the sea and not far from the port, with a long, curving entrance drive flanked by massive palms.

The commissionaire seemed impressed but not surprised by the style of my arrival: "Mr. Blair? Mr. Lindhausen asked me to tell you that he is waiting for you in the breakfast room." This proved to be a small dining room looking out upon a palm-fringed beach. It was well patronised but only one table was occupied by a single patron, whom I gathered was Lindhausen. We made eye contact at the same time and I moved toward him. He stood as I approached, standing an inch or two above my six feet—tall for a native, I thought, and of an unusually large frame, so that he seemed wider than he ought to be, neither slim nor fat, but of firm round chest and girth. A solid, strong man. His skin colouration and the cast of his features made it clear that he was Eurasian. By his name I guessed, correctly it proved, that he was the son of a Dutch father and a Tamil mother. He was well dressed in grey slacks, a precise shirt and tie of modest design, and a blue blazer— exactly right for an Englishman at breakfast on a holiday. He did not look at all out of place, as do some Eurasians in English dress in European surroundings; quite the contrary, he looked entirely at ease. I should have guessed from the introduction by U Tin Hlang that Lindhausen would be a burgher, and should have known—as I was soon to learn—the important stabilising role the burghers play in Ceylon in the three-way conflict between Singhalese, Tamils, and the English administration.

We shook hands and he said, "It is good of you, Mr. Blair, to accept such a peremptory invitation; but Lang was insistent that I meet you and I did not know how to give you advance notice. I suppose I should have sent an invitation to the ship by wireless, but Lang said you rather liked impromptu arrangements."

I assured him that I was delighted that he was helping me in my visit to Colombo and that otherwise I would have been at a loose end. He asked if I had breakfasted aboard. I told him I had. "Well, let us sit here and discuss plans for the day."

He gestured for more tea and a cup for me and lit another cigarette, not offering me one. Immediately, he recognised what he had done and holding out his cigarette case, said: "Oh, Lang tells me you like to roll your own and that this is detested in the mess. Do you wish to impress me with your dexterity, or will you have one of mine?" I took a cigarette.

As the day wore on I found that cigarettes were the only defect for me in Lindhausen's company. He seemed to be always enveloped in a cloud of smoke, cigarette after cigarette being implanted in a medium-sized holder which he kept smouldering away throughout the day. Otherwise I found him nearly as interesting as U Tin Hlang, and somewhat similar in style and outlook.

Lindhausen outlined for my approval the plans he had made for the day. We would drive around Colombo and its environs, call on several of Lindhausen's colleagues in the Ministry of the Interior, who would answer any questions I had about Ceylon and its people that he could not help me with, and in the evening we would dine at his home in Cinnamon Gardens with his wife and two daughters.

These plans rang well in my ears and I accepted them with expressions of gratitude.

"Oh, don't be too grateful, Mr. Blair. Like Lang, I rarely do anything without some purpose of my own advantage. I want something from you. I shall tell you about it later." I could not imagine what it could be, and it didn't seem to matter anyhow.

Lindhausen excused himself to tell the rickshaw men to go to his house and to send his car immediately to the Galle Face.

Lindhausen's car was an open Riley tourer, somewhat sporty for a tour of a city and its environs, but giving excellent visibility. He insisted that I sit in the front with the driver, while he occupied the rather cramped rear seat. He told me apologetically that his wife and daughters had their larger car that day. He did seem on the boastful side.

The driver was a Tamil, clad in village dress, barefooted, and with an affection for speed and risks that Lindhausen did nothing to curb. "Don't worry, Blair; he is a fine driver." I could not at first recall of whom he reminded me, and then it came to me—that awful Buddhist priest on the beach at Chinaka. But why? They didn't resemble one another at all. . . . Of course: the big toe of his right foot! The priest had used his preternaturally large, dirty, big toe with its broken nail to dig in the sand while I tried to negotiate about JayJay returning to Moulmein; this driver used his similarly oversized big toe in a prehensile fashion—it reached up and depressed the brake when necessary, which did not seem often enough to me. It was like an extra limb, the side of his foot fiercely on the accelerator, the big toe groping about and reaching up when it was necessary, in its master's mind, to slow or stop the car.

Understandably, I asked Lindhausen about motor accident insurance in Ceylon. "We don't worry about that. We leave liability to the ordinary civil and criminal law. The driver is liable if he is negligent, not the owner of the car. And the driver rarely has any money. So everyone who has a car also has a driver, which decreases unemployment but does make our traffic rather wild. And when the driver goes to gaol because he can't pay compensation to his victims, we send him foodstuffs and suchlike while he is there and find him employment, often again as a driver, when he comes out. It is a crazy system."

Lindhausen obviously both loved Ceylon and was perceptive of its many wild incongruities. I found him a delightful instructor on the country, its cultures, its laws, its arts, and its folkways. He did seem on the boastful side—the matched pair rickshaw, the allusion to the larger car elsewhere, and the several times that he informed me in one way or another that he was the senior non-English civil servant in Ceylon. Nevertheless, I found myself quickly at ease with him and even risked asking him about his ostentatious rickshaw: "That's an unusual rickshaw you have. I haven't seen one like that before."

"Lang told me about Blair, The Rickshaw Wallah, about your experiences with rickshaws," he replied. "I thought you would find my rickshaw distinctive. In city traffic it is much swifter than a car and certainly more reliable. I see you disapprove; Lang thought you would. He suggested my sending it for you."

I risked being direct; he seemed warmly amused rather than annoyed by my impertinence. "Well, I do find rickshaws somewhat distasteful, men pulling another man around, and to have two of them like a matched pair of horses. . . ."

"You would rather the two men starve, Mr. Blair, and their families? There is much unemployment here and no welfare system. Believe me, there are many wanting the wallahs' jobs. And my men and their unusual rickshaw have become well known in Colombo, which does my reputation no harm among the natives, though some of my European friends disapprove as you do. But it is what the Singhalese and Tamils think that matters to me; and they approve, I assure you."

I gradually came to understand that though he was a senior civil servant of the Raj, and therefore supposedly not involved in politics, his political base was all-important to him. And it was a base in the native communities, not in the English administration, for whom intelligence, efficiency, and subservience would more than suffice. Like Lang in Rangoon, Lindhausen in Colombo was planning and working daily for the day of independence.

The Riley tourer was well suited to the rutted roads of the villages around Colombo, as well as to the paved highways of the city—excellent visibility, highly sprung, the top of the door to hang on to as we bucked over the bumps. And as I managed to wrench my eyes from the driver's toe and pay attention to the surroundings, I settled down to a most interesting day.

Lindhausen crouched forward from the rear seat and poured information on village life and Colombo politics into my ears. Problems rather than achievements were in the forefront of his mind. There was, he assured me, a climate of violence throughout all of Ceylon. Village life particularly was torn by ethnic and religious hostility. The Hindu Tamils, a majority in the North, periodically slaughtered their Buddhist Singhalese fellow citizens; and the Singhalese, a majority in the South and in the country as a whole, returned the compliment with equal bloodiness.

With an abundance of bananas and coconuts, no one starved in the villages, but there were many malnourished children lolling about, many more than I would have seen in Burmese villages with their neat gardens and cared-for livestock, which were quite lacking here.

Lindhausen told me that the murder rate was extremely high in the villages, higher, he thought, than anywhere other than perhaps the distant country of Colombia, where, he had been informed, killing was a professional occupation.

I asked him why there was so much homicide in Ceylon, thinking that he might talk of the efficiency or inefficiency of British justice and of capital punishment. These matters, he said, had very little indeed to do with it. The causes, apart from the pervasive racial and religious hostilities, were simple enough: a combination of the lack of a reliable survey of the land, the absence of primogeniture, the formidable coconut knife, and the liquor laws.

It seemed an unlikely mixture, and I said so, but as he explained how these matters interacted, his argument made sense: The land has not been surveyed; hence boundaries are often in dispute; hence ownership of each particular coconut tree on or near the boundary becomes an important and highly contentious economic issue. Sons inherit equally so that smaller and smaller holdings precipitate more desperate boundary disputes. The wickedly curved, razor-sharp coconut knife is the tool of the villager's sustenance and also the instrument of his fury. And the high tax on beer and other alcohol drives the villager to brew his own "toddy" from the palm tree, and "palmyra toddy" proves to be a potent inflamer of brotherly disputes.

Many of these conditions seemed remediable by the Government. So they were, Lindhausen assured me, "but not until we have a government that cares about the villagers."

It was when we were discussing the villagers' penchant for homicide that I began to suspect what it was that Lindhausen wanted of me. And he now gave my suspicion better shape. He, like U Tin Hlang in Burma, was working toward and planning for the day of independence for his country, which, he assured me, could not be more than a decade distant. It would be then that the country would stand in need of a dedicated and efficient administration to prevent civil war between the Singhalese majority and the Tamil minority, with their different religions, languages, and customs, and their profound mutual suspicion. The better people in the current administration, and those in political groups like his that pressed for independence, were alike trying to get a few key administrators in positions of responsibility to plan for and lay the behavioural foundations for the early days of independence. Lang had written to him of my work in Moulmein and had spoken of me in terms of praise; he thought it might be possible to arrange a transfer for me to the service of the Government of Ceylon so that I could become one of those key figures of whom he spoke. It would, of course, mean a substantial increase of responsibility and a concomitant increase of salary; but he did not think I would object to that.

I expressed pleasure in Lang's opinion of me and made other noncommittal remarks.

"Lang has told me a lot about you; some of it you would like to hear, some you would not, but let us put this matter aside until after dinner tonight," Lindhausen said, and I was relieved to agree.

Lindhausen packed a lot into that day: a one-day narrative history of Ceylon, inspection of some of its main governmental buildings, brief meetings with several of his colleagues in the civil service, and lunch at Mt. Lavinia Hotel, built on a promontory beside a curved beach that reminded me of the beach at U Tin Hlang's home. A judge of the Supreme Court of Ceylon, the only non-European on the Court, if a burgher of mixed lineage like Lindhausen himself can be so described, joined us for lunch and gave me some sense of judicial arrangements and the law in Ceylon. I was immensely flattered and somewhat bewildered by all this attention, and kept thanking Lindhausen too frequently. It was clear that I was being entertained, instructed, and, to put no fine phrase upon it, inspected.

Dinner at his bungalow in Cinnamon Gardens, a suburb of luxury houses and substantial estates, with his wife and two daughters, also took me out of my depths. Lindhausen did everything lavishly, it seemed, and the meal was like an extended lecture on the culinary arts of Ceylon with Lindhausen, his wife, and his two daughters, who were about my age, all instructing me, often in chorus, as to what I was eating and its ethnic provenance, and inquiring of each dish, "Do you like it?"

After dinner, as he had suggested, he talked in more detail about the job he had in mind for me. He stressed again that it was his opinion that independence would come to Ceylon in a decade or thereabouts. I didn't have any idea if he was right, but it made sense to think about his proposal on that assumption. In outline, here is how he put it: The seeds of racial violence are planted everywhere in the fertile, racially mixed soil of Ceylon, and local petty politicians cultivate them assiduously. The English administrators know this, of course, but they continue to favour and to promote the Tamil minority, who are, on the average, better educated and harder working than the Singhalese majority, who in manner and leisurely pattern of life are closer to the Burmese villagers of the South I had come to know as a district officer. Racial hatreds intensify and are not at all ameliorated by an administration that goes by the book, treats all villages and villagers alike, and reserves all decisions of any significance for the central administration in Colombo. Lindhausen favoured regionalisation, with regional administrations sensitive to the particular and often distinct problems of each region, even of each village. He favoured bilingual education in English and Tamil or English and Singhalese, varying, if necessary, with each village.

And what all this led to for me was that he wondered if I would be interested in an appointment as regional officer for the South Central Region, which includes much of the area we drove through after we left the city of Colombo, as well as a considerably larger area to the North, East, and West.

Lindhausen said that he thought he was in a position to secure such an appointment for me and seemed to have made up his mind as to my suitability for the job on the basis of what Lang must have told him about me and the time we had spent together that day. It was not certain, of course; several in the administration would have to be persuaded, but he believed the job could be mine if I wanted it. I would be transferred from the Burma Police to the service of the Ministry of the Interior of the Government of Ceylon, of which, he repeated, he was the senior non-English officer—so we would be working together. I didn't have to make up my mind until a week or so after I was home in England, and this was a relief because I found myself both attracted to the idea and doubtful whether that was what I really wanted to do with my life—it seemed much like being a district officer but on a larger scale. Still, it would be wonderful to play a useful role in bringing peace to such a country.

I again was effusive in my thanks to Lindhausen and his family and assured him that I would think most seriously about the tempting contingent offer he had made to me. I said that I looked forward to hearing from him in London and began again on one of my bouts of expressions of gratitude.

"Oh, you've certainly thanked us enough, Blair. Off you go now. I have arranged that you will be taken back to the *Chitral* by my two rickshaw wallahs of whom you so deeply disapprove. But it is night, and no one will see you."

The mail had been pushed under the door of my cabin. I recognised Rosemary's writing on an envelope and opened it first. I had written to her of my home leave arrangements before I left Moulmein and had said I very much hoped to see her in London. I assumed this would be her reply. In a sense it was. She did briefly mention that she expected me to contact her immediately I arrived in London, but, that said, the letter went on for several pages about a very different topic.

As I knew from her earlier letters, she wrote, widowhood in London had been no burden to her; she had been renewing many old friendships and meeting many new people. It was like the time before she met and married George. But the past few months had been dreadful. She had noticed a lump in her left breast and had gone to her doctor; cancer had been diagnosed and confirmed by a second opinion, and within a few days she had been hospitalised and a mastectomy performed—her left breast removed. Recovery had been slow. She had gone to stay at her father's home in Sussex; they were kind to her but she was miserable and lonely. She was looking forward very much to seeing me and, again, I must contact her immediately I landed in England.

What a day it had been! It seemed ages since I had first seen Lindhausen's rickshaw on the dock. And, with this dreadful news, the night promised to be even longer. Yet, mercifully, I fell into an immediate, deep, and exhausted sleep.

The journey from Colombo to Aden and on to Marseilles was uneventful. Major Gorse had used his influence to protect me from the return to "my" cabin of the now recovered Mathew Links, who also had been given a single cabin in which to rejoice in his good health, restored by the skilled ministrations of his anaesthetist. So I had the cabin to myself and could read and write whenever I wanted to, which was often.

In the first few days out of Colombo I wrote to Dr. Veraswami describing my time in Ceylon. I tried to use the letter to him as a means of making up my mind whether I wanted the job in Ceylon if it was offered, setting out as best I could all arguments I could think of in its favour and all I could call to mind to the contrary. But it made no emotional sense—a contrived litany. I valued Veraswami's advice more than that of anyone I knew but he was not one to be consulted by mail; he guided by helping one guide oneself—a Socrates, not a Plato. I did not know how to engage myself with him in that process except by talk, and unhurried, diffusive, reflective talk at that, so that things would be seen clearly out of the corner of the eye rather than head on.

At lunch, two days before we were due to reach Marseilles, the table steward came hurrying to me with an envelope: "Sparks says this was marked urgent, Mr. Blair. He told me to bring it to you right away."

It was a cable from Rosemary. It read:

AM TAKING SHORT HOLIDAY IN SOUTH OF FRANCE STOP CONTACT HOTEL BRISTOL ON REACHING MARSEILLES STOP SUGGEST YOU DISEMBARK MARSEILLES AND TRAVEL LONDON VIA TRAIN

LOVE ROSEMARY.

I didn't know whether to be pleased or appalled. Remembering our times together in Moulmein and Rangoon, it would be wonderful to be with her again—she was, after all, the only woman I had known—in the biblical sense—who had seemed to love me. But how could I cope if she were ill? It was true, of course, that a few days on the Côte d'Azur and then the train to Paris and across to Dover and London would get me home at the same time as or before the *Chitral*, and the Bay of Biscay could provide unpleasantly rough sailing. But what was it that Rosemary expected of me? Marriage seemed quite out of the question—it had not really occurred to me—she was much older, and anyhow . . . What could I do? I could hardly not do as she asked, just not meet her in Marseilles; that would be too cruel. But she had given me no choice; I did not know where she was, in England or somewhere in France. I could make no reply to her cable other than to meet her in Marseilles.

The next morning I advised the purser that my plans had changed and that I would be disembarking at Marseilles.

The cable had said Hotel Bristol, and when I checked at the desk there was a room reserved in my name—but no Rosemary. "No," the desk clerk told me, "there is no Madame Brett registered with us." So I signed the register and was shown to my room. It was too large and obviously too expensive, a huge double-bedded room with a small entrance hall and a lavish bathroom, both the bedroom and the bathroom having splendid views of the promenade along the waterfront. My every inclination was to protest and seek more modest accommodations, but because Rosemary must have booked the room for me I thought it best to do nothing other than to tip the porter, probably too much, such was my insecurity, and settle in quietly.

After the cramped and somewhat spartan quarters on the *Chitral* it was a joy to have such comfort and such space, but how much it must cost! I had better find out. No, don't telephone the desk; better to ask when next at the desk.

The telephone rang—the front desk—a message: Mademoiselle Russell was waiting for me in the lounge. I had the sense not to ask "Who?" Of course, I remembered her father was Brigadier Russell; she must have dropped the Brett, whether for this occasion or permanently I did not know, and was using her maiden name.

I found her in a gloomy corner of the lounge beside the entrance to the hotel's restaurant, where one would have drinks before dining. And there was a glass in her hand when she waved to me as I stood peering about the room. I hurried over and awkwardly kissed her on the cheek. She patted the seat of the couch beside her and I sat down. "You look wonderful, Eric. The sea air agrees with you."

I started to return the compliment but found myself varying it to an expression of pleasure in seeing her again and some mumblings about what a difficult time she had been having since we met. The immediate truth was that the intervening months had not dealt kindly with the cool, crisp Rosemary of Rangoon.

"Don't look at me like that, Eric. I know I look awful. Don't stare. Just stop looking at me. Why don't you have a drink?" The orders erupted in a shrill, loud, and angry staccato. But then, equally suddenly she returned to the quiet warmth of her first greeting: "Oh, pay me no heed, Eric. Yes, the past few months have been miserable and I am so glad to be here with you now; I was really quite nervous waiting for you, and it made me angry." And linking her arm through mine, she moved closer to me on the couch.

I had been looking at her but I did not think I had been staring, and I had certainly determined in advance of our meeting not to be obvious about looking at her chest—and I did not think I had. But, even so, it was clear that she had changed. The firm lines of her jaw were fattened and rounded, her eyes were on the puffy side, and her clothes seemed to be loosely wrapped around her unlike the crisp-fitting styles I remembered. The fresh, feminine confidence that used to radiate from her eyes was no longer there, but she remained, undeniably, a most attractive woman.

A waiter approached. I raised my hand enquiringly towards Rosemary's glass. Yes, she would have another gin and bitters, which the waiter understood immediately, though I had less immediate success in making clear my preference for a beer, _bière_ not being apparently that which was expected to be consumed in the early evening on the Côte d'Azur.

As the waiter left I turned again to Rosemary, suddenly unqualifiedly pleased to be seeing her again and moved by the thought that she had gone to such lengths of planning to be with me. "It's wonderful to see you again," I said. "I've missed you so."

Her eyes misted and I thought she would cry. "You are very kind to me, Eric. I suppose I shouldn't have come to meet you, but it has been so lonely."

"Well, I'm delighted you did." And with a sigh of satisfaction, the anxieties of the past few days apparently behind me, I leaned back on the couch to savor our surroundings and the extraordinary fact of my being here with Rosemary, away from the world, so far as I could see without any obligations other than to be kind to, and take pleasure in the company of, one who seemed to be very fond of me, as I was of her.

She talked a lot of her recent time in England, a little of the weeks in Burma after George's death, and of "the wretched funeral in Rangoon" when we had been unable to meet. She talked not at all of the operation itself, merely of the convalescence at her father's home in Sussex and of how boring she found it to be unwell.

Her mood shifted when I spoke of the journey on the _Chitral_. Her mind seemed fixed on interrogating me about affairs she thought I must have had. I told her that I had come to know nobody aboard at all well, except perhaps Major Gorse and to a lesser degree Mathew Links, and I tried to launch into the tale of my success as an anaesthetist. But she did not pursue the clue I dropped and continued to interrogate me about unattached women. I said that there were one or two attractive enough females aboard, but that I had done little more than share a few words with them.

She persisted, pressing my memory for names and descriptions of the younger ladies on the *Chitral*. I did my poor best, but it became silly and I risked a nonsense bravura comment: "As you know, Rosemary, I am a vastly experienced Lothario; indeed, you taught me. I scarcely let a young lady pass by. And I never kiss and tell. It was, I confess, an exhaustingly busy journey. Let's draw a cloak over my many shipboard imbroglios."

To my dismay this absurd frivolity elicited the shrill, loud, and angry tone of her earlier orders not to look at her; but now she was even more vehement and astonishingly vulgar, using words I had never heard her use before. "You're a fucking rotter, Blair. I see how you look at women. You'd fuck a bird on the wing. God help those chippies of yours on that ship. You don't care a fuck for them or for me. That's all you do care for. I don't know why I came here." And now there were real tears, tears of anger and rejection, not the soft mist of affection that had threatened before.

It was becoming hard to bear. I felt like getting up and running away. But I just sat there. She was not shouting, but she certainly was not modulating her voice. A few people elsewhere in the lounge were looking around slightly puzzled, but I don't think they had heard that word, though they must have sensed the tension in our corner.

And I had not heard that word before from female lips. In the barracks it was used as every second word, every time an adjective or stress was required, and in the mess as an occasional expletive—and it in no way troubled me. But for Rosemary to use it with such evil force and such little sense! My stomach churned.

Mouth agape, I sat silent through her outburst and her tears, bewildered what to do. I noticed that she had not removed her arm from its interlock with mine, and I noticed further that though her words and her facial expressions were certainly those of deep anger, she nevertheless clutched me to her side even more tightly—and her body was trembling slightly, not with rage, I thought, but with fear. I started to pull my arm away so as to turn directly toward her to reassure her of the innocence of my days and nights on the *Chitral*, but decided not to, and just sat there trying by the steady pressure of my arm to give her comfort.

I offered her my handkerchief which, fortunately, was clean and folded. She took it and dabbed at her eyes as her anger and fear abated.

After a period of silence, I began talking again as if I had not heard her astonishing words, talking tritely of Moulmein matters, of Dr. Veraswami and U Tin Hlang and of Lindhausen in Colombo. I stayed clear of the *Chitral* and even of my experience as an anaesthetist, since I now wished to save that for her amusement when our moods were more attuned.

Gradually she relaxed, softened, and after another gin and bitters I managed to get her to talk about herself again. I think she must have had more than one gin and bitters before I arrived; her voice became increasingly blurred, and self-pity further eroded clarity. But I did begin to get a sense of her loneliness in England when the typical social pattern of her life as an attractive widow, the daughter of a wealthy Brigadier General, was disrupted by a dreadful illness. Like everyone, I had a horror of cancer; but I had never let my mind dwell on what cancer of the breast must mean to a woman. It must have isolated Rosemary completely from courting males, most of whom, like me, would be repulsed by fear of her disease. She said she was now free of those murderous cells; though one could not, she added, be too confident of the future. But until now I had not let myself think what a mastectomy (that is the word she used, gesturing toward her left breast) must have meant to her. And what *did* she look like? Undressed, I mean. . . .

The Rosemary I had thought I was to meet in Marseilles was the Rosemary I knew from U Tin Hlang's bungalow; but on and off this was a very different lady—one minute the Rosemary of Rangoon, smart, sophisticated and affectionate, the next an angry harridan, jealous and abusive. And how was I expected to behave? And what *did* she look like? And *could* I, even if in sympathy I wanted to?

I thought we should stroll the promenade and return to the hotel for dinner. Rosemary would have none of it. "Wandering about outside in the daylight? No, let's stay here until the lights are on and we can find a little cafe nearby."

By the time we left the hotel I had a better sense of the lay of the land. Rosemary had taken a room in the hotel for herself as well as having reserved a room for me, her cousin, a relationship of which the desk clerk had been informed—a customary relationship in such hotels, she said. She had also told the hotel authorities that she thought we would be staying for two or three nights, but since I had only a limited period of leave from Burma she was not sure about this and we might leave earlier. She implied that she did not expect me to spend a great deal of time in my room—hers was lavish, she assured me, though I had thought mine entirely too grand. But these apparent invitations were interspersed with bouts of annoyance at me for my past neglect of her—not having written often enough—and by occasional expressions of maudlin self-pity. She was a far from easy companion.

She did not invite me to her room before dinner, for which I was much relieved, saying that she needed to tidy up before we went out.

We met in the foyer of the hotel. She seemed more composed, though still clutching nervously at her shapeless, too-flowing dress.

We walked along the promenade toward the_____Square, where the commissionaire had told me there were several excellent outdoor cafes. It was a warm, soft evening; I found my spirits rising. Rosemary had again taken my arm, and for a while her jumpy monologue had ceased; indeed, turning to me and pecking me on the cheek, she said how good it was to be with me. And the easy, confident Rosemary, warm and friendly, was with me again.

We decided to walk around the square, looking at the menus of the several restaurants abutting it, some with tables outside on the square. We agreed it would be pleasant to dine alfresco.

We stopped to read one displayed menu, close to a row of tables gently lit and attractively set, where a few customers had already seated themselves, aperitifs in hand, eyes glued to the passing parade. My French was just equal to the challenge of the menu; Rosemary's was clearly much better. Smiling at her in easy familiarity, I saw that while she surveyed the menu she was reaching into the neck of her dress to resettle a string of pearls into their proper, more visible position.

"They're lovely, Rosemary. Did you have them when we were together? I don't remember them." It was an entirely innocent enquiry, but it had the most astonishing effect. Like a claw, her hand wrenched the pearls from her neck, breaking the string, and the liberated pearls flew, to the astonishment of the patrons, in a gleaming arc high above the row of tables, a vision set immutably in my memory. And she added to the onlookers' entertainment by screaming at me, as the pearls arced in the air: "You're always so fucking jealous. Yes, a friend gave them to me. He wasn't like you. He didn't hit me." And she swung her arm at my head, striking me quite heavily on the brow.

I had no idea what to do. The pearls seemed a suitable target of activity. So I moved to the tables of the restaurant and with a series of "pardon"s and "excusez moi"s scrabbled about among the feet of the patrons recapturing a few pearls here and there. One or two customers of the restaurant, their eyebrows near their hair lines, searched about on and beneath their tables, collected a few pearls, and handed them to me.

I rose from the search with a dozen or so pearls clutched in my hand, and looked for Rosemary. One of her high-heeled shoes was there, but not Rosemary. I was made to understand, by the patrons of the restaurant we had so amply entertained, that she had run off "in that direction"— toward the hotel, it seemed. I made noises of apology and gratitude to those who had helped me, picked up the shoe, and set off in pursuit. It was at this point that I realised that Rosemary was sick, very sick, not only physically but sick in the head, and that I had turmoil on my hands: no friends, no contacts, not much language, not much money, and a very sick Rosemary.

There was a message from Rosemary waiting for me at the desk of the hotel. She was not feeling well; she would see me for breakfast. It came as a relief. More than enough had happened that night. I had a cheese and fruit plate and a mineral water sent up to my room, and found myself both anxious and relieved. Relieved for the moment and anxious for the future.

I fell asleep wondering whether I should rejoin the *Chitral*, due to leave for the voyage around Gibraltar and across the Bay of Biscay, or adhere to the plan Rosemary had suggested and I had fallen in with: a few days in Marseilles and then the *Golden Arrow* across France to Paris and on to Dover and London. There was certainly space on the *Chitral*, even if I had to share my cabin with Mathew Links, but I had formally disembarked with my luggage and I suppose there would be some formalities required if I were to board again. Presumably I would have to make up my mind in the morning if I were to take flight on the *Chitral*.

It seemed only the briefest of sleeps before the telephone rang beside my bed. My sleepy "Blair here" was met by Rosemary's angry "Just checking if you had run out on me." And then, as I started to reply, her tone changed to a wheedling, coy "Why don't you visit me; I'm just down the hall."

My answer came without thought: "I'm exhausted, Rosemary. Let us meet in the morning and sort things out."

There was no reply. The telephone banged in my ear.

And now sleep seemed impossible. What in hell should I do? Though I knew that affection had cooled to a degree between Rosemary and me well before the funeral period in Rangoon, I had indulged myself by agreeing to what I saw as a harmless sexual encounter for a few days in the South of France on my way home. No, that was not accurate: I had agreed to meet her in England and she had arranged the South of France meeting in a way I could not easily avoid. I had known nothing of her apparent annoyance with me for, she said, neglecting her, and I suppose she felt a similar annoyance with all males for their neglect. In fairness, she had told me of her mastectomy before announcing her intention of meeting me in Marseilles, but at that stage there was little I could do to avoid meeting her—I didn't then even know how to contact her to tell her I wouldn't meet her, which anyhow would have been an unthinkable reply.

Perhaps if I did go to her room and make love to her, all would be calm. Probably that is all she wanted of these nights and days together. But the difficulty was that I felt quite uncertain that I would be able to make love to her, even if my mind told me that that was the easy way to buy a few days or hours of peace before escaping to my own life again. It wasn't my mind that would be called upon. And if I did try to reawaken our physical relationship and failed, as I feared I would, then her fury would know no bounds. Apart from the risk of failure, it would be cruel to pretend in that way—or so I told myself. I had liked her, indeed more than liked her; I had been in love with her, my first adult love affair. And I was now treating her most shabbily.

I needed help, that's what I needed. And this profound thought produced the glimmer of an idea. Perhaps in the morning I could take a taxi to the *Chitral* and see if Major Gorse was aboard and get his help, both as a medical man to advise me about Rosemary's condition and as a senior officer to be taken into my confidence should it be sensible for me to try to leave on the *Chitral* in the evening.

Somewhat comforted by this idea, I dozed off for what again seemed only a few minutes. Wakened by a knocking on the door, I got out of bed, went to the door, and though I knew who it was, asked, "Who's there?"

"Don't be a fool. Let me in."

Again words preceded thought and I said: "Do go back to your room, Rosemary. You will have us thrown out of the hotel if you go on like this."

Her reply was vigourous. The knocking on my door became a violent, open-palm banging, banging, banging, fit to wake the dead, to say nothing of the residents of the Hotel Bristol, and to alert the desk staff to the crazy behaviour of their recently arrived English guests.

Of course, I let her in.

She pushed past me and sat on the stool in front of the dressing table, clutching at her right hand, which she must have bruised on the door. Her night dress and dressing gown were awry, she wore no slippers, and she took no care to conceal herself as she sat on the stool. But her rage seemed to have dissipated and self-pity taken its place. I suddenly realised how extreme and swift were her changes of mood and feeling. This matter was clearly beyond me. I had better just play it calmly and get through the night any way I could, and hope for help in the morning.

"Rosemary dear," I said, "do let us talk quietly for a while."

She made no reply, but kept clutching at her hand.

I moved forward to take her hand.

She waved me away but then, quite peacefully, said, "You're right, of course, but I do get so lonely, so very upset. Be kind to me, Eric."

So I sat on the floor beside her, put my arm around her, and again tried to take her hand in mine, this time succeeding. It did not seem to be badly bruised, certainly the skin was not broken, but it must have been hurting; she had banged the door with extreme violence.

"Why did you not come to my room, Eric?"

"You left me a note telling me not to," I replied, which was hardly the true reason.

"Do you want to see what they did to me?" she asked, pulling at the shoulder of her gown and night dress.

"Not now, Rosemary. Later, when we have both calmed down."

"But I don't want to calm down. I've calmed down for too long already. Don't you remember at all our time together in Rangoon?"

I was becoming more and more troubled. It seemed necessary by almost any artifice to get her back to her room. But no artifice was necessary, or perhaps my strategy was a most mendacious artifice. "Let me take you back to your room, dear. The door made a fearful racket here. I shouldn't be surprised if the porter showed up. Let's go to your room."

She made no objection. I helped her up and, dressed only in my pajamas, wrapped an arm around her shoulders and walked her down the passage to her room, a distance of about twenty yards, hoping against hope that there was nobody else astir at the time.

Her room was a grander version of mine, similar in design but better furnished. I sat her down on the edge of her bed and pulled up a chair for myself a few feet away. She asked me to pass her handbag to her, which was on the dressing table. She peered into it and then, taking little notice of me, began to feel about for things in it.

Women's handbags have always fascinated me. Women carry so very much in them and find such difficulty in locating whatever it is they are looking for. Rosemary carried this to an extreme, taking in and putting out on the bed and then replacing in the handbag a great diversity of objects, including a few bottles of pills. She seemed disinclined to talk or indeed to take much notice of my presence. Finally I said, "Why not go to sleep, Rosemary? It will all be better in the morning," a sentiment I did not for a moment believe.

Again a soft concurrence but this time with a condition added: "Alright, but stay with me for a while."

I helped her to the bed, put out the light, and sat down beside her on the edge of the bed. I think I knew what she would do and am not even clear whether or not I wished to avoid it. She pulled me down beside her and kissed me, this time not a peck on the cheek, but a kiss I remembered from our earlier times together. After a while she took my hand and moved it over where her left breast had been. "See, it's nothing to upset you. Just a flat chest there like yours and quite a neat scar. If you want to you can hold the other one."

And it was as she said. I could feel a trace of a scar above where her left breast had been, and otherwise just a nippleless chest.

"I have a falsie I could wear if you like, but a bra in bed makes me feel like a tart."

I made no reply but found that I was now pressed up against her, body to body, with my hand holding her right breast. She snuggled even closer, with a soft noise of consent. It had been such an awful evening; this was the way to bring it to a peaceful and loving end. We could begin again with affection in the morning.

It had been a long time since I had been with a woman and I was quick to arousal. And she too. But the turmoil of the past hours and my anxieties for the immediate future were not to be denied. They remained in my mind and though penetration was easy and swift, that was all that was easy. My mind became an insuperable impediment to my body; I pretended to an intimacy and to a climax I did not feel. And I had no doubt that Rosemary knew exactly what had happened.

For a few minutes after our bodies were separated we lay silent, my head on her shoulder, my arm thrown across her body.

"I had better go back to my room, Rosemary, after the racket we made."

She made no dissent. "Yes, I'm exhausted. Get me a sleepy pill before you go. And call me in the morning when you wake."

I put on my pajamas, which I had earlier thrown on the floor, pulled the bedclothes up around her, found her handbag, and got a glass of water from the bathroom.

Looking vastly disarrayed, Rosemary sat up in bed, brushed her hair back from her face, and seeing a small bottle in my hand which I had taken from her handbag, said, "Yes, two of those please, Eric." And now, in the light and while she sat up in bed, I could plainly see the long scar of the mastectomy. It was exactly as I had felt it—not at all upsetting.

She took the pills and lay back in the bed, pulling the bedclothes around her. "You're a kind one, Eric. Don't be upset. I understand. Leave the handbag there. Now run along."

A sudden fear gripped me. I would not leave that bottle of pills by her bedside. I put out the light, kissed her demurely on the forehead and tucked the bedclothes around her. I put the bottle of pills in the pocket of my pajama coat and, peering out of her door in the hope that the corridor was clear—and it was—scurried back to my room, relieved that the night seemed to have passed safely.

I think I knew I was deceiving myself. Shortly before five, after only a few hours of sleep, I was wakened by another knocking on my door, less violent than before but vigourous enough, to find the hall porter and a policeman demanding my presence at a nearby public hospital where, they informed me, Rosemary had been taken an hour ago, overdosed with sedatives, her life in the balance.

The porter told me that Rosemary had called the front desk about two hours ago gasping weakly for help. The porter had found her unconscious, sprawled on her bed, several empty pill bottles scattered about. He had called for an ambulance and the police, which he was required to do. He had, he made clear, heard and reported our bangings and wanderings of the night before.

The policeman waited outside while I dressed. I rushed to the bathroom, pulled off my pajamas, and in doing so remembered the bottle of pills I had brought back from Rosemary's room. It suddenly seemed essential to get rid of them. I pulled on pants, shirt, socks and shoes, and then emptied the pills into the toilet and threw the bottle in after them, flushing the toilet to remove, as in my confusion I then saw it, any trace of my participation in her suicide, if such it should prove to have been.

I then hurried with the policeman down to the hotel lobby where the porter added another burden to my bewilderment. He had, he said, been instructed by the management that both Rosemary and I must vacate our rooms before noon. There had been a mistake in the booking. The hotel was overbooked. A maid would pack Madame Russell's effects, unless I wished to. Would I look after her suitcases or should they store them for her? It seemed the last straw. And, he added, with what seemed like satisfaction, of course I would be responsible for both accounts, hers and mine, since the rooms had been reserved for Madame Russell and her cousin, and we had arrived together, which we hadn't.

Even in the misery of that morning I noted with amusement that overnight Rosemary had changed in the collective view of the Hotel Bristol from a mademoiselle to a madame. Adversity can have an aging effect.

I did not argue with the porter. It was not the time to confront innkeepers' law, certainly French innkeepers' law, which I had no doubt gave little protection indeed to the tourist. I hurried out with the policeman to his car and we were driven to the hospital.

I thought I would be taken immediately to Rosemary's bedside, but not at all. There was another policeman waiting for me, Inspector Rowlandson, senior to my first police escort and speaking fluent English, so that we didn't have to make do with the mixtures of French and English I had been struggling with earlier that dreadful morning. Rowlandson seemed a strange name for a Frenchman; surely it should be Rolandfils? He must have had an English male progenitor somewhere in his ancestry. It was an irrational thought, considering the situation, but it had been an irrational night and morning generally.

"Would you mind making a statement?"

"About what?"

"Why, everything about the sick lady and your relationship with her. For a start, where did you or she get all those pills?"

"She brought them with her from England."

"Did you give her any?"

And, of course I had. But how to tell him that? To my astonishment it became suddenly clear that Rowlandson was interrogating me about what might be seen as a homicide—they thought I might have killed her: gotten rid of an old flame! Or helped her to kill herself!

Now I knew that the path of caution was to say nothing on such occasions, but the path of caution bore no attraction for me. The whole story poured out of me in summary form, from our earlier meeting in Moulmein, through Rangoon and U Tin Hlang, and then the funeral, Brett's death, and last night. It sounded coarse, gross. But Rowlandson was an attentive listener, particularly when he knew I too was a policeman, or so he classified me. He listened, made notes, asked an odd date or time, but in no way cross-examined me.

When I say that the whole story poured out of me, that is not quite true. I made no mention of my having given Rosemary the sleeping pills, nor of the bottle of pills I had taken back to my room. It seemed unnecessary to burden myself with that bit of incriminating evidence.

Several times I asked to be taken to see Rosemary, each time being refused. "The doctors will let us know when you may see her."

When I spoke of Rosemary's mastectomy Rowlandson looked up in surprise and seemed to become more understanding, but then asked, "Why did you not stay with her last night, at least until she went to sleep? Did you not suspect what she would do?"

Had I? I am unsure. At one level I suppose I must have. But she had seemed so calm and sensible when I left her. But then I had noted the violent shifts of mood. I must have suspected. Otherwise, why should I have taken the bottle with me?

Word came from a nurse that Rosemary had had her stomach pumped out, that she was sleeping, that the doctors believed that she was now out of danger, and that I should come back in the afternoon. My sense of relief was immense, but was it for Rosemary or myself? It did not seem worth the trouble to think about that.

I told Rowlandson of our notice of eviction from the hotel. He said he would speak to the management of the hotel and arrange that I could stay on. He added that even though Rosemary now seemed out of danger I was not to leave Marseilles without first checking with him, and he gave me his card. He would, he said, prepare a written statement for me to sign when I returned to the hospital later in the day. Such is necessary, he said, in every case when a foreigner is involved in homicide, suicide, or attempted suicide.

"Do you want to be driven back to the Hotel?" Rowlandson asked.

"Not unless you can arrange matters with the hotel first," I replied. "I don't feel like arguing with them now." But he had to draft my statement and report in to his headquarters before he could go to the Hotel Bristol. I said I would walk about for an hour or two and try to get my head clear.

The hospital was less than a mile from the hotel, but I set off, unshaven, coatless, in crumpled shirt and pants, to walk to the waterfront. Perhaps I would see if Major Gorse was on the *Chitral*; perhaps I could confide in him as I had planned the night before about what now seemed a very minor difficulty compared to my present predicament. But then I realised that the more people knew of my role in Rosemary's attempted suicide—I could not let myself think that she might die—the worse it would be for me in the future. The Ceylon appointment would be quite unlikely if this scandal were known, for scandal it would be turned into, though in Marseilles, at least, I had done nothing scandalous.

Or had I not indeed done grievous wrong? Why had I not recognised her need and been more generous of my affection both in outward display and in the act of love? Was I so proper that I would deny comfort, even the comfort of what in the past I had myself so much wanted, to one in need who had certainly been a close and loving friend?

Nevertheless, there seemed no point in broadcasting the miserable story, and I decided I had to face my troubles without help from Gorse or anyone else. How I longed for Dr. Veraswami. He would have helped me straighten my thoughts without telling me what to do.

What should I do? One course, probably the most sensible, would be to return to the hospital in the early afternoon, make certain that Rosemary was out of danger, read and sign Rowlandson's draft of my statement if it were accurate, pick up my luggage (pay my bill? both bills? I wonder what Rowlandson would arrange about that—after all, Rosemary had no lack of funds—my meanness revolted me), and catch the next train to Paris. I would leave a note for Rosemary but would not include a forwarding address. That would certainly minimise the number of people knowing about and spreading the word about my delinquency. I suppose I would have to tell Rowlandson what I was doing and bear the brunt of his disapproval, but that was a slight punishment compared with the possible consequences of this affair becoming known to my masters in London or Burma or my potential employers in Ceylon.

Rosemary would not talk about it, I assumed. Her role was even less laudable than mine; but then I realised that she could present it as my importuning her to meet me in Marseilles, thinking she was a widow anxious for sexual companionship, and when she came, taking advantage of her and then leaving her in the lurch, so that in despair she tried to kill herself. Oh yes, she could turn the tale against me alright.

Would it help her for me to stay in Marseilles and look after her as best I could? Perhaps it would, but my every nerve revolted at the idea. This was not the Rosemary I knew. She needed psychiatric care, not coerced masculine companionship. My presence would probably just make things worse for her. If I didn't mean to pursue a protracted friendship with her, I had better leave now; it would be more cruel to desert her the longer I stayed. . . . What a convenient thought!

To my horror I saw approaching a face I knew—and knew very well from peering down at it through a cloud of ether—Mathew Links. He had seen me and was crossing the street to accost me. "Didn't expect to see you here, Blair. Thought you were hell bent for home, though Major Gorse did tell me to look out for you and to say he wanted to see you if we crossed paths in Marseilles."

"A friend has had an accident," I replied, beginning a path of evasion and lies which I knew would shift beneath me. "I may have to stay here a day or two—but I'll still get home before that *Chitral* tub."

My effort to appear nonchalant was probably unconvincing; I had to get rid of him quickly, particularly if Gorse wanted to see me. Perhaps

Gorse could help me with the medical aspects of Rosemary's case, or even be helpful in advising what I should do. Yes, despite my earlier decision not to consult Gorse, I knew I had to confide in somebody, and he seemed the best available confidant. "If Gorse wants to see me," I continued, "I'd better hurry to the ship. Let's meet for a drink in London. After all, you owe me one; I saved your life."

Links was a nice man. He saw my distress, I think, and did not detain me. And, yes, in a way, I had helped him in time of sickness; why would I not do the same for Rosemary? Because I was scared to be her lover? Yes. All said and done, that was it. Leaving her now might just as likely blight my career, such as it was, as staying for a few days to try to help her.

Gorse was in his cabin, and, despite my bedraggled and haggard appearance, my coming aboard and asking to see him had presented no difficulty. He seemed pleased to see me, sat me down with a beer, and gave me the surprising news that he had seen Rosemary earlier that day in hospital. There had been no strange coincidence in this; as I knew, he visited a major hospital in each port. An Englishwoman who had taken an overdose of drugs had been admitted here, and it was quite ordinary that he should have been brought to her bedside.

I tried to tell him the story of the events of the previous evening and night, and not to embroider or gloss my part in it. I even described my sense of guilt when flushing the pills down the toilet.

"Is she mad?" I asked.

"If you mean certifiably insane, fit for commitment to a mental hospital against her will, certainly not. But if you mean a very disturbed and mentally troubled woman, then, from what you have told me, she certainly is. A psychiatrist could treat her and help to give her some calmness, could perhaps reduce her intake of alcohol, and could reduce the wild swings of mood you describe, but only if she wished it. And I don't think she does now."

"So what should I do? Can I help her?"

"I very much doubt it. If you take my advice you should get away from her just as quickly as you can. Get tonight's train. Or come back with us on the *Chitral*."

I doubted I could now abandon her without seeing her. I would have to wait until she was in a position to look after herself, possibly when she was safely back from the hospital at the hotel. Gorse said he understood how I felt, but still didn't think I would be able to be of much use to her.

It struck me that, if she was due to leave the hospital today, as Gorse suggested, perhaps he would call on us both at the Hotel Bristol in the early evening, before the *Chitral* sailed. He had seen her in hospital; it made sense that he should at my request visit her when she was discharged to see if she needed any further help. He said he would call in about six. I should phrase it as a social visit, to say farewell to me, not an unsolicited medical call.

I thanked him and checked with the purser that the *Chitral* would be sailing at eight and that, provided I could be on board before then, my passage could be arranged.

I walked the mile or so back to the hotel, arriving hot and exhausted, and, I'm sure, looking and smelling so. I was far from confident how I would be received and whether a room would be available for me; but Rowlandson, as he had promised, had been in touch with the hotel about my room, and he and the British Consulate had interceded for Madame Russell, so that there would be no difficulty at all about our staying on.

So now even the Consulate knew of our secret dalliance on the Côte d'Azur. Our tumultuous affair was taking on the character of a public performance!

There was also a message for me from Rowlandson to the effect that Rosemary would likely be discharged from the hospital shortly after the four o'clock medical rounds and requesting that I please meet him at the reception desk at the hospital at that hour.

I had a bath, shaved, and lay down on the bed to decide what to do. It was clear to me that I could not just walk out on Rosemary while she was in hospital, as Gorse had suggested. If she needed help to get back to England, I must give it. And, anyhow, Rowlandson's request to meet him and presumably sign, if it were accurate, whatever statement he had prepared was not rationally to be ignored. Perhaps he wanted to stop me from walking out on Rosemary—he must have realised how tempted I was.

I thought wryly of my earlier daydreams of administering the Southern Region of Ceylon, of presiding with wisdom and esteem over the lives of grateful natives, bringing concord to previously warring native factions, and amusing with poise and confidence the charming Lindhausen girls. What a fine and pleasant life it might have been! But then, acknowledging the misery of my present situation, I forced myself to face the blunt truth that under French law I probably had already been arrested on suspicion of assisting a suicide, that this would in due course be recorded in police files and thus become available to all law enforcement agencies of the United Kingdom—and that had Rosemary died, a homicide charge would have found its way there too. An ultimate acquittal would not help much: either charge was enough to preclude the Ceylon posting.

So I would have to go to Rowlandson at the hospital at four. It was now a little after one. I had not eaten and I did not want to. Perhaps the best course would be to take a brief nap and then try to decide what to do. I was certainly exhausted; there had been little sleep last night and the events of the early morning seemed to have drained me. I set my alarm clock for three and fell immediately to sleep, a sleep deeply troubled by confused, kaleidoscopic dreams of courtrooms, of bewigged and fierce judges, and of myself confessing to shameful but imprecise crimes.

For reasons that were not clear to me, I dressed carefully in my uniform to meet Rowlandson and to bring Rosemary back from the hospital. Rowlandson met me at the hospital reception desk on time, expressed his pleasure in what he had heard of Rosemary's complete recovery, and led me to a small room off the foyer to study the two sheets of typescript he wished me to sign.

I read them through. They were accurate enough. Certainly there were no clear errors of fact, though my explanations for what I had done were omitted. It was not what I would have written, though as I say, there was no clear inaccuracy to which I could point.

"Is that reasonably accurate?" he asked.

"More or less. Nothing wrong with it, though it does make me out somewhat of a fool."

"Perhaps that's the best you can hope for," he replied. "At one stage I had it reading a lot worse for you."

"I don't see how it could be much worse," I foolishly responded.

"Well, tell me about those pills in your toilet. Don't you know they float? I guess the bottle went down, but not the pills you emptied out. Of course the hotel reported them to me when the housemaid found them. They are exactly the same pills your girlfriend swallowed. What were they doing in your room?"

I made no immediate reply. I think a helpless gesture of raised hands and shaken head escaped me. Rowlandson took pity: "Oh, don't feel so miserable. You're in the clear. At one stage I thought you weren't, but your girlfriend saved you. I believe her. She told me you gave her only two and probably took the bottle and the rest away fearing she would do what she did. But why the hell didn't you tell me? And is there anything else I should know?

"No. No. Any sense had left me. It just seemed so awful to have the pills. I think I told you everything else."

"I, too, think you have," Rowlandson replied, "but the pills do mean that you must have known there was a risk she would try to kill herself. Why didn't you stay with her, at least until she went to sleep?"

I really didn't know why I hadn't, and said so. He said that the statement need not be changed to include all this, hinting that it was courtesy to a fellow policeman in need that led him to this decision, and suggested I should sign the statement as it was.

So I signed and dated it; he signed as a witness. And then, immediately, but with kindly demeanor, he departed, urging me to contact him if we had any trouble with the hotel or, indeed, any other problems.

I thanked him and returned to the reception desk to ask for directions to the ward or room where I could find Madame Russell.

"But she was discharged earlier this afternoon."

"That cannot be. I was told she was to be discharged at the afternoon medical rounds."

But it was so. The nurse looked at the medical register and confirmed her memory. Rosemary was no longer at the hospital.

"Did she leave a note for me?"

"No. No messages."

I hurried back to the hotel. No, Madame Russell had neither returned nor telephoned any message.

I was quite bewildered. Perhaps I should check at the Consulate; but that did not, on reflection, seem sensible since it was at least possible that they had not been informed of my involvement, just of Rosemary's over-dose and hospitalisation. There seemed no sense in drawing unnecessary attention to myself.

I realised I was hungry, having missed both breakfast and lunch, and thought a light snack might be a sensible way to occupy time until Rosemary returned to the hotel. I set off in the same general direction that Rosemary and I had walked the evening before and came to the same square and the same restaurant where Rosemary had thrown her pearls to the sky.

I am unsure why, but I was not surprised when I heard Rosemary hail me. "Eric," she called, waving me to the table where she sat with a man of about my own age. "Meet a new friend of mine, Geoffrey Pollit. He is in the Consulate here. The hospital told them of my accident and Geoffrey came round to see if he could help. He arrived just before I was to be dis-charged and has been kind enough to bring me here for a drink on my way back to the hotel. I told him this is where I wanted to come since we didn't quite get here last night."

Geoffrey Pollit muttered the usual formalities in my direction, and I in his, and we performed the customary limp-handed shake of Englishmen who don't particularly want to know one another.

Rosemary gestured towards the chair opposite her—she and Geoffrey had been sitting on the same side of the table looking out at the square. I sat down, enquiring how she felt. "Oh fine," she said. "Did me the world of good. Nothing like a little stomach pumping when you're unconscious. And I think I've lost some weight, too, which does no harm. But I really must be careful about sleeping pills when I'm exhausted."

Geoffrey remained silent and ill at ease, with me rather than with her I thought. Rosemary pressed on with excessive gaiety: "I met a friend of yours this morning. A Major Gorse, or some such. He came on rounds with my doctor. Said he knew you. Talked to me for some time. Said some rot about you giving an anaesthetic to someone. Said he hoped to see you before the *Chitral* sailed."

Genuinely concerned, but thoughtlessly, I blurted out: "Should you be drinking, Rosemary, after such an experience?"

And her sudden aggression again engulfed me: "None of your damn business. What would you care? Why don't you run along. I'll be back at the hotel sometime before dinner. Geoffrey and I can get along quite well together without you. See you later perhaps."

I sat bewildered. Rosemary turned to her new escort and tried to absorb him in chatter whose content I could not follow. Suddenly disgusted and angrier than I recall being before, I stood up and said, "All right. I'm off." And without waiting for a reply headed back towards the hotel.

Rosemary shouted something but in my rage and speed of departure I did not hear it.

She had told me what to do. Fine, a relief, I would do it. Let Geoffrey worry about her for a while, I had had enough for the time being, perhaps forever.

I had not managed to tell Rosemary that Gorse would be visiting the hotel in the early evening. It didn't seem to matter now, anyhow. If she didn't come back reasonably soon to the hotel, then I should take Gorse's advice and embark again on the *Chitral*. He would, I felt sure, help me get myself and my baggage back on board. And, if she did come back, I could then tell her of Gorse's likely visit and ask her to see him with me.

These thoughts calmed me slightly as I returned to the hotel; at least I would not be entirely alone and would have professional help on hand for Rosemary if she needed it.

I left a message addressed to Madame Russell at the front desk asking her to call me as soon as she returned and went up to my room to try to plan sensibly.

Rosemary called me about thirty minutes later, apologetic for "biting my head off at that restaurant—it doesn't seem to be a very good place for us." She would, she said, take a nap; she found herself on the tired side. "Stomach pumping is quite exhausting." And yes, she would not mind joining me for drinks before dinner in the lounge. "Let us start again at the same place, see if we can make it work better this time."

"Is that Pollit man still with you?" I heard myself asking, knowing it was a foolish question and fearing an immediate outburst of rage. Instead, she laughed warmly, "Of course not, Eric; you're becoming as jealous and silly as me. I got rid of him quite soon after you stormed away."

I told her I did expect a visitor at the cocktail hour, that Dr. Gorse from the ship was coming to say goodbye to me and that he hoped to see her then to check that she was recovered completely.

She made no objection, even volunteering that she had liked Gorse at their encounter early that morning, though she was then feeling quite poorly.

I set my alarm clock, checked it carefully, took off my outer clothes, lay down, and was immediately asleep.

Shortly before six I telephoned Rosemary's room. Yes, she would meet me in a few minutes in the lounge where we had met the night before.

She arrived in a relaxed and friendly mood, a joy to be with. Perhaps the experiences of the past twenty-four hours had cured her entirely. She ordered her usual gin and bitters and the waiter did not even make a performance out of getting me a beer. Without rancor she suggested that we had better cut short our time in Marseilles. The Consulate seemed anxious that she should return to England; that had been the burden of Pollit's message to her. From her passport, which, like other foreign visitors, she had had to deposit at the hotel, both the police and the Consulate knew that her father was her next of kin and she thought that, since generals seemed to impress them, there was a real possibility that he might already have been advised of her hospitalisation—Pollit had said he was unsure about this. "Daddy is a dear. He will be worried. He looks after me well. But I don't get much room to maneuver." Pollit had said that the Consulate could obtain reservations on tomorrow's *Golden Arrow* to Paris, on which he had already arranged to travel for some business. She thought we should both go. "And, Eric dear, if Daddy has been informed, he may meet us when we reach London. You had better brace yourself; he can be difficult—I won't find it the easiest—he thinks he owns me because he loves me and no one else."

I found I was not troubled by the thought of the angry general; the Rosemary of Burma was with me and nothing else seemed to matter. My moods began to shift with hers. Why had I been so anxious? Everything was now wonderful. A joyful leave here and in London and then back to Moulmein or to Ceylon. There was no rush about changing my work; I had a lot of growing up to do. The *Golden Arrow*, London, and later Asia would do very well indeed.

I saw Gorse entering the foyer of the hotel and waved to him. Rosemary greeted him cordially and thanked him for his help in the morning. "It was great to have an English doctor there. The French doctor seemed efficient enough but I was never sure what he was doing."

Gorse complimented her on how well she looked after such a trial. He avoided reference to the cause of the problem, I noted, and she, too, spoke of her "accident" and of her silliness in not keeping more careful track of her pills. And then, to my dismay, he said, "Blair here has been worried sick about you. He told me about your time together in Burma. He's a good chap; don't be hard on him or on yourself. These things change, you know; they often don't last a lifetime."

And her fury was in full force again: "I don't know what he said to you, Doctor, but it sounds like a bloody lot of lies to me. He's a leech, hanging around me when he's not wanted. Telling lies about me, saying I tried to kill myself. I know; that policeman told me. I'm sick of this talk; it's really none of your business, Doctor. If you'll excuse me, I'm off to the ladies room to tidy up while you two get done with whatever you have to do." And pulling her clothes around her in the same desperate way as the evening before, she made off towards a corner of the lounge where, I supposed, the ladies room was to be found.

Gorse turned to me: "You see. You really had better clear out now. You must see what a danger she is to you, how sick she is."

I was annoyed with him. I had told him the broad story of our relationship but I had avoided details; I had not really been indiscreet. He seemed to me to have deliberately suggested that I had.

"Why did you do that, Gorse?"

"I thought it might set her off. She is on a very close fuse, in a deep despair. You won't be able to help her much."

"Is there a risk she will try again to kill herself?"

"Of course there is, and you being with her probably increases it. If you can get her back to England, and hand her over to whoever she has there, that would be the best for her, but it is obviously quite risky for you. Her father is a general, you told me. That won't help you much if all this comes out as a scandal."

We sat in silence for a while. I caught sight of Rosemary in the distance peering around a pillar in the lounge to see if Gorse was still with me. I thought it unlikely that she would rejoin us. I thanked Gorse for his kindness to me on the ship and for his efforts to help me here in Marseilles. I promised to call him in London and tell him the denouement of the Rosemary affair.

He left and I sat there, sipping occasionally at my beer, Rosemary's half-full gin and bitters on the table beside me. She returned, apparently composed. "I'm glad that Gorse doctor has gone. He annoyed me, treating me as if I were dotty. But you were naughty to have blabbed to him."

"I really didn't blab. I had to tell him we knew one another in Burma. How else explain the two of us here and my leaving the *Chitral?* I told him nothing that was not obvious."

"Don't worry, dear," she said, in a calming, child-comforting manner, as if I were graciously to be forgiven my minor fault, her outburst entirely ignored.

What a contrast our second evening in Marseilles was from the turmoil of the first. Rosemary was obviously very tired; she had slept very little the night before, only a brief period in the early morning after her stomach had been emptied of the lethal drugs. She was content after dinner to go for a brief ride in one of the horse-drawn carriages which carry tourists up and down the promenade of the seemlier parts of the Marseilles waterfront and then to retire to her own room, suggesting that I not accompany her, and pleading exhaustion like an importuned but loving wife temporarily rejecting solicitations to intimacy.

I was very content to fall in with her inclinations.

Early the next morning she called my room. "Come in for a cuddle before we get up, Eric dear." And I did. And it went well enough; I was becoming attuned to her moods and found myself able to respond to her affection.

We had breakfast together in the hotel dining room, chattered like we used to about very little, packed, and paid our respective hotel bills, which far exceeded what I could properly afford, and made our way by taxi in midmorning to the railway station.

Pollit had done as Rosemary requested and purchased tickets for us to Paris on the *Golden Arrow* and on to London on the boat train, and he had made appropriate sleeping-car and dining-car reservations. When Rosemary told me that he would be on the same train to Paris, I was surprised. Did the Consulate really care that much about seeing us out of their jurisdiction? But by the time we met at the station and I paid him for our tickets, I had accepted what Rosemary had told me: that Pollit had already planned to make the journey to Paris on consular business and that she, not he, had suggested our accompanying him.

In the event, I was pleased. Rosemary and I had not rediscovered the easy conversational mode and the easy silences of the springtime of our affair; to have him occasionally with us, particularly at mealtimes, tended to smooth conversation by reducing emotional pressures.

The details of that journey are not fixed in my mind. I remember most clearly a sense of caution in everything I said and much that I did. I remember how careful I found myself in my choice of subjects and words; any faint hint by glance or word of sexual attraction by either of us for anyone else (and in my case the fact that there was no one else didn't insulate me from the hazard) risked precipitating one of Rosemary's furies. And I remember, too, the warmth of affection that she gave me when I was careful of my words and solicitous of her well-being.

I came to understand just how difficult life was now for Rosemary. George Brett had been the ideal husband for her. She had been born to the life they shared, trained for it, acculturated to it. He had been pleased that she should continue her role of charmer of the regiment, the beautiful daughter of the distinguished general, adept in society, capable in transient affairs of the heart, fashionable, intelligent, but troubling herself not at all with anything other than the light and inconsequential. George gave her room to nourish these talents and to bring them to full bloom. Now they were swept away, or so she seemed to think, and she had laid the foundations of no other pattern of life.

With the mastectomy and the idleness of convalescence, she might understandably have turned even to me, but I had clearly been a disappointment. What was she to do now with her life? It would be easy to suggest countless ways in which she might fashion a happy and productive life, but I knew that I, for the time being, would be the last person who could counsel her in matters of reason and sensible planning. But I could well see how she had tired of life and, certainly on the night we met in Marseilles, how she might see no point in its continuance. And if, added to that, there were the pressures of what Gorse had told me was a "manic-depressive condition just short of psychosis," one could have only sympathy for the pain Rosemary must be enduring.

On that long train journey, I tried to assuage her pain. I did my best, but it was not good enough. Shortly before the boat train docked at Dover, she shot herself.

I found my hand shook quite visibly as I opened the letter from Veraswami; it struck me he had never written to me before, all our communication had been oral. How could he possibly capture his spritely insight in writing?

> My Dear Eric:
> I rejoiced in your letter from the *Chitral* after you left Colombo, and that it changed ships in mid-ocean, which you are not supposed to do with horses in mid-stream, added drama to its contents.
> You, an anaesthetist! What a stupid fool I am! I should have known: you could have doubled your stipend as a district officer by assisting in all my operations. Such talent, and that it should so long have been unrecognised, dormant, hidden. Hurry to Harley Street, they need you there.
> As you see, I enjoyed your letter. And now I need every bit of pleasure I can get here in Moulmein. It is most lonely without you. The beer is warmer and my mind emptier. It was a cruel kindness to enliven my life by your company and to challenge my mind with the problems you shared with me—and then to abandon me here.
> So, I have decided. That is to say, my dear wife watched me for a few weeks since your departure and decided for herself, and then told me how very wise I was to have reached the same decision for us both. We will leave Moulmein in a fortnight. We go home. Not home in the sense you British use it, to your country, but home in our more particular usage, to the village in the Punjab where I was born. I will be the villagers' probably esteemed and certainly poverty-stricken doctor. One day you must come to see for yourself; you will always be utterly welcome.
> I think I helped you as you helped me; but I am not deserting you. I know now that if you do return to Moulmein after your present leave, it will be only for a very short time. Your letter with its mention of a possible job in Ceylon started my mind in that direction, though you

know that I have often been troubled about how long you have stayed in Burma. And a telephone call from U Tin Hlang this morning to the hospital convinced me of it. So, if we meet again, as I so very much hope, it will be in the Punjab.

U Tin Hlang told me all he knew of the death of Rosemary. It is sad, but you must not for long blame yourself. I know you well enough to know that you are not capable of being deliberately unkind. You will, of course, think of many ways in which you could have saved her, better protected her, as we all do when such tragedies strike. But you did not make man or woman; one of our Gods, or one of them with Darwin's help, did that. You are responsible only for the realities of choice within your own potential. I have watched you; I do not know the details but I am absolutely sure that you should not blame yourself too severely, that you should not indulge yourself in too much self-recrimination. Some, yes; then put it behind you.

What a pretentious preacher I am! But let me keep on—after all, you do not have to take any notice of what I write. Please do not stop U Tin Hlang going to England to help you. He tells me the enquiry by the Coroner can be delayed on his application to represent you. He very much wants to come. I know it will hold up the whole matter and that you are anxious to get it over with, but he needs to be of help to you. He blames himself to a degree. Please let him be your counsel; you know he will do excellently well, and I believe it will be good for both of you.

If it helps, write to me about this whole miserable business; if not, write to me and tell me about it when it is over.

As you must know, I miss you. The acting district officer is a meticulous fool, meticulous about regulations and ignorant of everything else. And patronising, too; no doubt I deserve it, but he does not merit the giving out. I look forward to going home to my village; I have had enough of sharing even a small part of the white man's self-imposed, much resented burden.

I do hope this letter is not good-bye, but just in case it is, let me write what I feel and could never say, though it will not surprise you: I long admired you, and then I came to love you, not as David loved Jonathan, but as a father loves an adult son who has become also a friend.

May all the Hindu Gods, and the God of the Muslims and of the Buddhists, and even your ascetic God, may all of them—perhaps they are all one—Bless You.

I had met U Tin Hlang once before at a railway station—at the same time that I had met George and Rosemary Brett. Indeed, I had gone to Moulmein Station to receive them and had not expected him at all. I remember that George Brett had disapproved of my enthusiasm when I then saw and unrehearsedly embraced U Tin Hlang; I think Rosemary had approved.

Now it was very different. He was coming to help me—not to compli-cate matters for me, as he so often had—coming as my counsel, coming at his insistence, for I certainly could not afford his usual fees, coming despite my earlier assurance that I needed no counsel since I had done nothing wrong, an opinion he swept aside as childish: "If you don't see how badly you will appear at the coroner's enquiry, then you are in desperate need of my services."

He had said that he felt some responsibility for the whole miserable affair since he had facilitated my friendship with Rosemary and had been a friend of us both—and he had certainly not been of much help to Rosemary after George was killed. So I had ceased protesting, had as usual done as Veraswami advised, and accepted his help with gratitude.

As his train drew into Victoria Station, I saw Lang's head poking out a window through the smoke. What a joy to have such a friend! Whatever came of this, my time in Burma had blessed me with the friendships of Veraswami and Lang.

In London, Hlang set himself up in some state in a suite at the Savoy, which has always been willing to receive Indians and Asians. Indeed, when I had asked Hlang whether there was any colour bar at the leading London hotels he had replied, "I am not sure, but here at the Savoy they would take an alligator if it could pay the bill."

On the night of his arrival, Hlang insisted on my joining him, as he phrased it, "for a light dinner and a heavy interrogation, little to drink for you and some good claret for me." And he was true to his word.

"So you slept together when she came back from that rendezvous with Pollit?"

"It wasn't a rendezvous. He had been sent to the hospital by the Consulate. The police must have notified them of her overdose. They checked with London, I think, and wanted to get her safely back to England. Perhaps her father had a hand in it; I don't know, and he and I have never met. And no, we did not sleep together that night. She said she was exhausted, and that was not surprising considering her previous night and that day."

"Well then, did you sleep with her at all after she left the hospital?"

"Yes. Early the next morning she telephoned my room and I went to her and joined her in bed. I had little choice if she were to behave herself."

"So, you slept with her to be kind to her. Come off it, Eric. That will never wash with the Coroner."

"Wash or not, it was so. Of course, I had been very fond of her, as you know, and it was no hardship to make love to her; but I was certainly inse-cure and inept and, I suppose, scared much of the time that she would fly into one of her furies."

"Did you share a compartment on the train?"

"No. Pollit had booked three compartments, one for each of us. I don't think he realised until we met at the restaurant that I was with her at all. Rowlandson had been pretty discreet, I think, which was kind of him."

"And you had similar arrangements on the train from Paris to London?"

"No. Pollit left us in Paris. We had neighbouring compartments on the carriage from Paris to Calais, which was loaded on the boat for Dover during the second night of our trip."

"And that was the night of the tragedy?"

"Yes."

"Tell me about it," he said, and sat back, brandy balloon in hand, looking away from me. "Take your time. Try to remember some words; don't just describe."

I did my best but it was not easy, not at all. That night should be etched precisely in my mind, but in fact it is jumbled together, bits here, bits there: warmth, fear, failure, and lasting pain. I certainly remember the evening departure from Paris, with both of us relieved to see the back of Geoffrey Pollit, who had proved a bore, an oversolicitous, self-righteous bore. And eating in the dining car through the Normandy countryside was a joy, but when we returned to our compartments difficulties had begun.

Rosemary had again consumed too much alcohol—several aperitifs before dinner and more than a sampling of wines with the meal. I had avoided any remonstration about this, remembering the effect such a comment, no matter how well meant, had had in Marseilles; but I am sure she saw my unease. "Oh, don't worry, Eric. I'm used to it by now."

She had suggested that we bed down early since we might not sleep well if there was a swell on the channel when the carriage was shunted onto the channel ferry. And she added, "Little Eric might like to play. You could bring him to visit me if you like." I was puzzled for a moment; she had not before used this euphemism. She said I blushed. I suppose I did. Anyhow, of course I did return to her compartment later and found her in the darkest of moods.

I was not the butt of her depression; it embraced the world and all that therein lay. But I certainly figured in her indictment of life. I did not love her; that was clear. I had not even mentioned marriage and I had to be persuaded even to make love to her.

I did my best to comfort her. I took her in my arms and tried to gentle her to peace, but it did no good. I did not lie to her, as I perhaps should have, I did not tell her I loved her, I did not talk of marriage. If I had, I think she would have known it was deceitful. I tried to tell her of my affection for her, of my enjoyment of her company, and these lesser lies (though they had at one time certainly been true) did have a calming effect. Words progressed to endearments, endearments to caresses, and before long we were naked in her bunk bed on the now gently rocking boat train.

"How to phrase this, Lang? Perhaps as she did. The problem was that, after some preliminary show of energy, Little Eric remained Little Eric, and stubbornly refused to offer a testament of love. Though coaxed, he persisted in his flaccid denial. We did not rush; she was gentle and helpful with me, but Little Eric remained Little Eric."

I tried to tell her I was exhausted. That the past few days had been a strain for me. That I was very fond of her. But the more I talked the more her body stiffened away from me. I asked if I might stay there until she went to sleep, to hold her in my arms until she went to sleep; but she said that the bunk was narrow and peculiarly uncomfortable and I had better go back to my compartment.

Rather literally, tail between my legs, I did. My sympathy was then with myself rather than with her.

I think it was about five minutes later that I heard the shot.

U Tin Hlang stayed silent as I fell silent. Then, a deep sigh, "And you think, Big Eric, that the Coroner's jury will listen to that story and not try to find some guilt on your part in her death?"

I was angry now, with Hlang. "I don't think anything at all about that, Lang. I told you the truth as best I could. I still am not clear what I should have done differently. I couldn't control much of what happened. She was a very sick woman, I am sure of that."

"Oh, don't go all English and huffy on me, Eric. I was merely thinking what a challenge you present me with. But have no fear, I am equal to it—you could not have better representation, I am sure of it."

"You really are a cad, Lang; but it may be as you say—you do these things well. Anyhow, thank you again for being here to help me. I'm sure I do need it."

"Where did she get the gun?" he asked.

"I don't know. It was not mine and my fingerprints were not on it, so the police at Dover told me rather regretfully. They thought it might belong to her father, but he says he has no knowledge of where she got it. Possibly she had had it for some time; she could easily have acquired one sometime during her army days. But she never mentioned it to me."

"When you left her on the night of her death, did you think she might try again to kill herself?"

"I suppose I should have, but I didn't. Since Marseilles the overdose had been passed off between us and with Pollit as an accident, a product of too much alcohol and forgetfulness of what had earlier been swallowed, and I had half believed it. And there had been no further mention or appearance of sleeping pills. No, I was worrying about myself, a sense of shame and failure, and not at all about her. Of course, as I heard the shot, I knew immediately."

Hlang smiled pensively at me. "I'll do my best; I hope I can bring it off. I'll certainly not play the overconfident, too-smart-by-far cad, as you described me. But perhaps you would like to know the legal heart of the matter."

I waved my head about in Veraswami's circular motion to stress how much I would like to understand.

"It is simple enough. Whatever the Coroner finds of Rosemary's state of mind when she shot herself, your criminal liability turns on this: Did you, by affirmative action or affirmative word, aid or encourage her in that act? That you failed to stop her, or did not try to stop her, or did not try to dissuade her, is not, as the law stands, your legal obligation. If you had been married to her, it would be different. But such is the moralistic state of your English criminal law that, since your relationship was illicit, you owed her no duty of care to stop her killing herself, none at all. A bright line is drawn between action and inaction. What is essential is that I should persuade the Coroner that nothing you did was an act, and nothing you said was a word, that aided, abetted, or positively encouraged her suicide."

I would need to think about all that. A bright line, Hlang called it: it did not seem all that easy a line to draw.

Hlang saw my exhaustion and chased me away: "Call on me for lunch tomorrow; sleep in in the morning. The Coroner's Court is only two days off. The rest is up to me, though you will have to listen carefully tomorrow when I tell you how to behave in court. It won't be quiet and friendly like that caricature of a court you ran in Moulmein."

I risked a further question, a question probably best left unasked: "Tell me the likely outcome, Lang."

His usual roguish manner returned. "Oh, I doubt that the Coroner will recommend further action against you. He will probably think you have been punished enough by his enquiry. You will come back to visit me, my horses, my elephants, and my mistresses in Burma either soon or later, when I am Prime Minister."

I could see what Hlang had meant about the Coroner's Court; it was indeed nothing at all like my little court in Burma. The Coroner took to himself some pomp and ceremony, though he was not, as I had thought, both a lawyer and a doctor—just a local Magistrate, not an honourary but a paid professional Magistrate, a Stipendiary Magistrate, whose medical expertise came from the testimony of pathologists and other medical professionals giving evidence before him on all unnatural deaths.

The courtroom—bench, dock, jury box, counsels' table, spectators' seats, royal insignia, and all—was a courtroom of the Dover Magistrates. The Dover Coroner had jurisdiction because Rosemary's death had occurred in English waters and the body had been brought ashore in Dover. The jury box was empty since Hlang had waived the jury: "They would never understand your behaviour; let's hope the Coroner does."

There were a few spectators, but none gave me pleasure by their presence: a general in full uniform and many medals, obviously Rosemary's father; three well-dressed gentlemen who, I later learned from U Tin Hlang, were observers from the India Office, the Foreign Office, and the Burma Police; Geoffrey Pollit; one or two journalists, according to Hlang; and the rest local citizens with nothing better to do than watch me suffer.

There was another counsel at the table to which Hlang led me. Hlang introduced himself and then returned to my side: "He is representing Rosemary's and her father's interests. He will not be sympathetic to you.

His name is Percival." And Hlang led me round the front of the table and formally introduced me to Percival.

Hlang had told me to enter the courtroom with him a few minutes before our case was to be called, to sit beside him at the counsel's table, not to recognise anyone or speak to anyone in the court without his guidance, and to preserve a quiet, confident, but not cocksure manner. I told him that in the circumstances I disliked his choice of words. He replied that that was precisely the sort of smart comment I must at all costs avoid—just be simple, direct, and accurate. Don't volunteer.

What sticks most in my mind from that morning is the extraordinary difference in Hlang's manner and behaviour in the Coroner's Court from his usual forensic style. In Moulmein, and when I had seen him in the Superior Court in Rangoon, he was a florid and dramatic advocate, relishing his own wit and not concealing his confidence in the outcome of the case. This morning he was subdued, reflective, cautious and considered in speech, preferring the homely syllable to the orotund, and not concealing, in fact exaggerating, that he was a stranger to English courts who practiced in a simple colonial jurisdiction and was here now solely at the command of friendship. Even his scar, slicing from below the eye across his cheek, blended circumspectly with his round, brown face and had lost its dramatic flair.

From the *Chitral* to the Hotel Bristol to the hospital to the train journey and on to Paris and Dover, the Coroner helped the witnesses to get the sad story told. Throughout I seemed to have been selfish in my behaviour towards Rosemary, taking advantage of her vulnerability and not sufficiently protecting her. This was true even when Hlang put me on the stand to tell the story myself; he did not open up opportunities for me to defend my conduct, and neither did the Coroner or Percival when they questioned me.

Percival called only one witness—a Dr. Florey, a psychiatrist. Rosemary had never mentioned him to me. Apparently, after the mastectomy and while she was convalescing at his home, her father had persuaded her to see Dr. Florey. It was good for me that he did, but I was surprised that he had managed to persuade Rosemary to see a psychiatrist—she was such an independent person, taking pride in her self-reliance. But her depression and her drinking had apparently begun to trouble her to the point that she was willing to consider the need for some outside assistance.

Dr. Florey had seen her on some seven occasions. His evidence was that she was not psychotic, that she was clinically depressed, and that he had done his best to cheer her up—a very English treatment modality.

Percival asked him if she had ever spoken to him of suicide. "No, she didn't." Did he have that possibility in mind when he was treating her? "Yes; but I did not then regard it as a serious problem since she seemed to recognise that her life could and would be restored to reasonable happiness."

Percival persisted, and reached the central issue of his interrogation of the psychiatrist: "So, in your professional opinion, Mrs. Brett was not a person who would rationally plan to take her own life?" And with Dr.

Florey's reply, "That is right," fixed, he hoped, in the mind of the Coroner, Percival sat down with a stagey sigh of relief.

The evidence completed, both Percival and Hlang asked leave to address the court. Percival made much of Rosemary's clinical depression in the wake of her husband's tragic death and the cruel blow of her cancerous condition and its treatment; but he did not spare me. He strongly suggested that my ill-treatment of her had pushed her over the brink of sanity and had been the trigger for her self-destruction. She was, he stressed, "a very sick lady in need of care and consideration, which she was denied."

Hlang remained subdued and exaggeratedly respectful. He made no effort to justify my conduct, detail by detail. He agreed with Percival in his analysis of the background causes of Rosemary's illness, and, as to my part in her suicide, he fixed the blame on our earlier adulterous relationship in Burma from which all our subsequent behaviour flowed. He made her death sound like a Greek tragedy, with Rosemary and me the captives of our earlier-formed characters, which we both were powerless to change. Neither of us, in the South of France or in our journey north, had intended to do any wrong; it had all been done before.

The Coroner did not delay his verdict: Mrs. Brett had taken her own life "while the balance of her mind was disturbed" and there would be no recommendation for any further legal proceedings in relation to that death. As the law stood, only positive acts of encouragement or assistance to a would-be suicide were indictable, and he did not find that I had engaged in any such conduct.

I had my doubts. I was relieved that it was the Coroner's view that I had done no wrong, but law or no law, I felt I had done very wrong; certainly I could have done a great deal better. But I was glad I was not to be punished for it. Or was I to be punished? At least not by the law.

Commentary to
"The Curve of Pearls"

You are under no general legal duty whatsoever to assist your neighbour in an emergency, and, if you do, you incur risks of civil liability to him—so, pass by on the other side! The parable of "The Good Samaritan" has escaped the attention of the Common Law of England and of all but one state of the United States. Law, ethics, and morality overlap; they do not coincide. What is ethically and morally desirable may or may not be legally enforceable, and good samaritanship is one area where the law stands mute.

To test the matter, let us move the parable of the Good Samaritan to this country and this time. You have, of course, a cellular telephone in your car. You are driving through a section of the badlands of the Southwest. You see a foreign-looking gentleman prostrate beside his car, alone, in the sun. You draw close enough to see that he is still breathing but in a sinking condition.

The road is deserted, no car in sight. You decide "not to get involved." You consider calling for help for him on your telephone, but reject that too—that might get you involved since your phone can be traced. You pass on. He dies.

As the law stands, his family has no legal recourse against you and you have committed no crime.

That would be the result even if you were a licensed medical practitioner. Unless the man needing help was already his patient, a doctor is under no legal duty to help him. (In order to encourage such assistance, several states have passed laws to shield doctors from liability in negligence if they do intervene.)

You may remember the case of Kitty Genovese, knifed repeatedly unto death while some 45 New York citizens, in their apartments beside the vacant lot where she was attacked, heard her screams for assistance but neither went to her aid nor telephoned the police.

Lest the law sound too barbarous and uncaring, as I have set it out, let me explain it a little further. You may have a legal duty to help your "neighbour" if that neighbour is related to you or if you are under a contractual or other legal duty to go to his aid. For example, parents have duties to care for their children, and older children for their parents. Husbands have duties to wives and wives to husbands. Different states spell out the range of these duties in different ways, but by and large the closer relationships are covered. Likewise, the police and firemen, by their contracts and by their established roles in the community, are under a generalised duty of good samaritanship. And there are other similar categories—lifesavers at the beach, gatekeepers at grade crossings, and so on.

And a final obvious qualification to the apparently uncaring posture of the law on this subject: If the doctor under no duty of care to the injured pedestrian does go to his aid, thus preempting the help of others, he may not thereafter glance at his watch, conclude that he will be late for his golf foursome, and abandon the poor wretch in mid-operation. Going to aid creates duties to provide reasonable aid, even though there was no such duty to begin with, and that principle goes for all of us, not just doctors.

European systems of law go further and have defined a generalised duty of good samaritanship when the aid is within the samaritan's power and he does not thereby put himself at risk. Vermont, alone among the states, has done likewise. But there is little empirical evidence from Europe, or from Vermont, to suggest that such statutory obligations make much difference.

Eric Blair's situation in relation to Rosemary's obvious risk of suicide raises a problem where the law *would* make a substantial difference; that is why I chose to explore it in this story.

Were they married, as distinct from having an affair or having had an affair (and even if they had been cohabiting without benefit of clergy, though this is more doubtful in some common law systems), Blair would have been under a well-established legal duty to care for Rosemary and to do his best to prevent her suicide—you will judge whether he failed in this regard.

It is clear that his military, police, and bureaucratic superiors thought that he had failed, ethically and morally, and believed that he should have done more than he did; but since he lacked any legal duty of care there was no legal remedy they could pursue.

This parable raises the question of the wisdom of the common law on good samaritanship and, it is my hope, raises that question in a situation where the pressures on Eric Blair to distance himself as far as possible from Rosemary are very great. She has become a substantial threat to his career. No, that is not fair; their past sexual relationship and her continuing dependence on him have become a substantial threat to his career. How great is his duty of good samaritanship in such a situation? And, if he fails to meet whatever standard you propose, what should be the sanctions for that failure?

Perhaps the common law is right. Perhaps these are situations best left to ethics and morality, situations where the law would do more harm than good.

An historical aside may be of interest. In the formative years of the common law there was the crime of "misprision of felony," whereby the citizen was under a duty promptly to notify the police of any crime of violence committed in his presence. Failure to do so was itself a misdemeanour. Perhaps, at the very least, we should resurrect that crime which has fallen into desuetude—it would surely serve as a useful educative tool to minimise moral failures of the type exemplified in the Kitty Genovese situation.

Epilogue

A few weeks later a letter arrived from Bhatinda in the Punjab.

My Dear Eric:

You know already. You saw my dreadful handwriting and the Indian stamp on the envelope and, clever policeman that you are, immediately deduced that I have returned to my village—as I said I would, to end that sad affair of Mr. Chanduri and his need for heroin. My family and I are home at last. I was right to wander, lusting after strange Gods, but it is now right to come home.

There were no farewell celebrations. A few patients did seem perturbed; but the representatives of the Raj maintained their usual stiff-upper-lip composure in the face of my departure, and the Club tried to suppress its collective satisfaction. I do not regret my years in Moulmein, though I wish I had managed to persuade our masters in the Raj that I was not the disloyal fellow they thought me.

But I am sad that you have had such a troubled time since you left the *Chitral*. U Tin Hlang wrote to me on the day the Coroner gave his verdict about Rosemary's death. He is far from your harshest critic—you probably are—but I am sure he reports faithfully. I know you are perceptive and sensitive, but I also know that a tired man, under pressure, alone, unsure of his affections past and present, troubled by sexual insecurity, and bewildered as to his duty, does not always make the best decisions. But this I can write in honest consolation: I have never met anyone I would trust more than you in such circumstances. So, try

336

to put it behind you. You will probably do worse things in your life, and certainly many better things. Work is the best anodyne.

I could be more helpful to you on the verandah of my bungalow in Moulmein with a Watney's in my hand, waving it about in the air, while you pretend to fear a beery inundation. I hope one day there will be such a meeting for us, but I cannot now see how or when. I think you should not come this way soon. Though you are as a son or a younger brother to me, and I would dearly love to see you again, your life should now be in England, not in the East, and not in the police or the law. They are fine occupations, but no longer for you. Your canvas is larger.

I have been reflecting on our time together in the moments I can grasp for myself between moving a family and setting up a modest medical practice in the township of my birth. I have persuaded myself I have been of use to you. I am probably an egotistical old fool, but let me tell you how my ramblings of mind proceed.

As one grows older, one's reading moves from fiction to biography; not entirely, but to a substantial degree. And so it has been recently with me. So far as I can see, *everyone* who achieves anything of note reports having had a mentor, someone to whose spark of encouragement and teaching he owes his achievement. Now I am not claiming this for myself, not at all. You will achieve greatly, of that I am sure, and it will have little to do with me except in one respect, and it is that respect that I cling to.

When I was a medical student in London I lived, like so many other Indian students, in the Earl's Court district, where, you will recall, there is a large ice skating rink. This was so foreign a pastime for one from Bhatinda that I tried it, liked it, and used to exercise there occasionally in the winter evenings when I could no longer study. Before we tottering amateurs were allowed on the clear ice prepared for the evening session, I would observe a very few of the most skillful skaters, those who later would leap and dance and twirl, now huddled in twos and threes around the rink doing what they called their "compulsory figures." These consisted of precise, superimposed eights and other shapes, many intricate and small, done forward and backward, slowly, meticulously, anxiously. I came to realise that they could dance and leap and twirl largely because they had laid this foundation of precise balance and firm control.

I think I pushed you to perform the compulsory figures for your work as a policeman and magistrate combined, forcing you to be sure your moral compulsory figures were meticulously cut.

The general view is that moral issues need no such training for their resolution—just do what is right, let your conscience be your guide, that's all there is to it. But that is far, far from the truth. All knowledge requires training and reflection, and for moral issues the need is overwhelming, since we all have immense capacities for self-deception when our interests are even remotely involved—and in making moral judgements they are always to a degree involved.

I am sure you have a distinctive quality of moral understanding. It seems to me that over our years together in Moulmein that quality has grown and intensified in you, and it also seems to me that I have helped you in its development. So, could it be possible? Have I served as your mentor in moral development?—certainly never by suggesting what you should do in those troubling dilemmas you were kind enough to share with me, but by enquiring, by probing, by helping you think through moral issues, so that you avoided automatic, swift, self-centered reactions, and let your decisions and actions wait until you saw them in their complexity. How wonderful for me if that is true!

If it is true, pass it on. Make war on simple solutions to subtle human problems; help others to think through feelings as well as facts. Pass it on. And there will be many you teach, Eric, of that I am sure.

So, perhaps it is really so. Certainly, I have persuaded myself I think it so. I have been a moral mentor to you and you will be such to many thousands. I count on it. I expect it of you. It fills me with joy.

My dear wife says to wish you well though she does not know you at all. She has seen you often as she rushed to hide in the back rooms when you visited me, and I have talked to her of you until jealousy stirred in her breast. Nevertheless, she says to wish you well. And I think she really does. I know I do.

Write if you want; but don't feel you should. Ours has been a wonderful relationship for me; if it now ends, so, sadly, it must be. With gratitude and lasting affection.

Your friend,
Veraswami